ISRAEL IN FOCUS

Images of Israel through the photos of The Jerusalem Post

1932-2015

THE JERUSALEM POST

ISBN 978-965-91209-4-9

Compiled by **Marc Israel Sellem, Chaim Collins, Sarah Levin**
Edited by **Ilan Chaim**
Front cover photos, **Marc Israel Sellem/The Jerusalem Post**
Design by **Hana Ben-Ano**

CEO Jerusalem Post Israel, **Ronit Hasin-Hochman**
Production Manager, **Dror Ronen**
Jerusalem Post Archives Manager, **Elaine Moshe**
Printed at Hadfus Hahadash

EDITORIAL OFFICE: The Jerusalem Post, 206 Jaffa Road, Jerusalem 9438302
Telephone 02-5315666, Fax 02-5389527.
MANAGEMENT OFFICE: 15 Ha'achim Mislavita, Tel Aviv 6701027.
Telephone 03-7619000, Fax 03-5610777

Photographers: Marc Israel Sellem, Ariel Jerozolimski, Isaac Harari, Zvi Roger, Israel Hadari, Gur Salomon, Gideon Markowicz, Israel Sun/Yael Somekh, Meir Kfir, Dan Hadani/IPPA, Lester J. Millman, Rolf Kneller, Fred Csasznik, E.F. Ilani, Jerusalem Post Archives

The power of photography

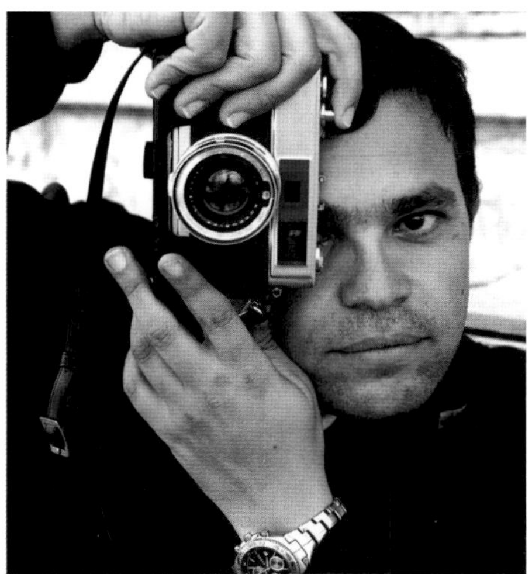

When I was 12 years old and helping to clean my home for Passover, I found an old camera in a plastic bag inside a closet. It became my best friend, and provided me with the greatest education I could ever hope to have.

Fast forward 24 years to September 2010, two months after I began working as the chief photographer for *The Jerusalem Post*. Then-Knesset speaker Reuven Rivlin (now the president of Israel) called me into his office after I had photographed him for a story.

"You have a heavy responsibility on your shoulders," he told me. "Every time you take a picture that appears in the paper, it will form the image of how the world thinks about Israel."

It only took a few months on the job before I understood how right he was and how powerful photographs can be.

When I began to work on this book and sort through the thousands of photographs in my own archives as well as that of the *Post*, our choices became clear. I quickly understood that this was not going to be a book of standard news photography, but a collection of photos that interact with the reader and provoke reactions, whether it be laughter or astonishment.

Some of the photos are the result of long hours of effort that involved waiting for the right moment, like the cover photo showing shadows on the walls of the Old City. Other photos fell into my lap – all I had to do was pick up the camera and shoot, like the photo of the helmet and the Dome of the Rock on Page 84.

And then there are the magical moments derived from being in the right place at the right time and having the intuition to snap the shutter, like the cover photo that made world headlines of German Chancellor Angela Merkel appearing with the shadow of Prime Minister Benjamin Netanyahu's finger over her lip.

I hope you will be entertained by the photos in this book, but I also hope that you will be moved by them and come away with a new appreciation for Israel.

I would like to thank the management of *The Jerusalem Post* for making this book possible, and my colleagues at the paper, especially the gifted team that worked on this book.

MARC ISRAEL SELLEM
Chief photographer, *The Jerusalem Post*

Introduction

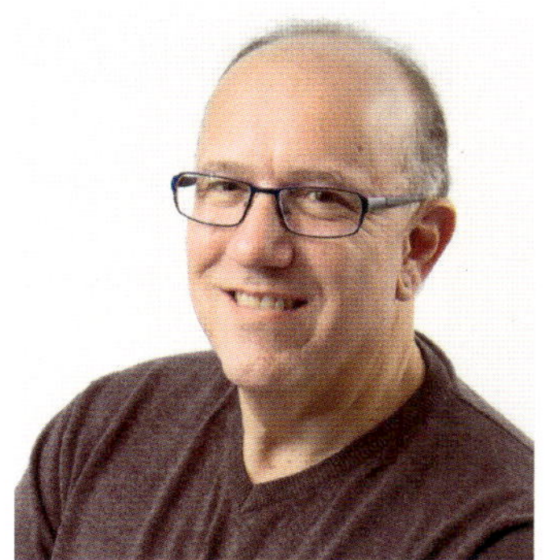
(Debbie Zimelman)

Beginning in 1932, 16 years before the establishment of the State of Israel in 1948, *The Jerusalem Post* has been faithfully chronicling the dazzling array of events unfolding in this dramatic region of the world.

The use of photographs to accompany the stories was a gradual development in the paper, but has become an integral form of journalism that complements and sometimes summarizes the importance of certain historical events more succinctly than words.

Some of Israel's top photographers devoted their lives not only to documenting the news taking place, but the people, the character, and the flavor of the country. When one captures an image of Israel in their mind, it can be any number of scenes – the historic Western Wall, the rugged desert, the breathtaking coastline. Or it can be of any type of person – urban hi-tech visionaries, Beduin tent dwellers, traditional hassidic Jerusalemites, 18-year-old soldiers.

Israel in Focus – Images of Israel Through the Photos of The Jerusalem Post presents the Israel beyond the headlines – with hundreds of evocative, revealing photos by its chief photographer, Marc Israel Sellem, and from the extensive Post photo archives, that encapsulate the robust and diverse character of the Israel experience throug the ages.

We didn't attempt to provide a historical narrative of Israel, but instead to offer views of the country that exemplify its uniqueness and its attraction to so many people around the world. We hope you enjoy it as much as we did putting it together.

DAVID BRINN
Managing Editor, *The Jerusalem Post*

Editor's note

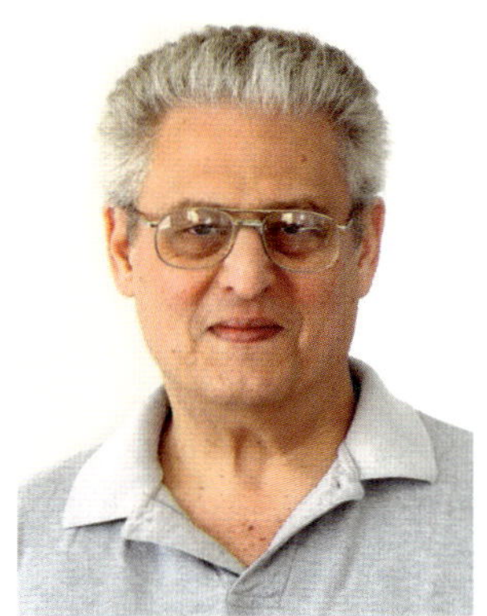

Many of the exciting photos in this album are familiar to readers of *The Jerusalem Post* as the work of its chief photographer, Marc Israel Sellem. Through his keen eye, the rich tapestry that makes up the Israel mosaic comes into clear focus. From news-making events to intimate captures of a candid moment, Marc's photography has carried on a time-honored tradition at the *Post* of vividly chronicling the development of the country.

He has not been the only one. Other timely images were recorded by our photographers from stages in the paper's history, including past chief photographer Ariel Jerozolimski (1999-2010) and various respected agencies that have contributed to the paper, some of which no longer exist.

Occasionally, however, non-professional photographers have made valuable contributions to our pages.

This volume reflects such a combination of efforts since the *Post* was founded in 1932, with the bonus of a series of exceptional photographs by a young pioneer, Ralph Fried, whose work preceded the paper's debut by a decade.

Ralph Fried was a Hungarian-born missionary who began a more than 20-year pastoral career in Mandatory Palestine in 1923. A keen amateur photographer, he took hundreds of historic photos in the ensuing decades – his pioneering photojournalism producing a rare history of the time and its people. Fried's 1923 panorama of Jerusalem is one of the first full-color photos of the city, while his 1935 color videos are perhaps the first ever of the region. His videos of the first Independence Day, May 14, 1948, are classic. Now, many years after his passing, his legacy lives on in some of the wonderful images he took, graciously made available by his great-grandson, Paul Freed, to his fellow *Jerusalem Post* readers.

ILAN CHAIM

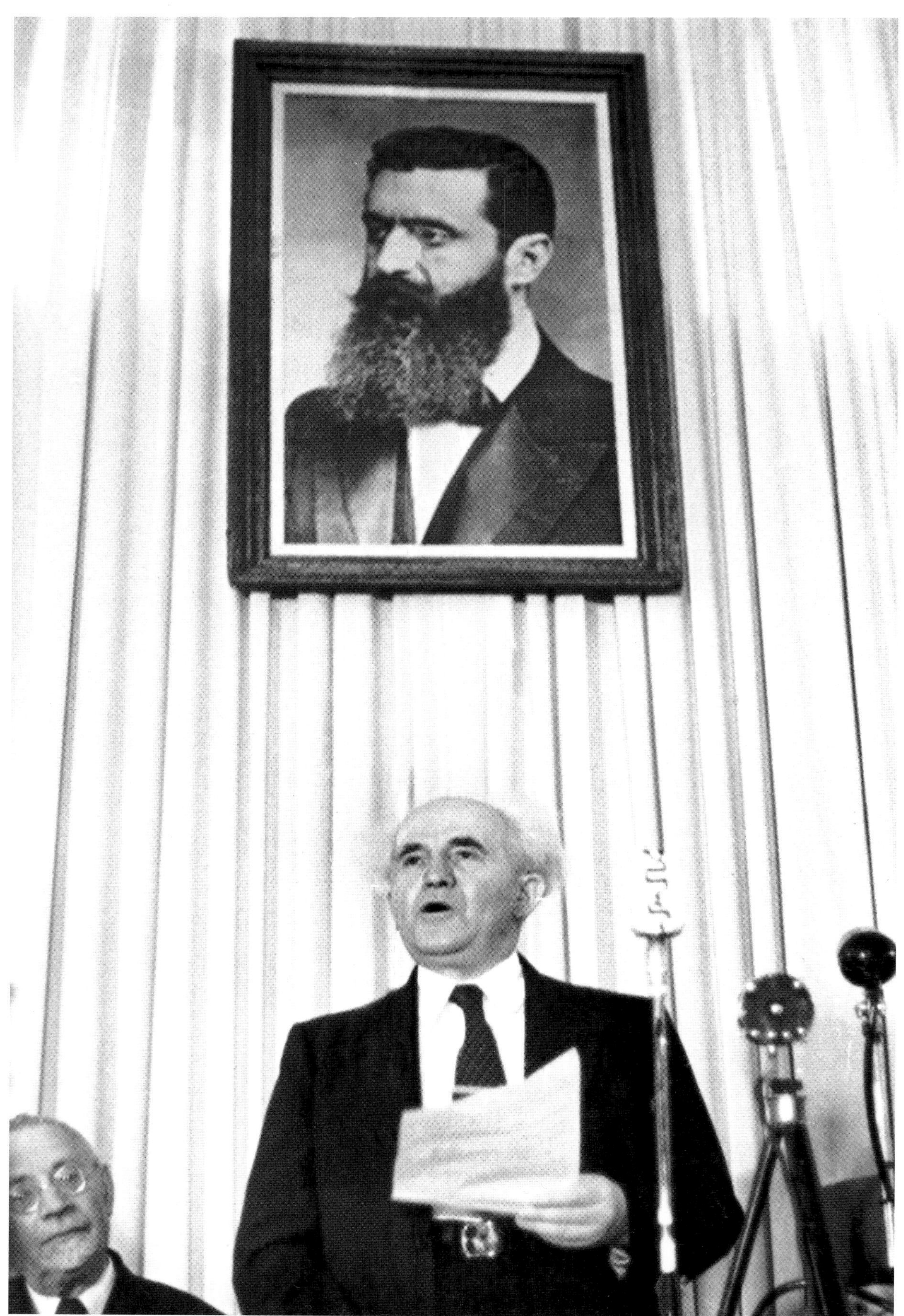

David Ben-Gurion proclaims the Declaration of Independence.
Jerusalem Post Archives
1948

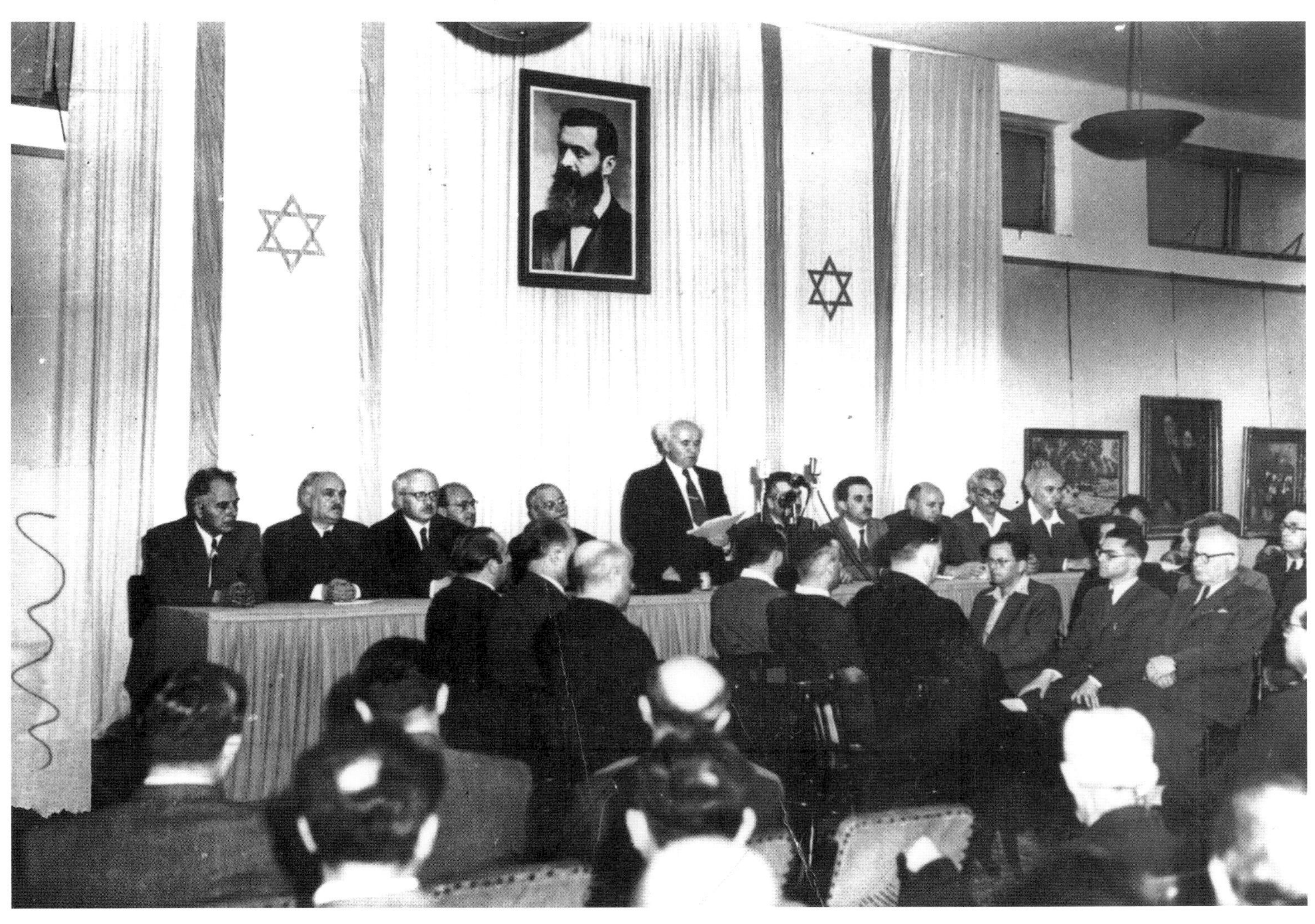

A broad shot Ben-Gurion's
declaration at Tel Aviv Museum
(today known as Independence Hall).
Jerusalem Post Archives
1948

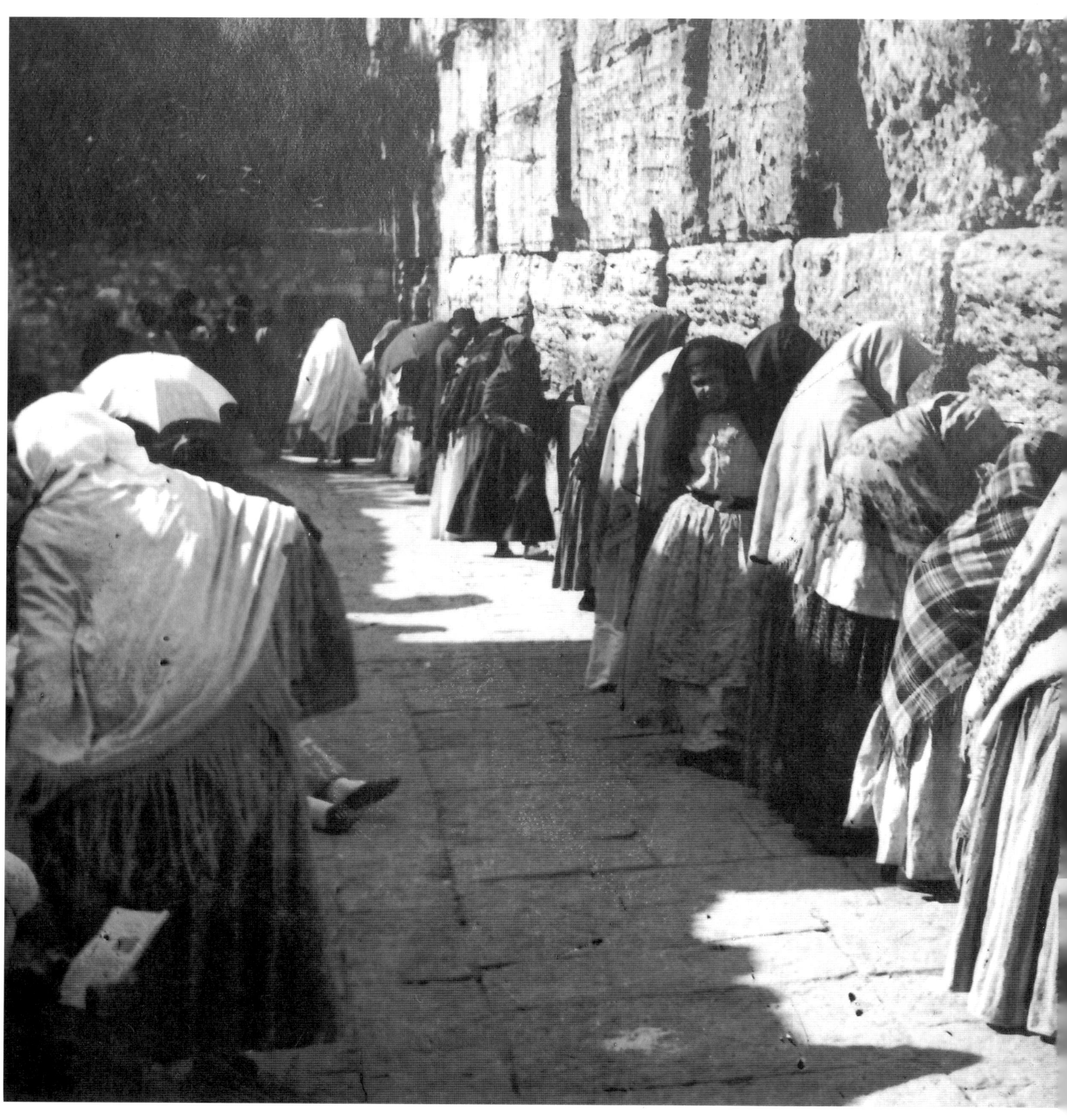

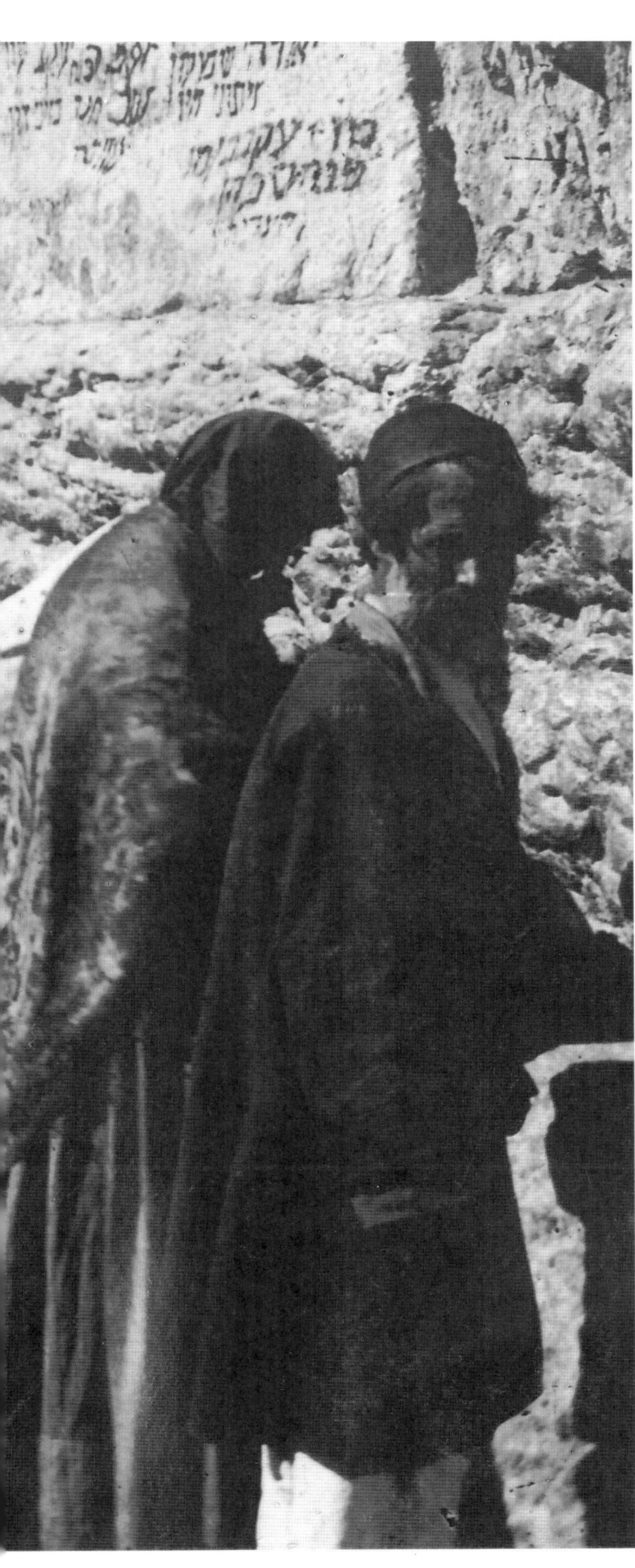

Men and women pray together at the Western Wall a century before the Women of the Wall.

Ralph Fried

1923

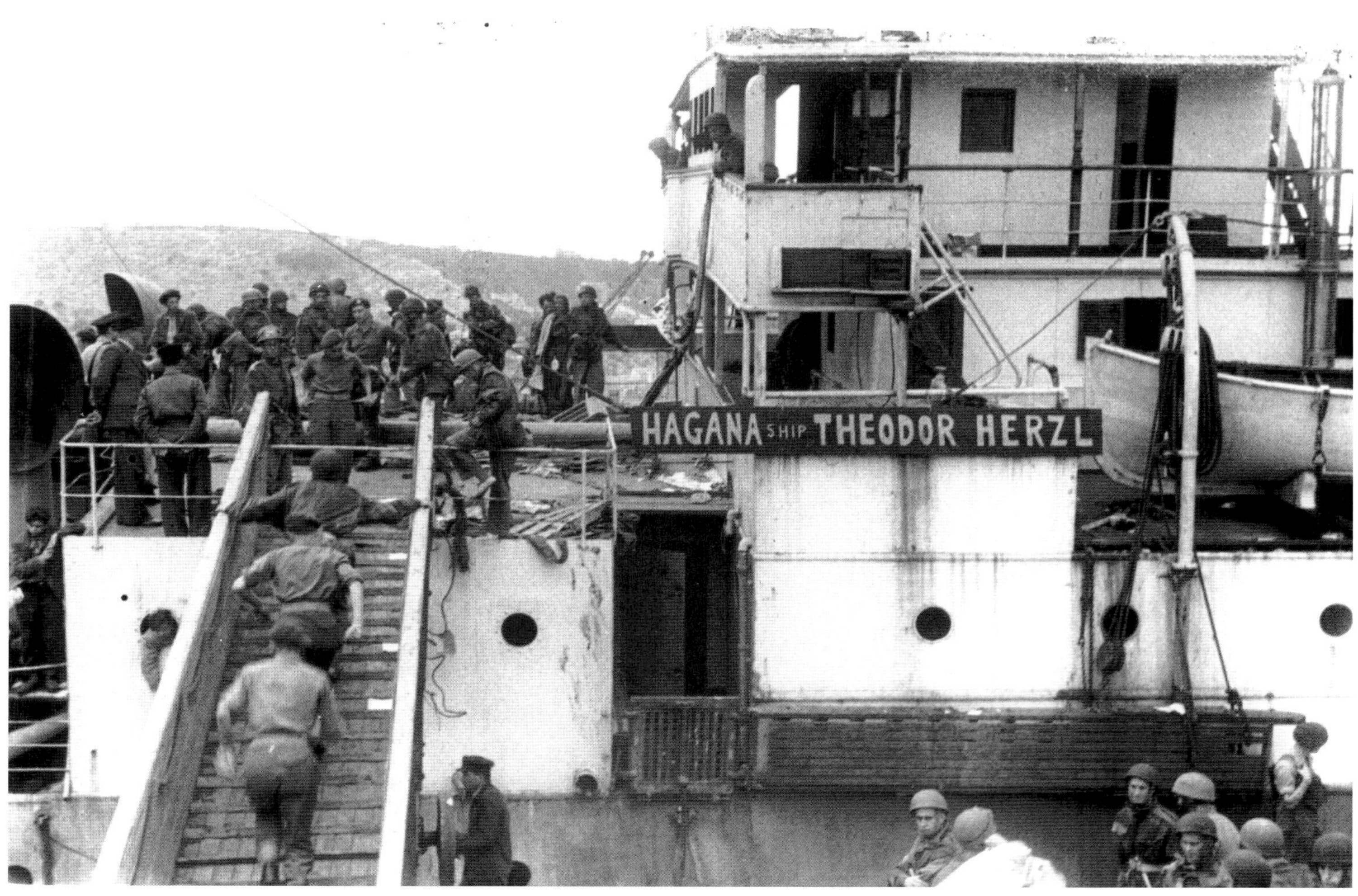

British troops board the
illegal immigant ship
'Theodor Herzl.'

Rolf Kneller

1947

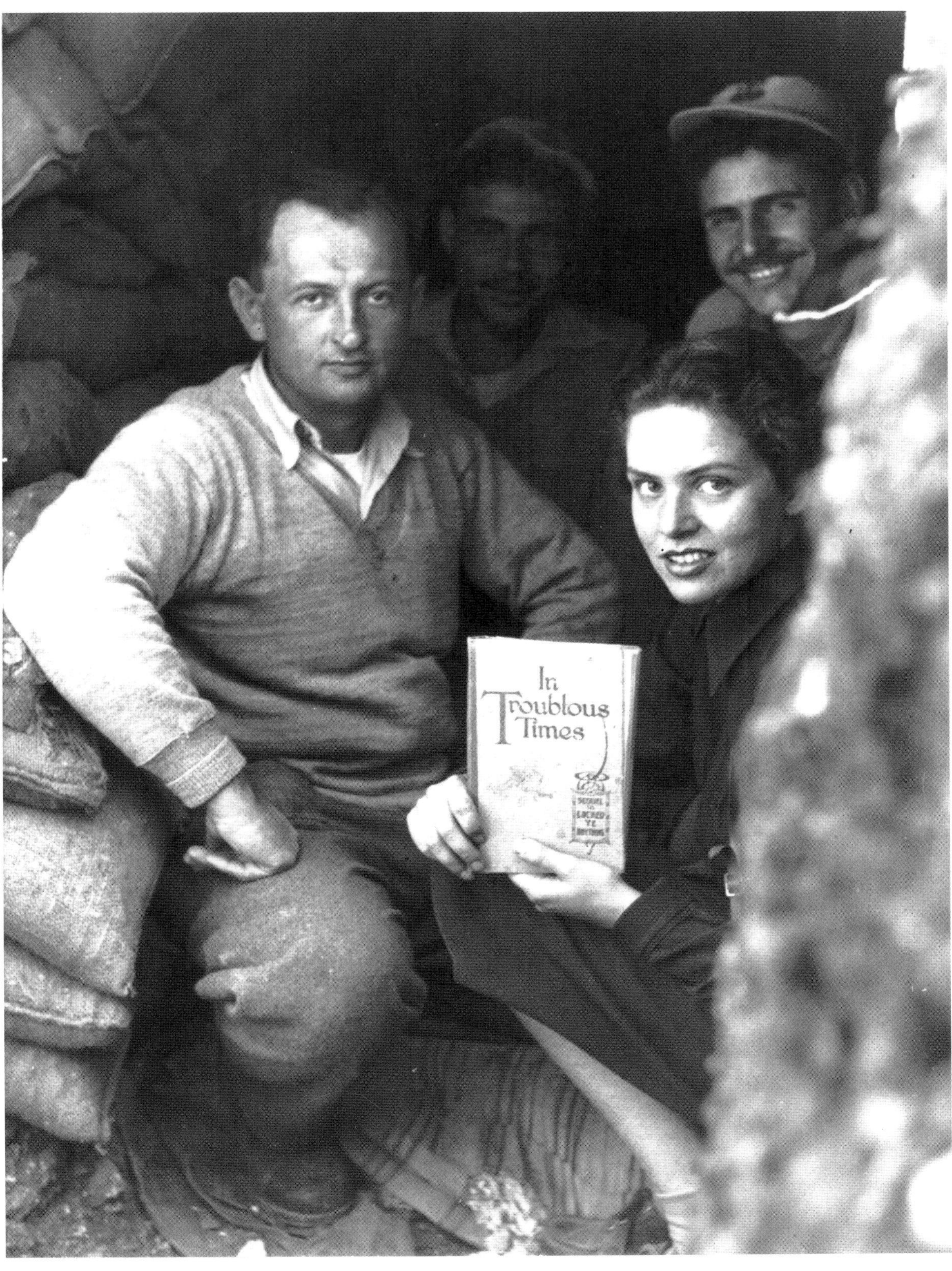

Kibbutz Ramat Rahel
under siege.
Jerusalem Post Archives
1948

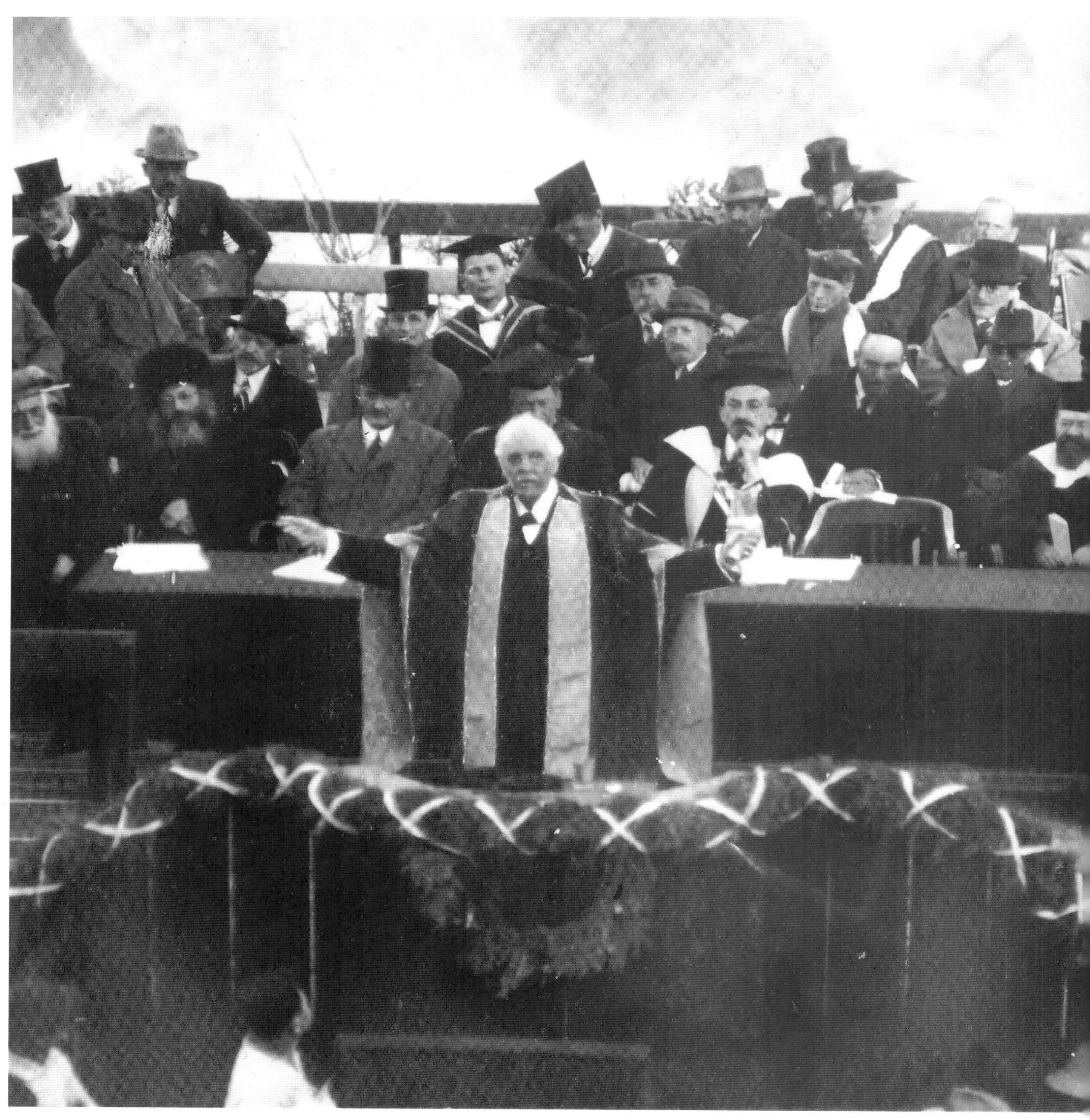

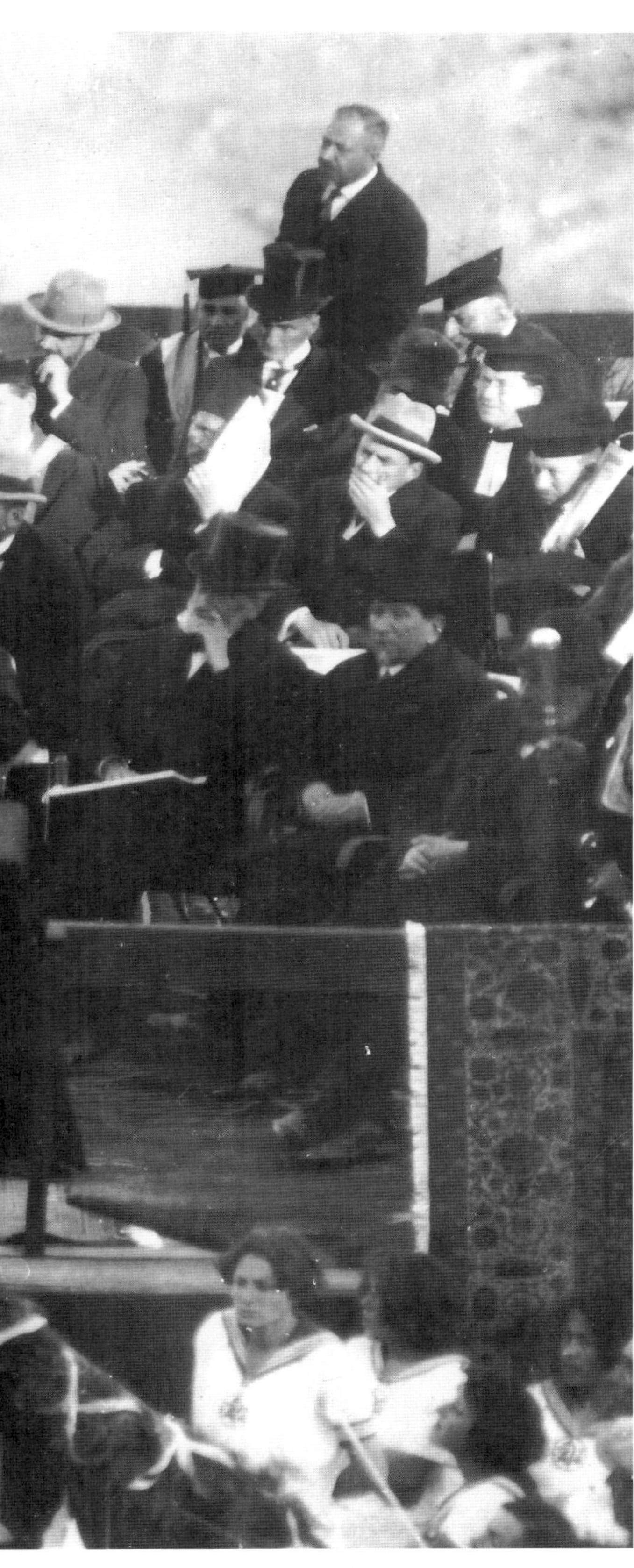

Lord Balfour proclaims the opening of the Hebrew University of Jerusalem on Mount Scopus.

Ralph Fried

1925

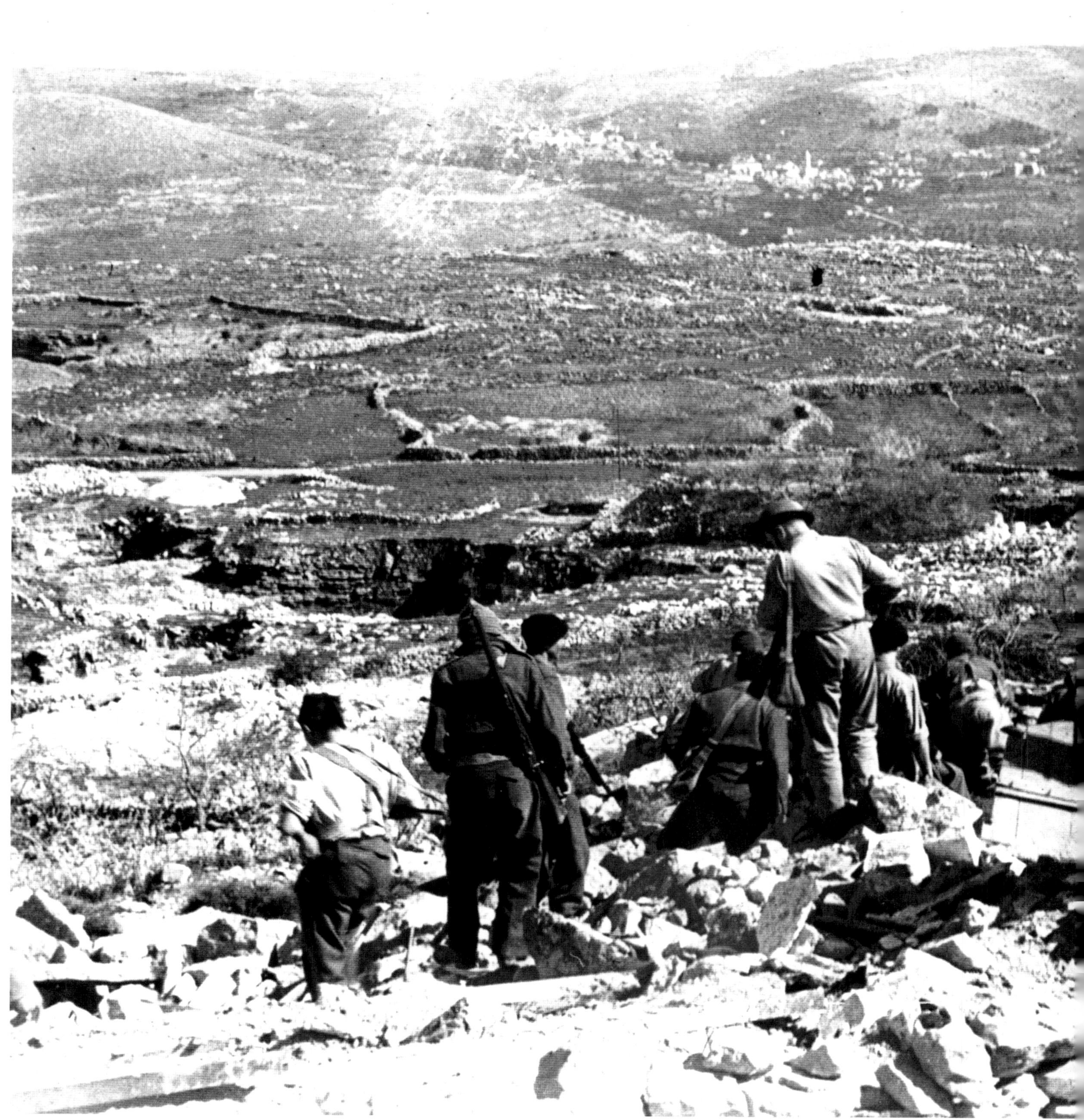

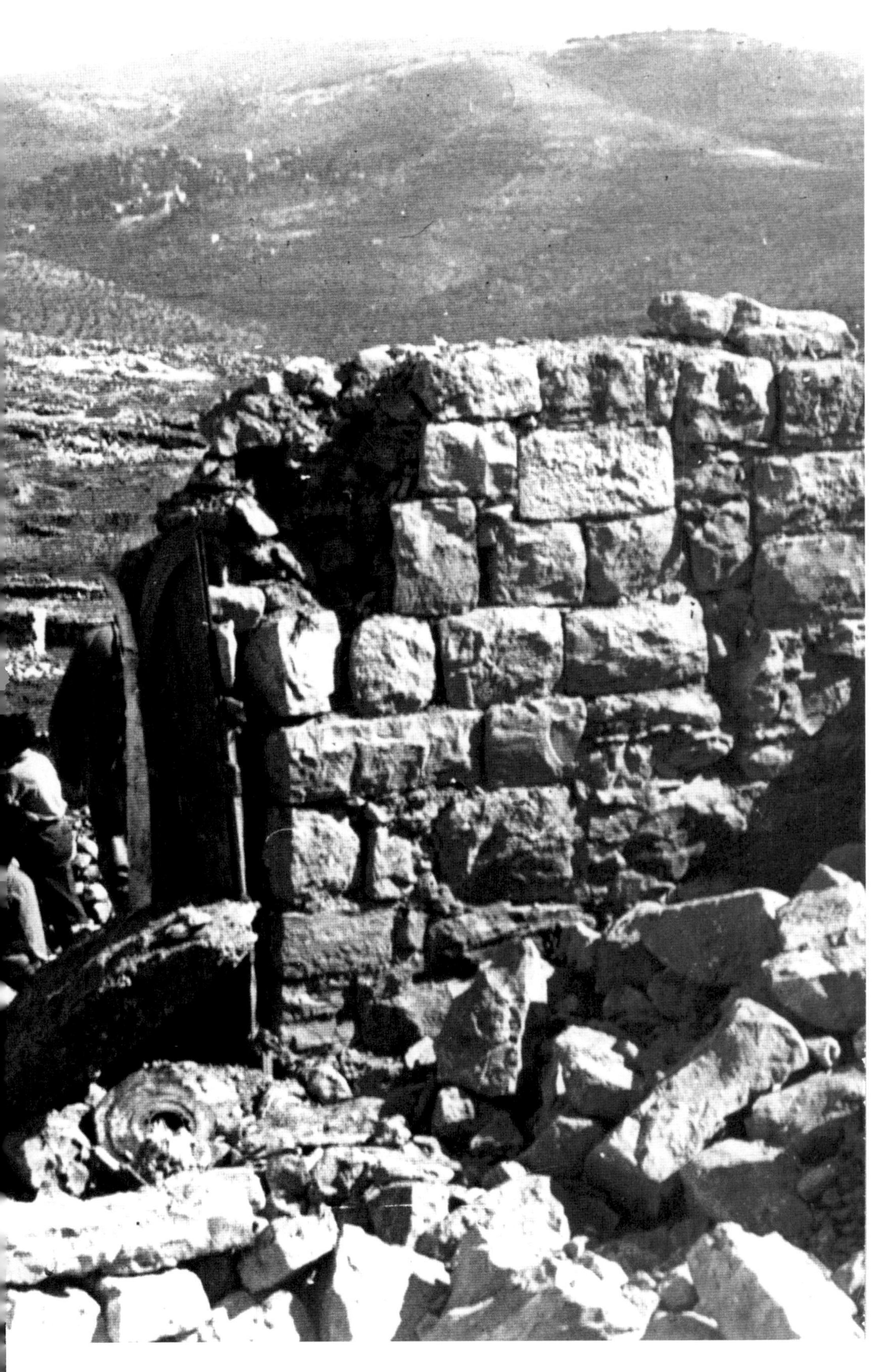

The Battle of Katamon for the southern approach to Jerusalem.

Jerusalem Post Archives

1948

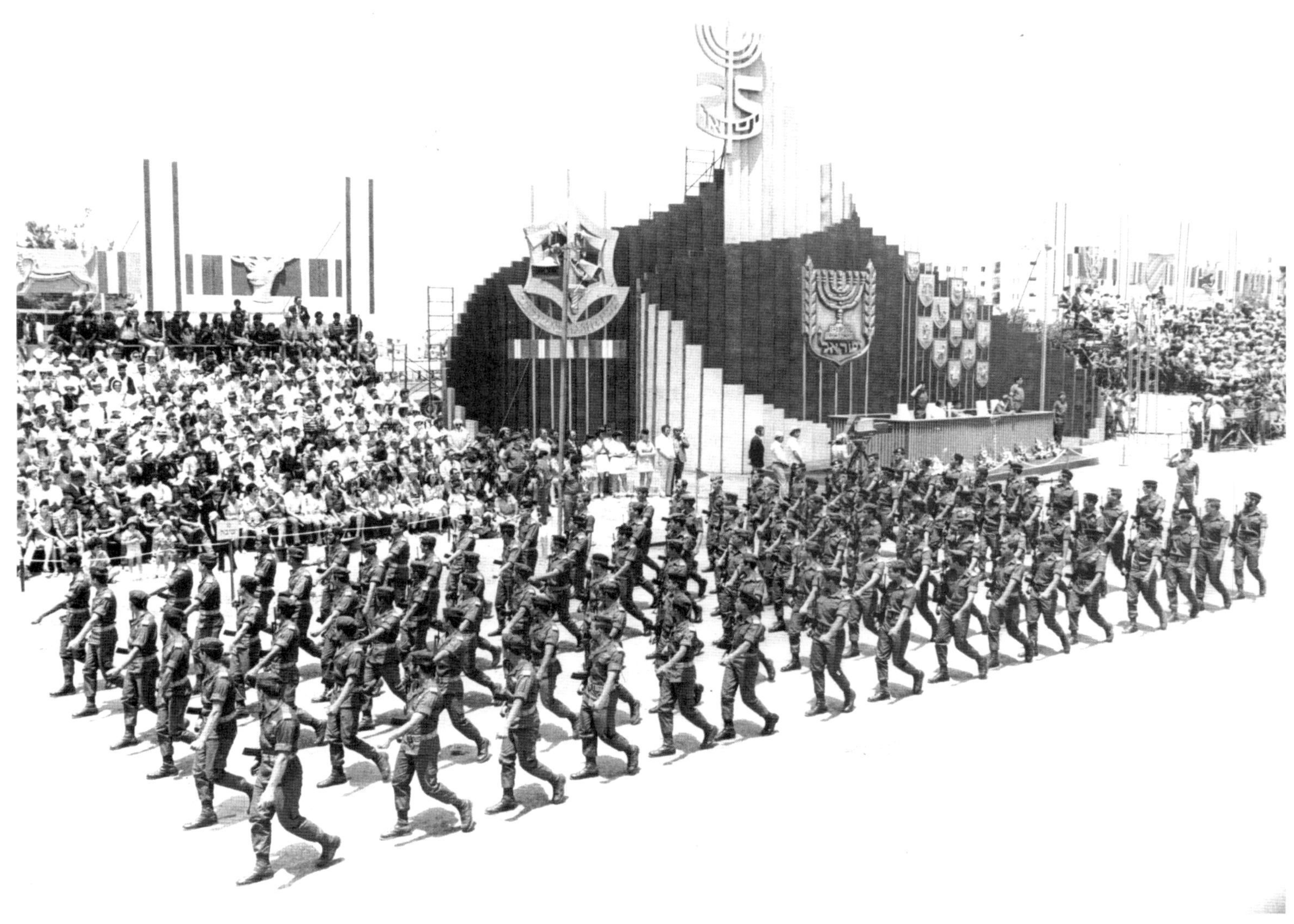

Troops march past the reviewing stand and mobile artillery units pass in review in Jerusalem, on Israel's last Independence Day military parade, marking the country's 25th anniversary.

Jerusalem Post Archives

1973

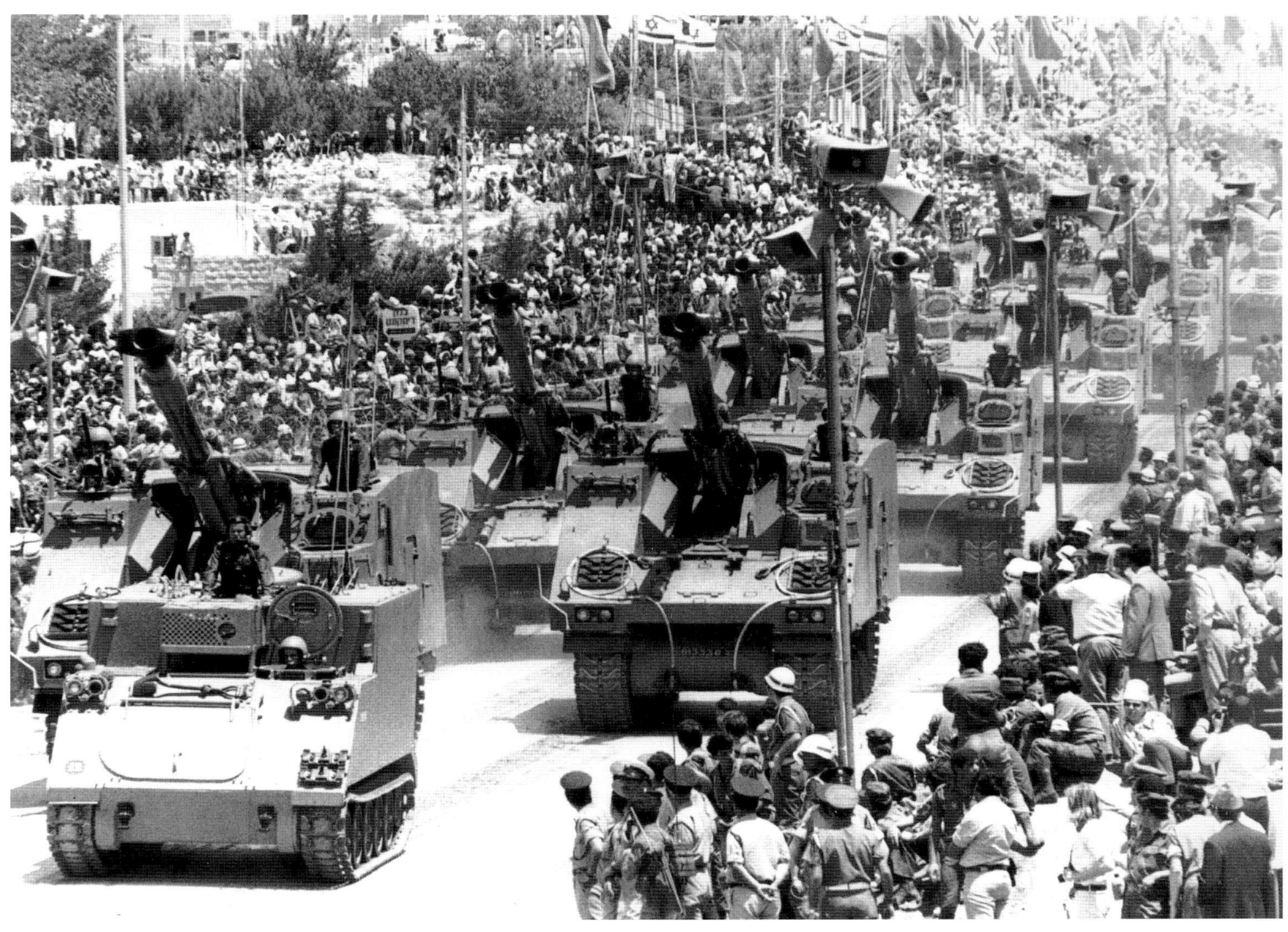

A display of tanks at that 1973 Independence Day military parade.

Jerusalem Post Archives

1973

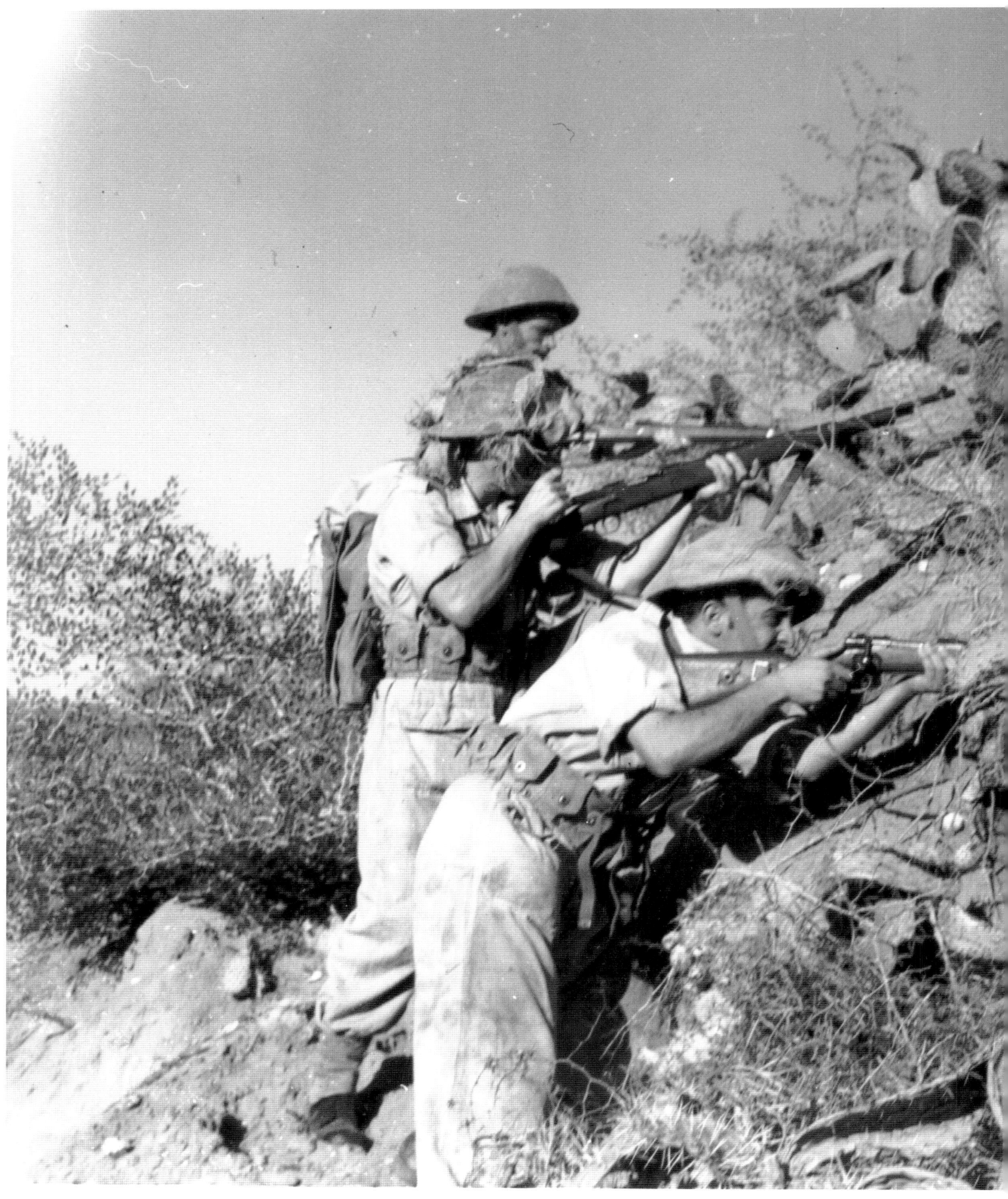

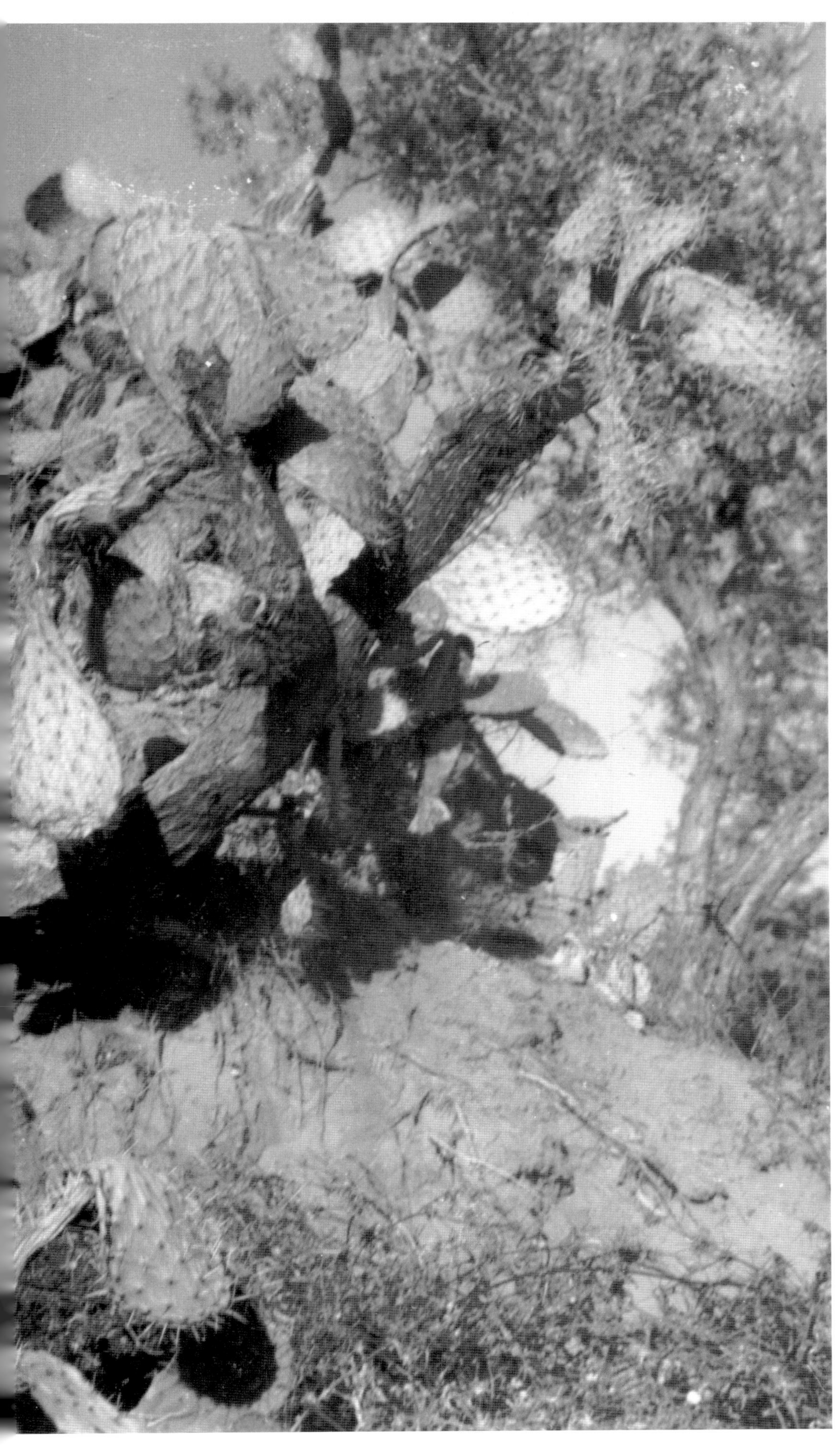

Hagana troops fight in the battle for Ramle.
Rolf Kneller
1948

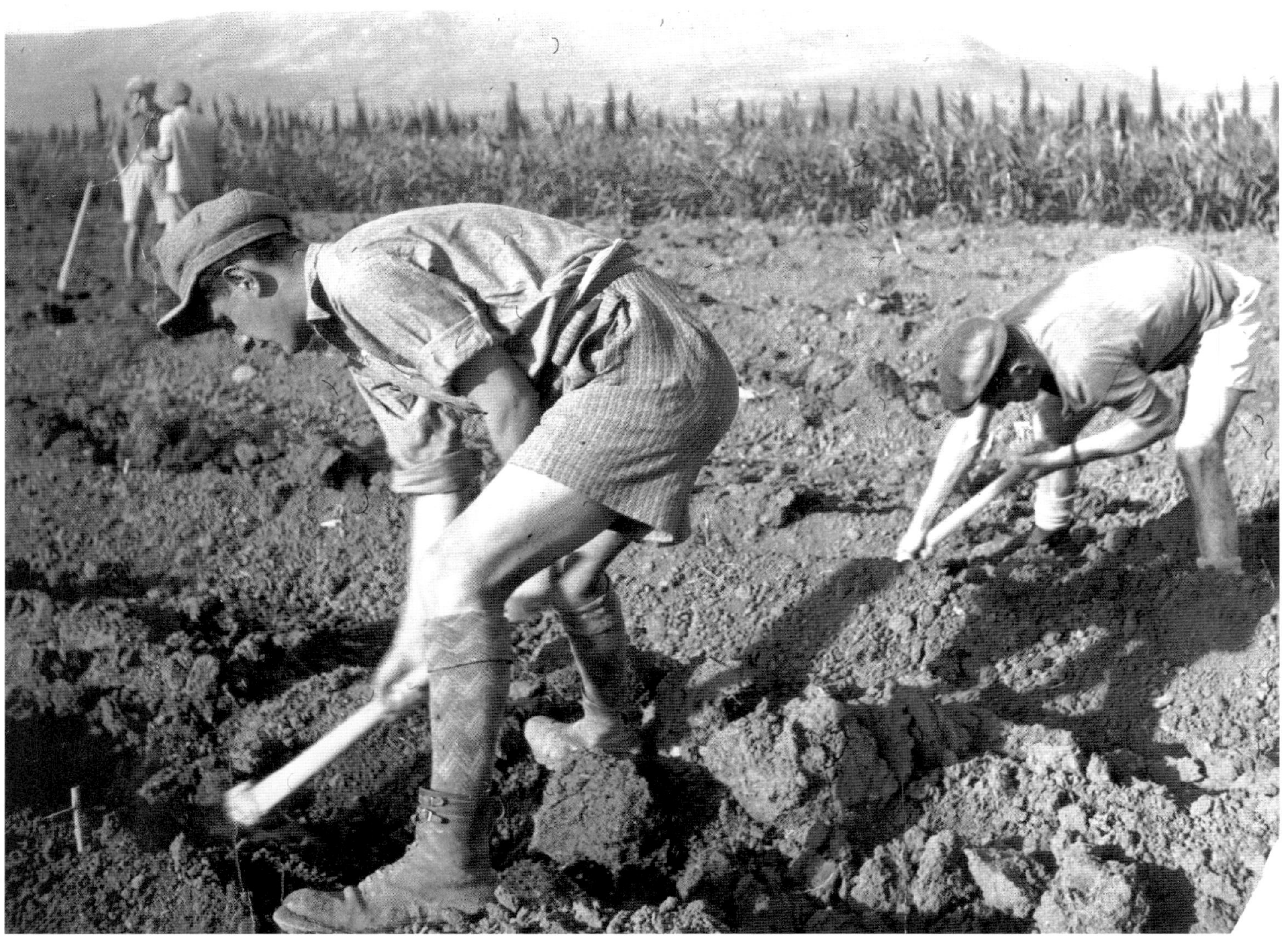

Preparing the ground for banana trees at Kibbutz Degania Alef.

Keren Hayesod-UIA

1927

Members of Agudat Yisrael from Eastern Europe.

Jerusalem Post Archives

1950

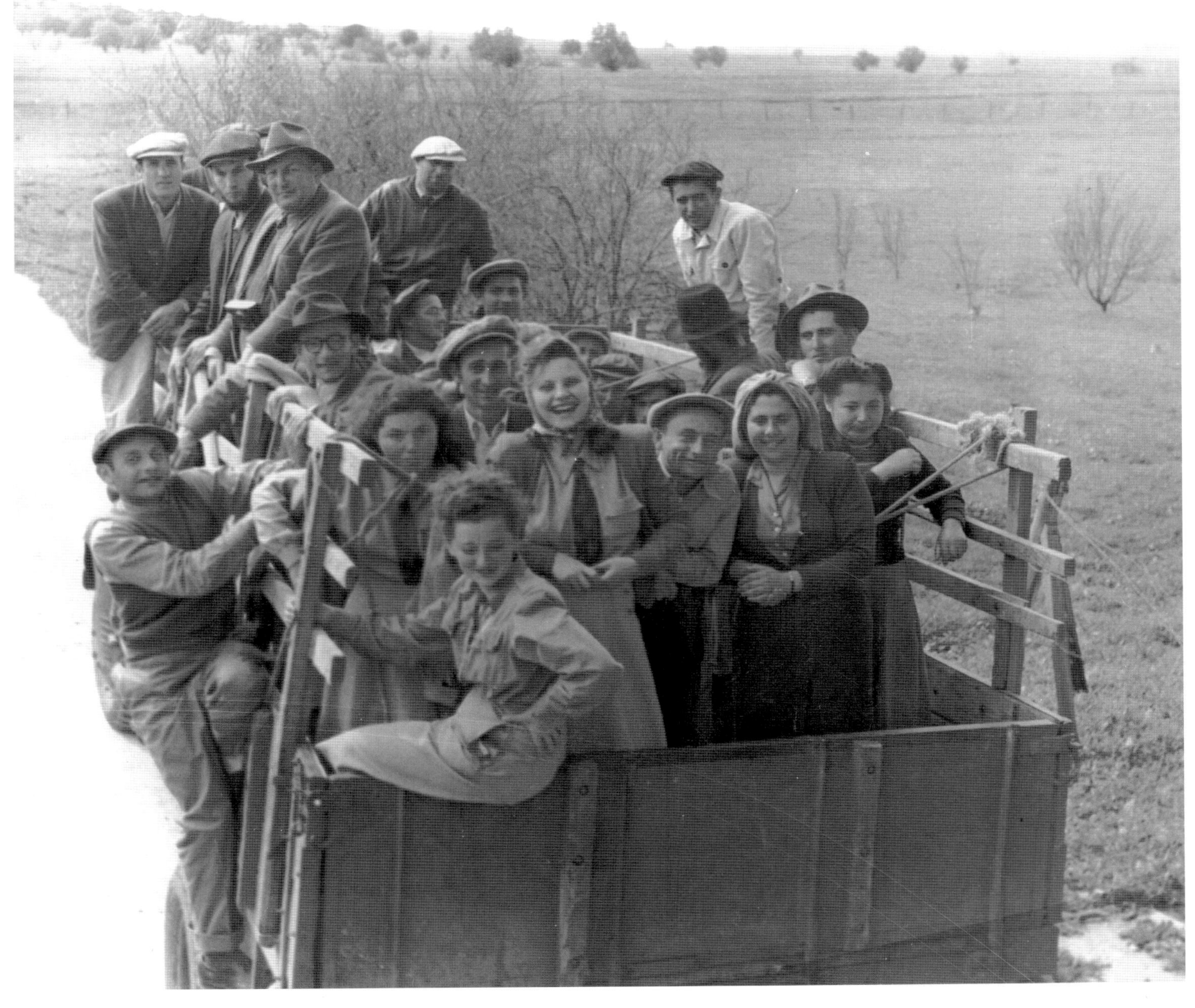

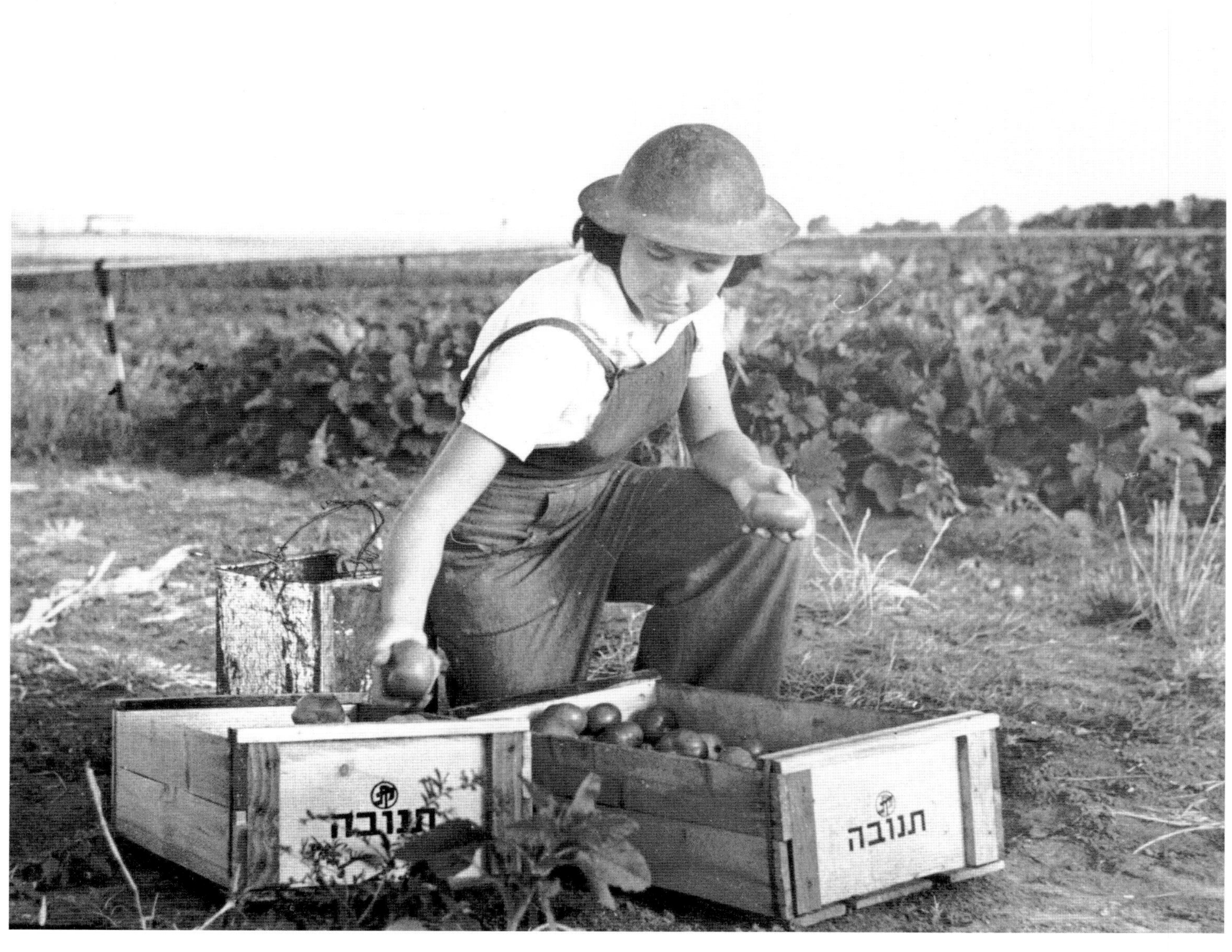

A member of Kibbutz Hazor
picks vegetables shortly
before the cease-fire.

Fred Csasznik

1949

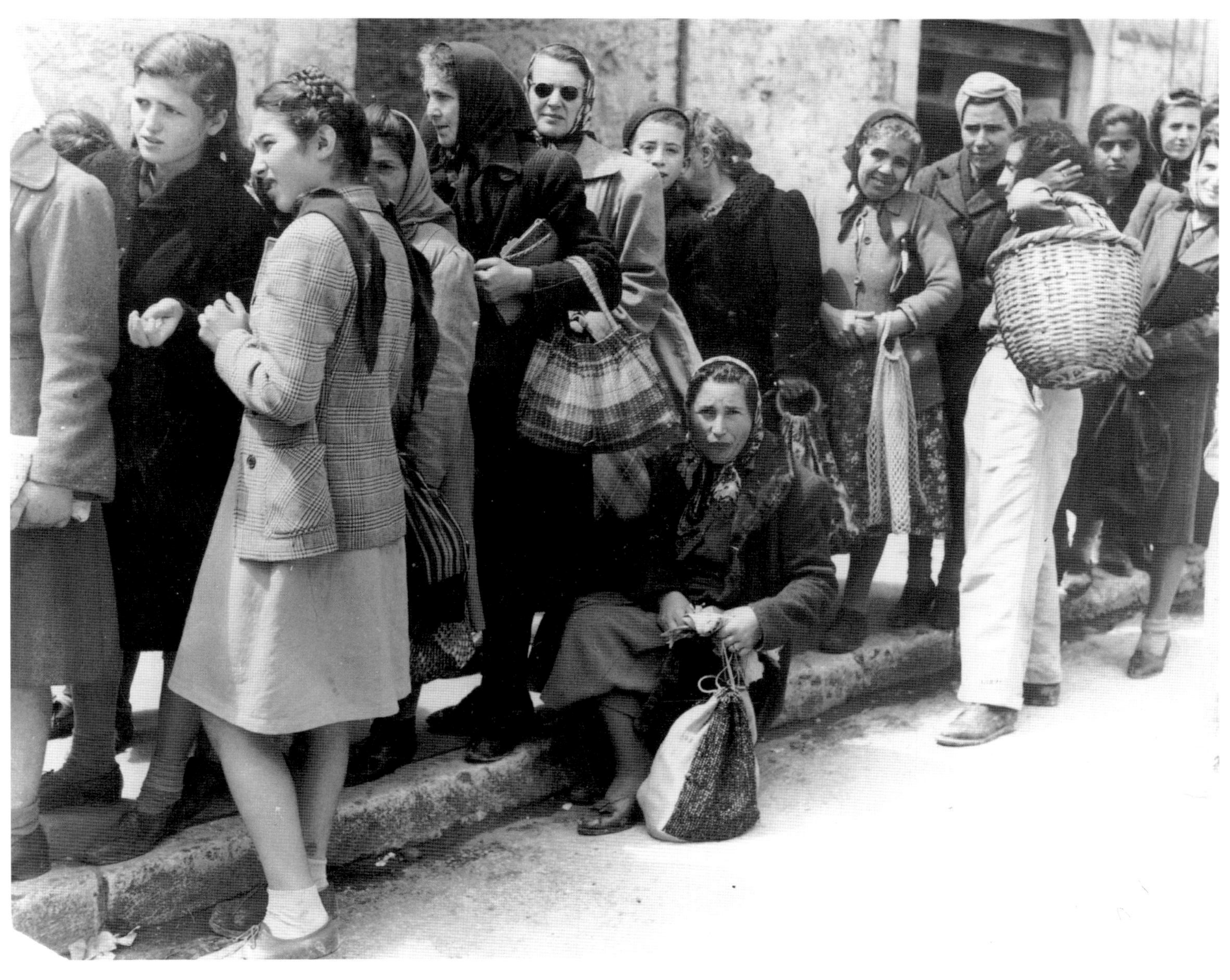

Queueing for food distribution in besieged Jerusalem.

E.F. Ilani

1948

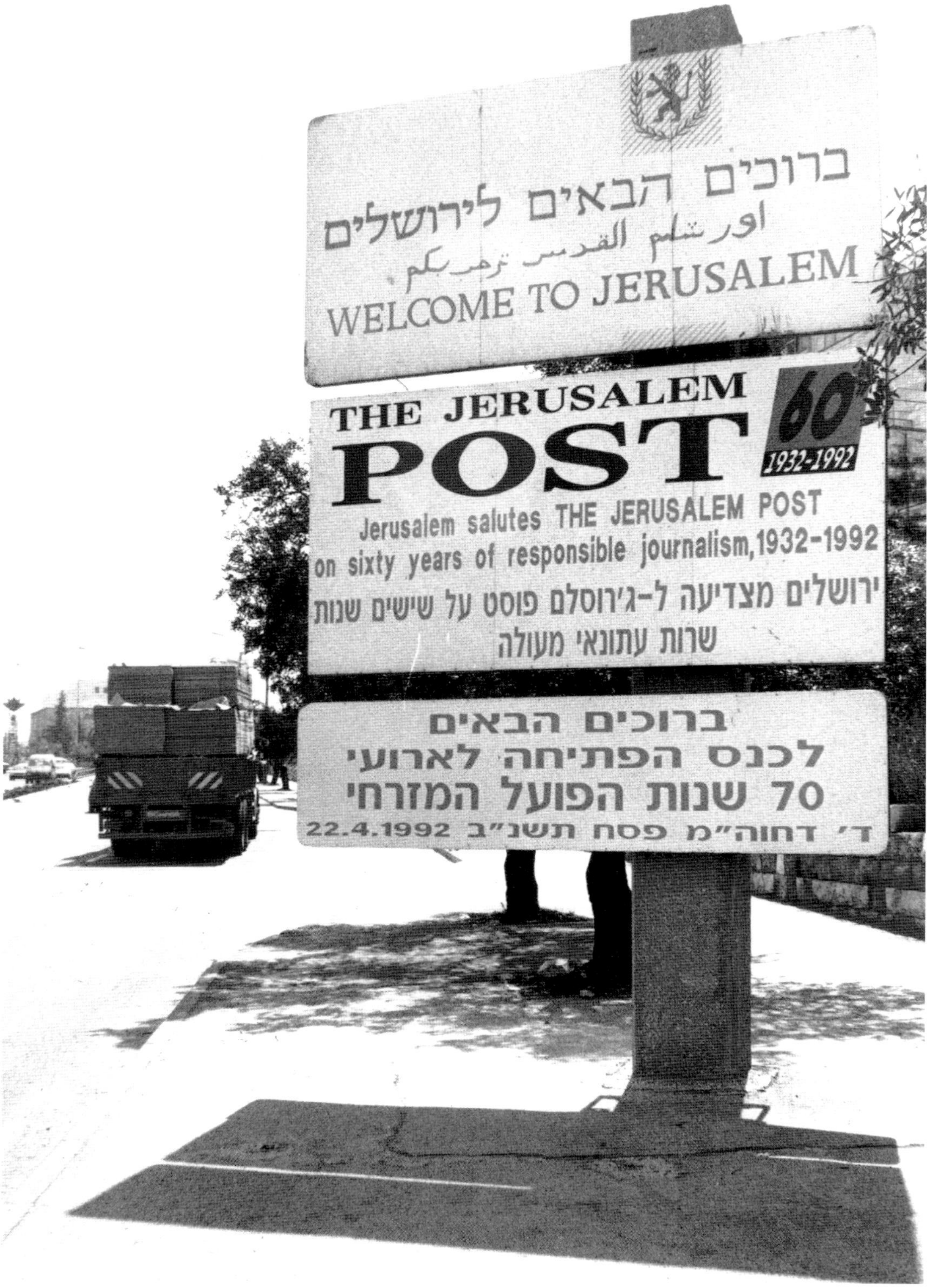

Jerusalem salutes the Post's 60th anniversary.

Isaac Harari

1992

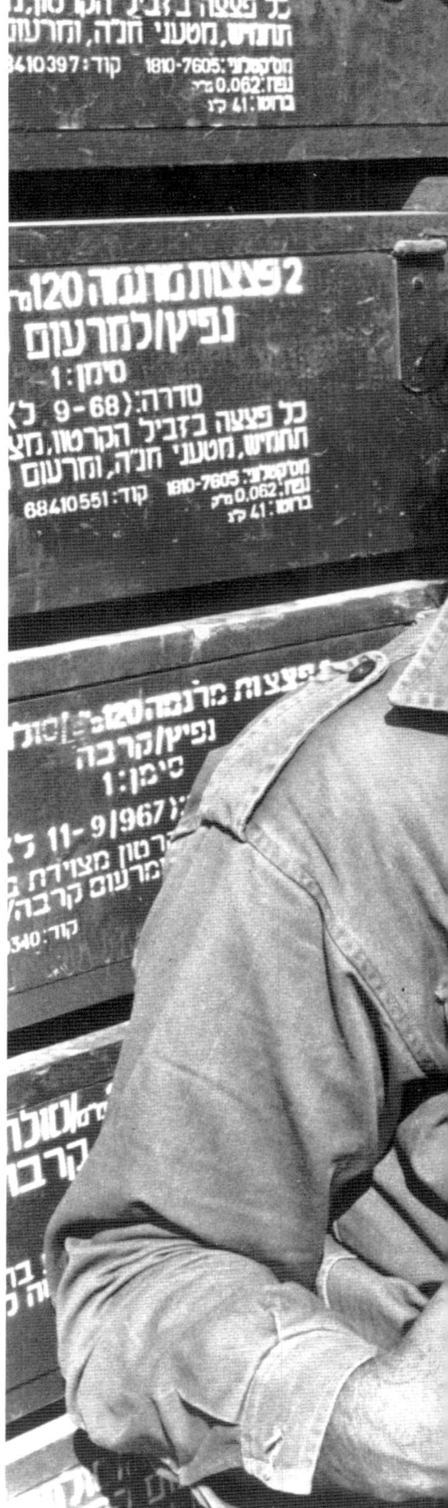

Keeping informed at the Suez Canal.

IPPA

1973

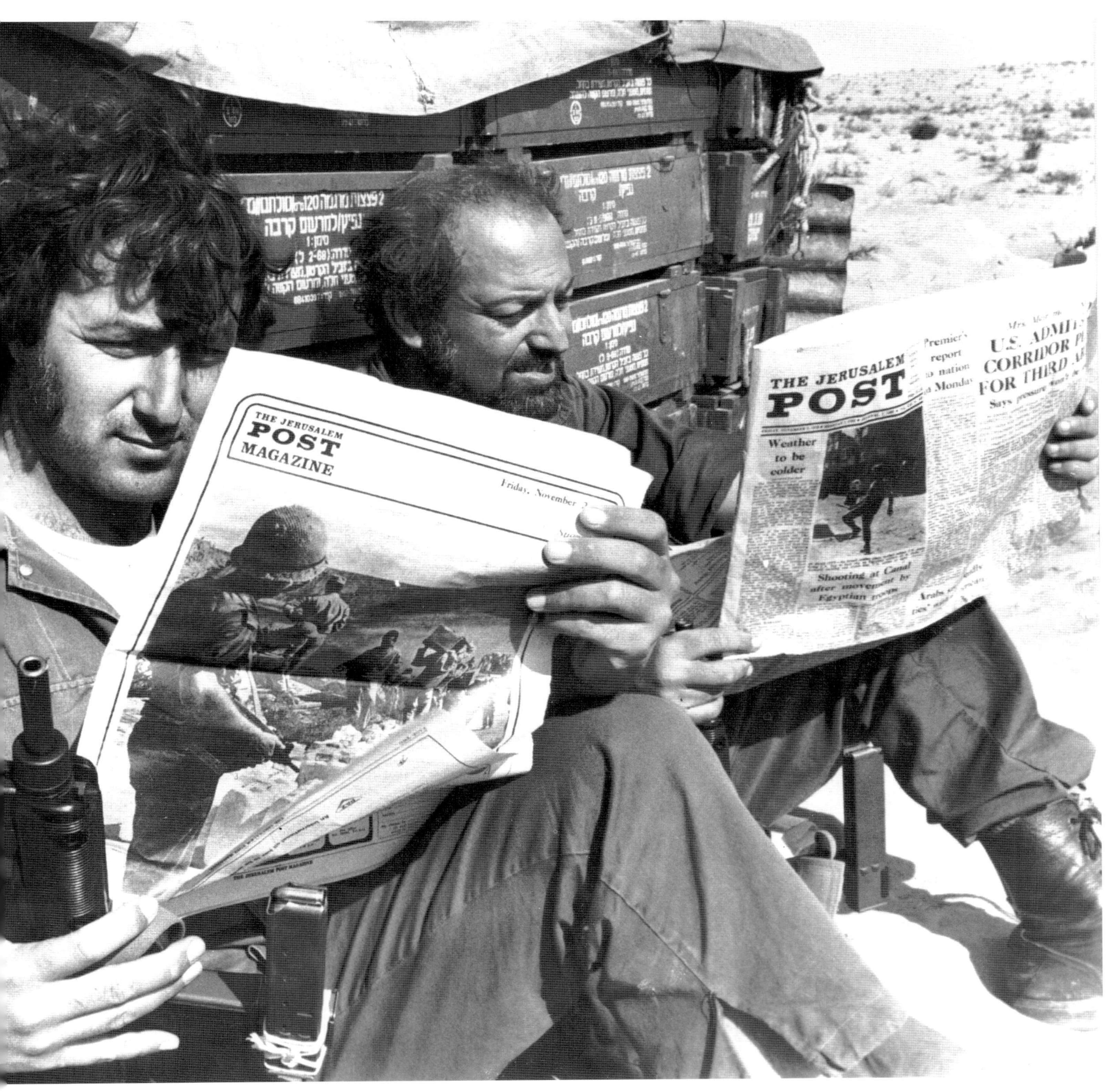
THE JERUSALEM
POST
MAGAZINE
THE JERUSALEM
POST
Weather
to be
colder
Shooting at Canal
after movement by
Egyptian troops

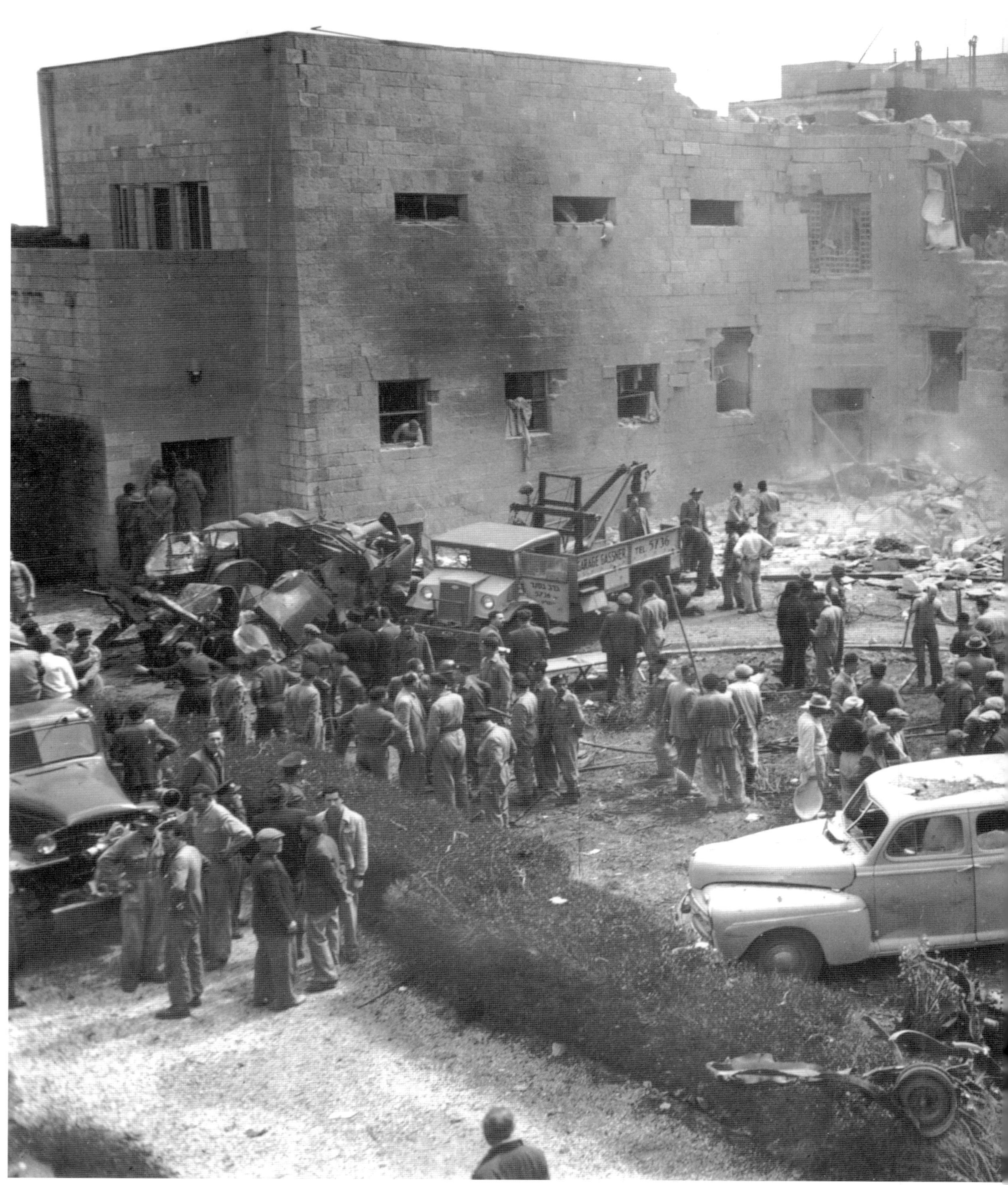
GASSNER
TEL. 5736

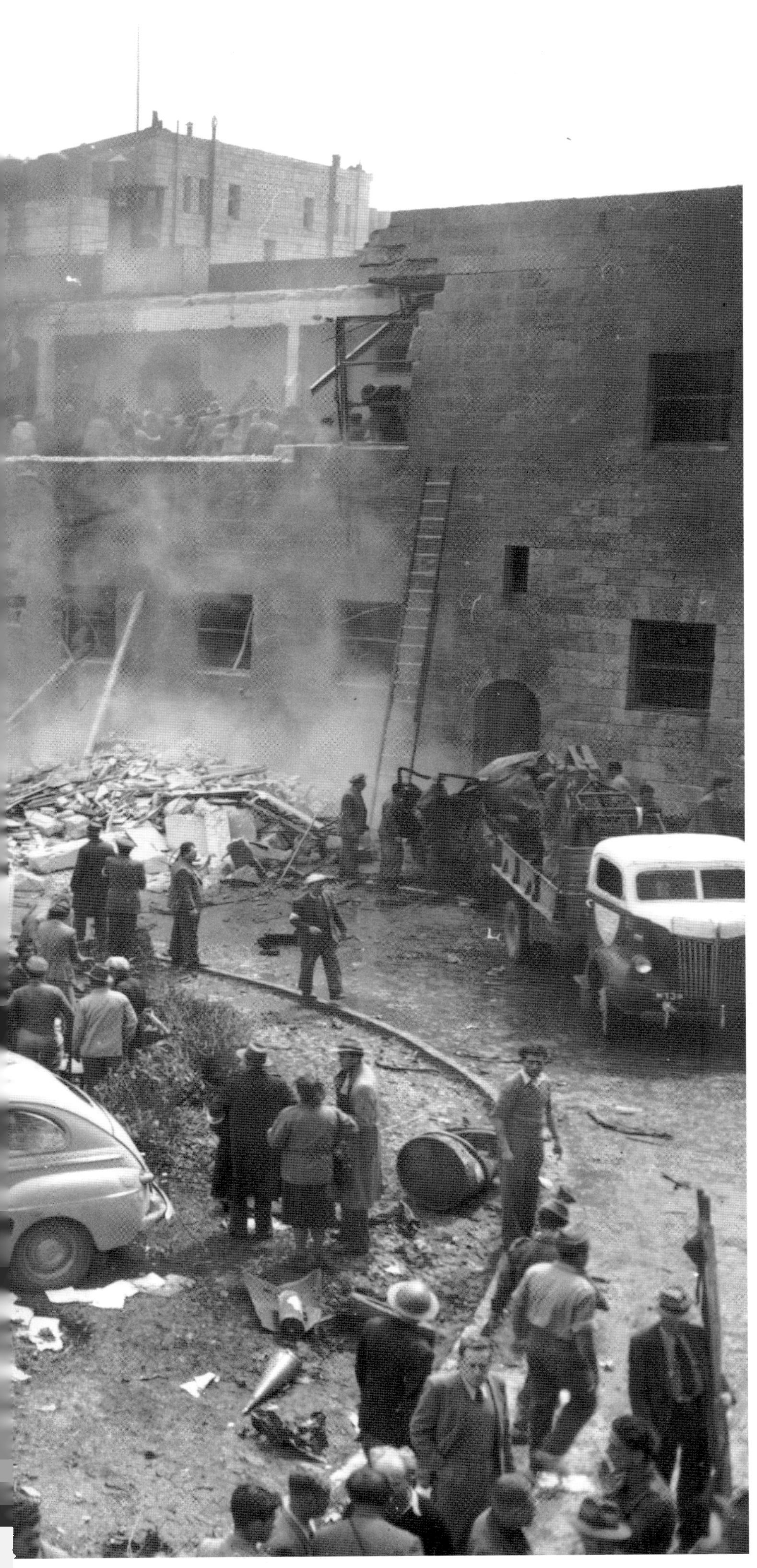

A massive terrorist car bomb damages the Jerusalem headquarters of the Jewish Agency on March 11, 1948.
Rolf Kneller
1948

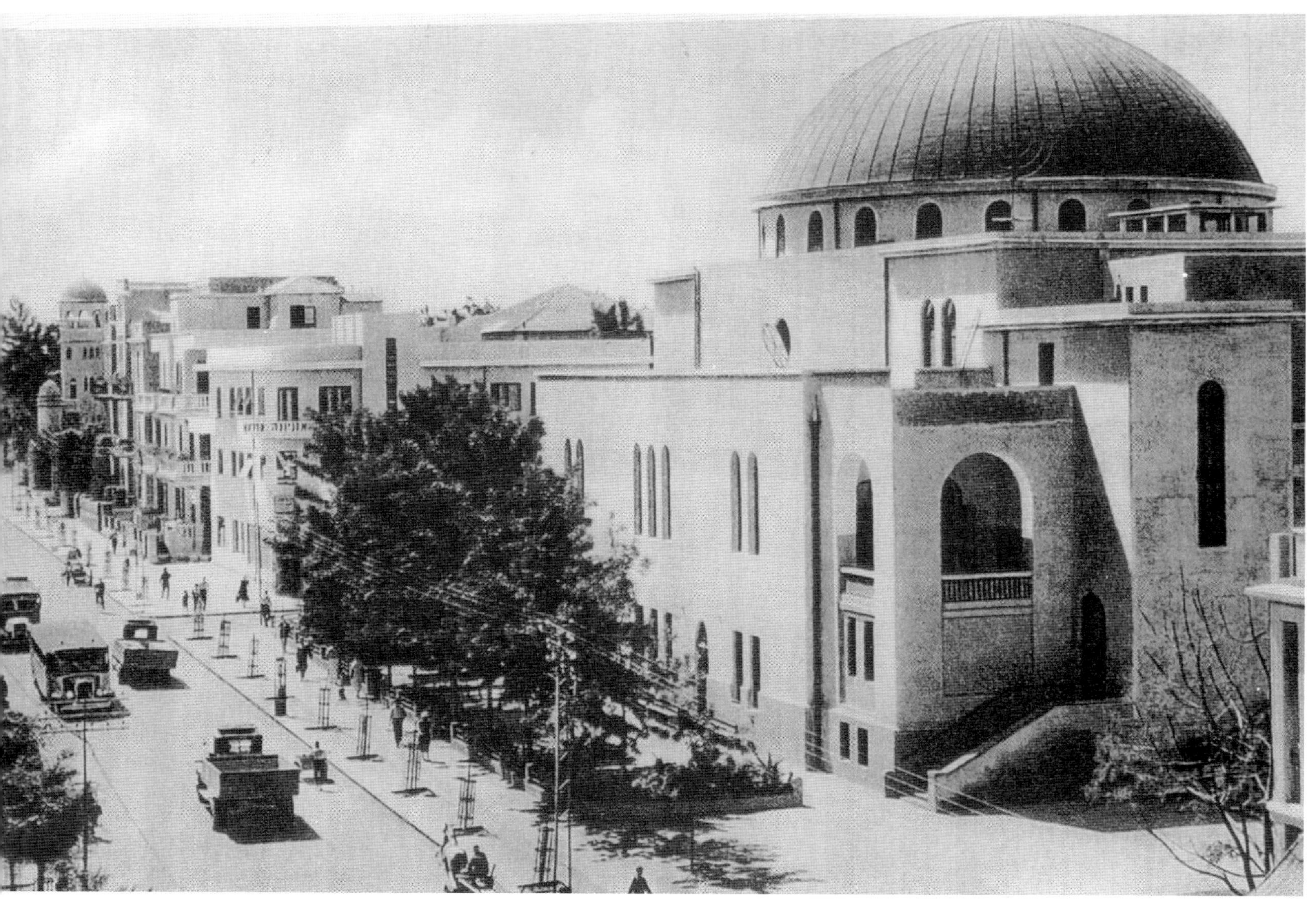

Tel Aviv's Great
Synagogue in the 1940s.
Jerusalem Post Archives
1940

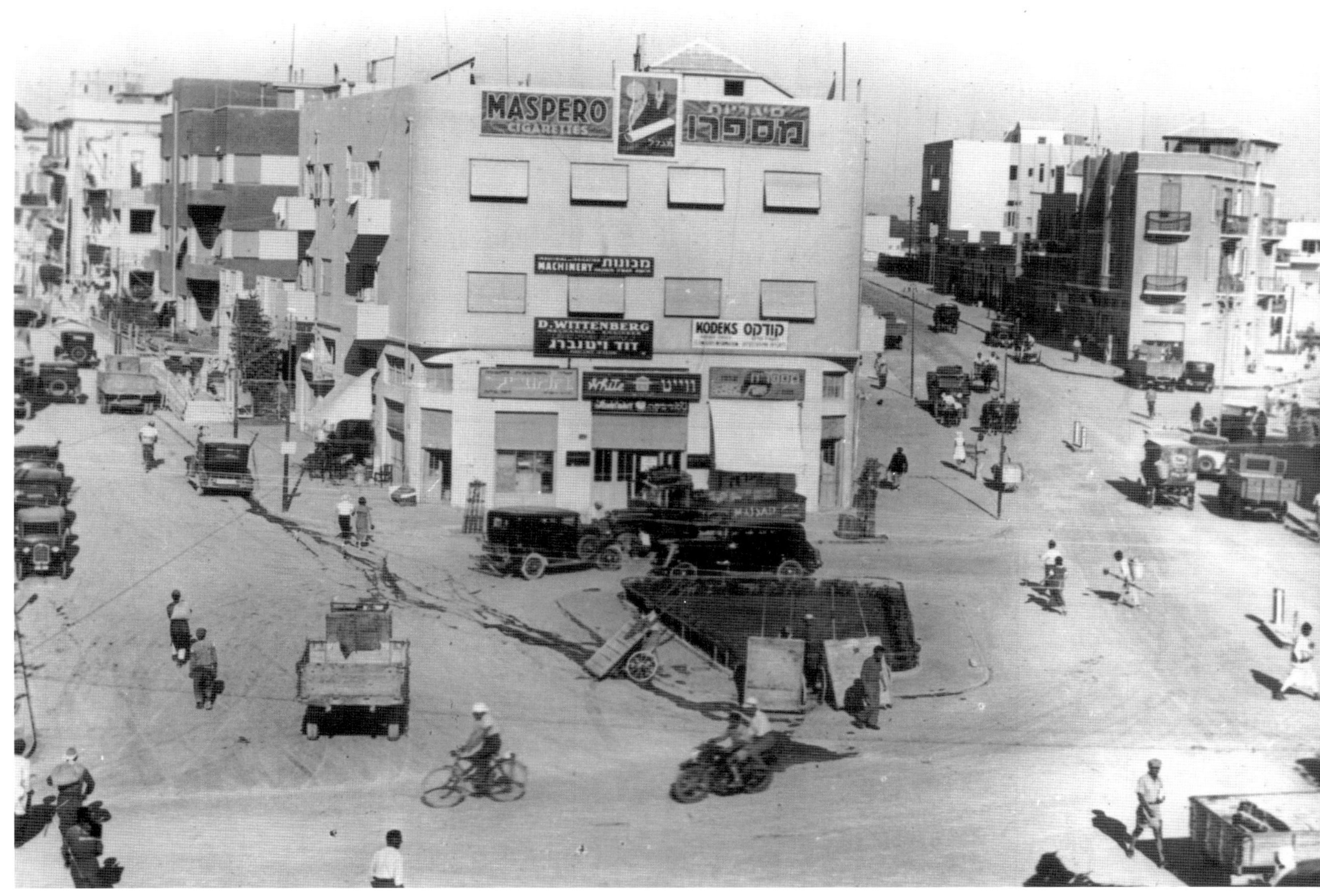

Kikar Hamoshavot in Tel Aviv.
Jerusalem Post Archives
1934

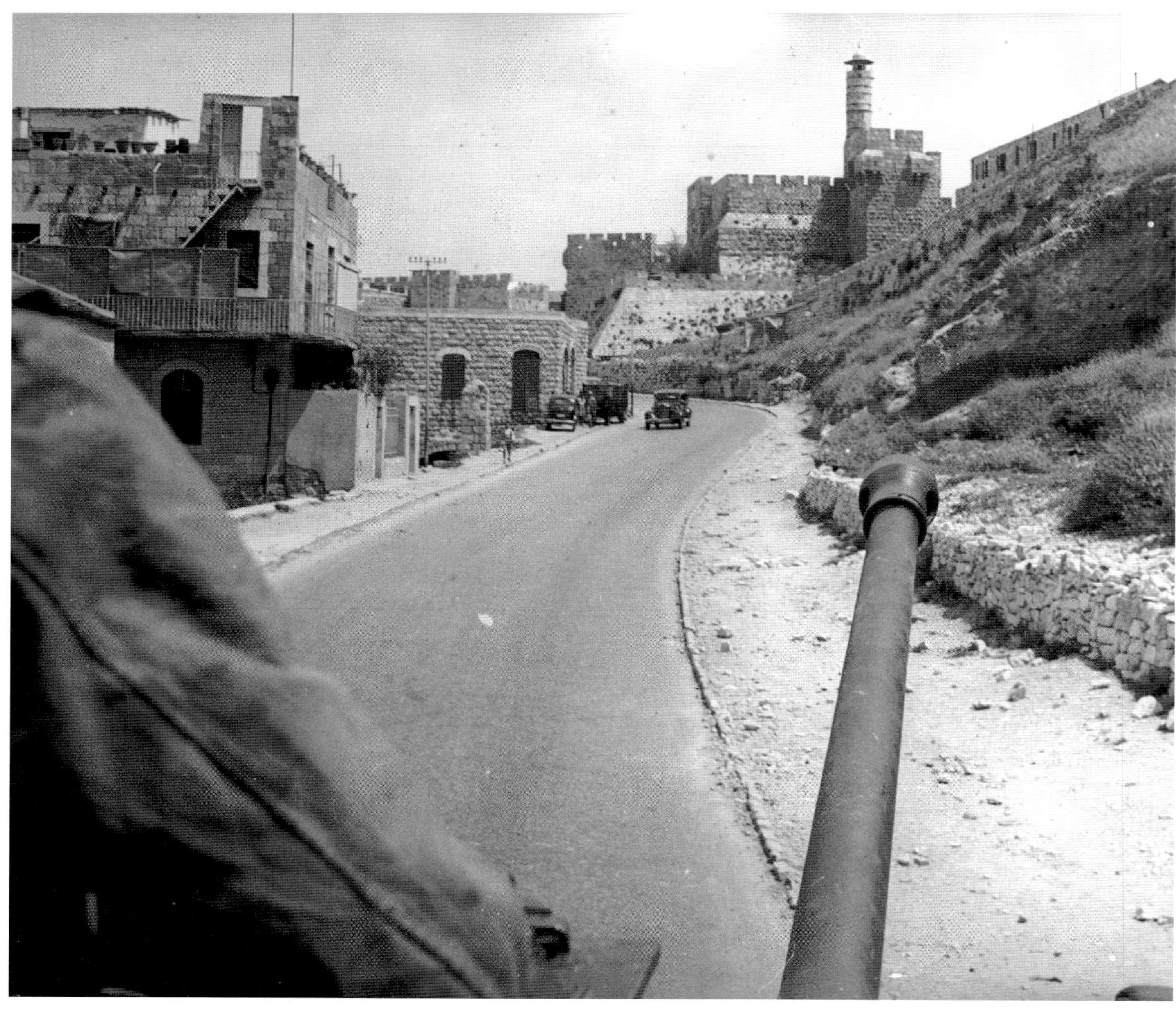

A British tank approaches
the Old City of
Jerusalem's Jaffa Gate.
Fred Csasznik
1946

IDF paratroopers get
their first glimpse of the
Western Wall.
Jerusalem Post Archives
1967

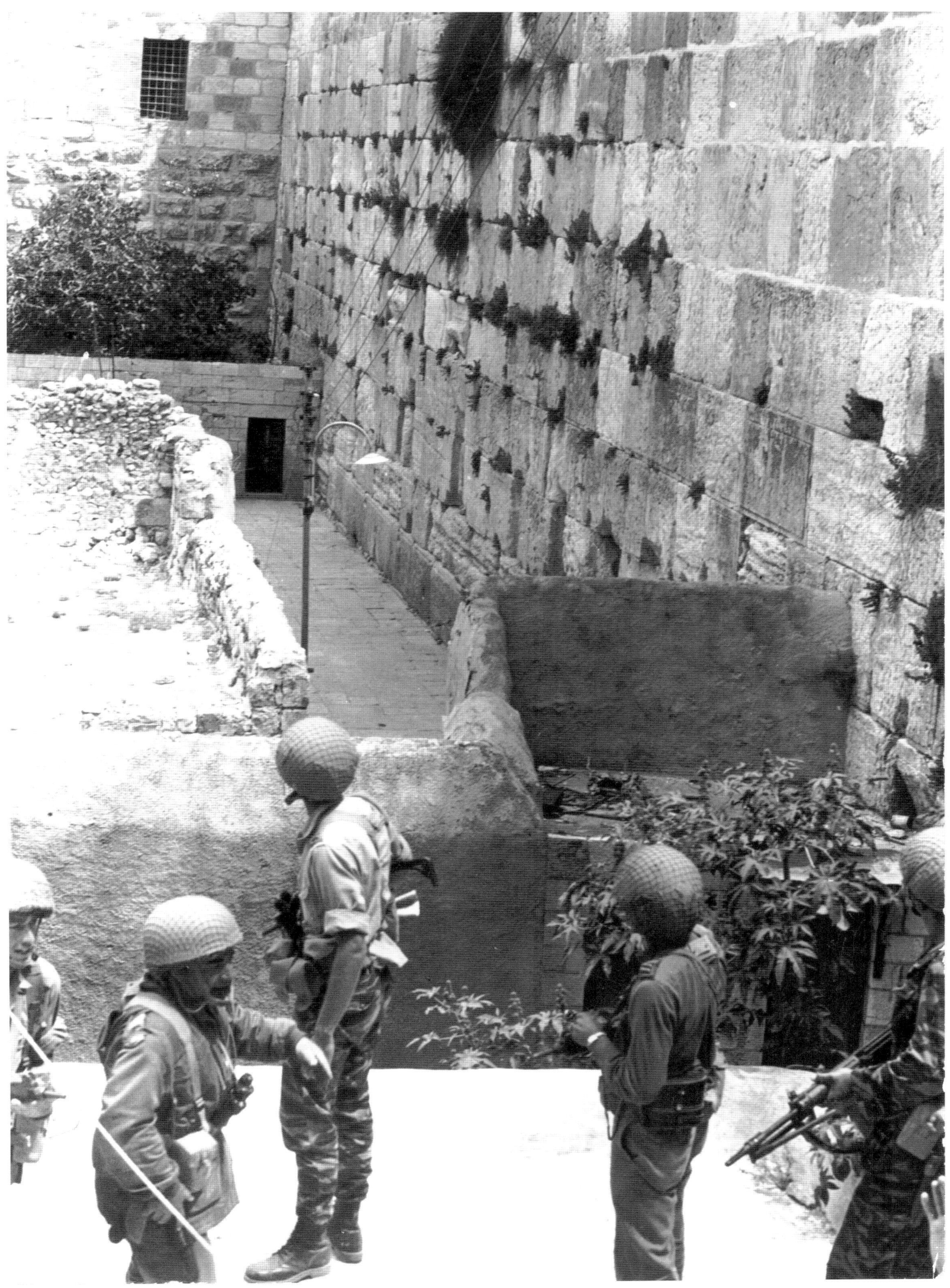

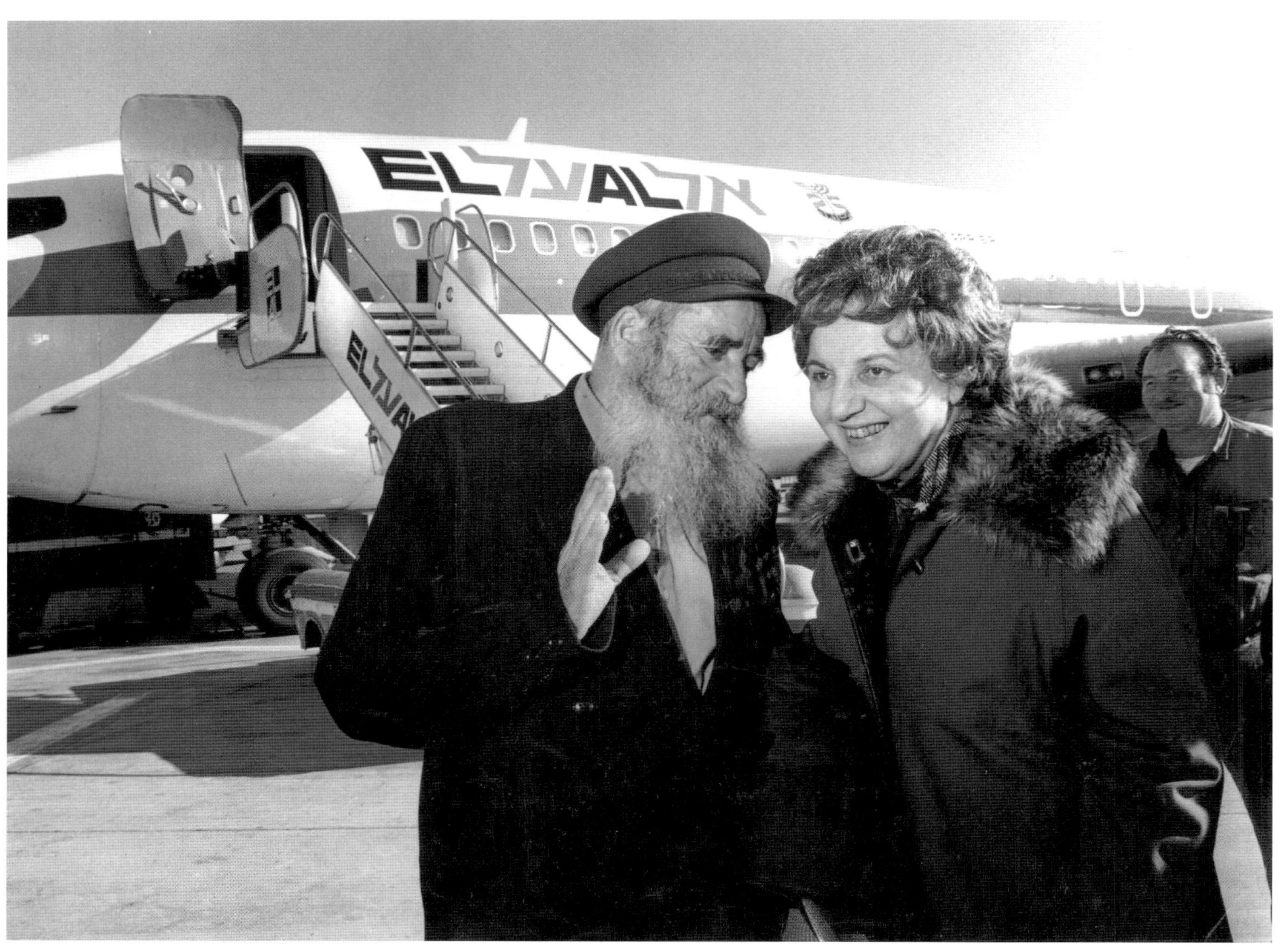

New immigrants arrive in Israel.

Jerusalem Post Archives

1990

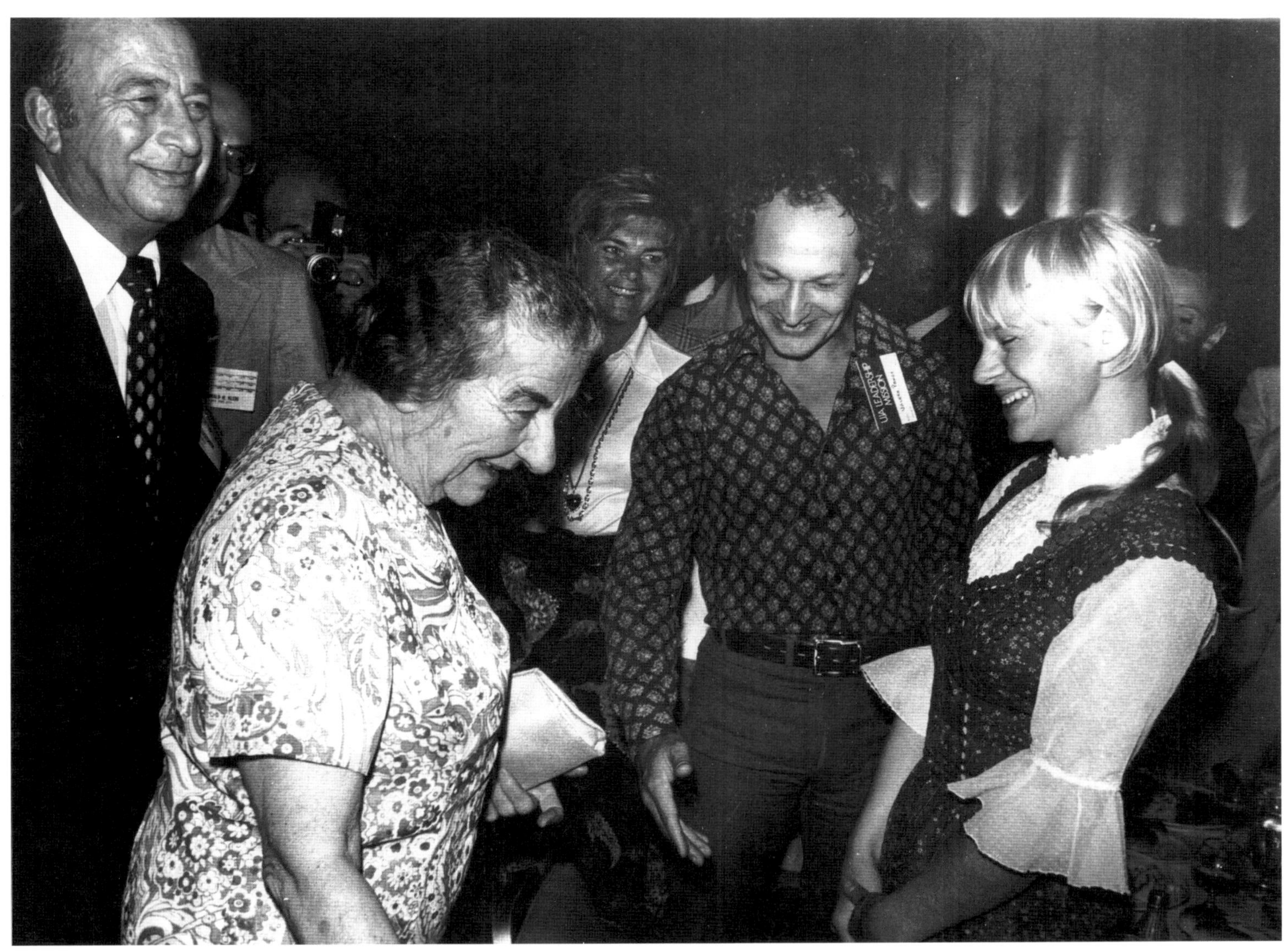

Prime Minister Golda
Meir attends a reception.

Lester J. Millman

1974

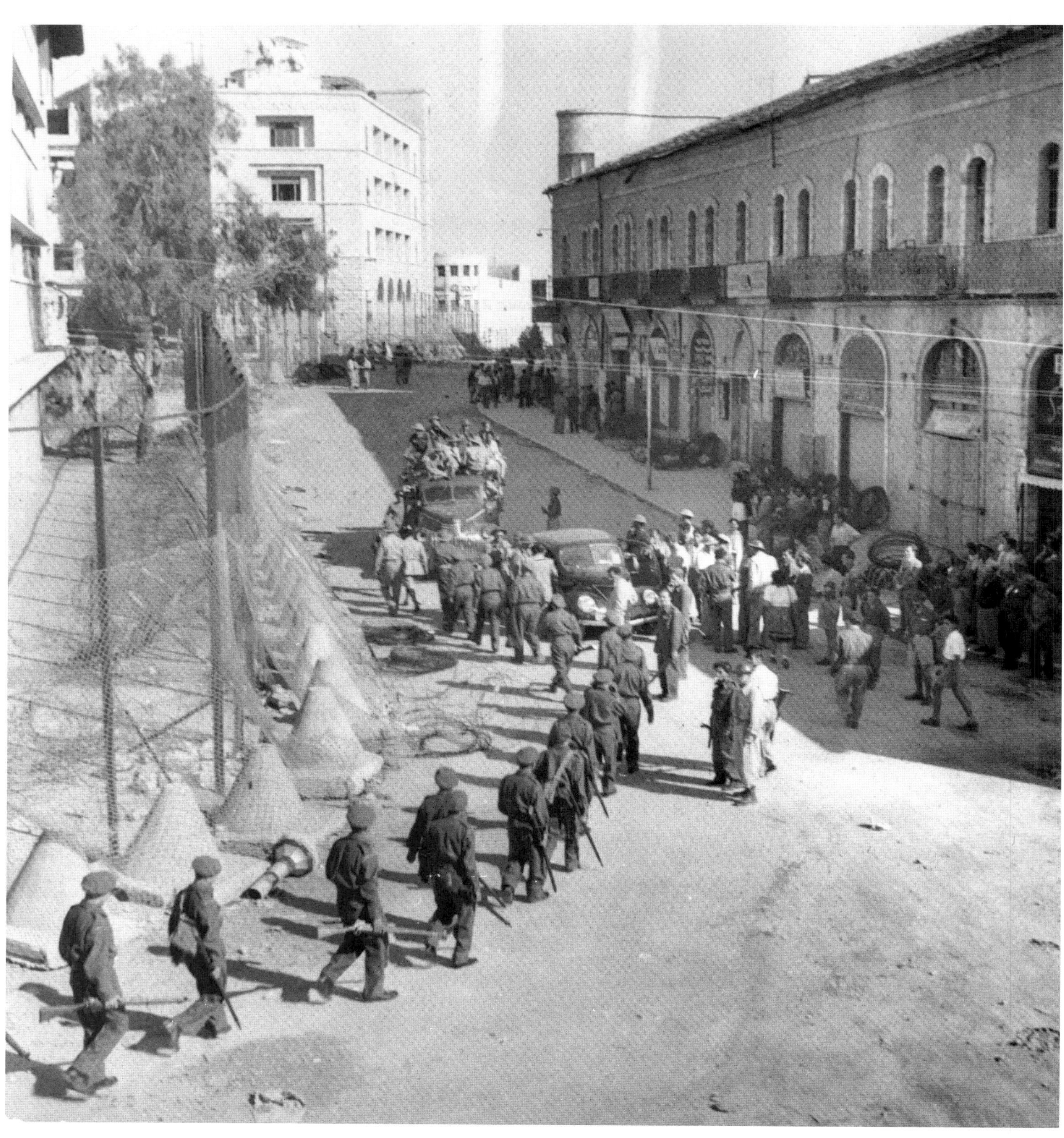

British troops march along the perimeter of the 'Bevingrad' compound in downtown Jerusalem.

Jerusalem Post Archives

1948

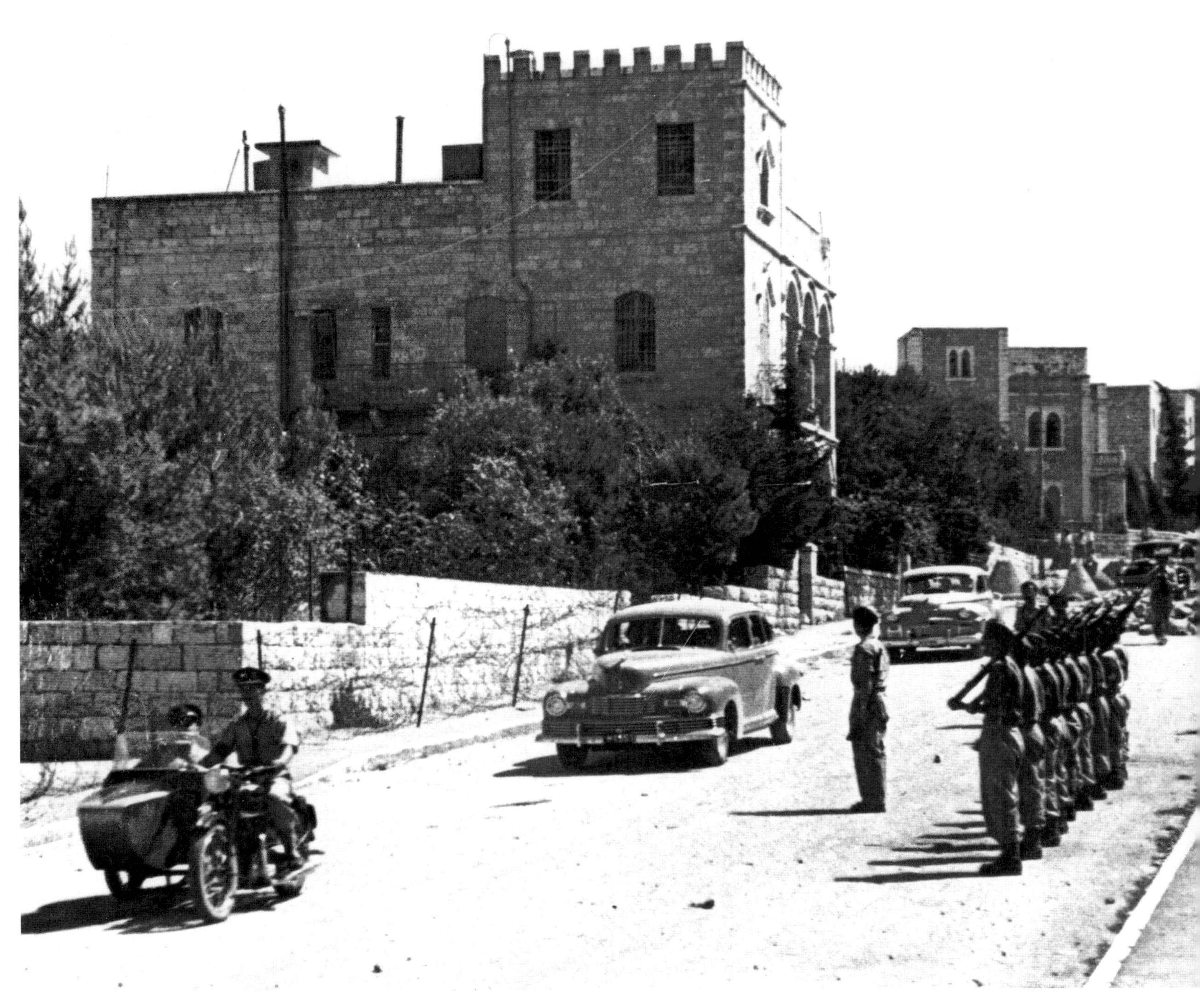

The Jewish military commander and UN officials arrive in Jerusalem for truce negotiations.

Jerusalem Post Archives

1947

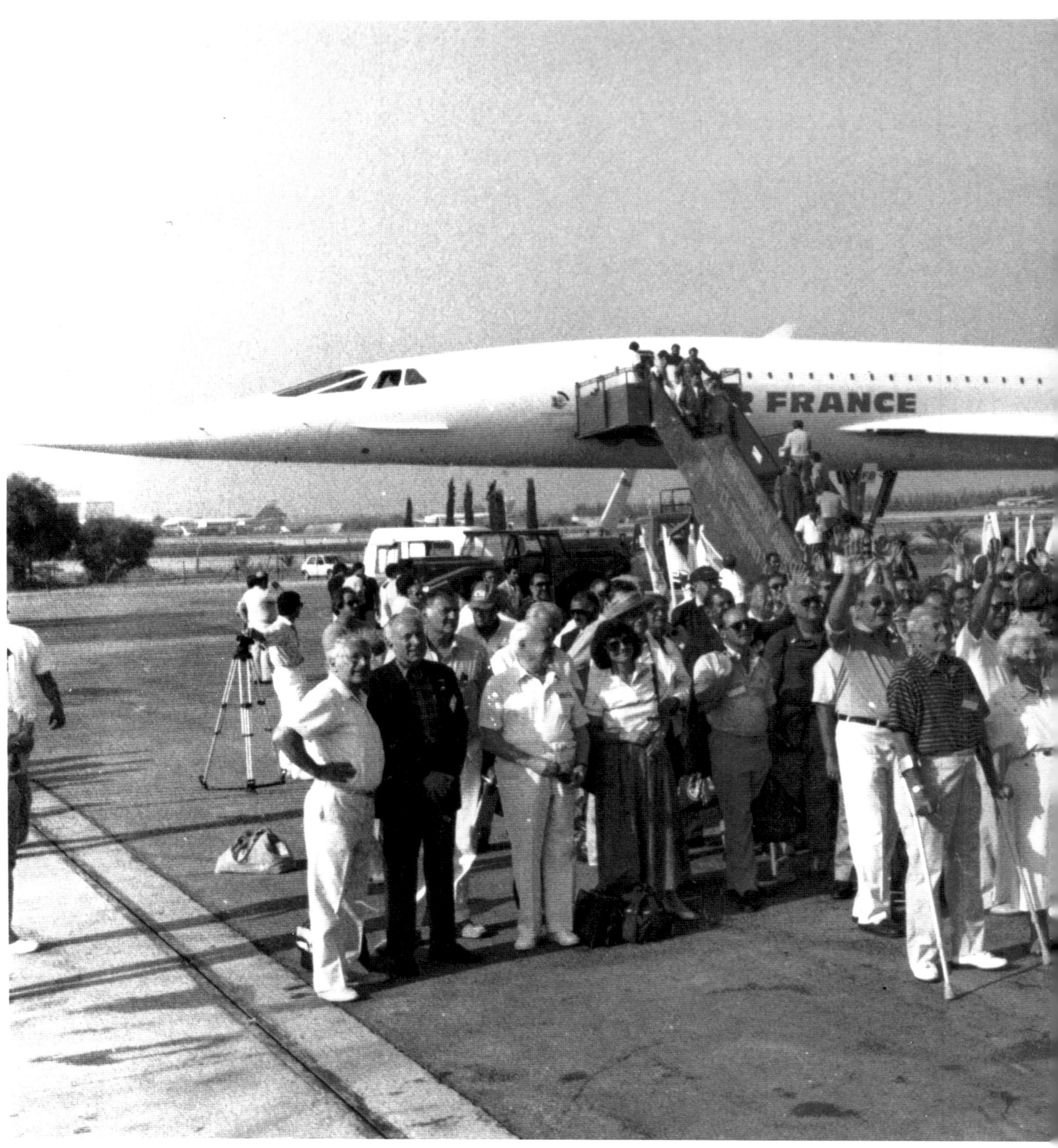
R FRANCE

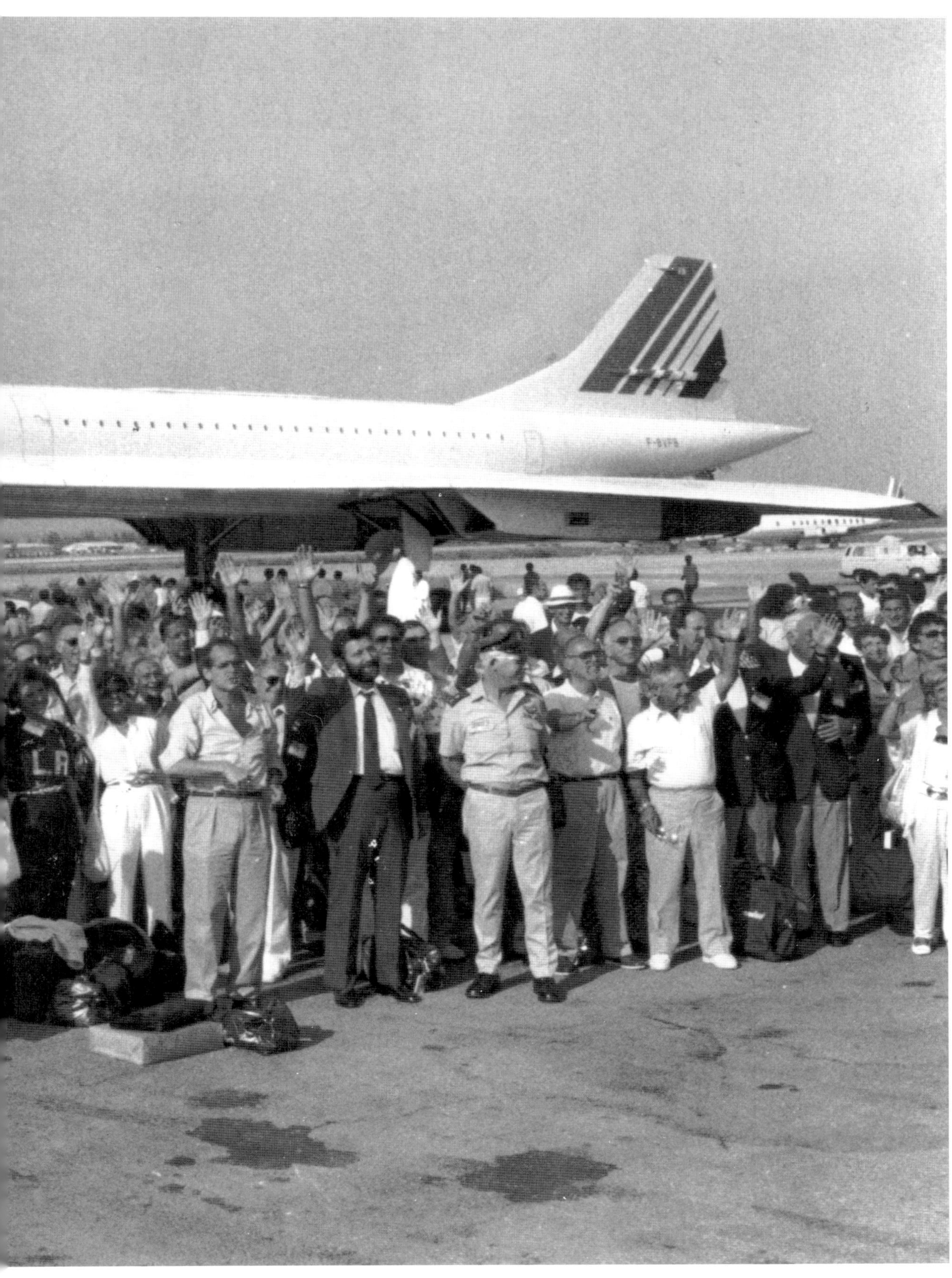

A UJA mission arrives on a special Concorde flight.
Meir Kfir
1987

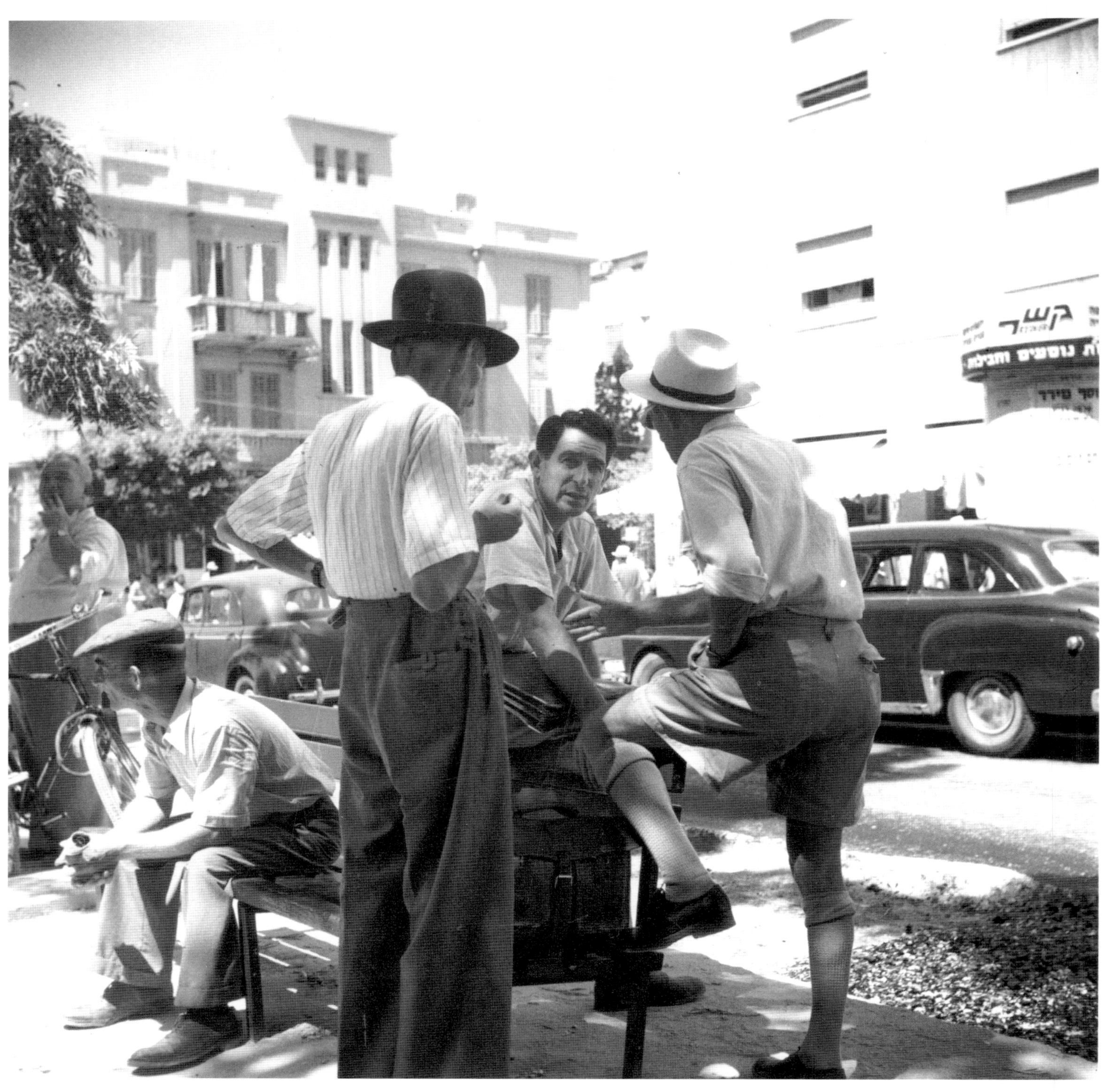

Taxi drivers confer at the intersection of Rothschild Boulevard and Allenby Street in Tel Aviv.

Jerusalem Post Archives

1950

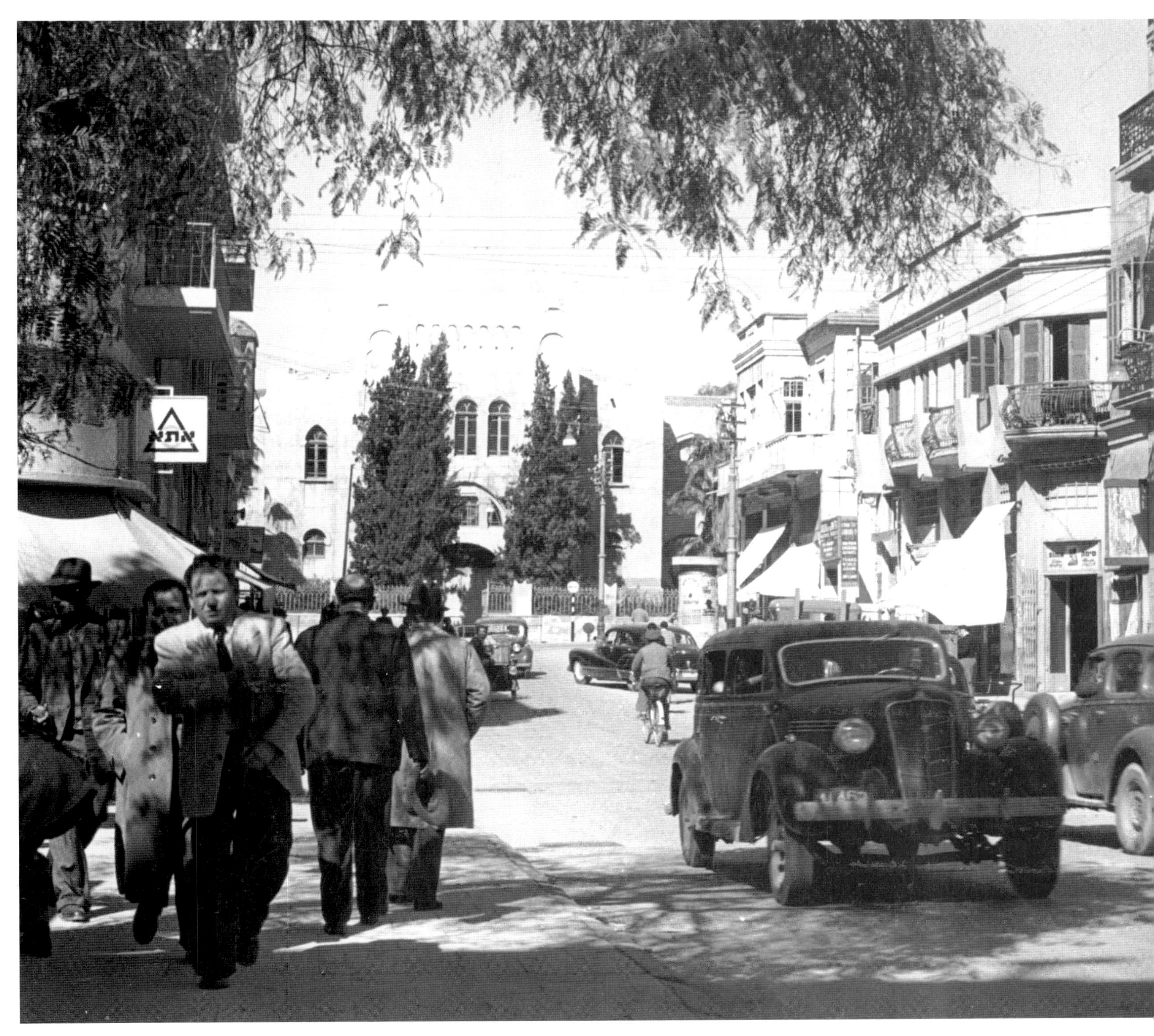

When parking spaces
were available in Tel Aviv.
Jerusalem Post Archives
1950

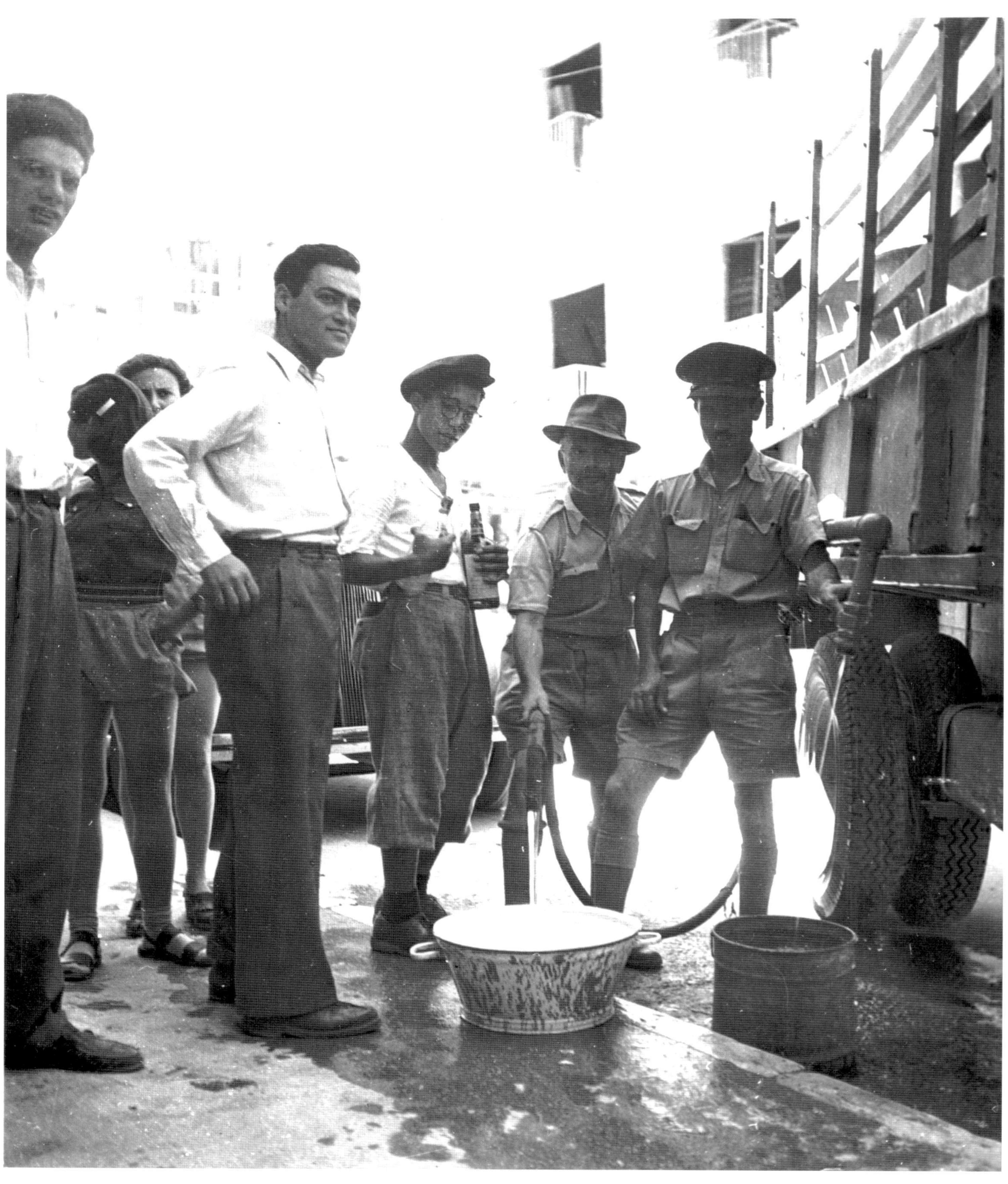

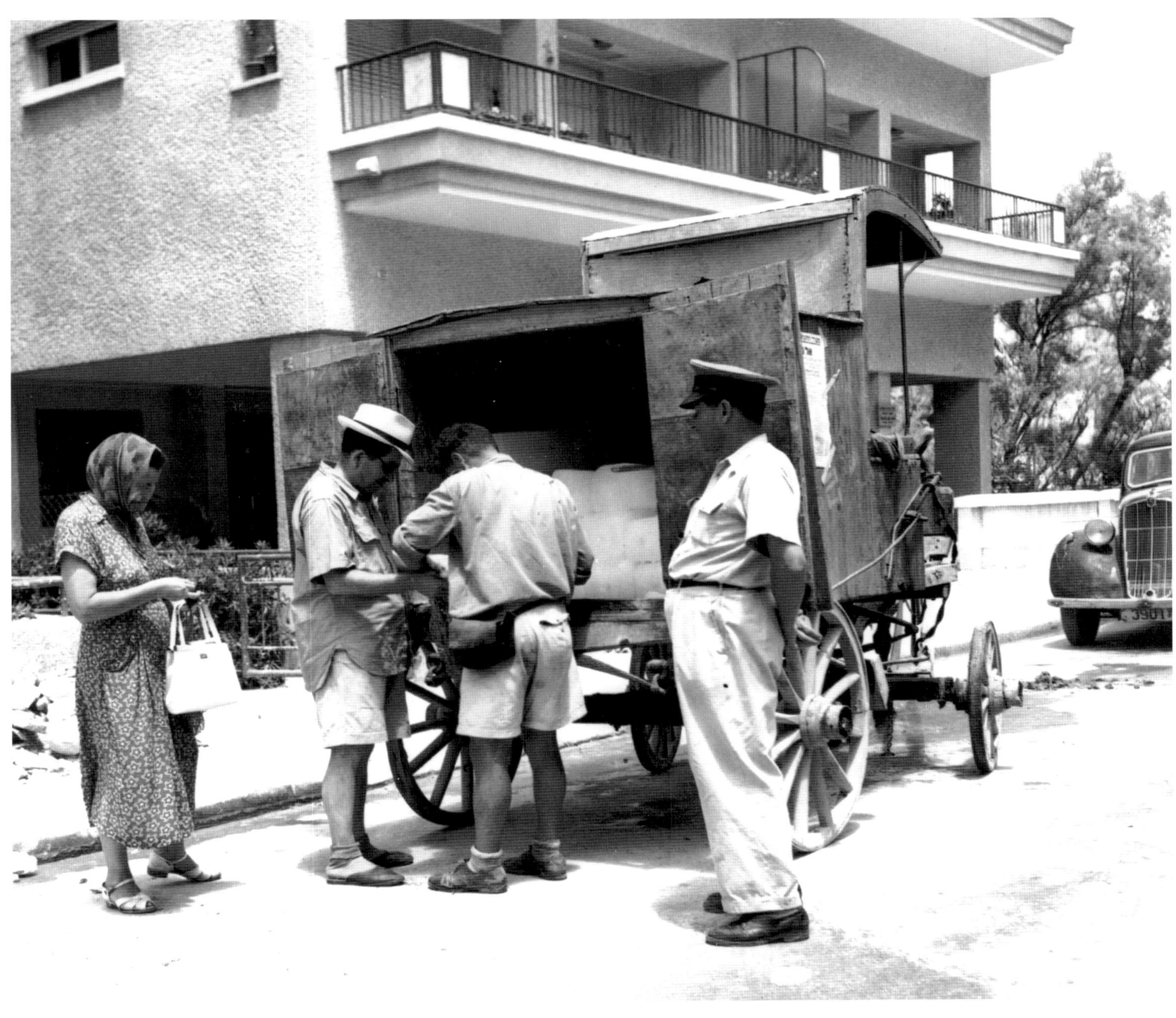

The ice man arrives.
Government Press Office
1951

Rationing water during
the siege of Jerusalem.
Rolf Kneller
1948

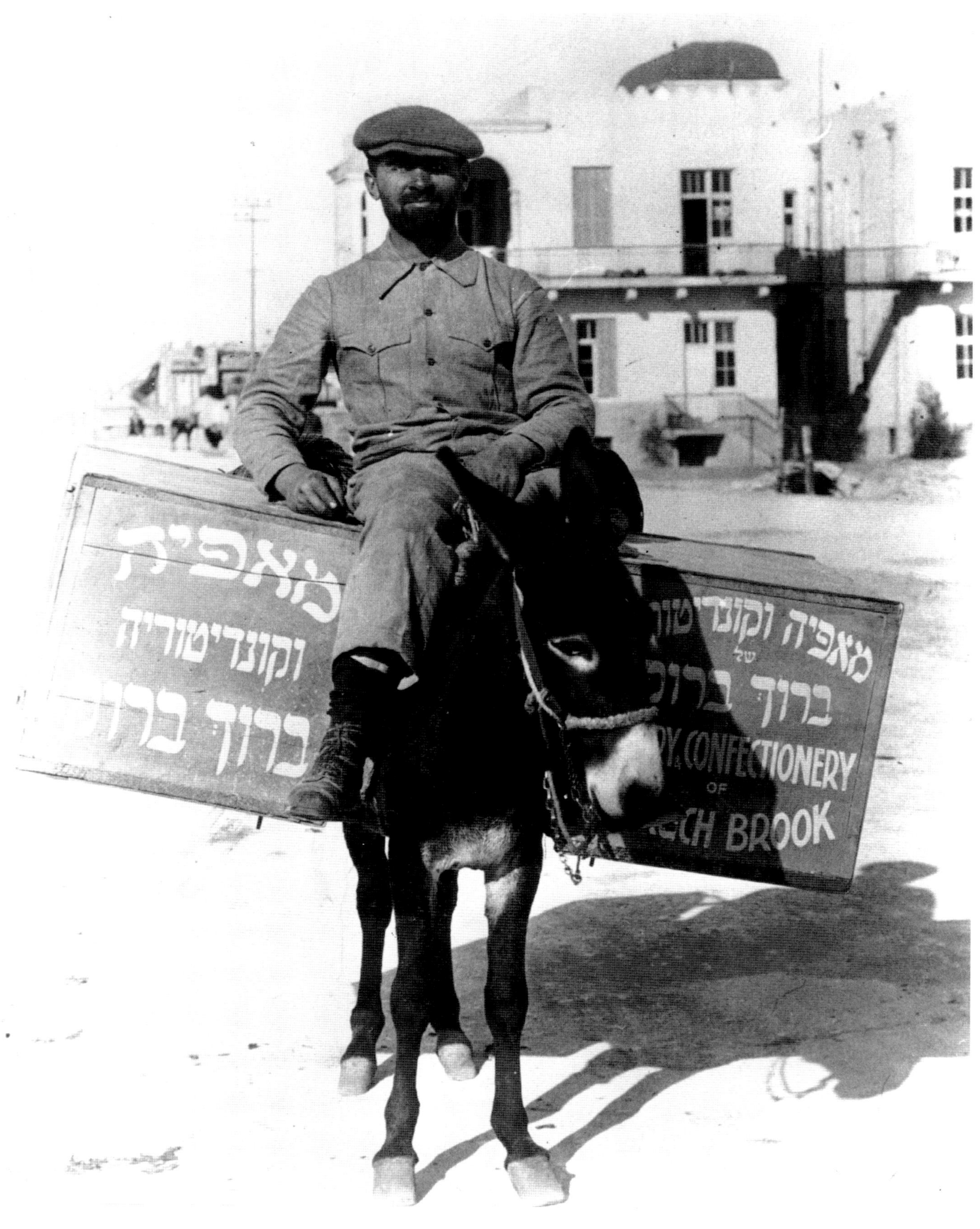
מאפיה
וקונדיטוריה
ברוך
מאפיה
של
ברוך
CONFECTIONERY
OF
BROOK

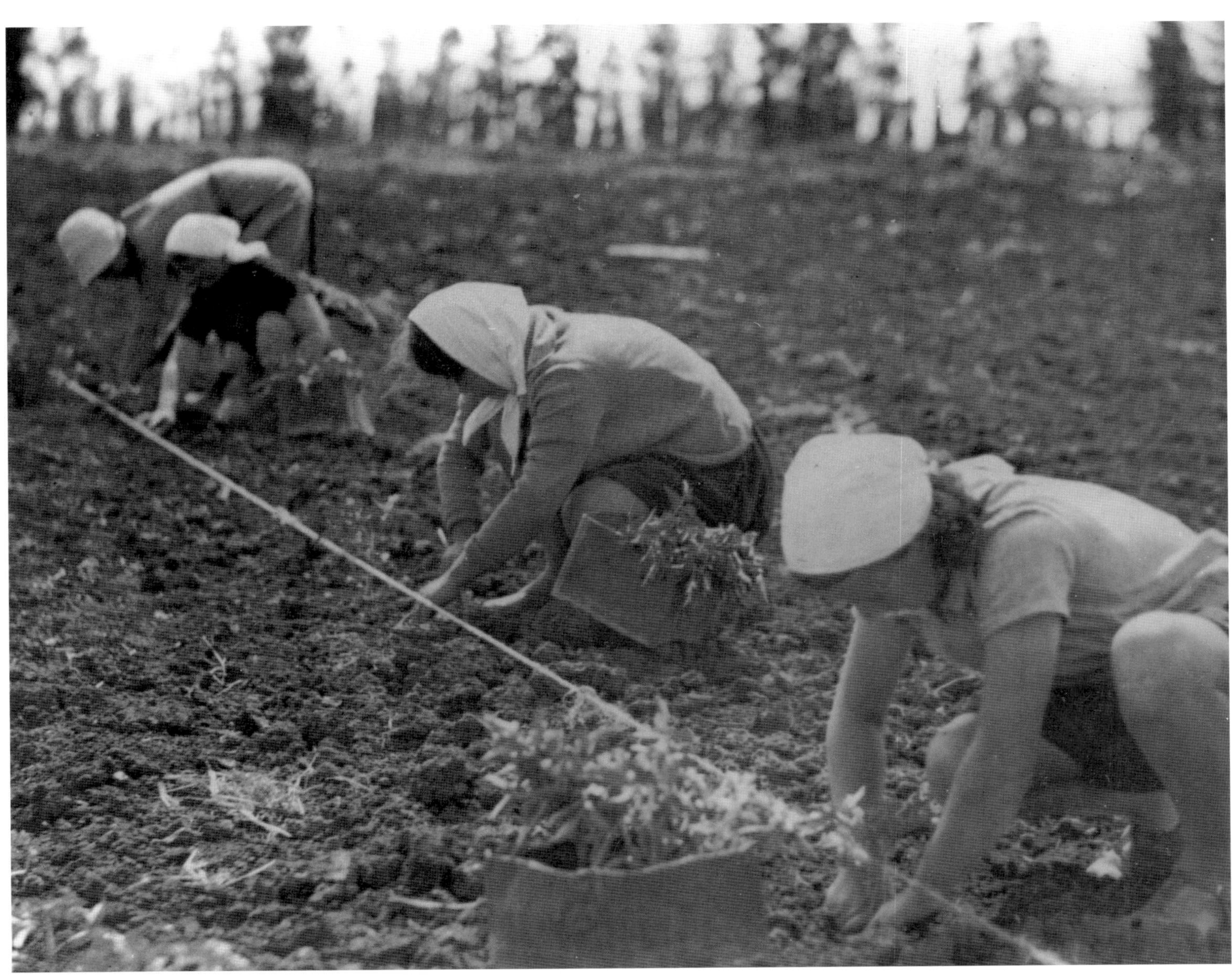

Women farm workers learn the basics of agriculture at Jerusalem's Havat Halimud.

Jerusalem Post Archives

1925

Making deliveries for the Baruch Brook Bakery in Tel Aviv.

Jerusalem Post Archives

1921

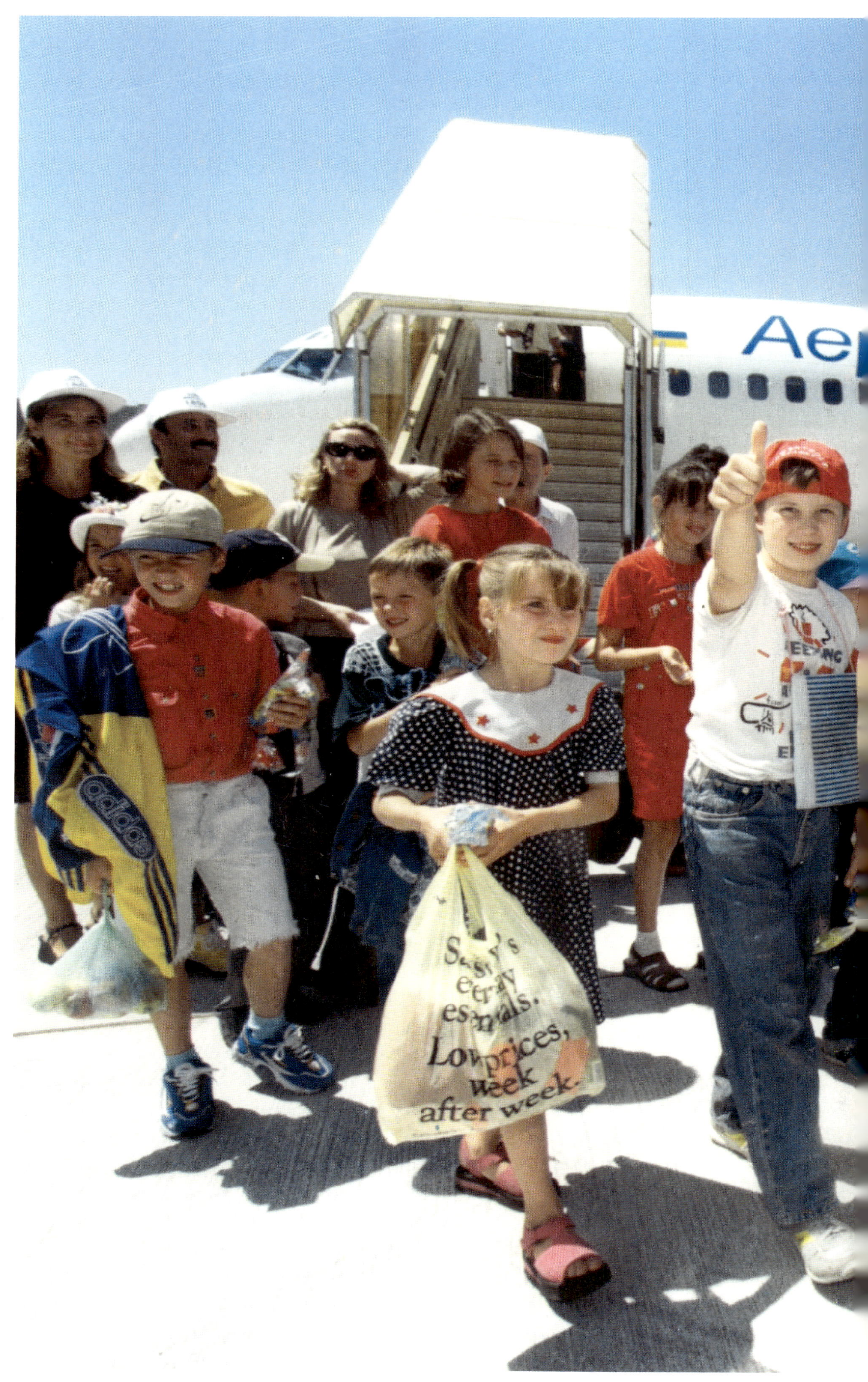

Chabad brings children from the Chernobyl disaster area to Israel.

Israel Sun/Yael Somekh

1999

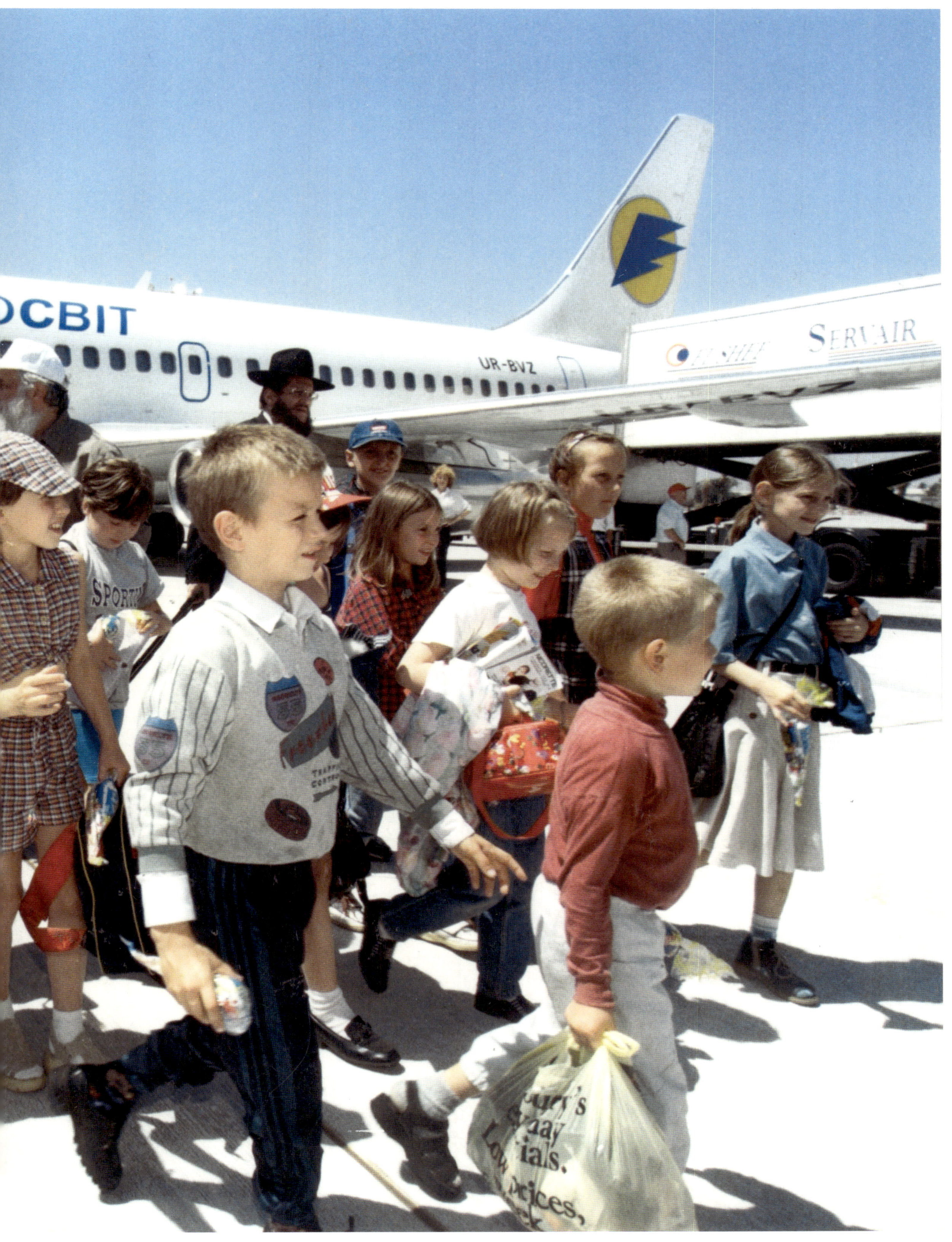
OCBIT
UR-BVZ
SERVAIR

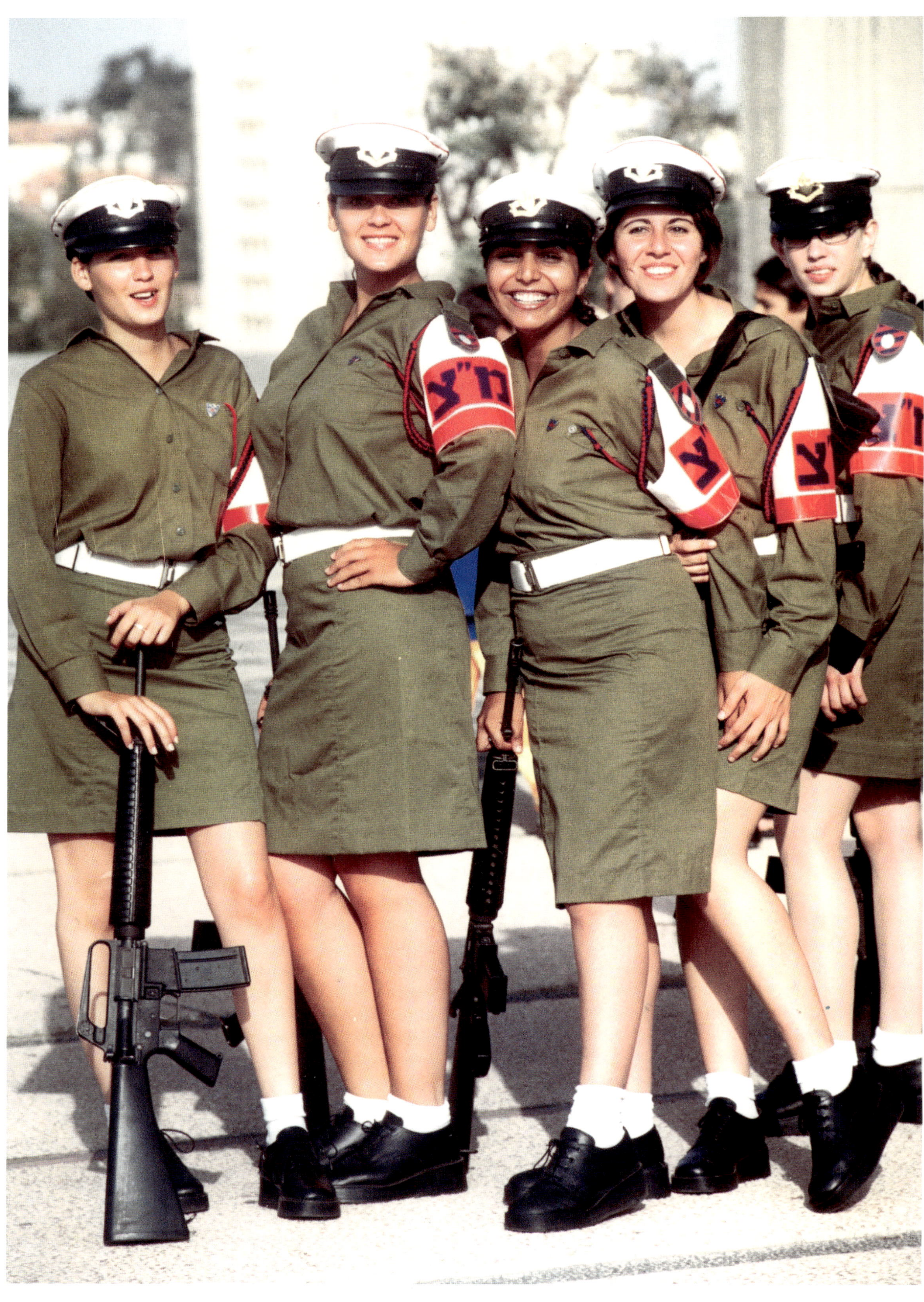
מ"צ

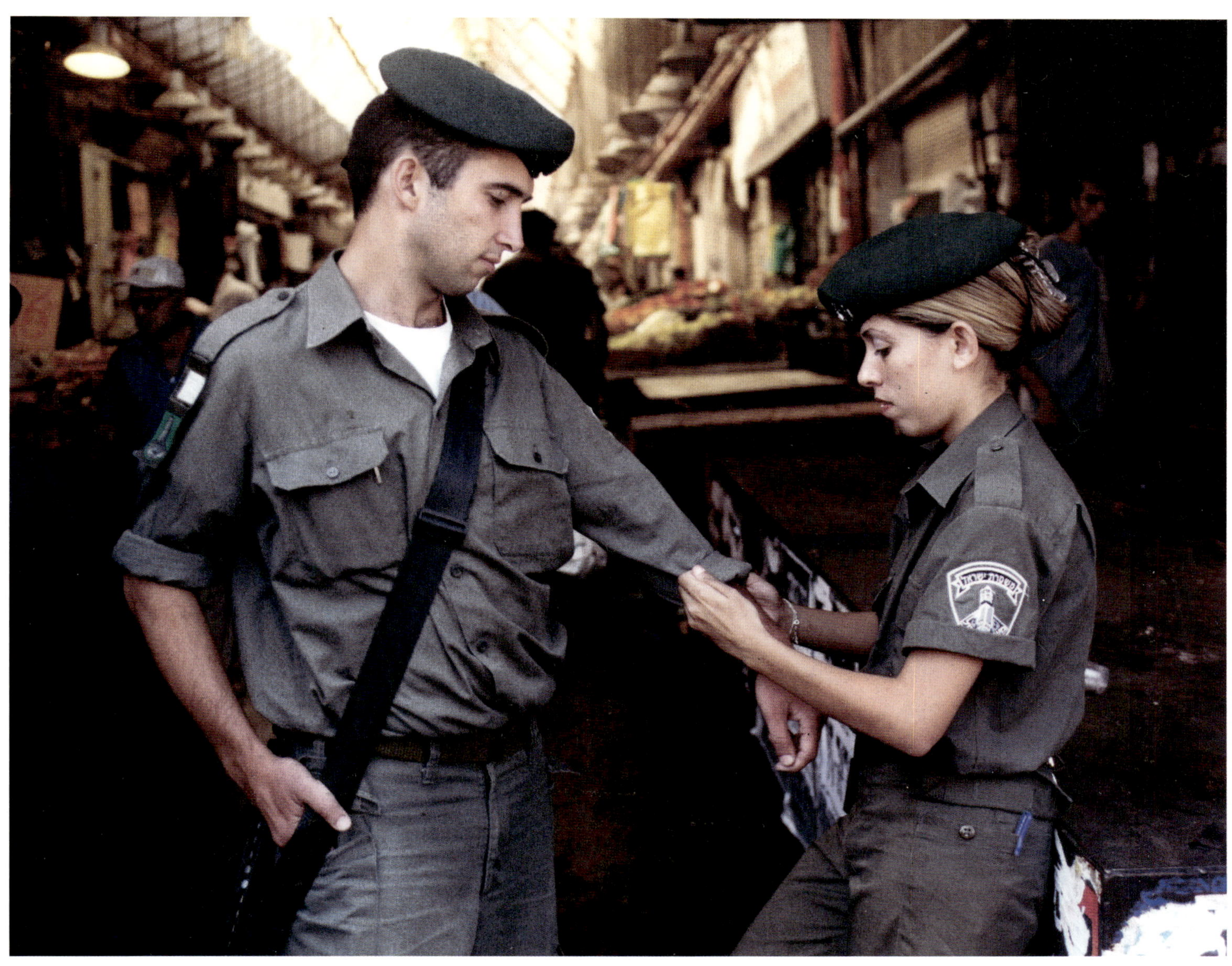

Border policemen
stand guard.
Ariel Jerozolimski
2000

Military policewomen strike
a pose.
Ariel Jerozolimski
2000

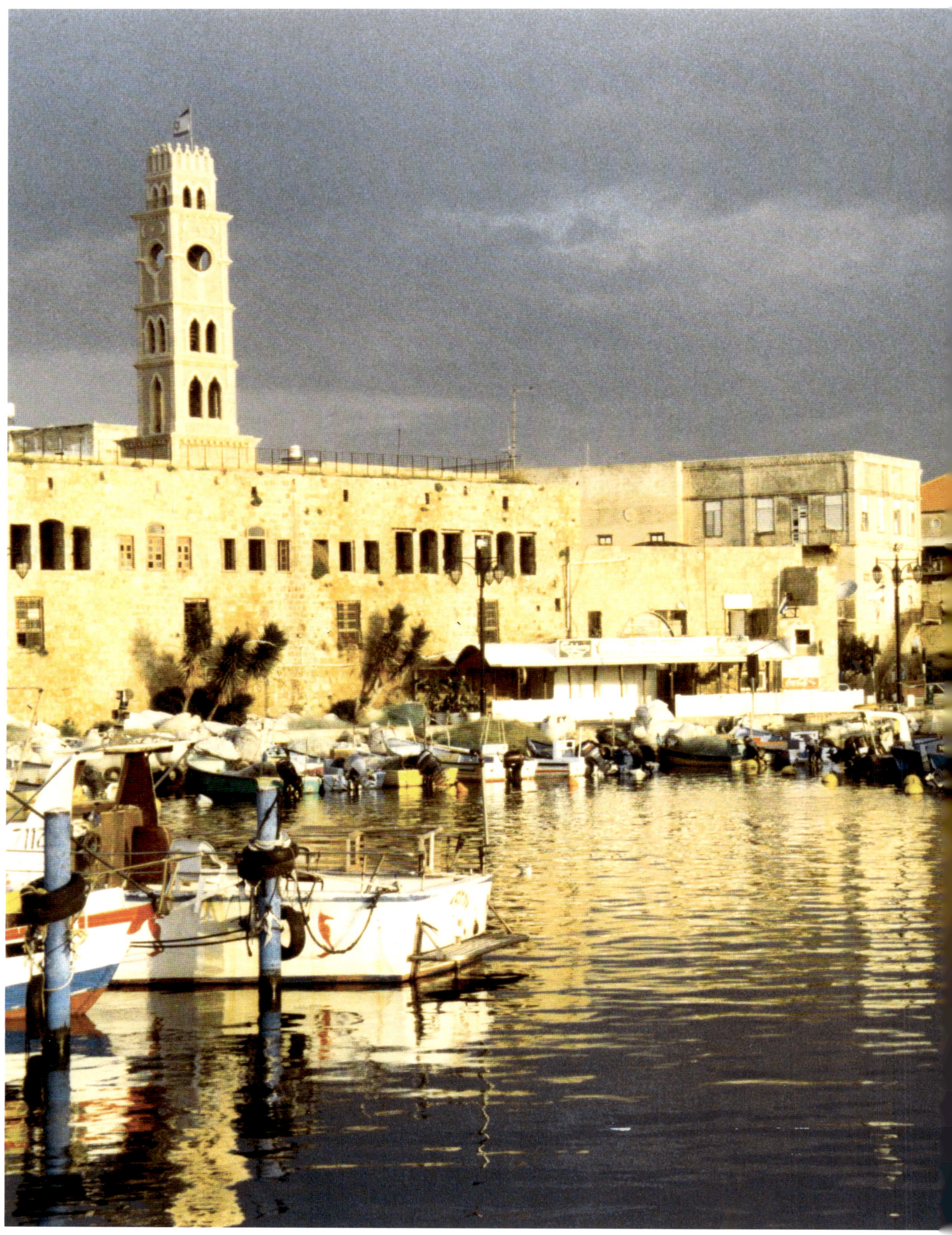

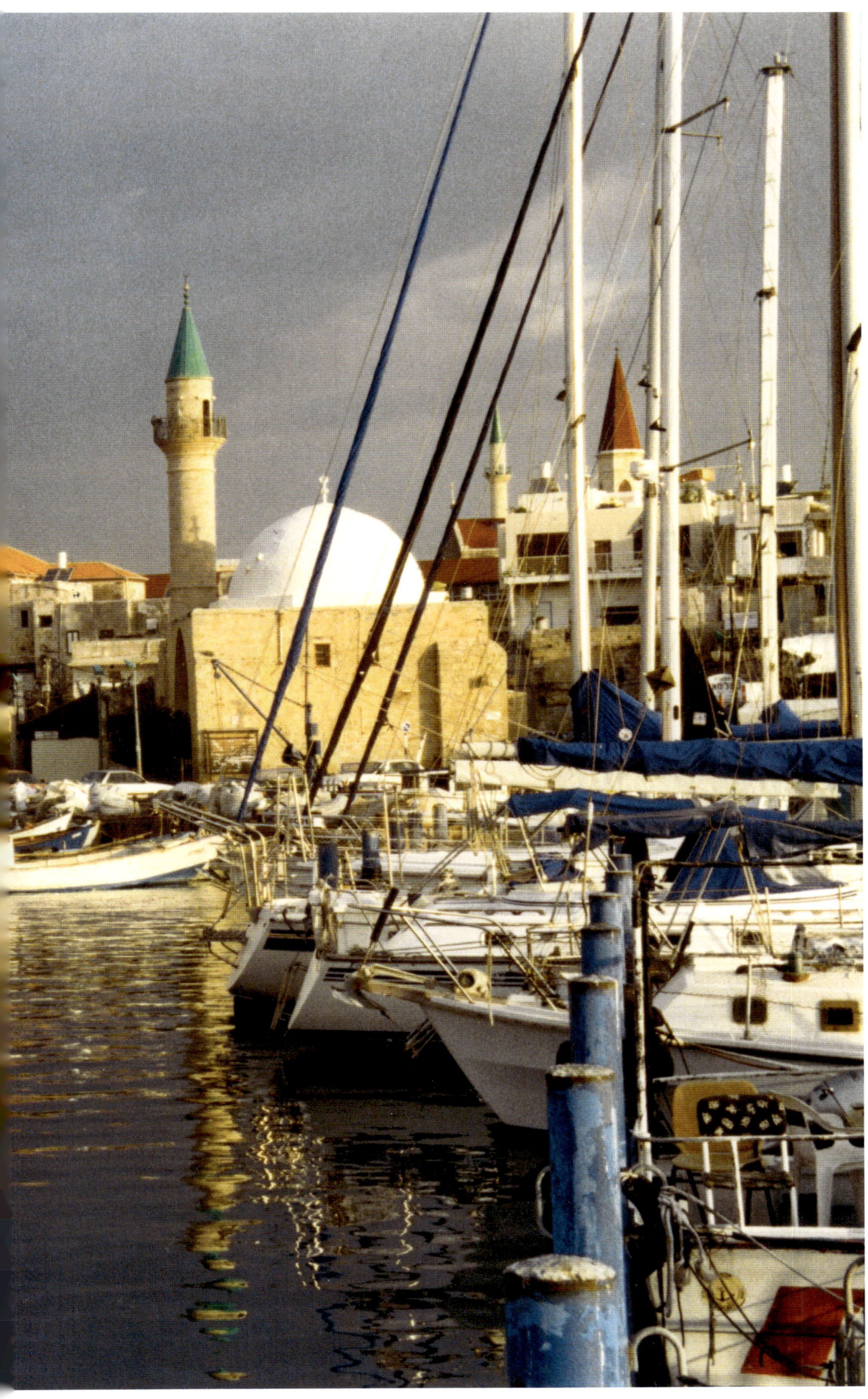

A view of Acre from the harbor.
Gur Salomon
2001

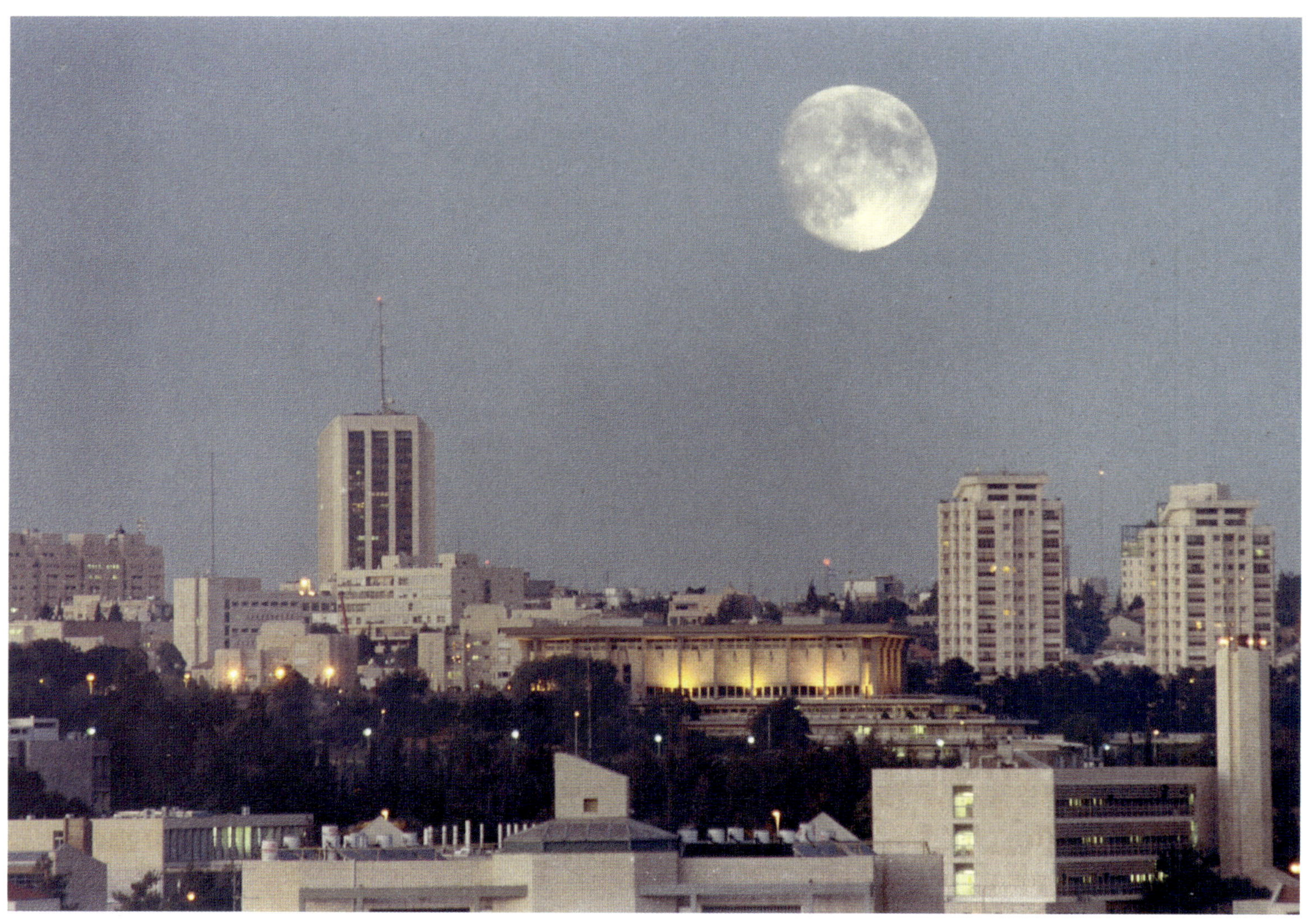

Moonrise over the
Knesset.
Jerusalem Post Archives
1983

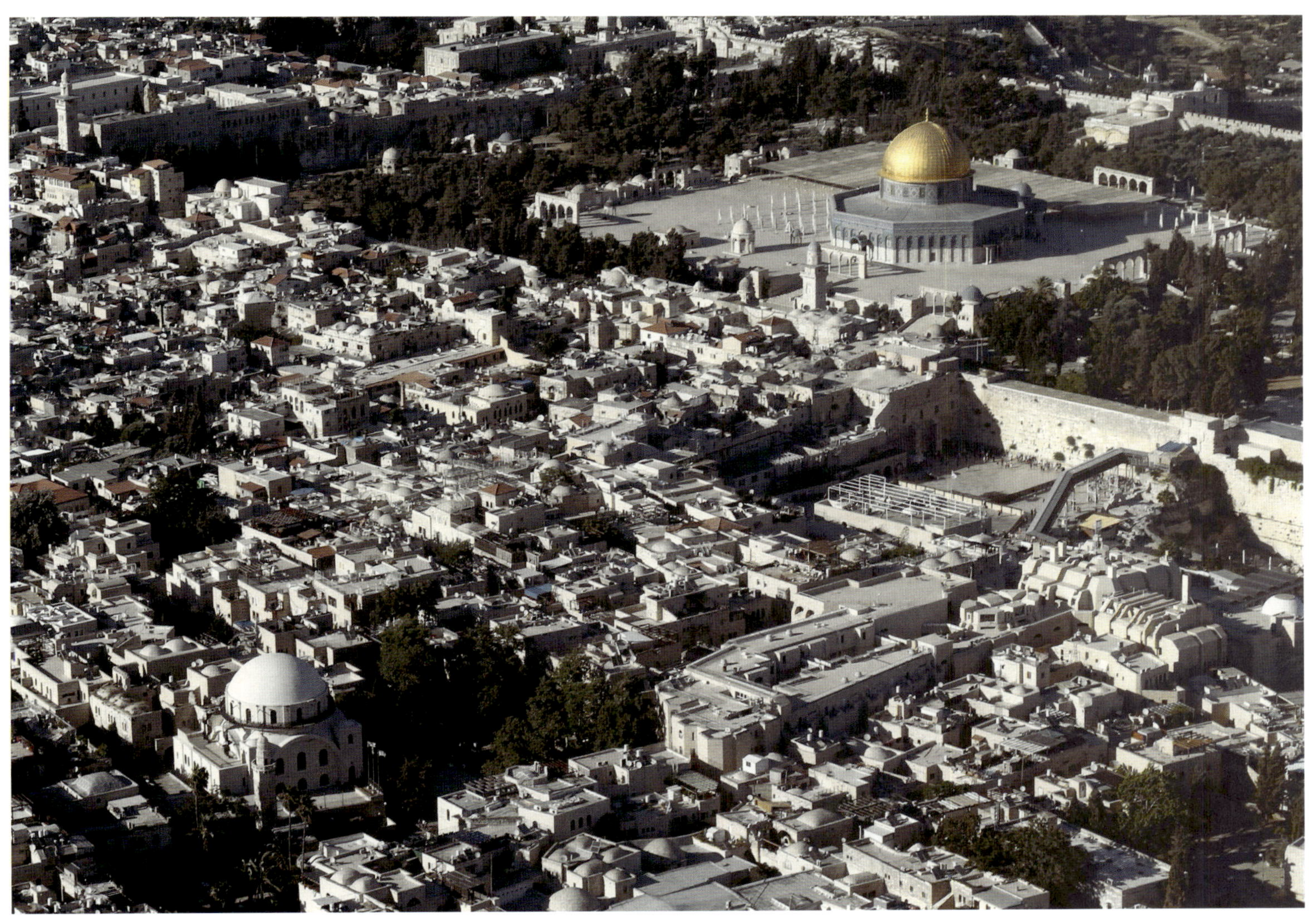

A helicopter's view of
Jerusalem.
Marc Israel Sellem
2014

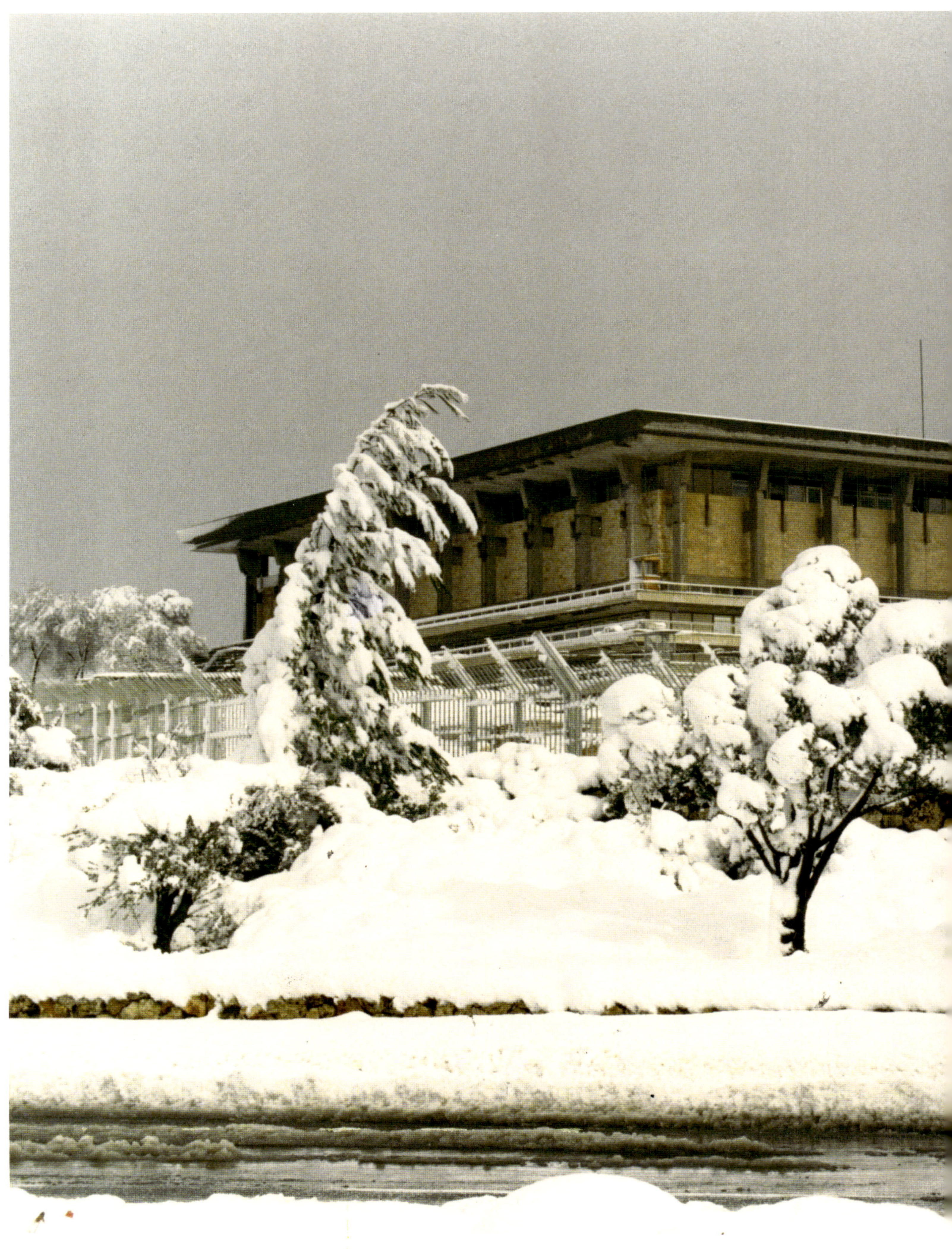

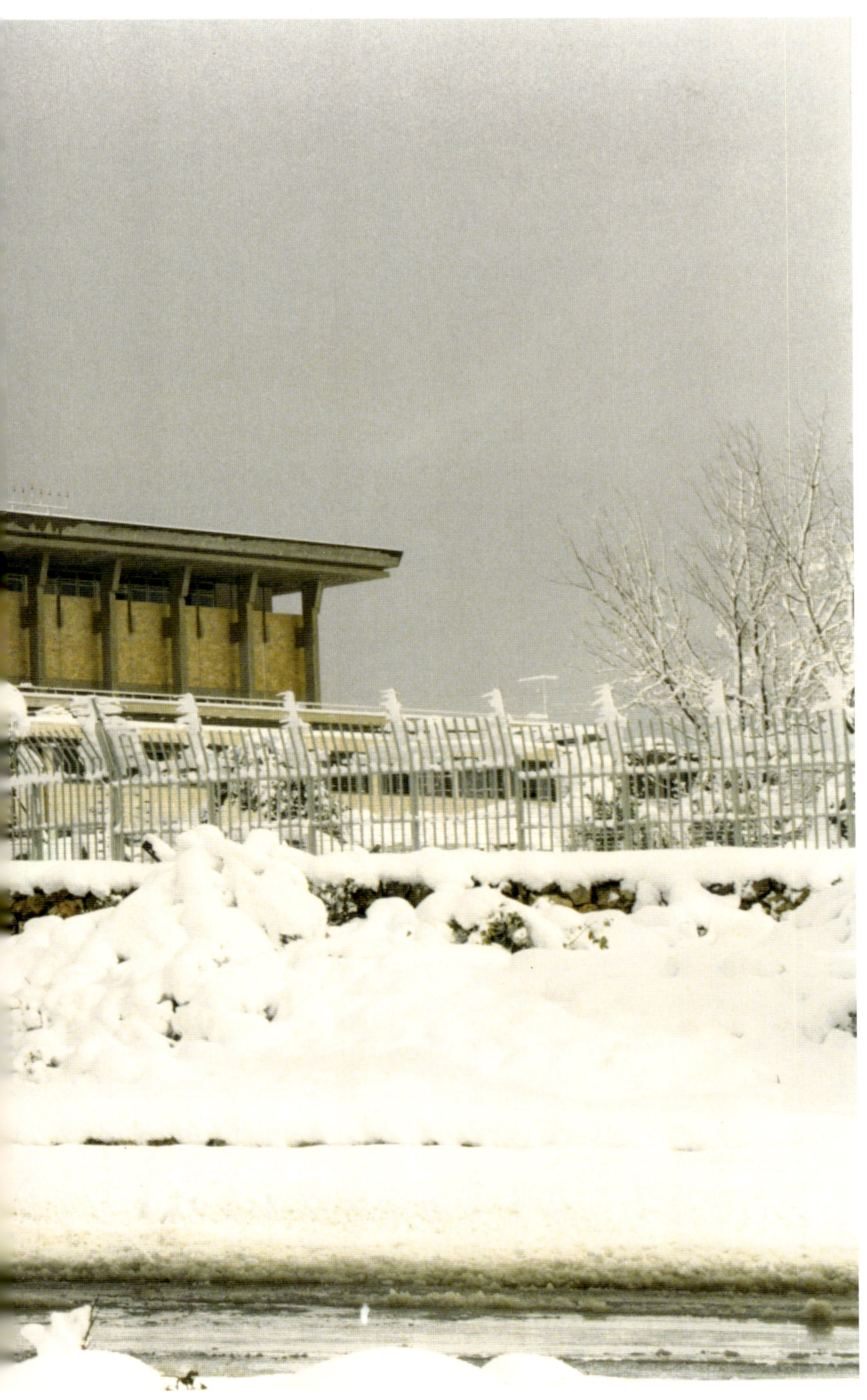

The Knesset after a rare winter snowfall.
Jerusalem Post Archives
1998

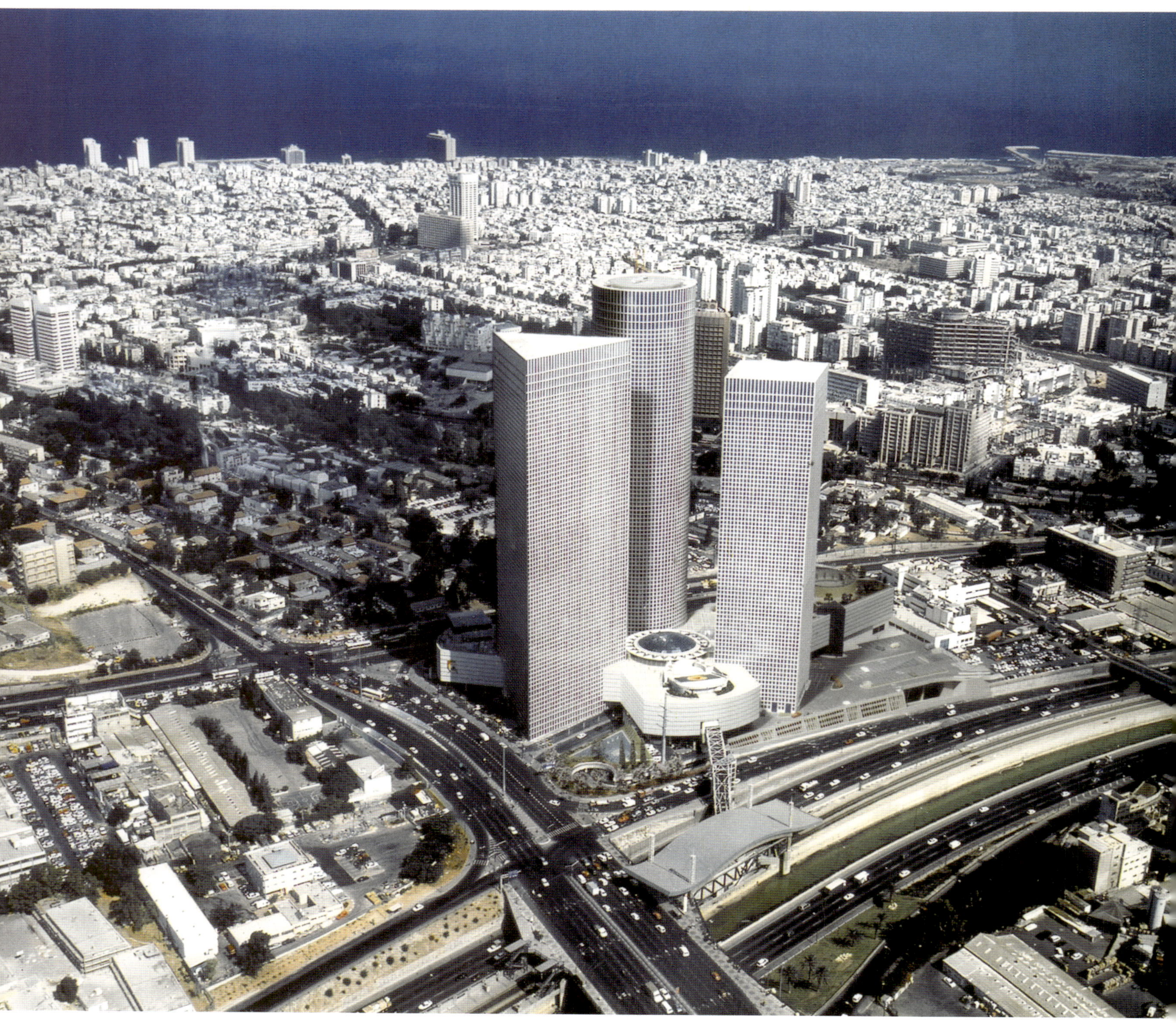

The three Azrieli towers dominate the Tel Aviv skyline.

Jerusalem Post Archives

2001

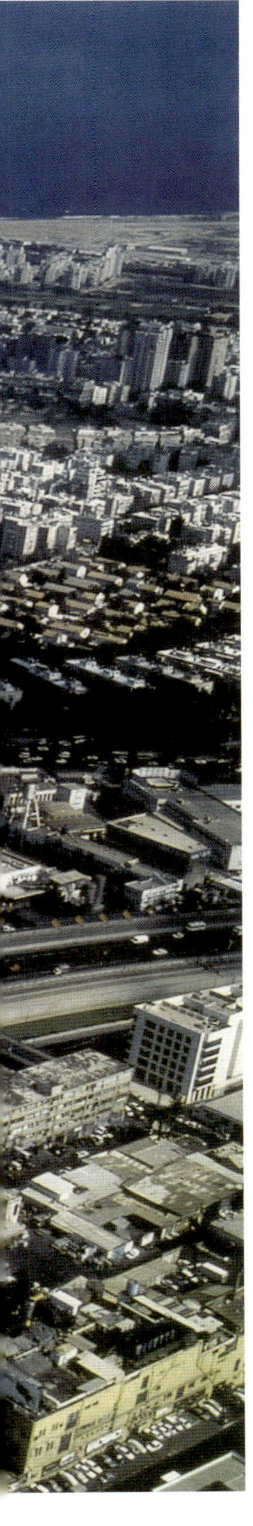

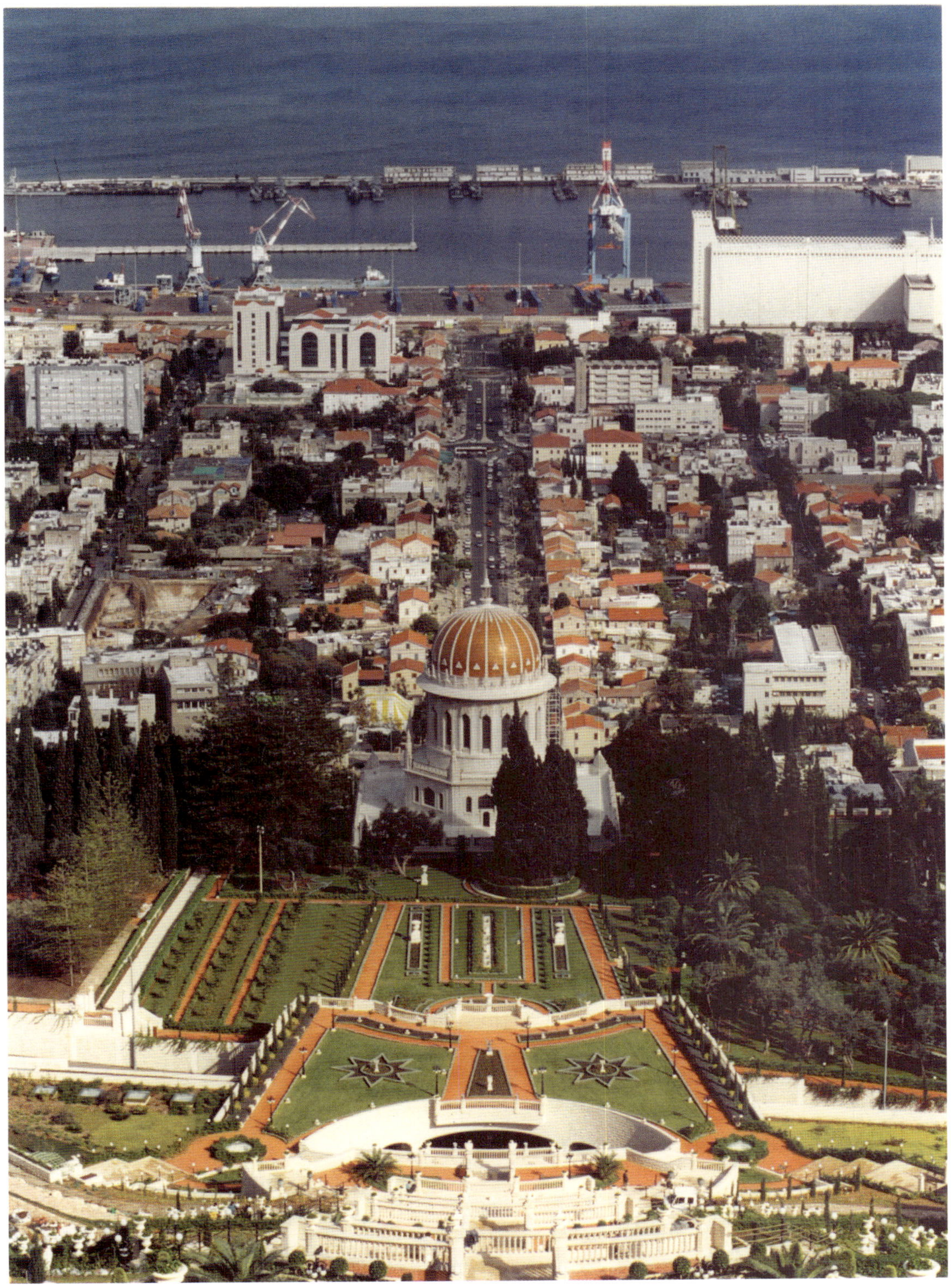

The Bahai Gardens
in Haifa comprise a
staircase of 19 terraces
extending up Mount
Carmel.
Zvi Roger
2004

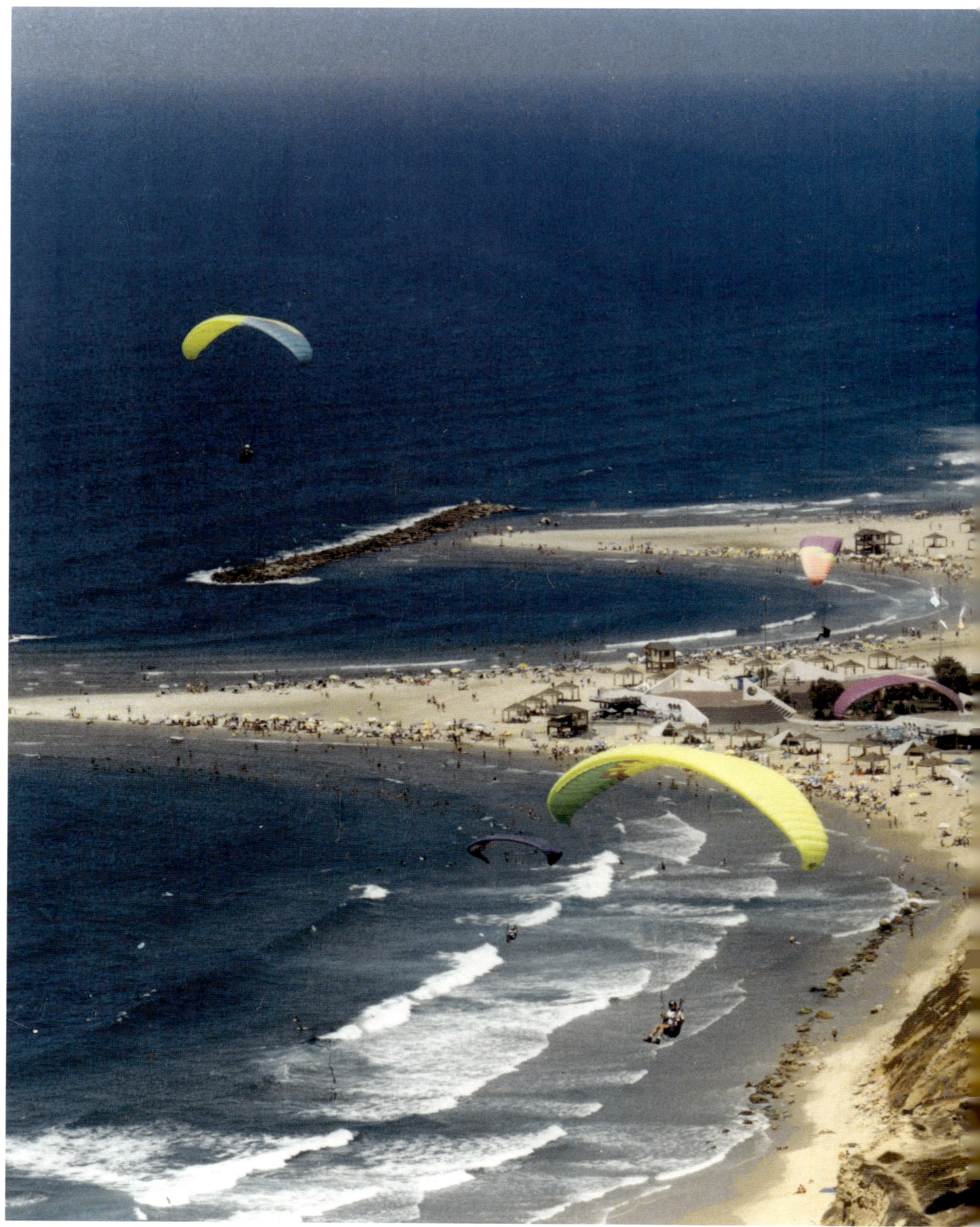

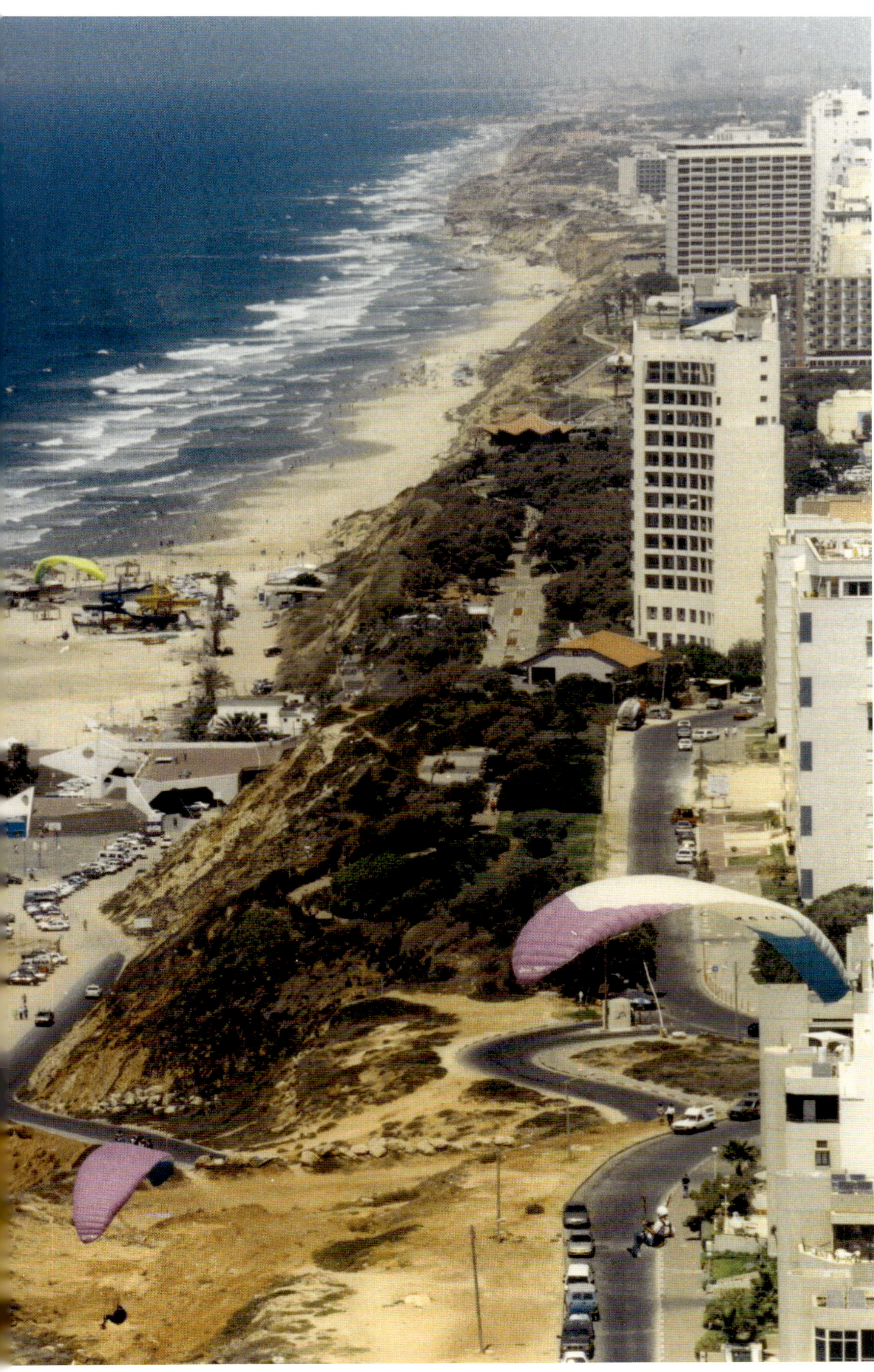

The cliffs above the Netanya shore are ideal for parasailing.
Gur Salomon
2001

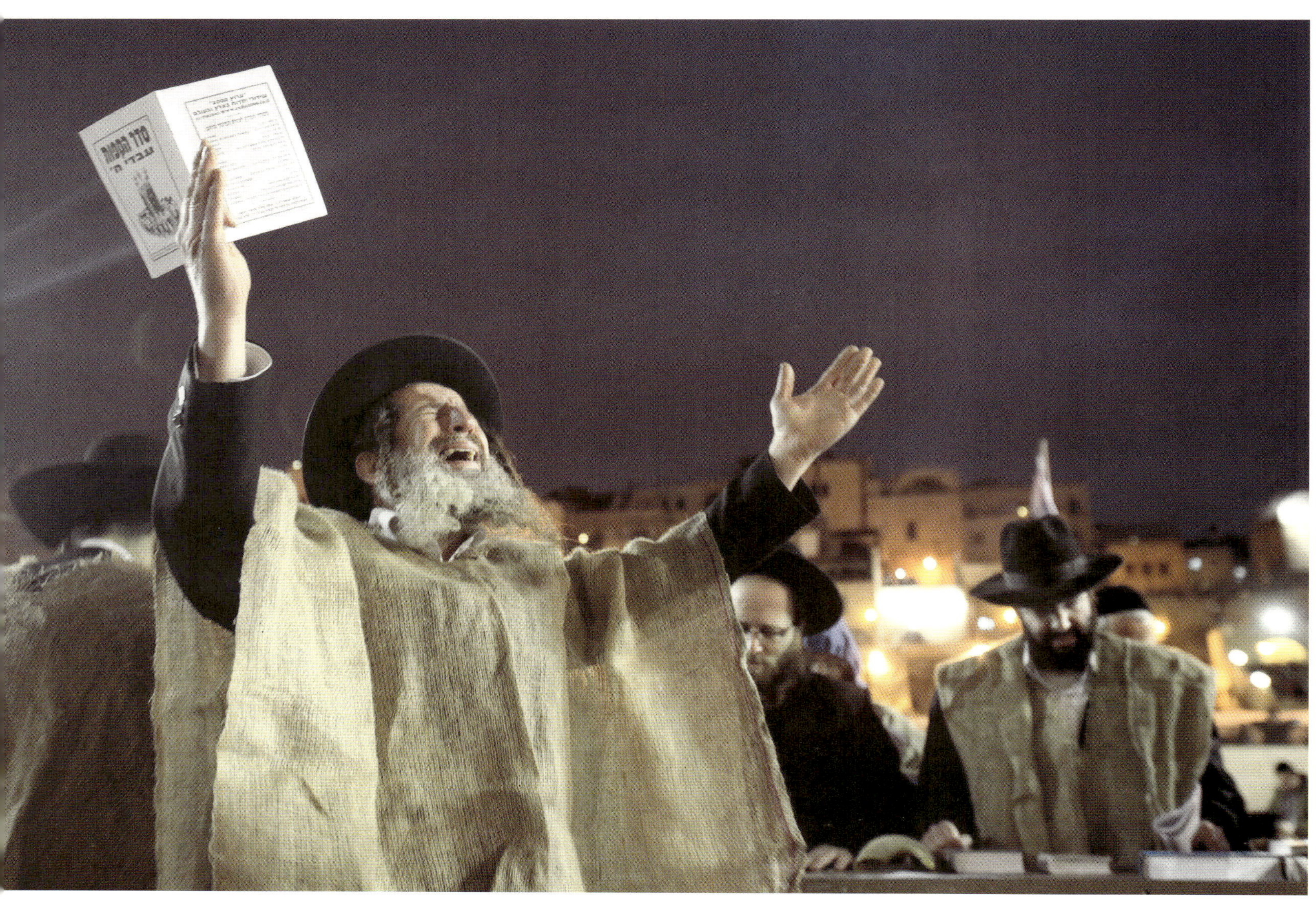

Worshipers at the Western Wall observe the Fast of 10 Tevet, commemorating the Babylonian siege of Jerusalem in 425 BCE.

Marc Israel Sellem

2012

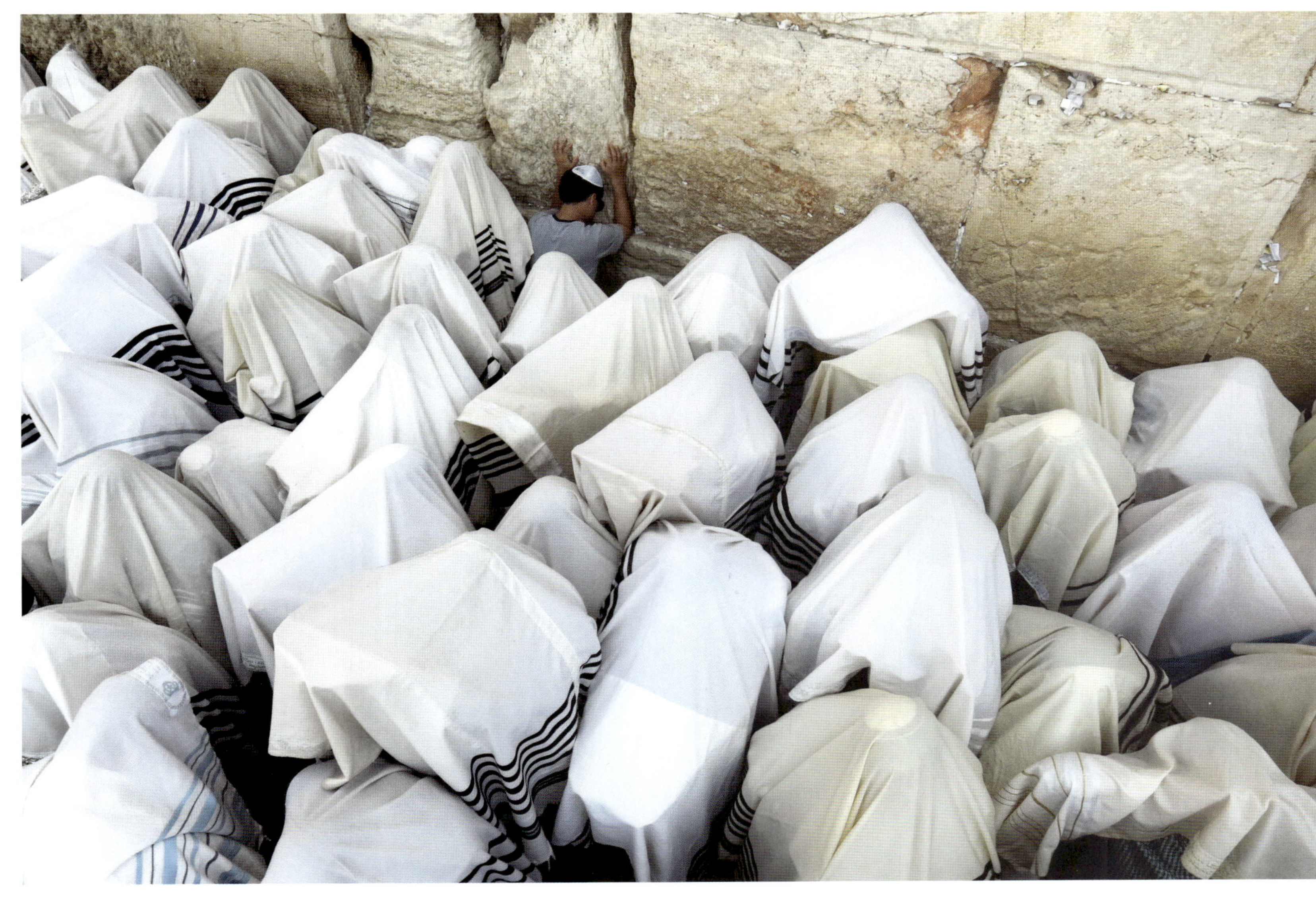

The Priestly Blessing is given at the Western Wall on the intermediate days of Passover and Succot.

Marc Israel Sellem

2013

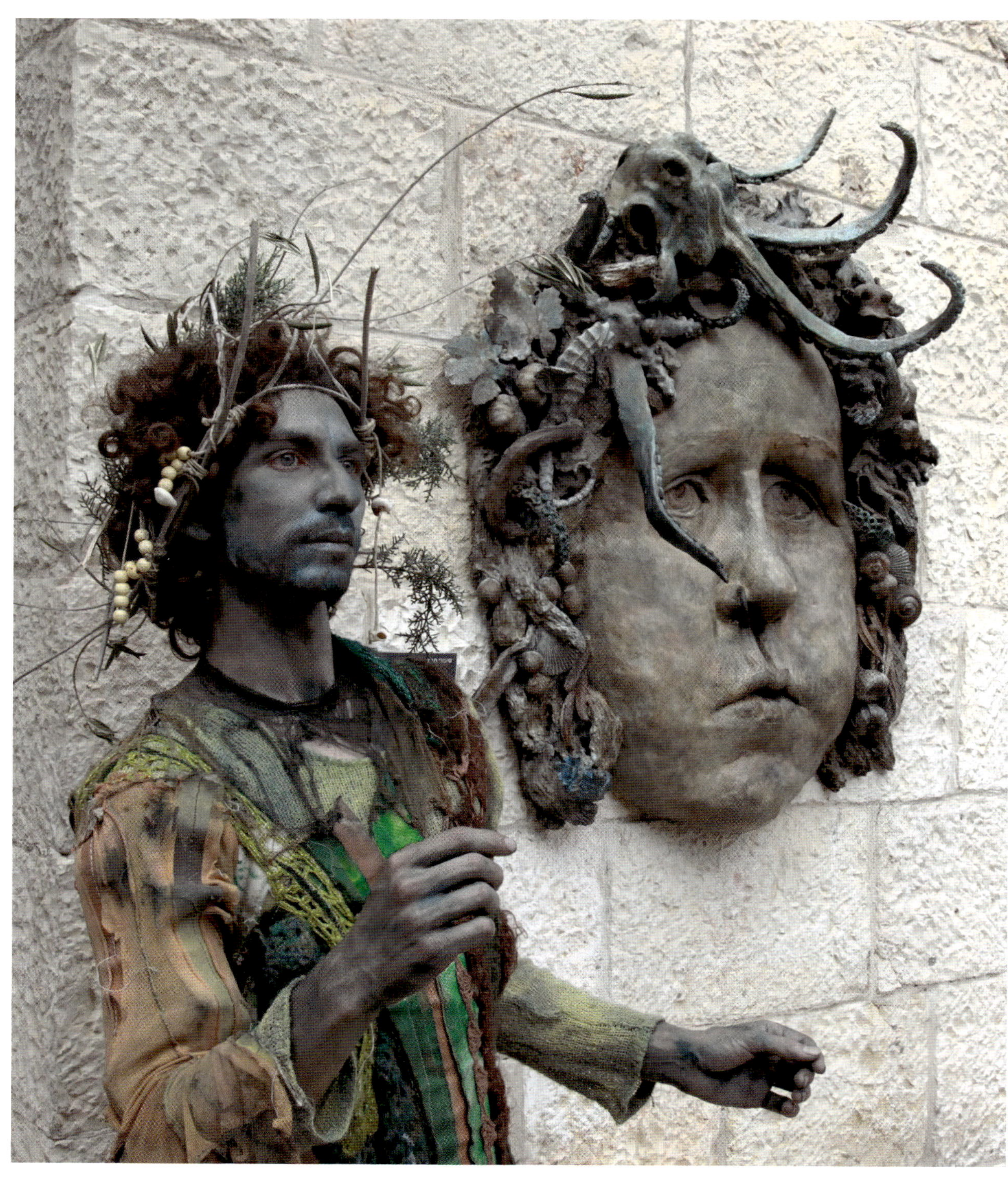

Statues come alive on
Jerusalem's Mamilla Mall.

Marc Israel Sellem

2011

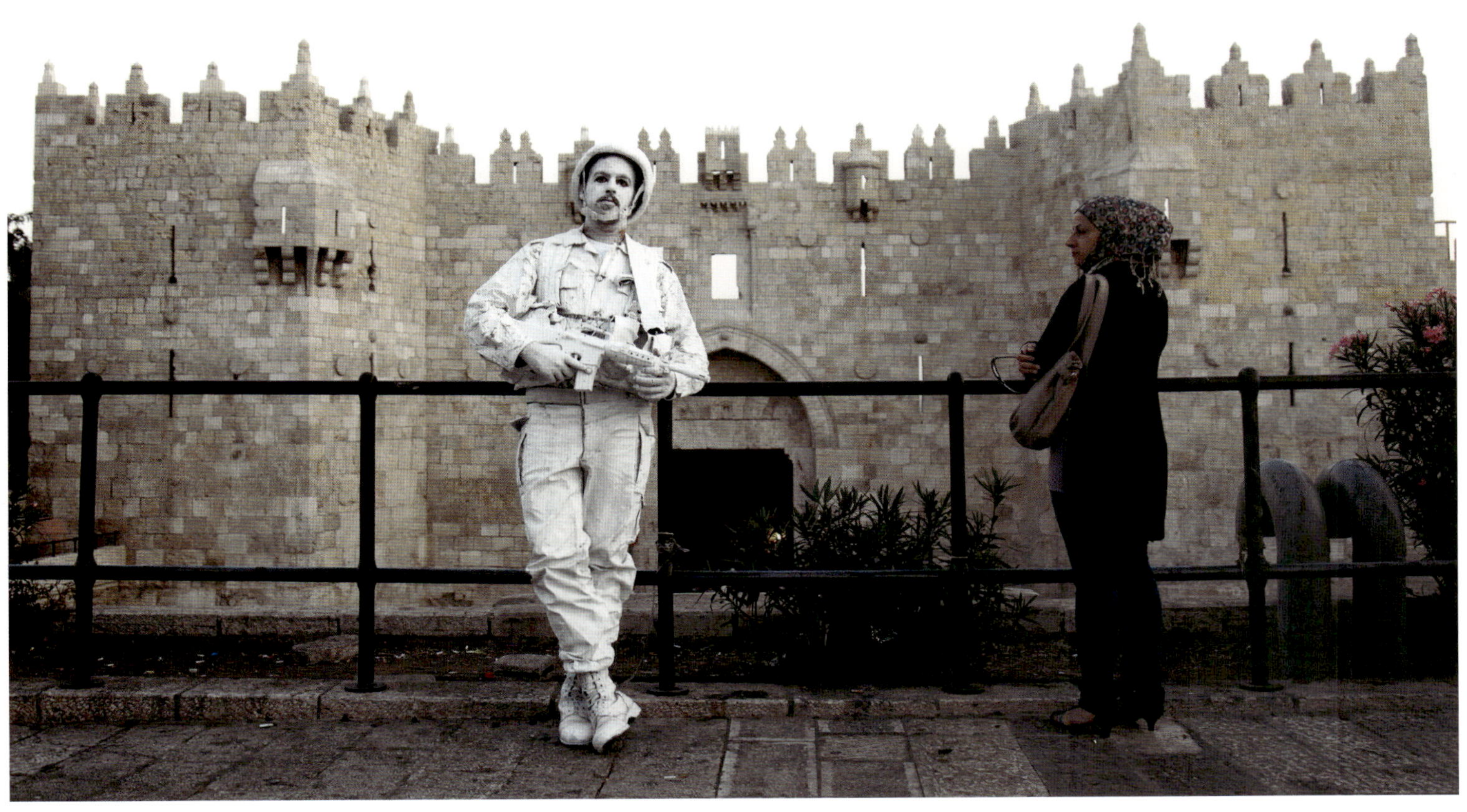

The mythical soldier in white stands guard at Jerusalem's Damascus Gate.

Marc Israel Sellem

2011

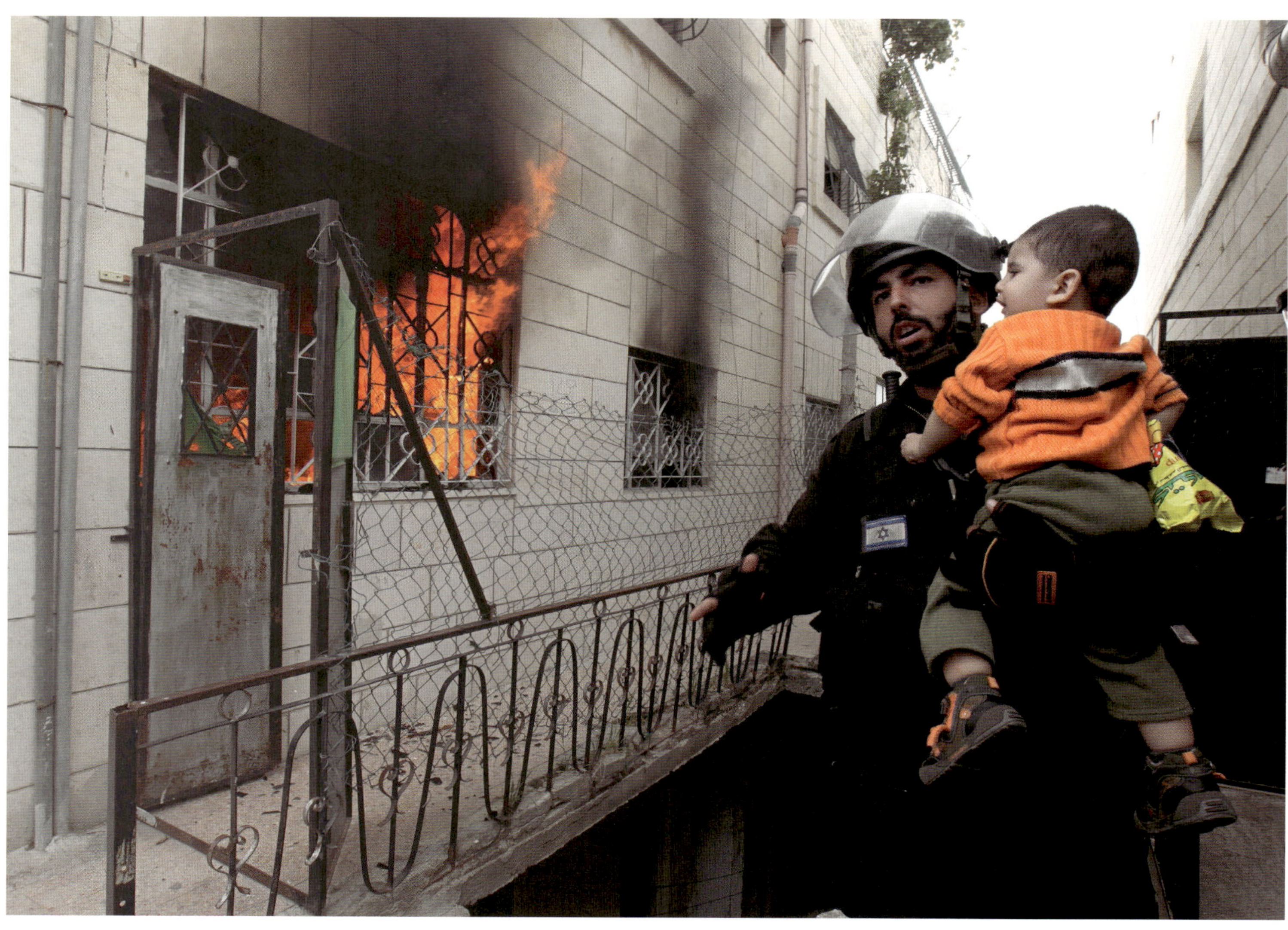

A Jerusalem firefighter rescues a resident of Issawiya.

Marc Israel Sellem

2011

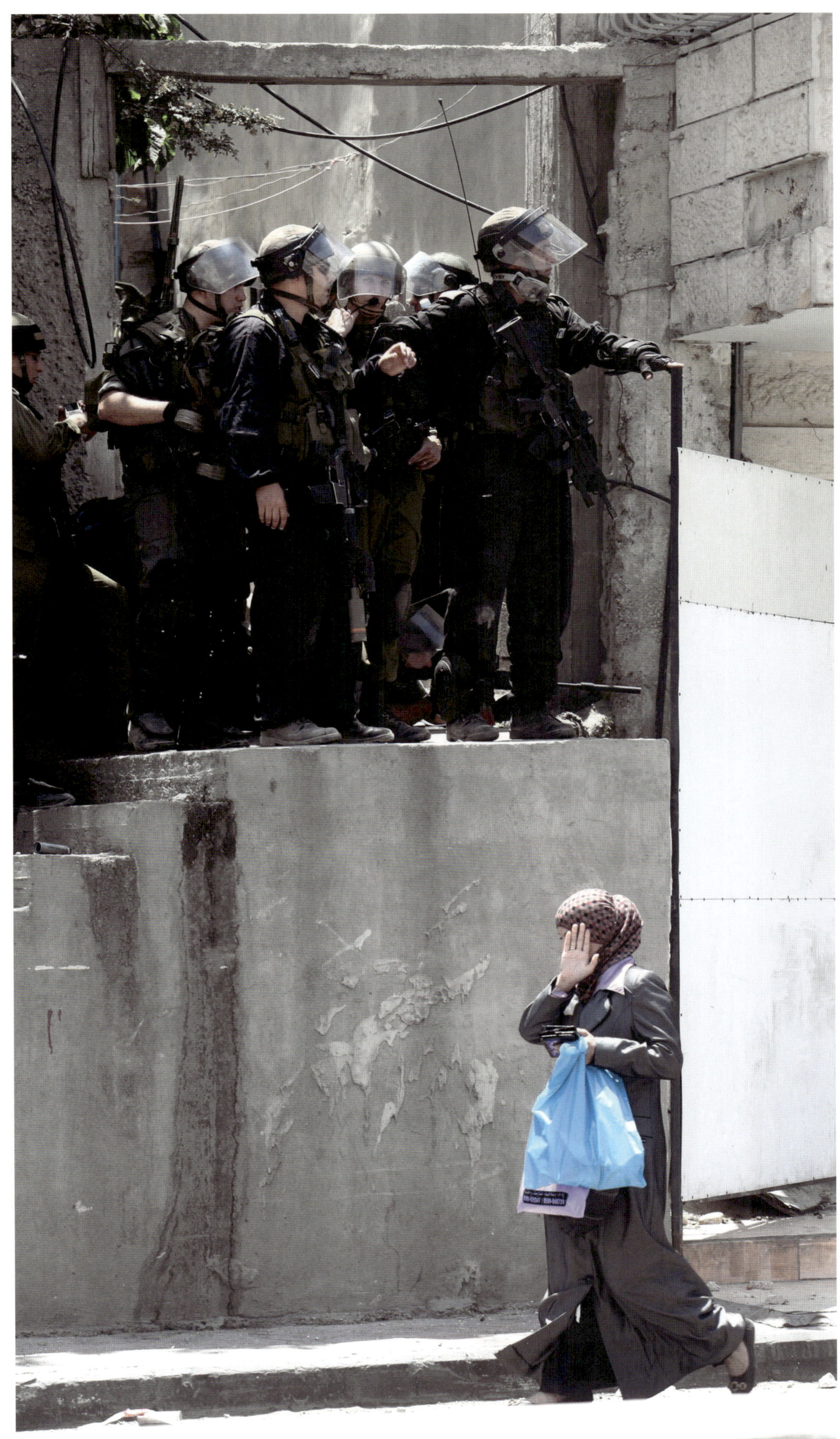

War and peace in Kalandiya.
Marc Israel Sellem
2011

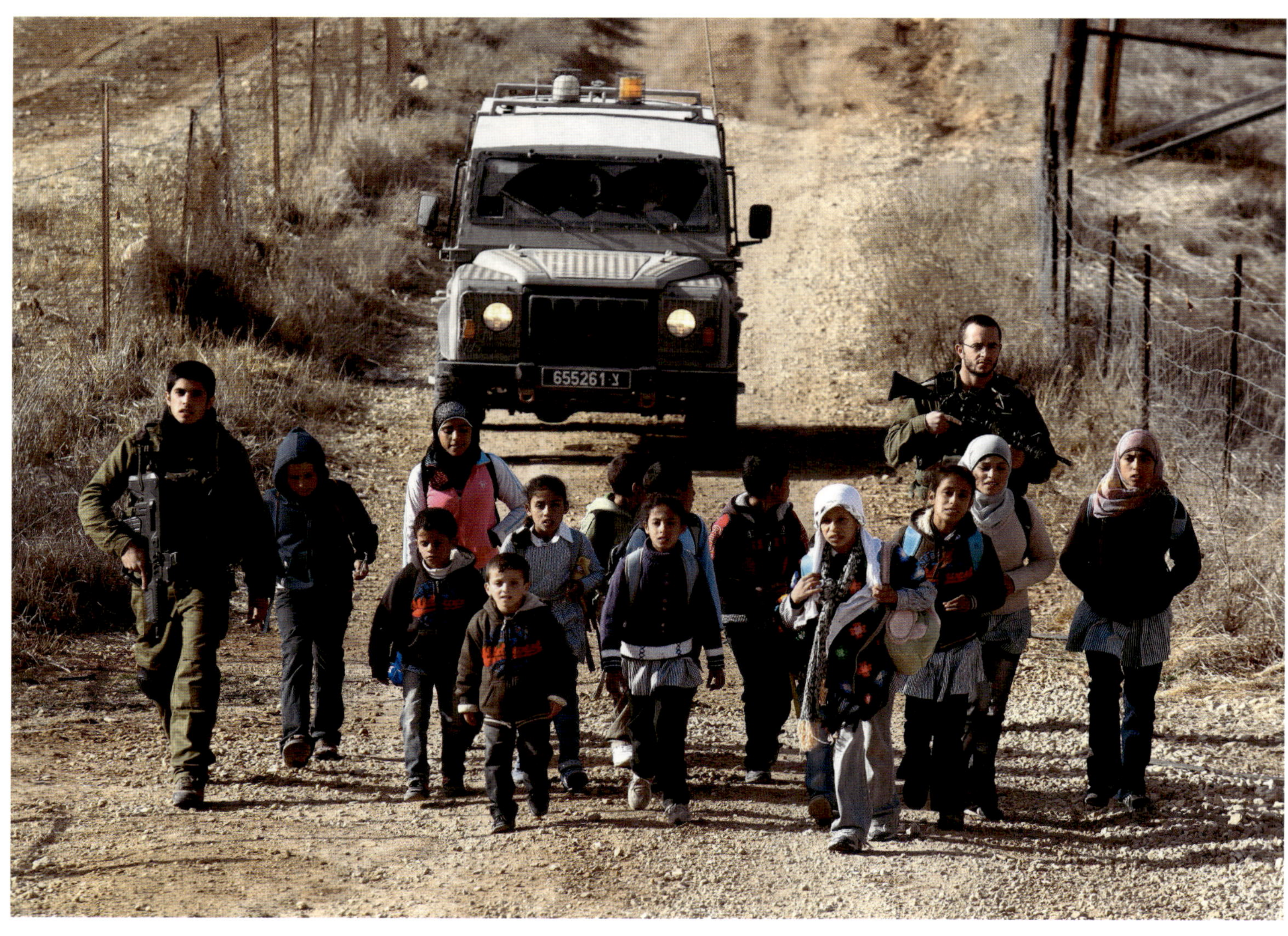

Soldiers escort
Palestinian kids to
school past a West Bank
settlement.

Marc Israel Sellem

2010

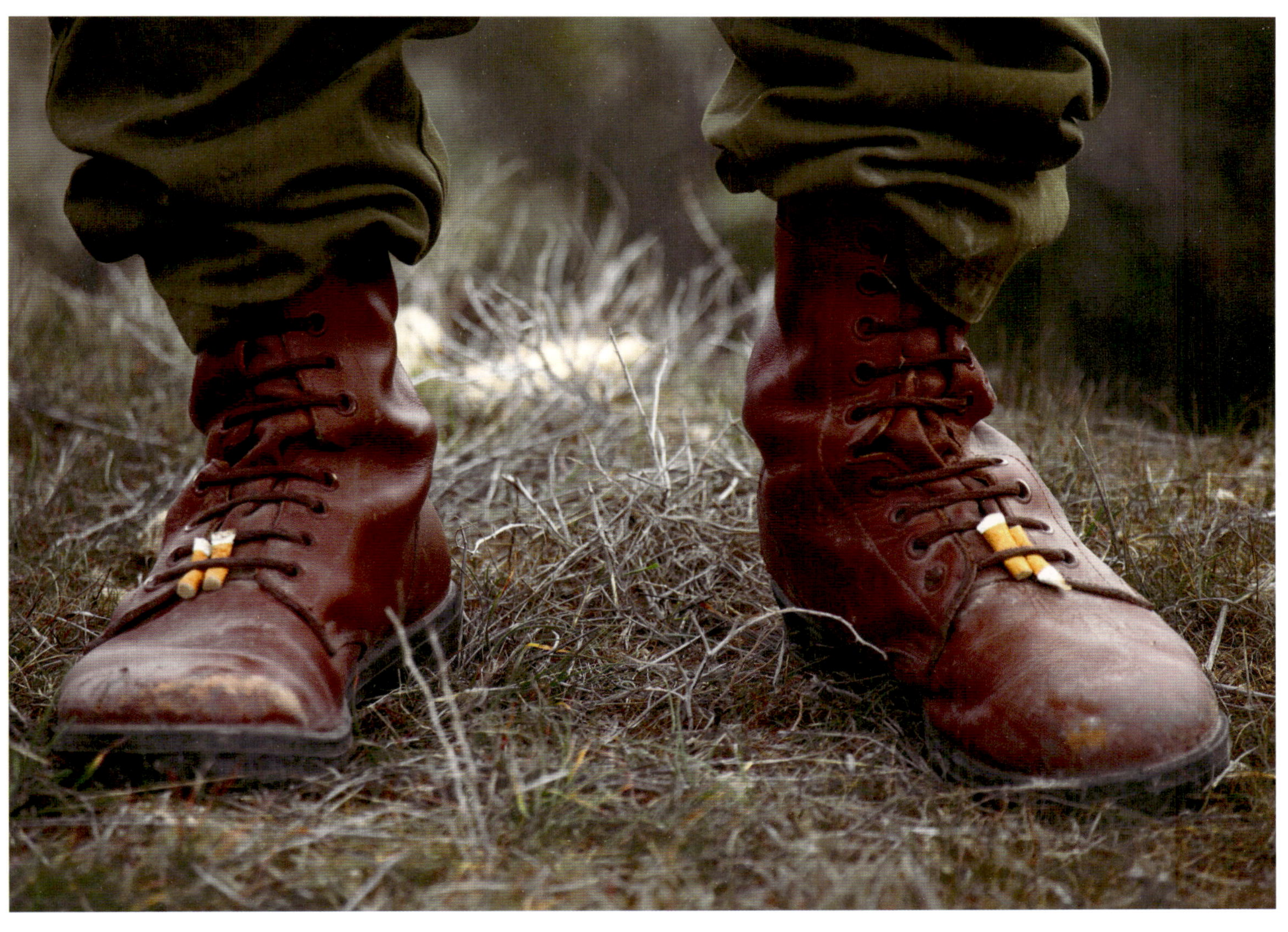

An ecologically minded
paratrooper saves his
butts to dispose later.

Marc Israel Sellem

2011

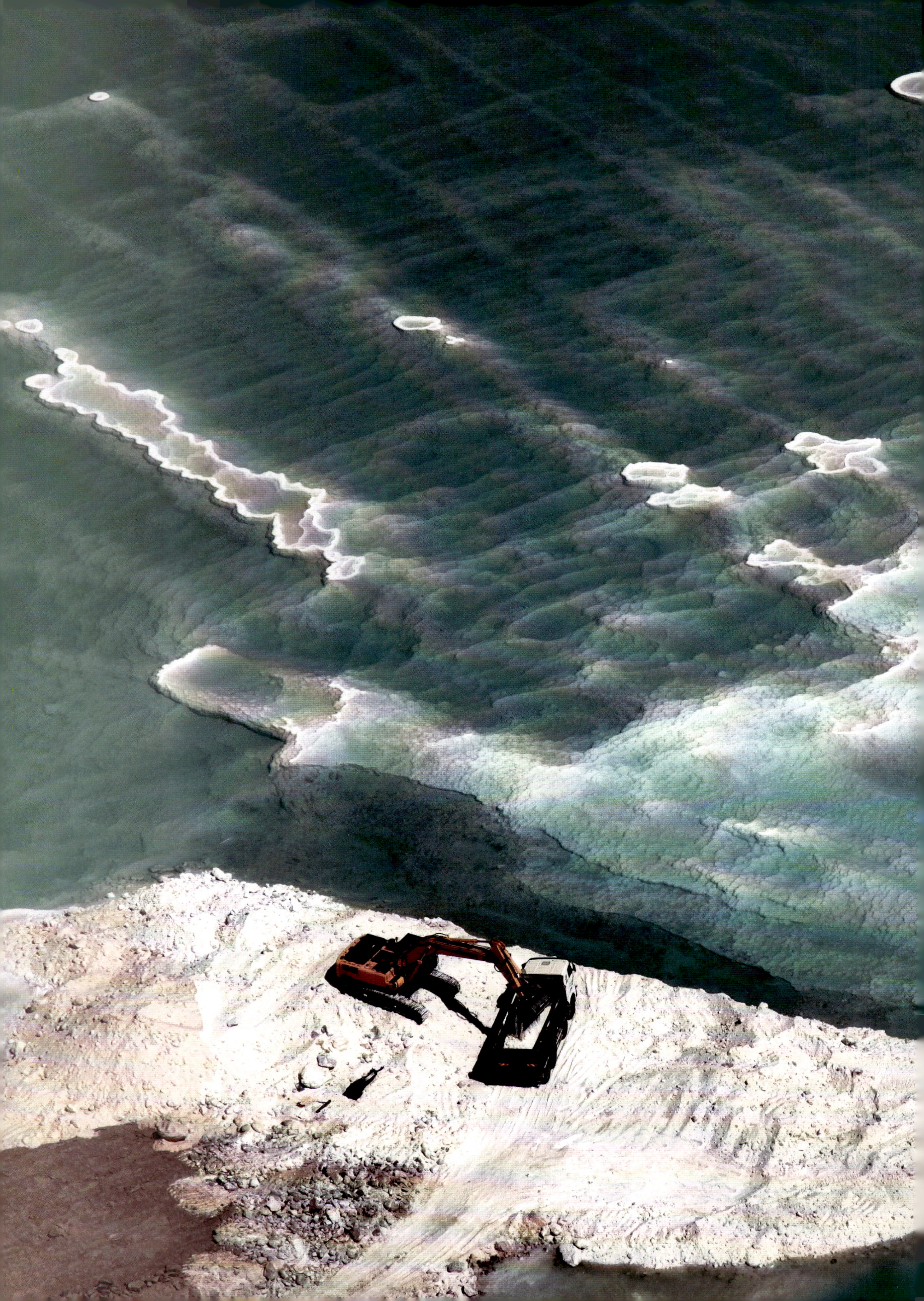

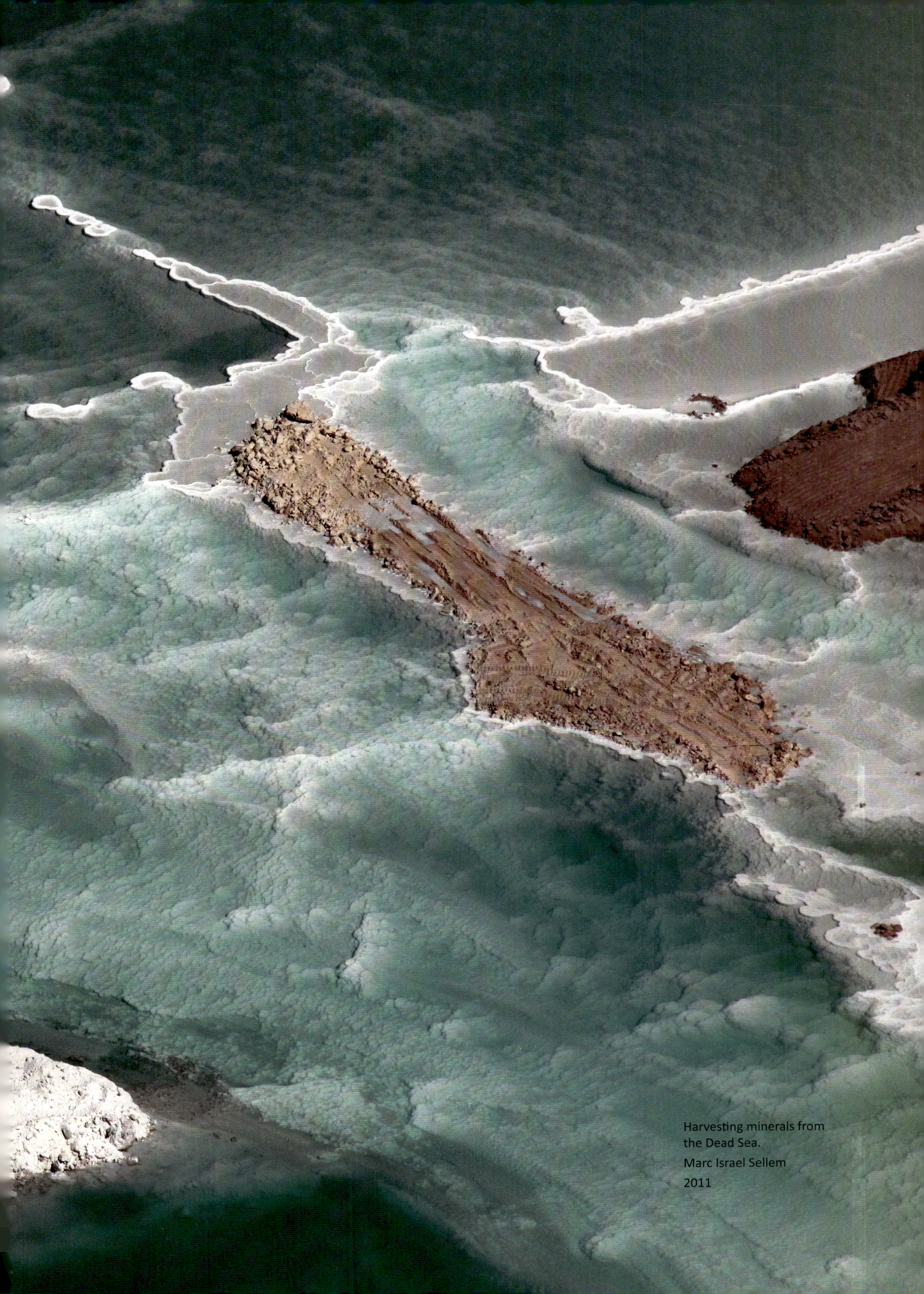

Harvesting minerals from the Dead Sea.
Marc Israel Sellem
2011

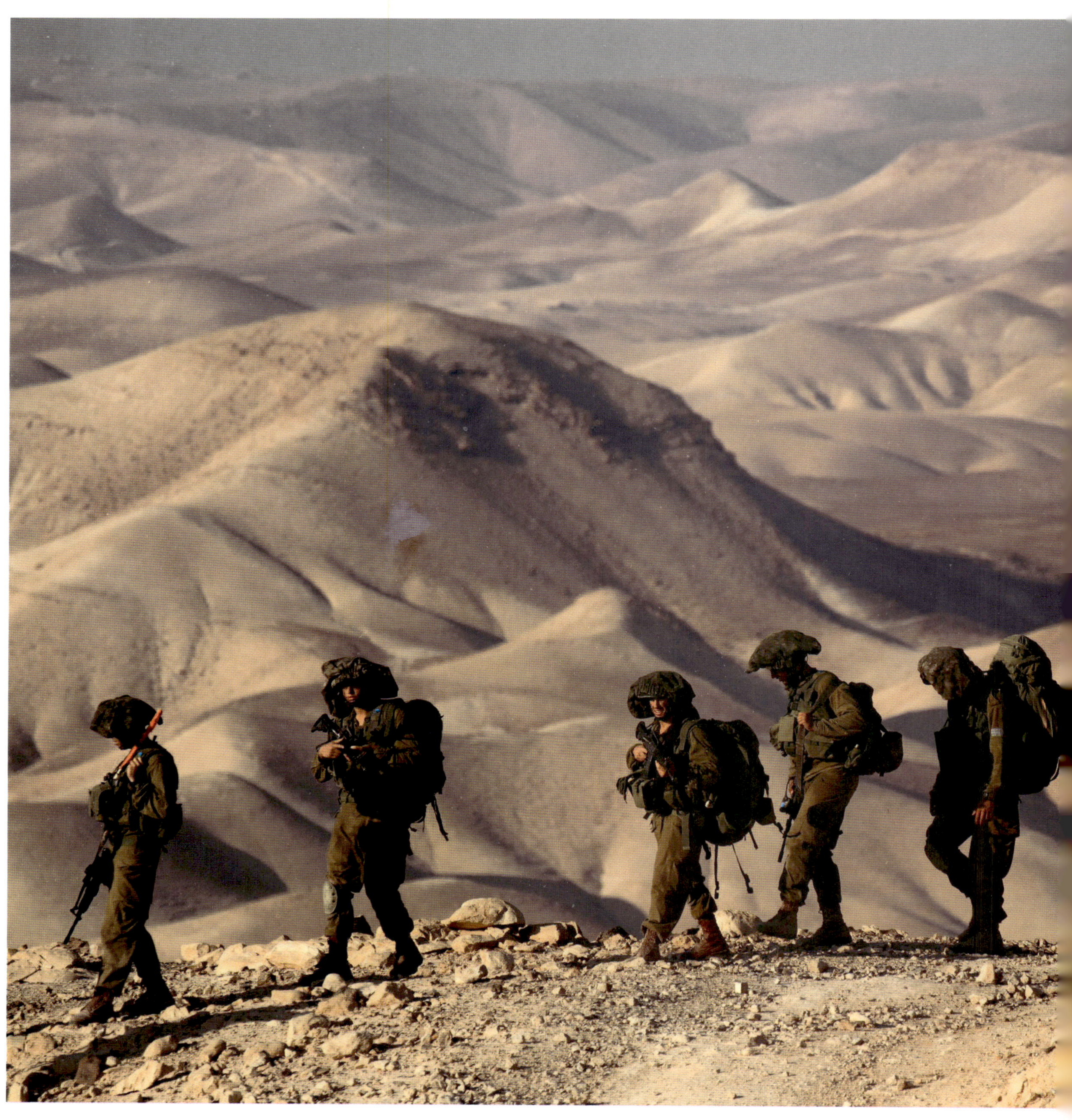

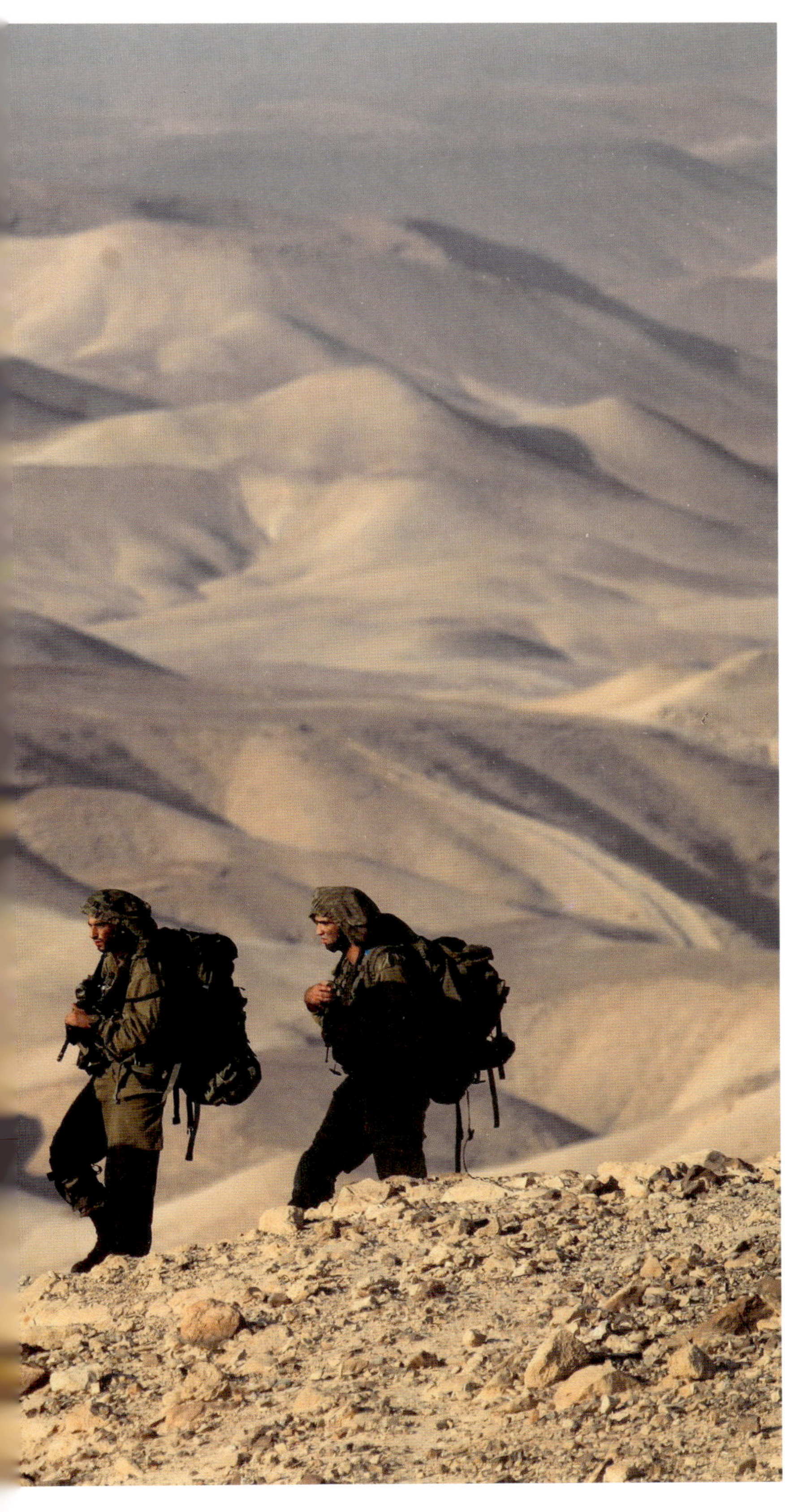

A training march in the
Judean Desert.
Marc Israel Sellem
2010

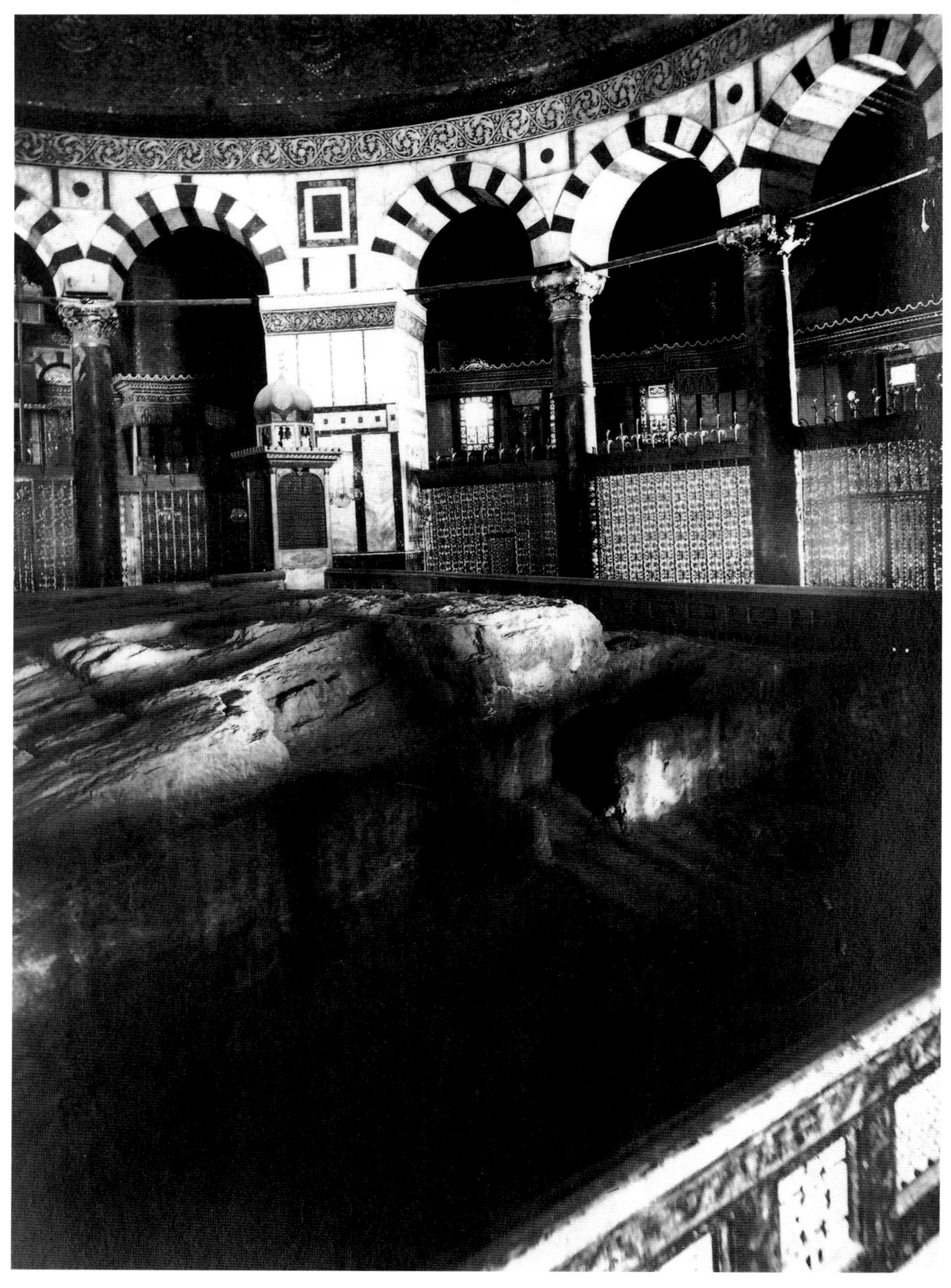

The Foundation Stone inside the Dome of the Rock and its surroundings is the holiest site in Judaism, the location of the First and Second Temples.

Ralph Fried

1923

Standing in the shadow of the Dome of the Rock.

Marc Israel Sellem

2010

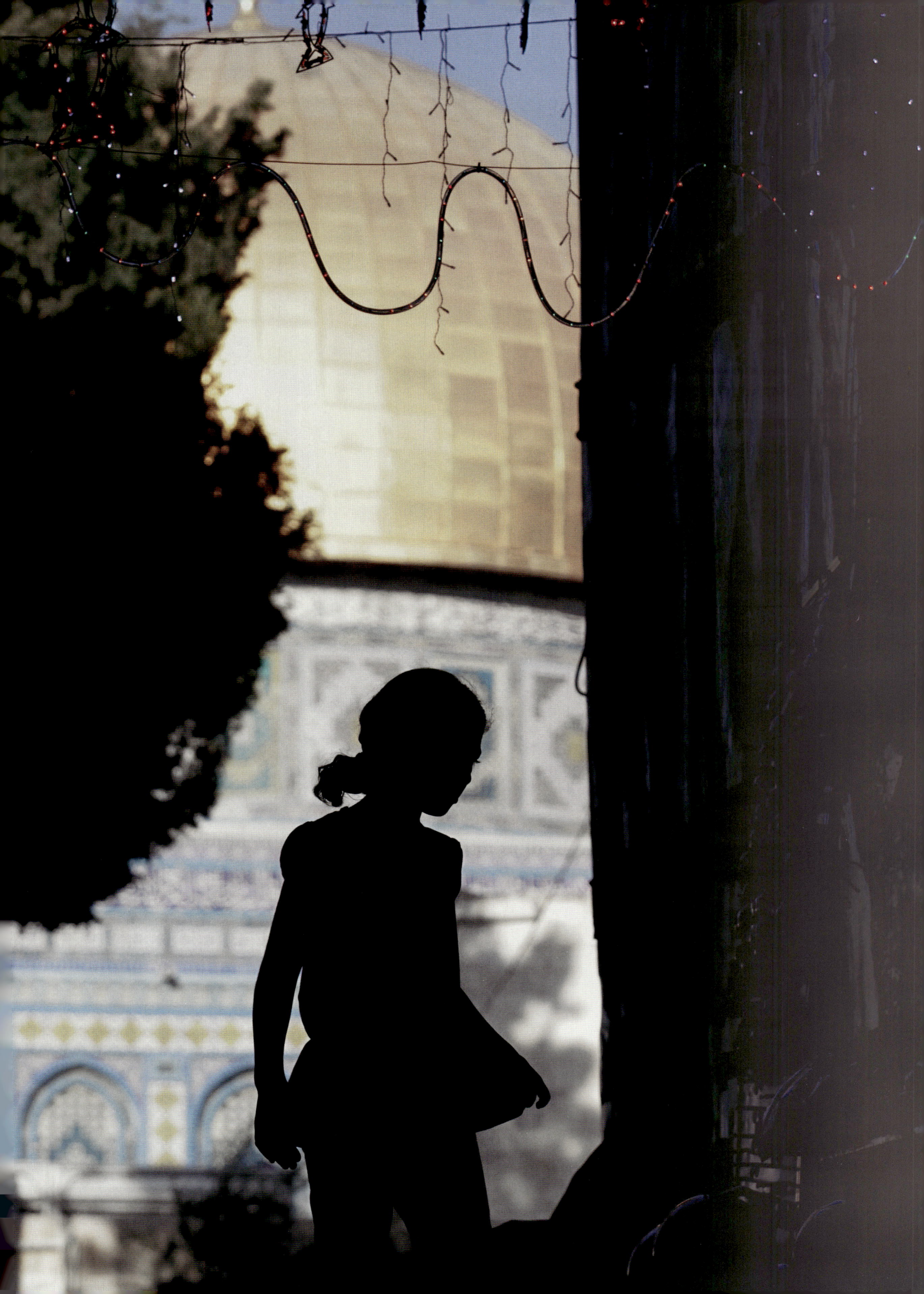

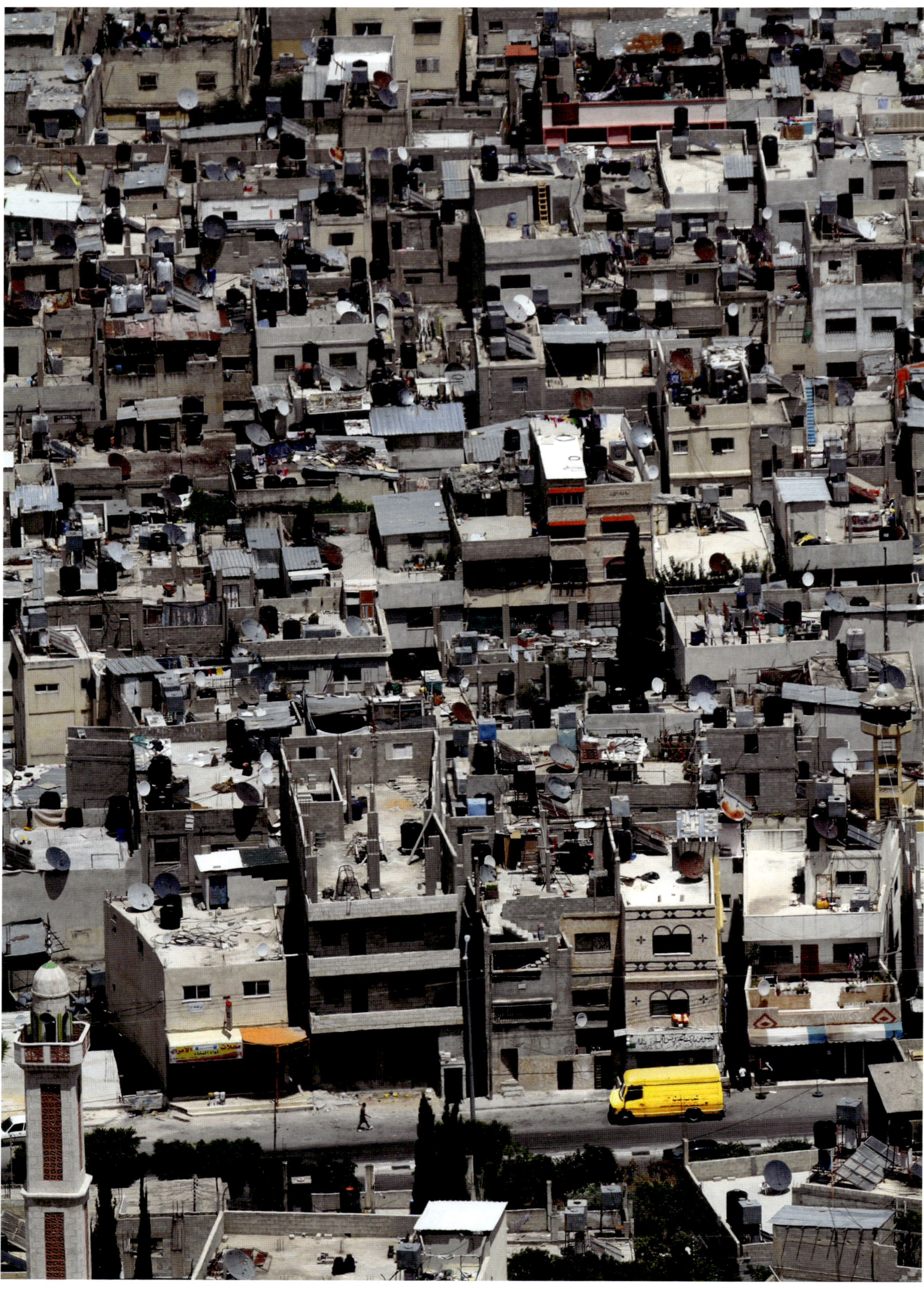

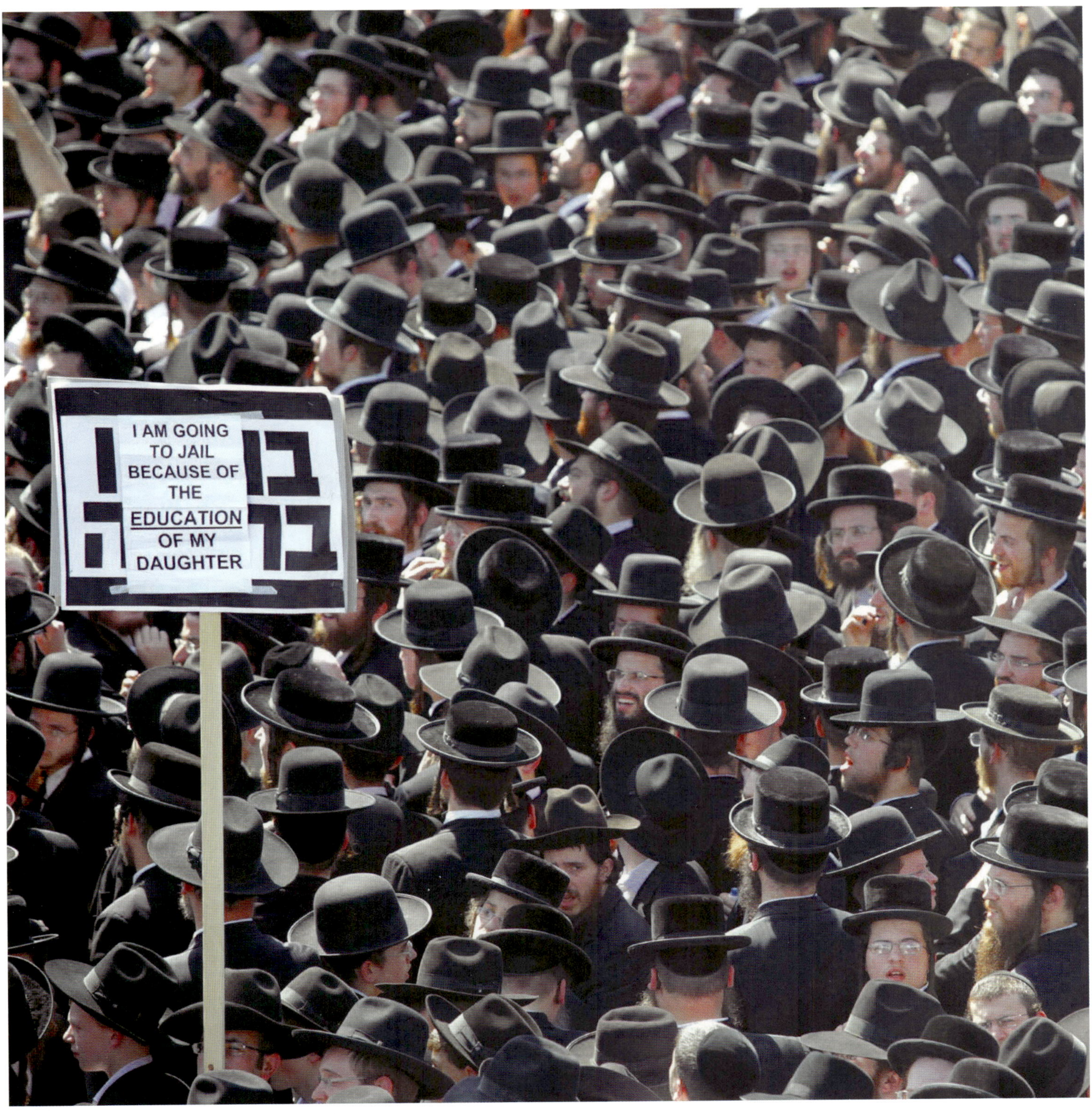

Ultra-Orthodox rally in Jerusalem to protest against military conscription.
Marc Israel Sellem
2011

An aerial view of Nablus.
Marc Israel Sellem
2010

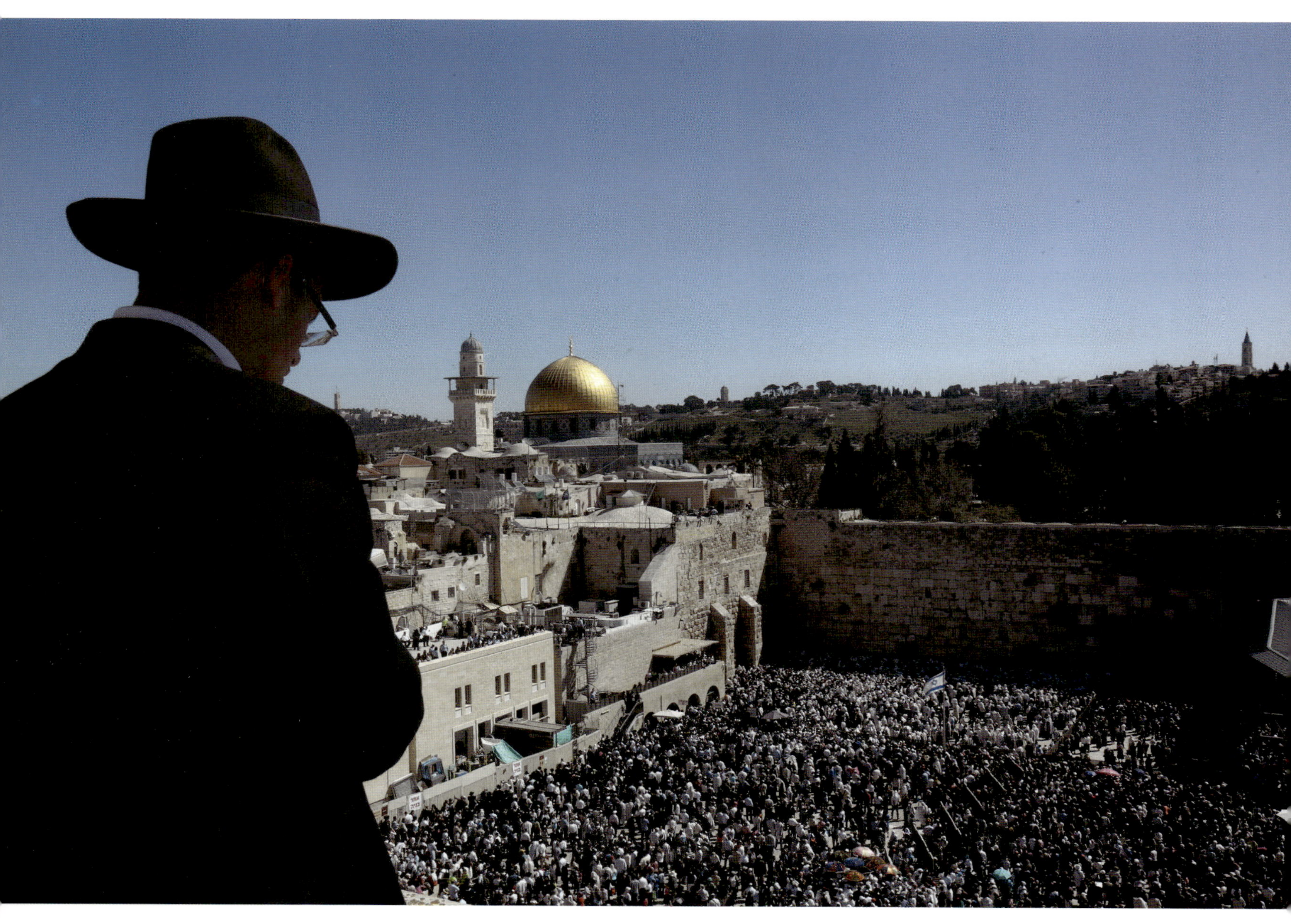

Thousands gather at the Wesetern Wall for the Priestly Blessing, delivered on the intermediate days of Passover and Succot.

Marc Israel Sellem

2015

Where do you park your reindeer in the Old City?

Marc Israel Sellem

2014

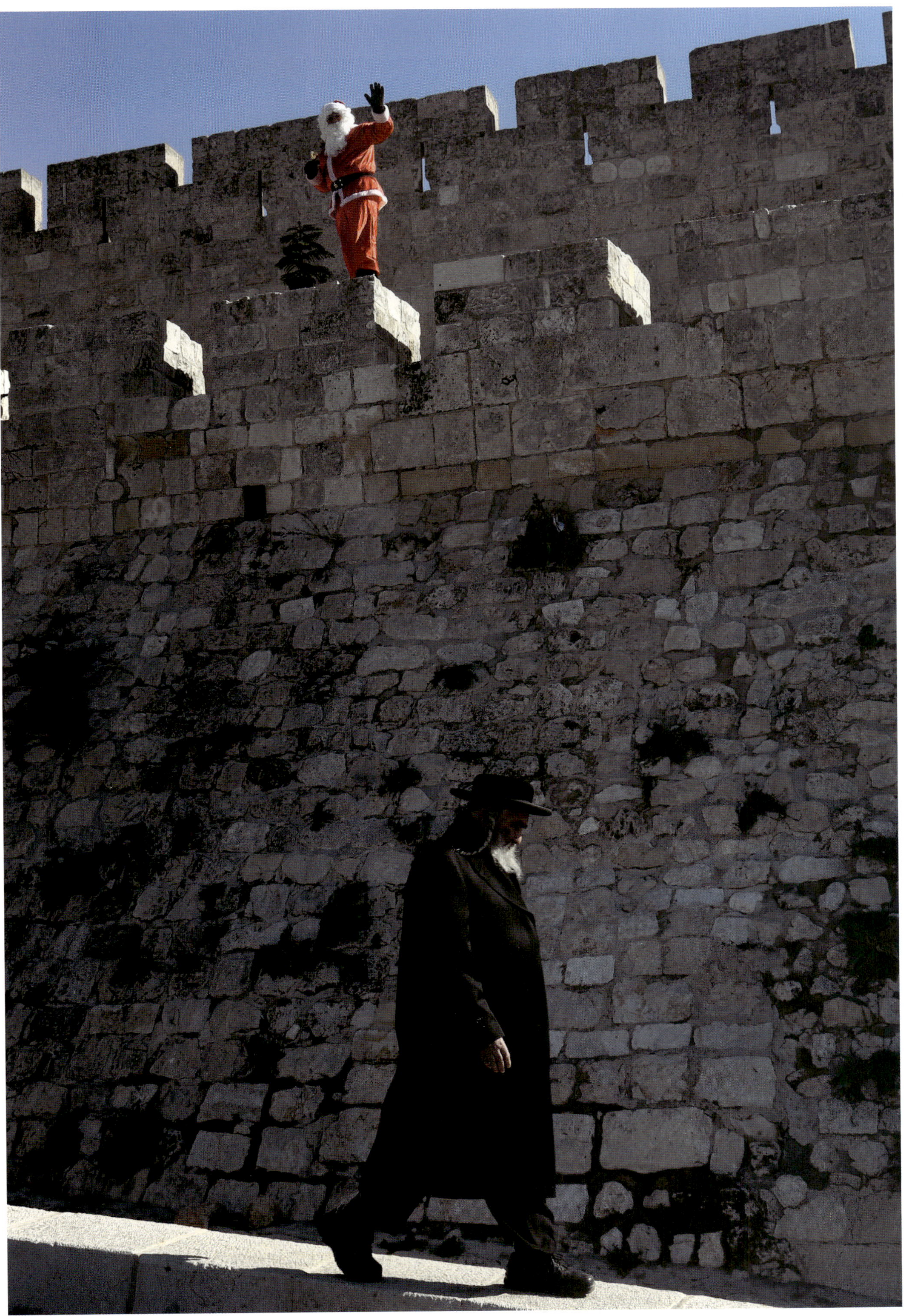

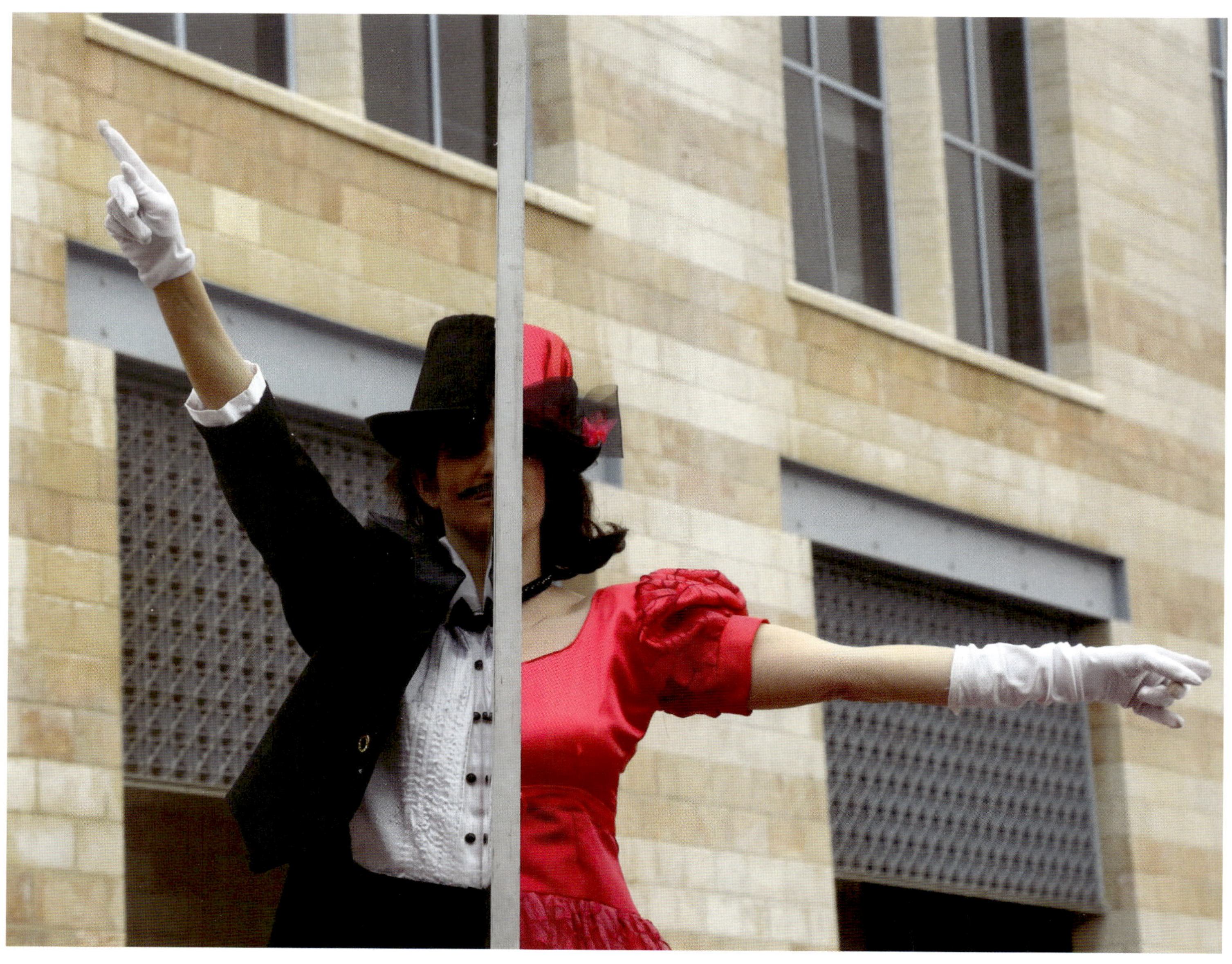

Can't decide what to
wear on Purim?
Marc Israel Sellem
2014

A Yemenite bride carries
a lot of weight.
Marc Israel Sellem
2014

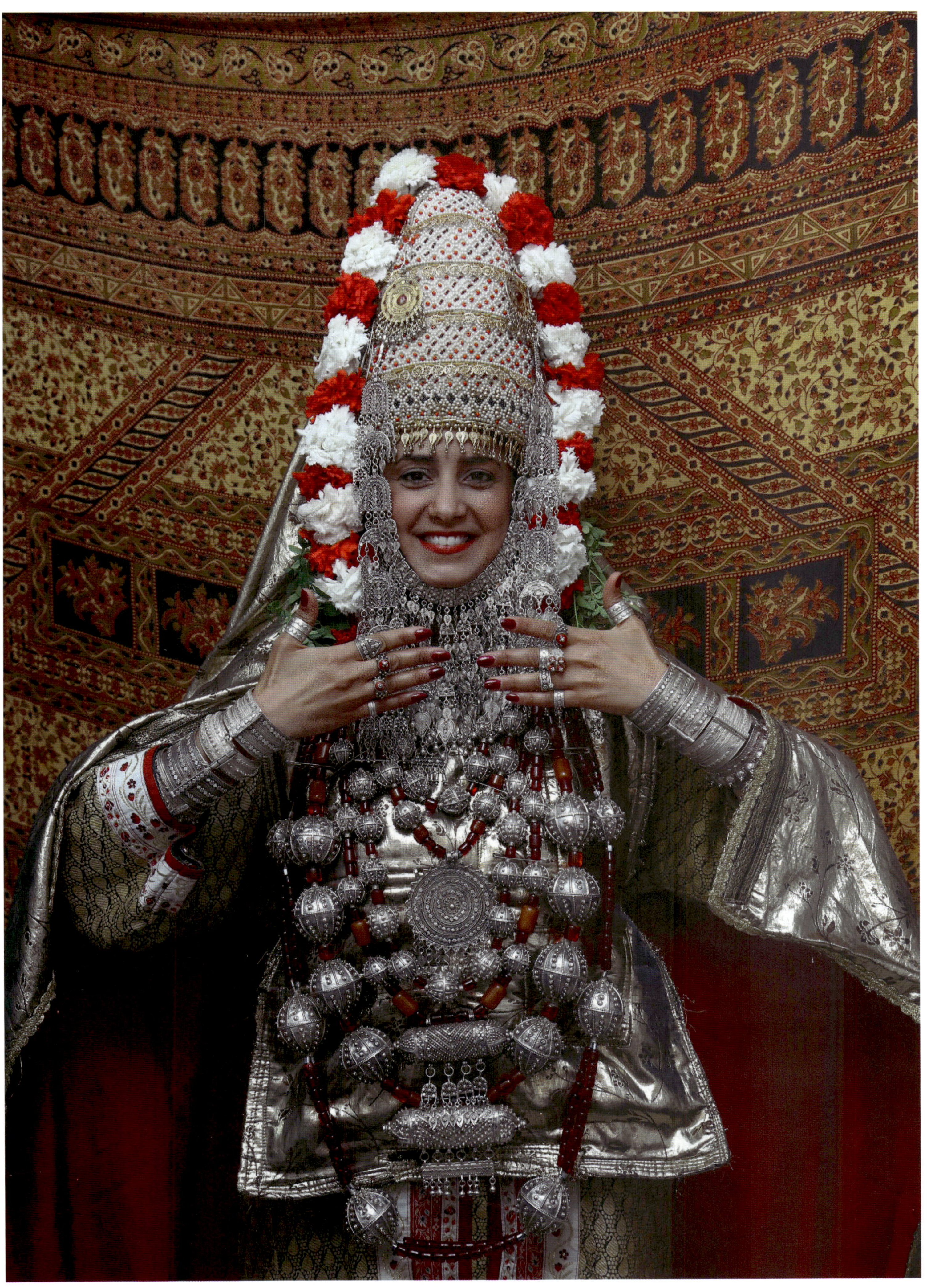

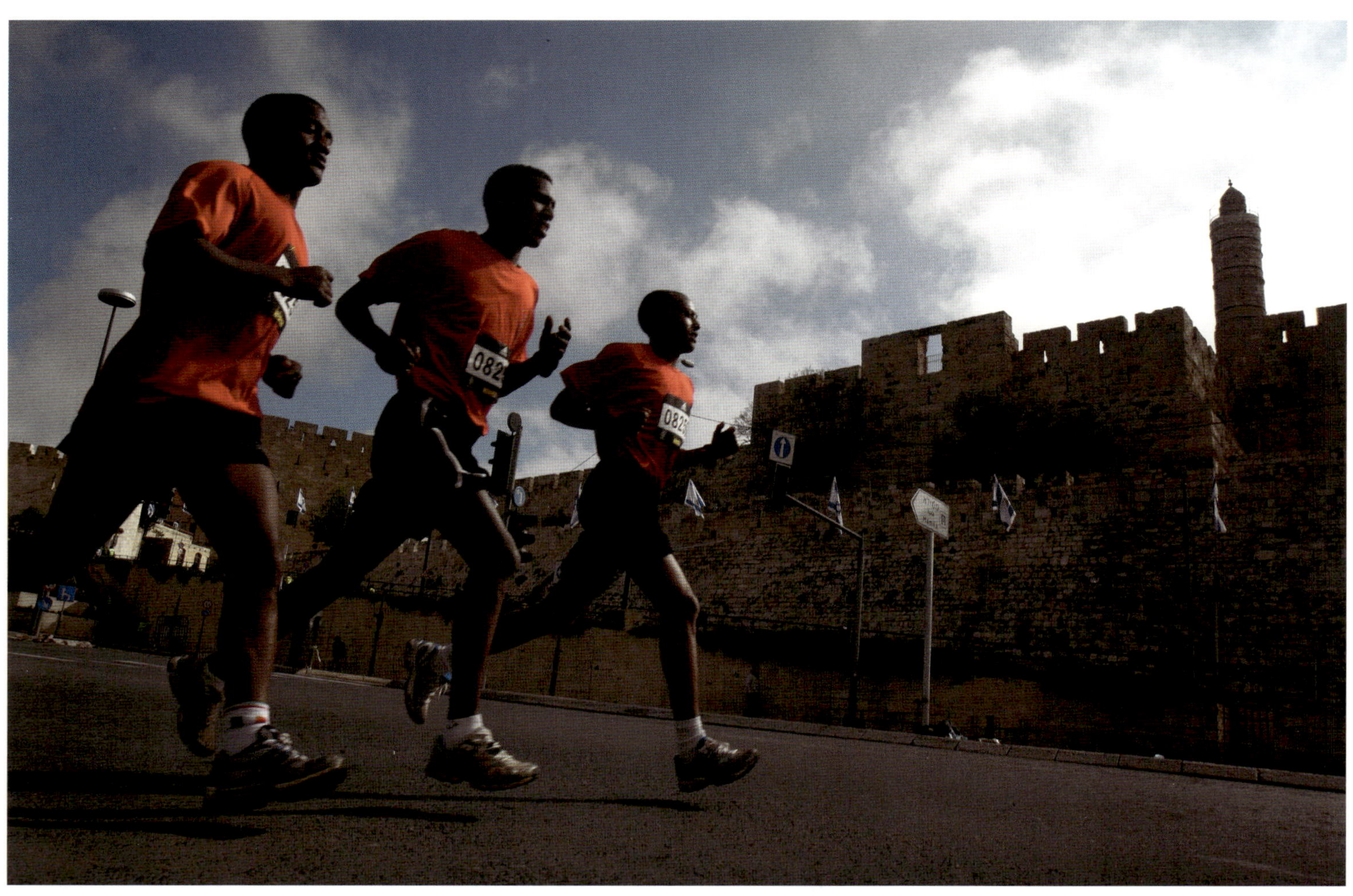

Runners in the Jerusalem Marathon
pass David's Citadel.
Marc Israel Sellem
2011

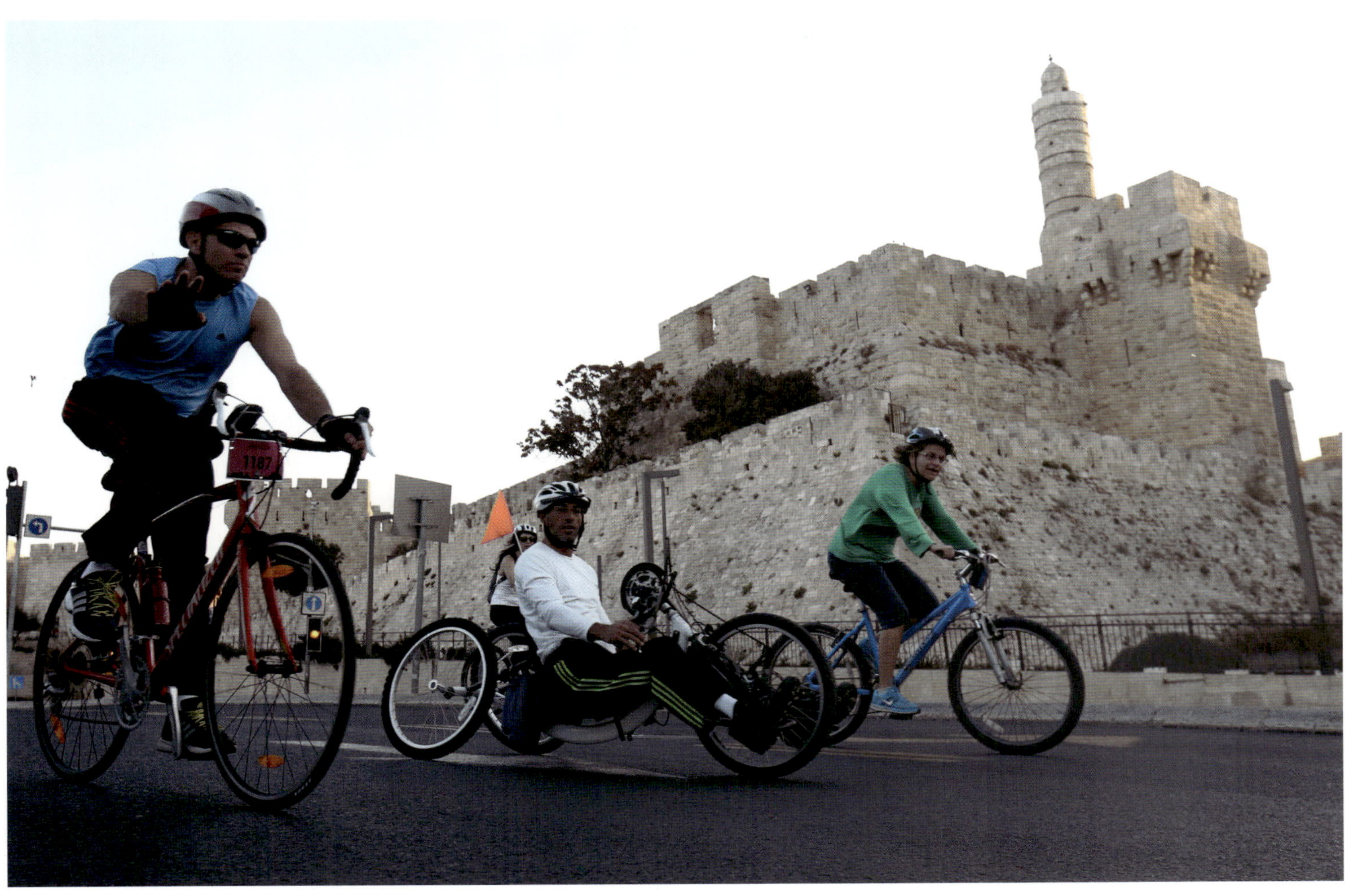

The Gran Fondo Giro Ditalia international bicycle race takes place in and around Jerusalem.

Marc Israel Sellem

2013

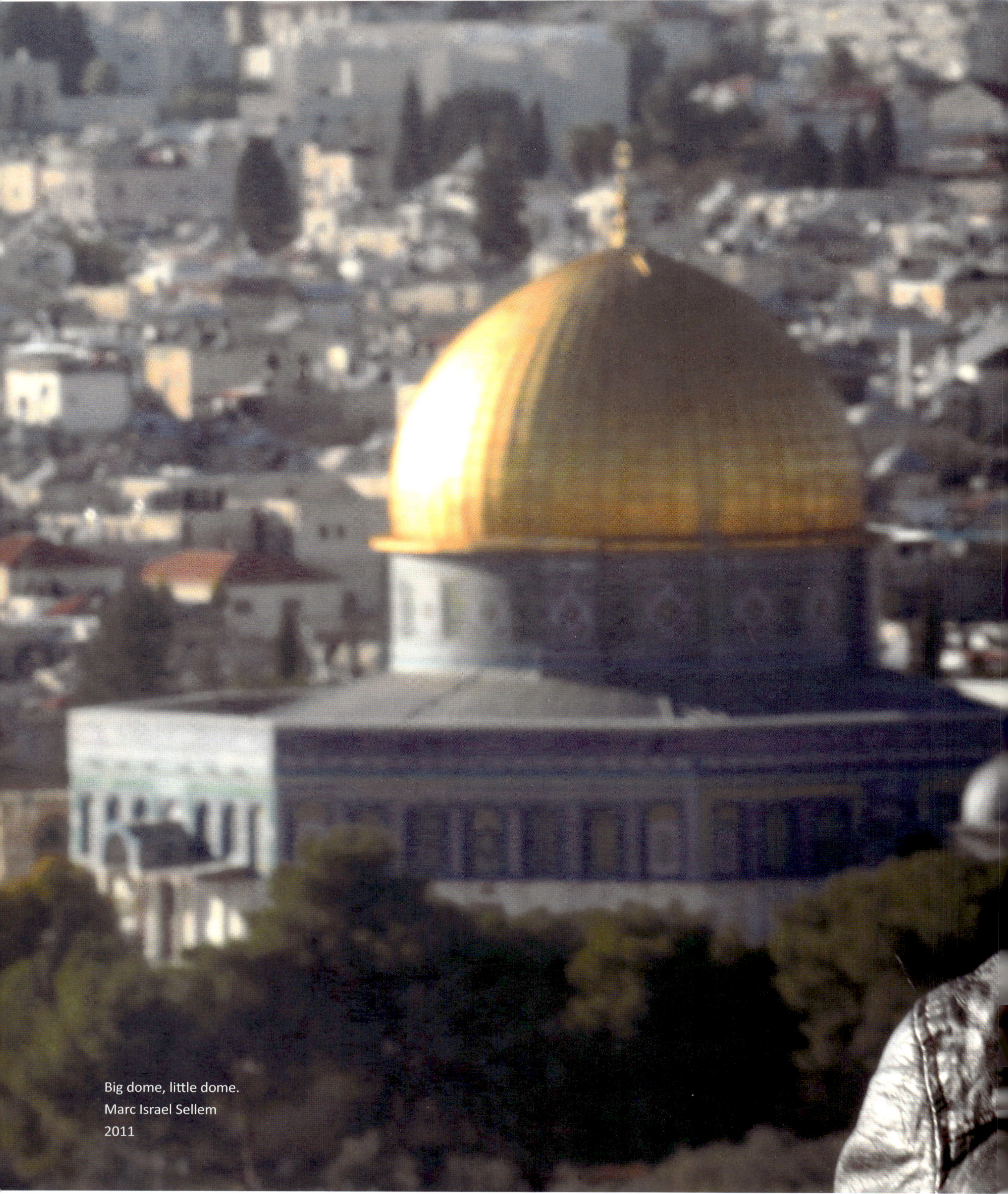
Big dome, little dome.
Marc Israel Sellem
2011

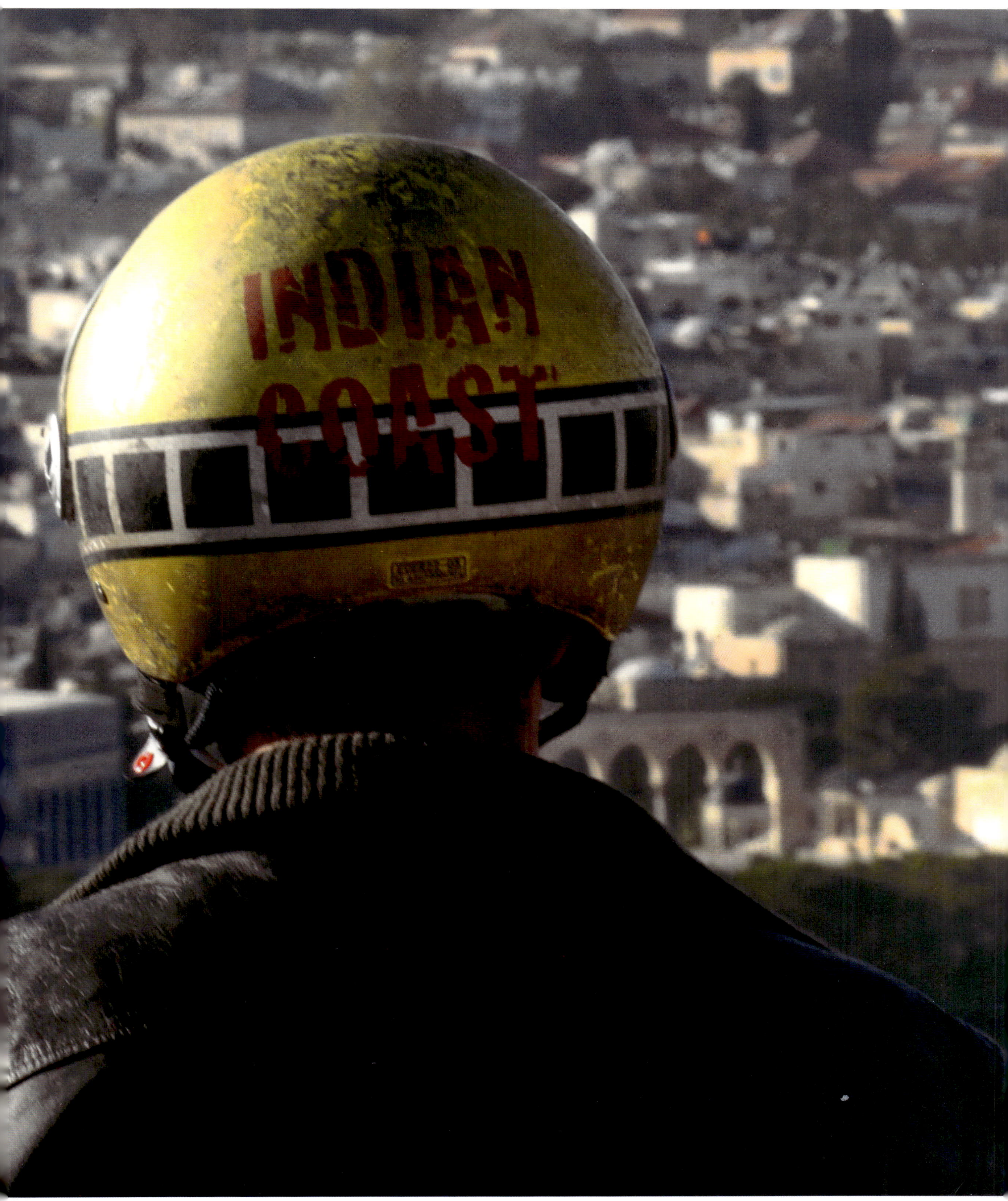
INDIAN
COAST

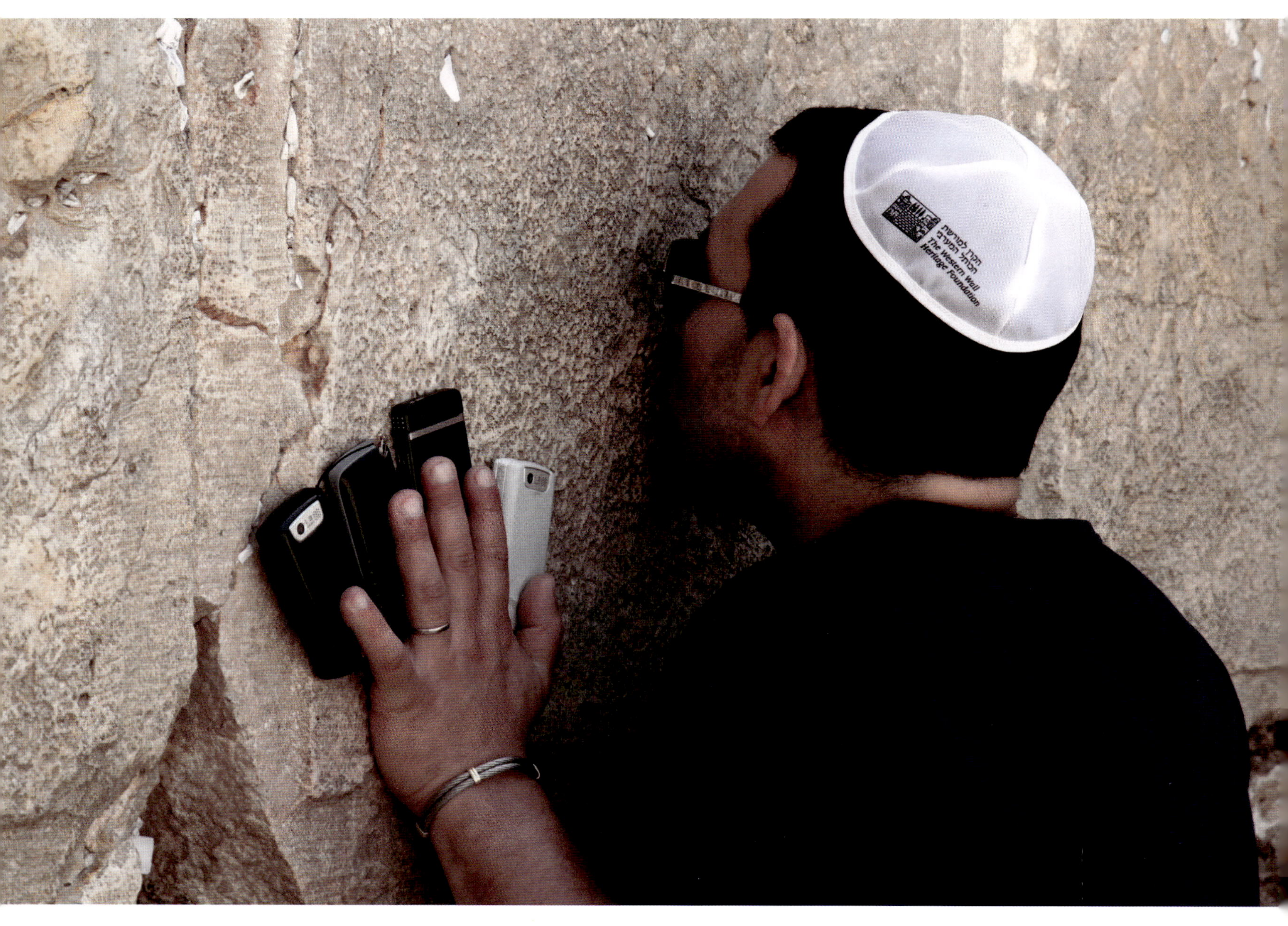

God is a toll-free call at
the Western Wall.

Marc Israel Sellem

2011

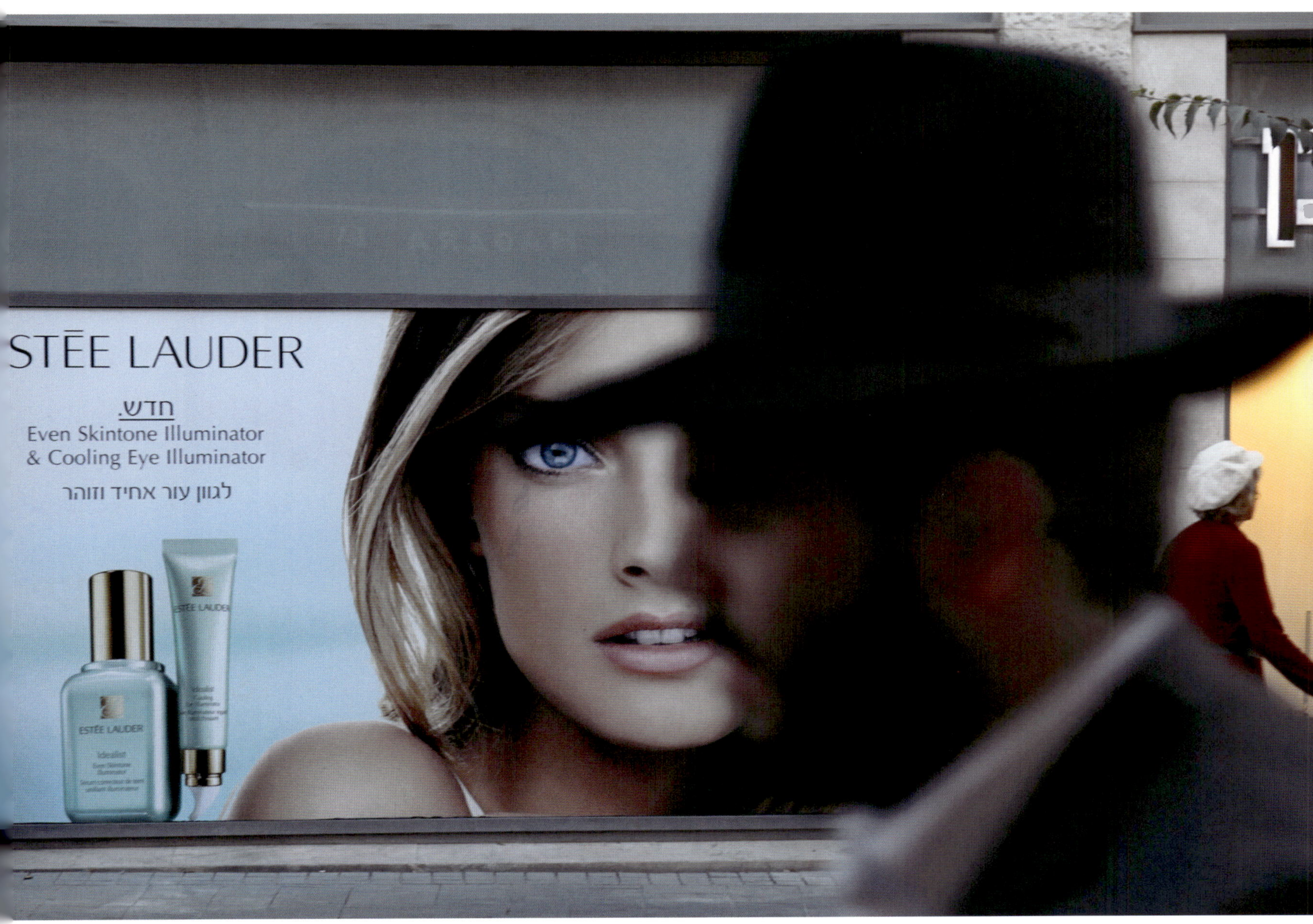

No eye contact.
Marc Israel Sellem
2011

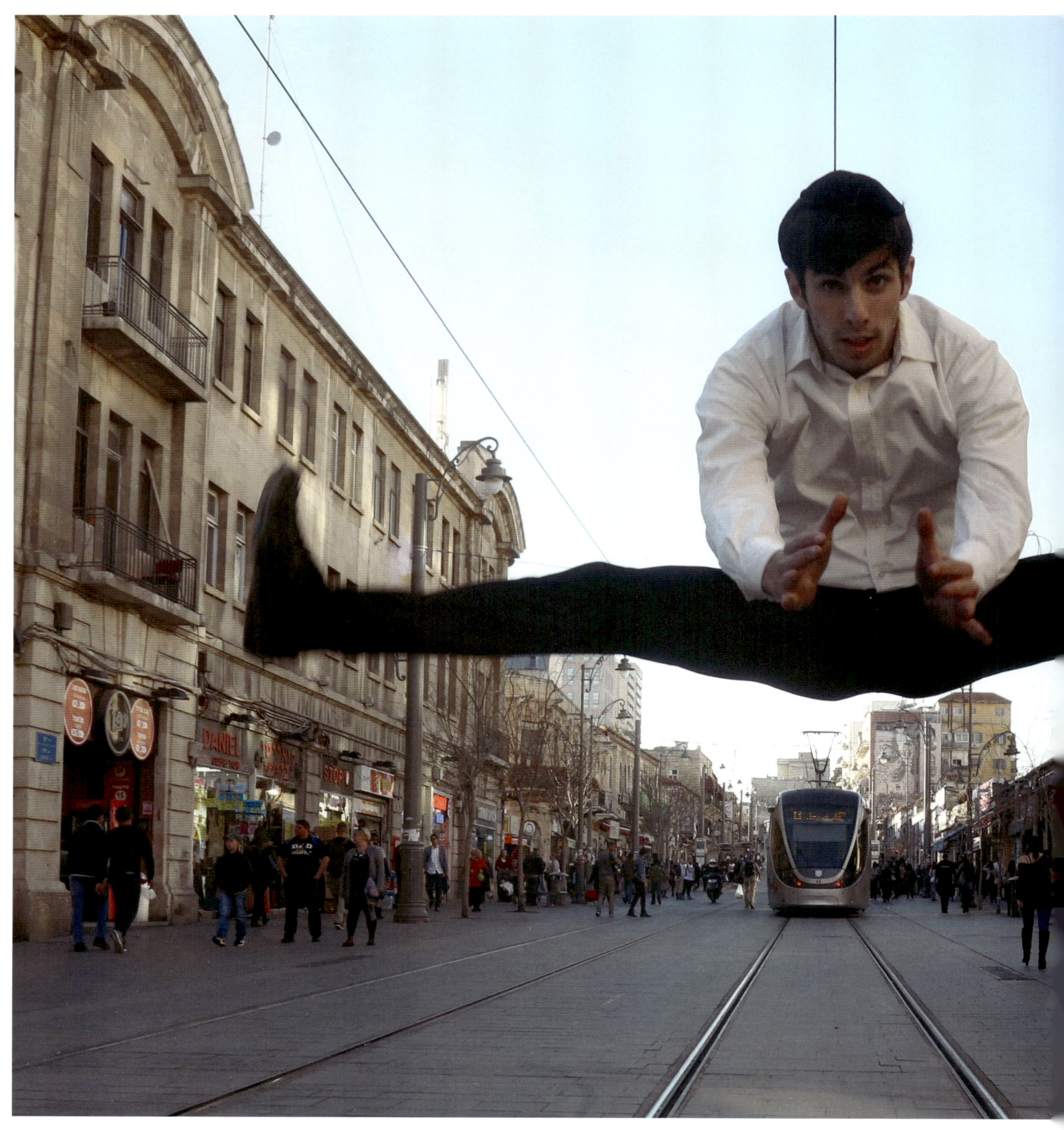
DANIEL
STOP

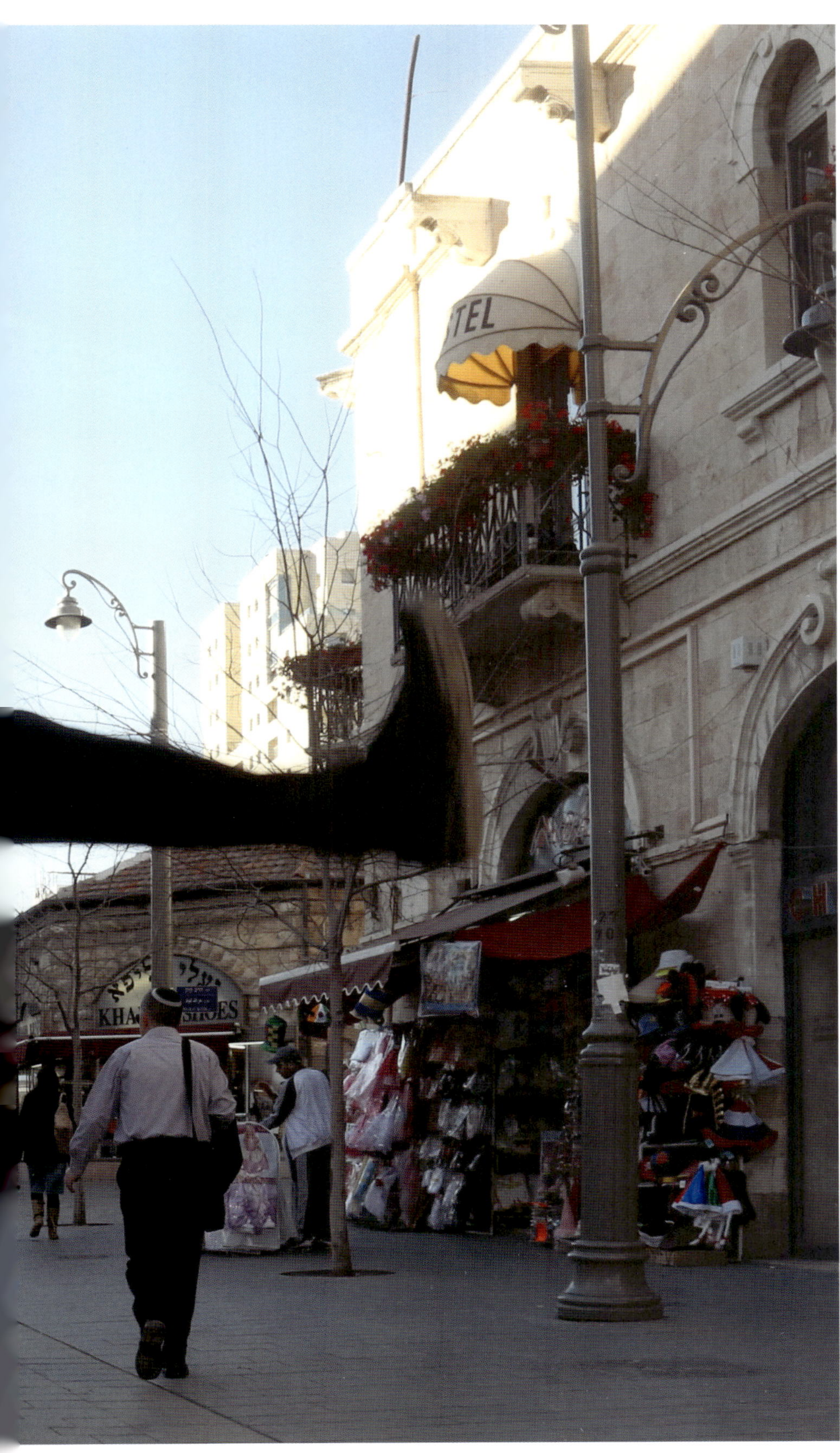

A martial arts enthusiast does a split on the tracks of the Jerusalem Light Rail.

Marc Israel Sellem

2014

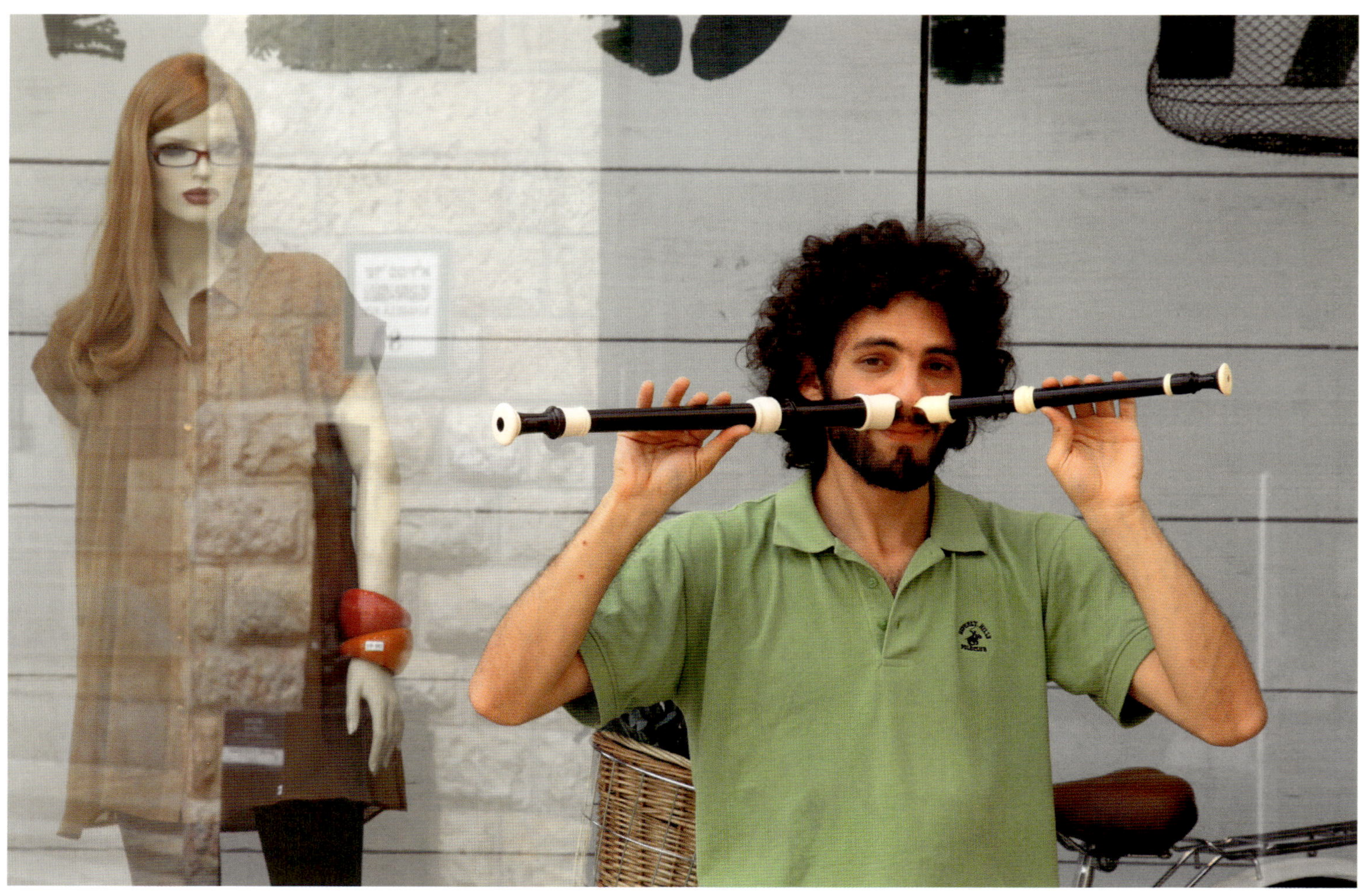

Not everyone can play a
duet with their nose.

Marc Israel Sellem

2011

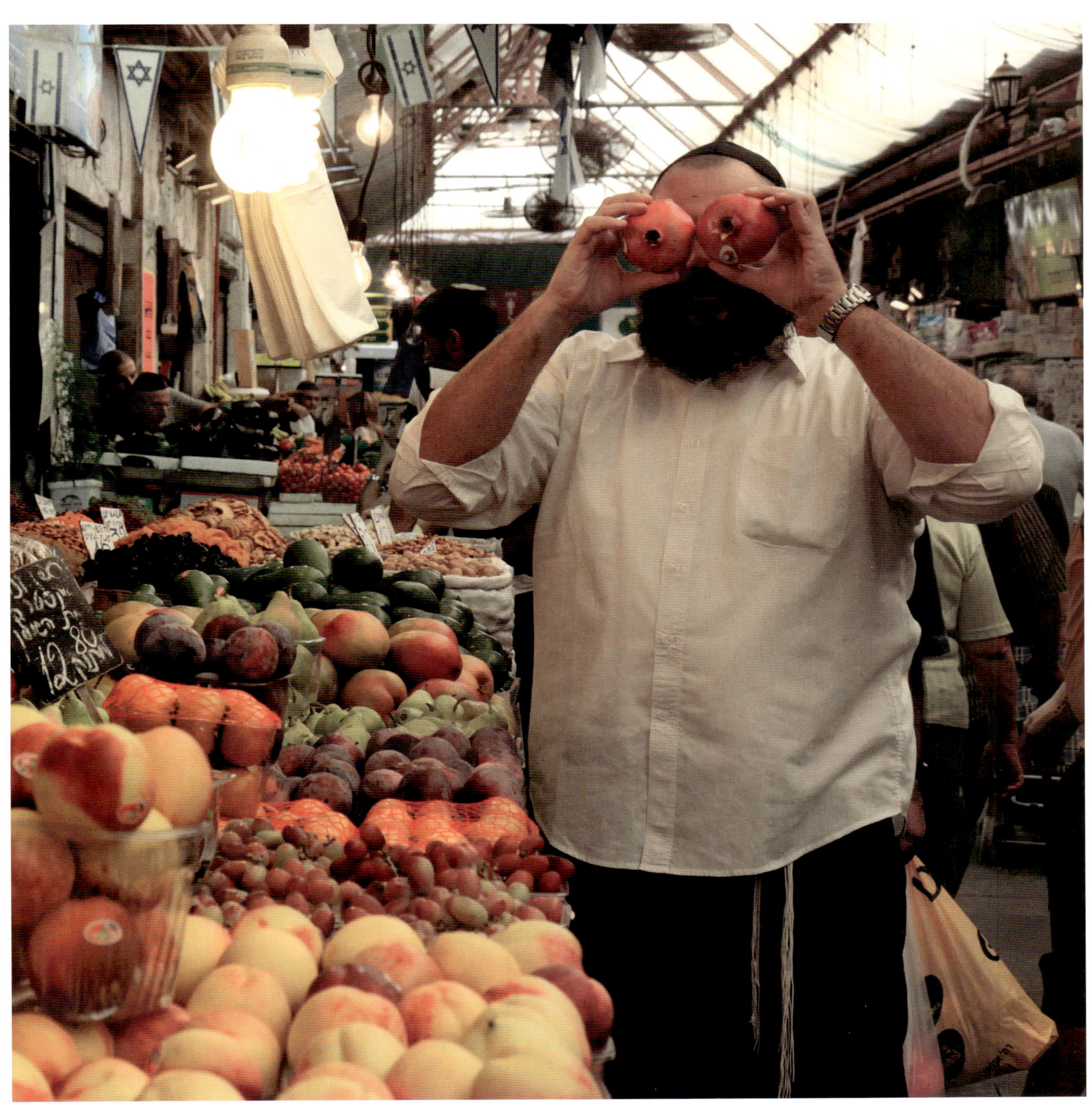

Jerusalem's Mahaneh Yehuda market is bursting with fruit for Rosh Hashana.

Marc Israel Sellem

2011

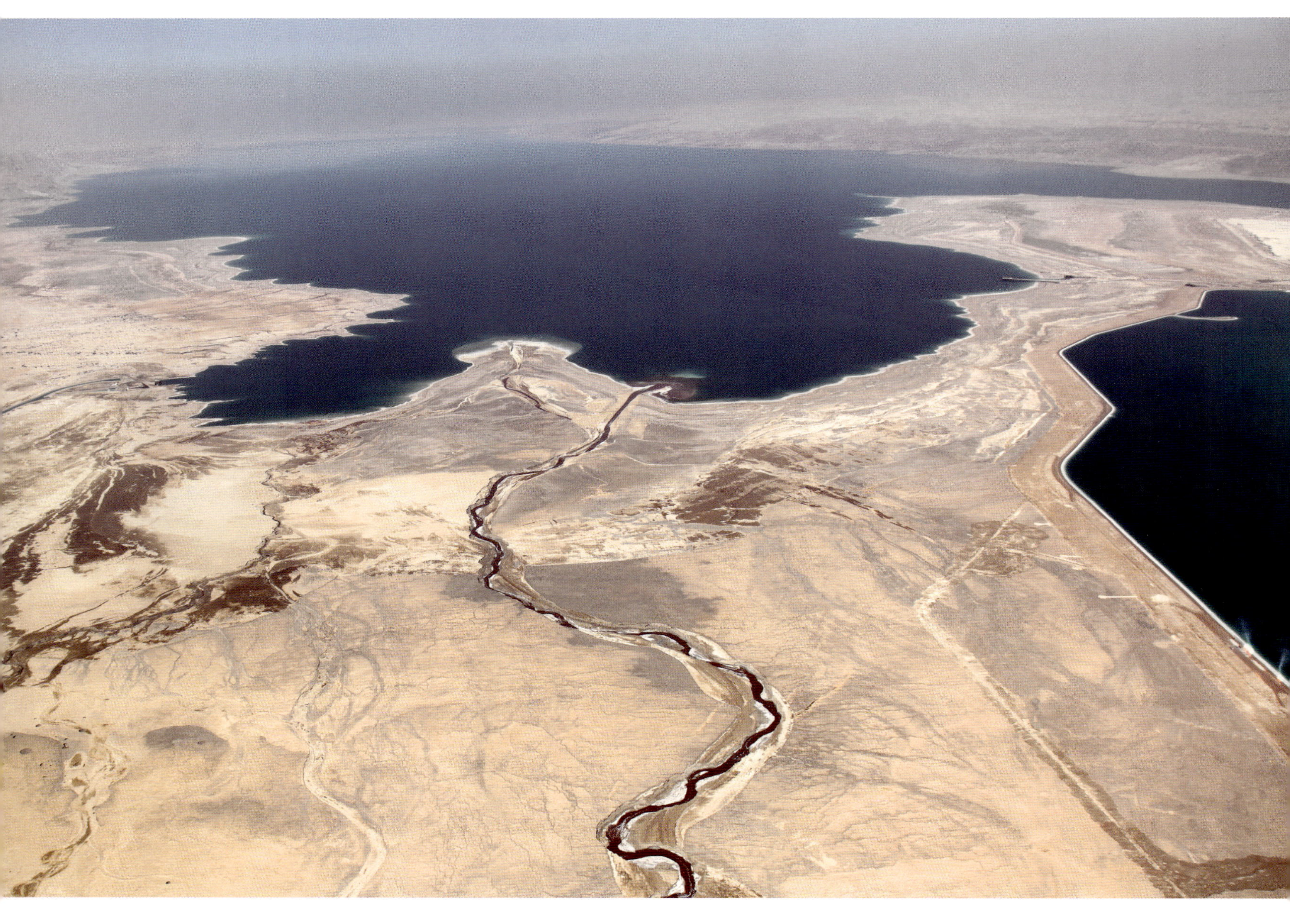

An aerial panorama of
the Dead Sea.
Marc Israel Sellem
2011

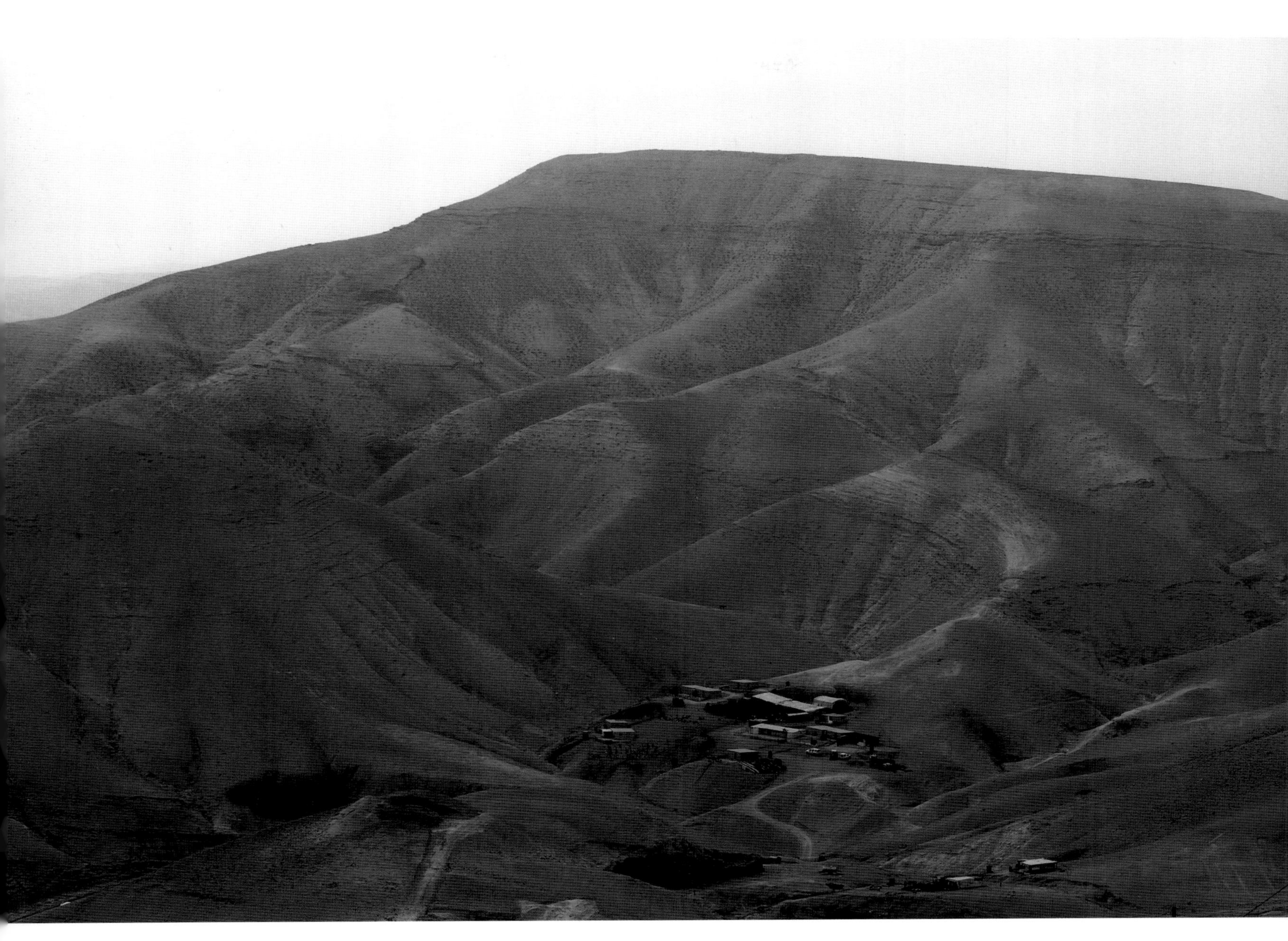

A Beduin encampment
in the Judean Desert.
Marc Israel Sellem
2014

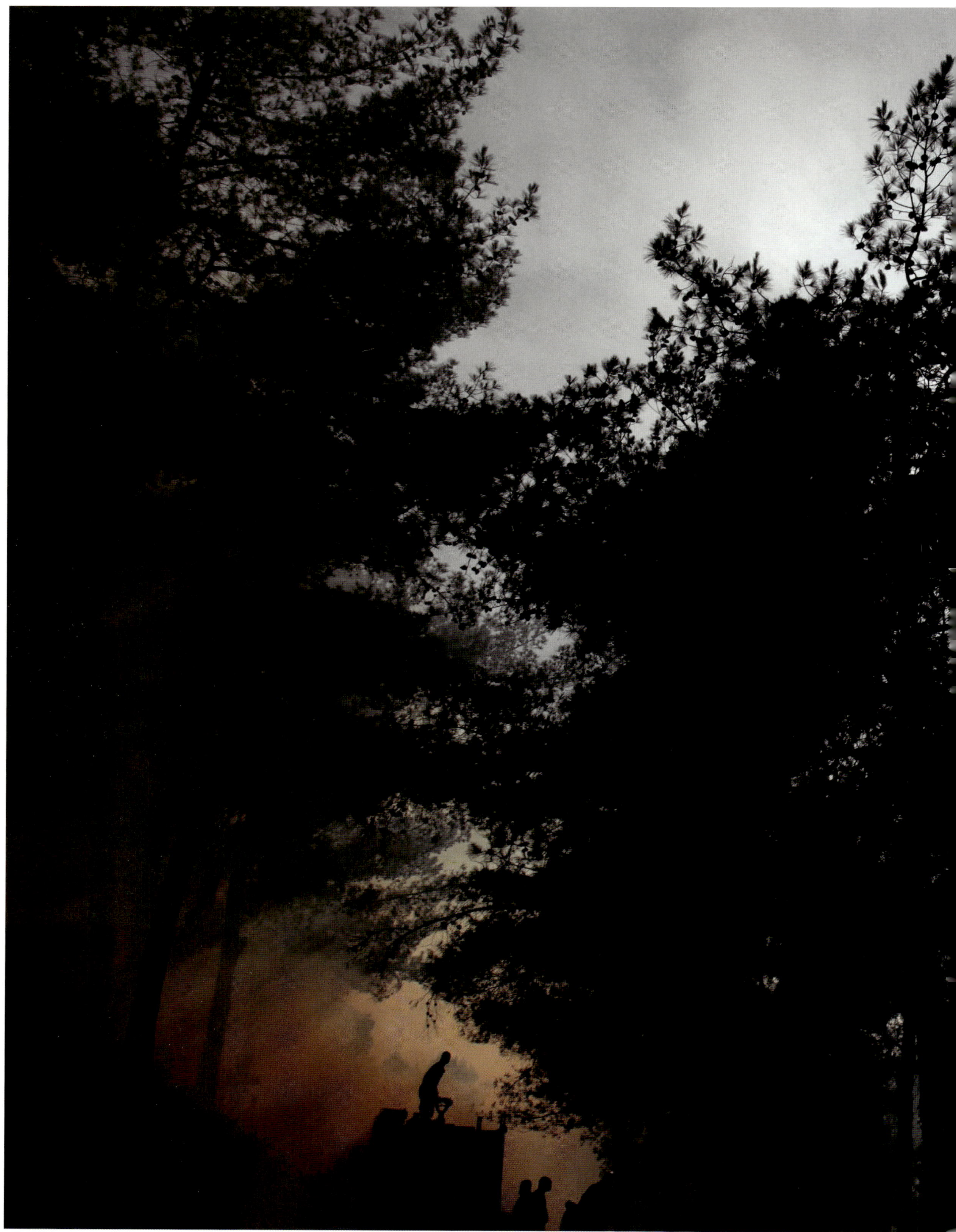

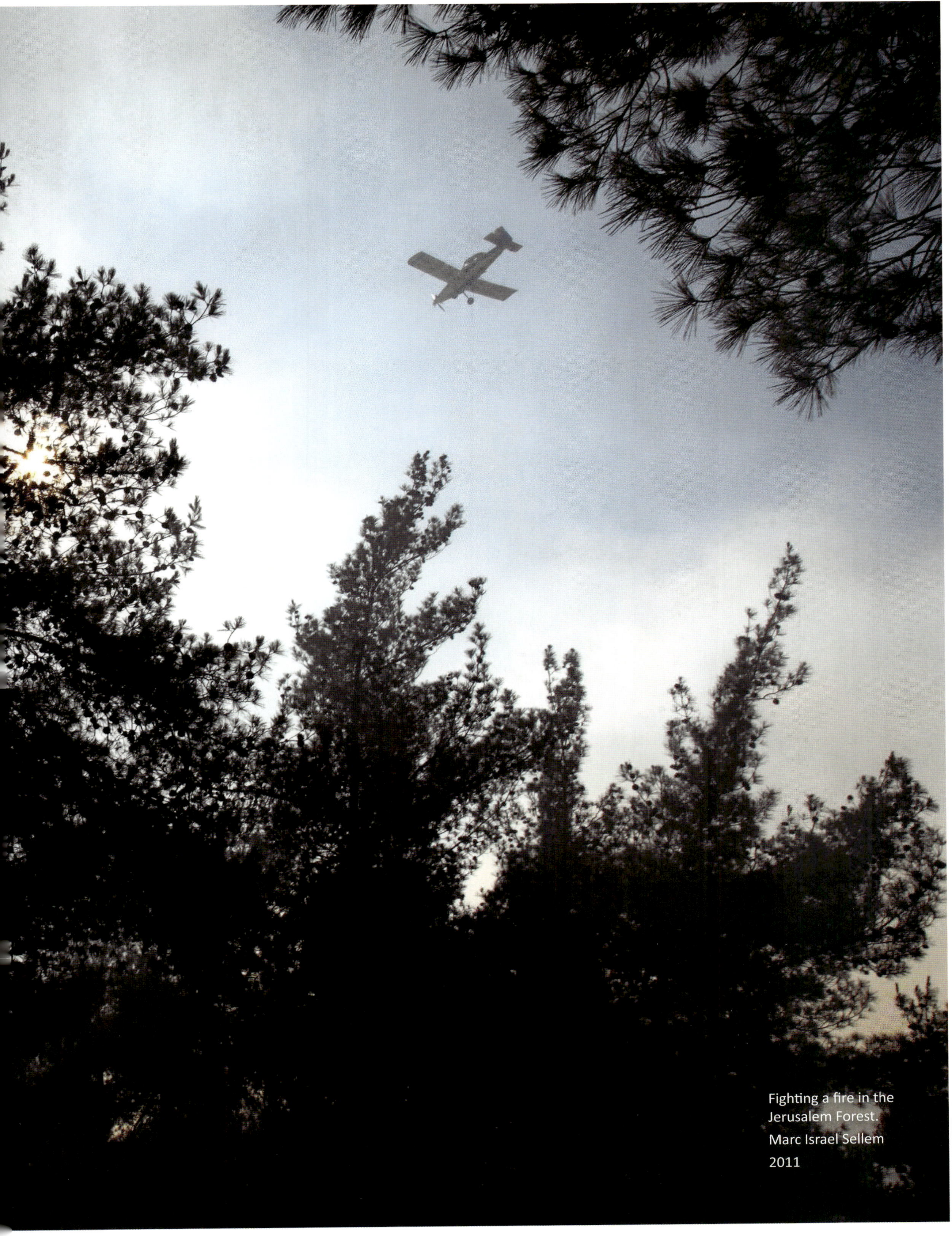

Fighting a fire in the Jerusalem Forest.
Marc Israel Sellem
2011

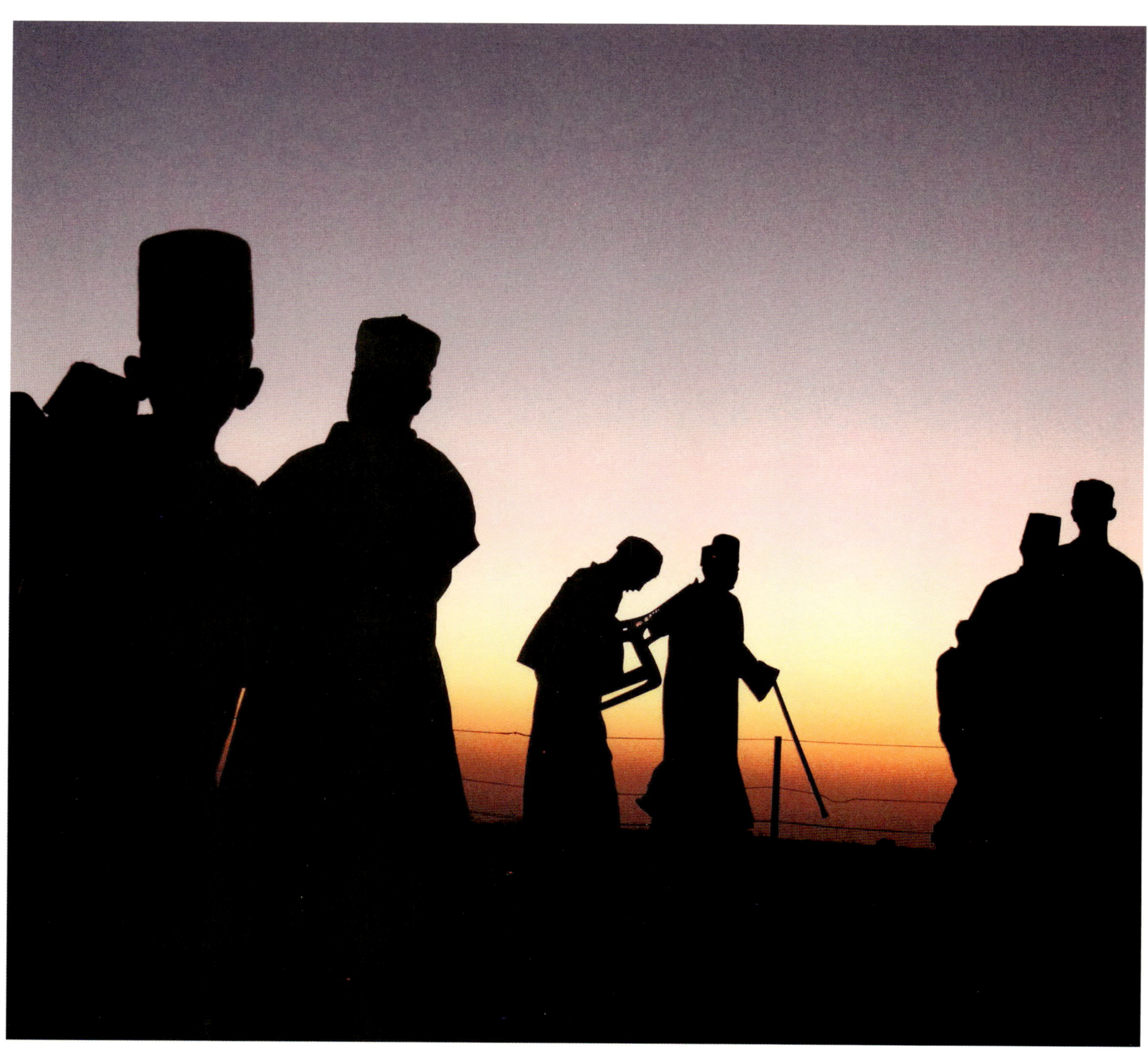

Samaritans
Marc Israel Sellem
2011

Shadows on Jerusalem's
Old City wall.
Marc Israel Sellem
2010

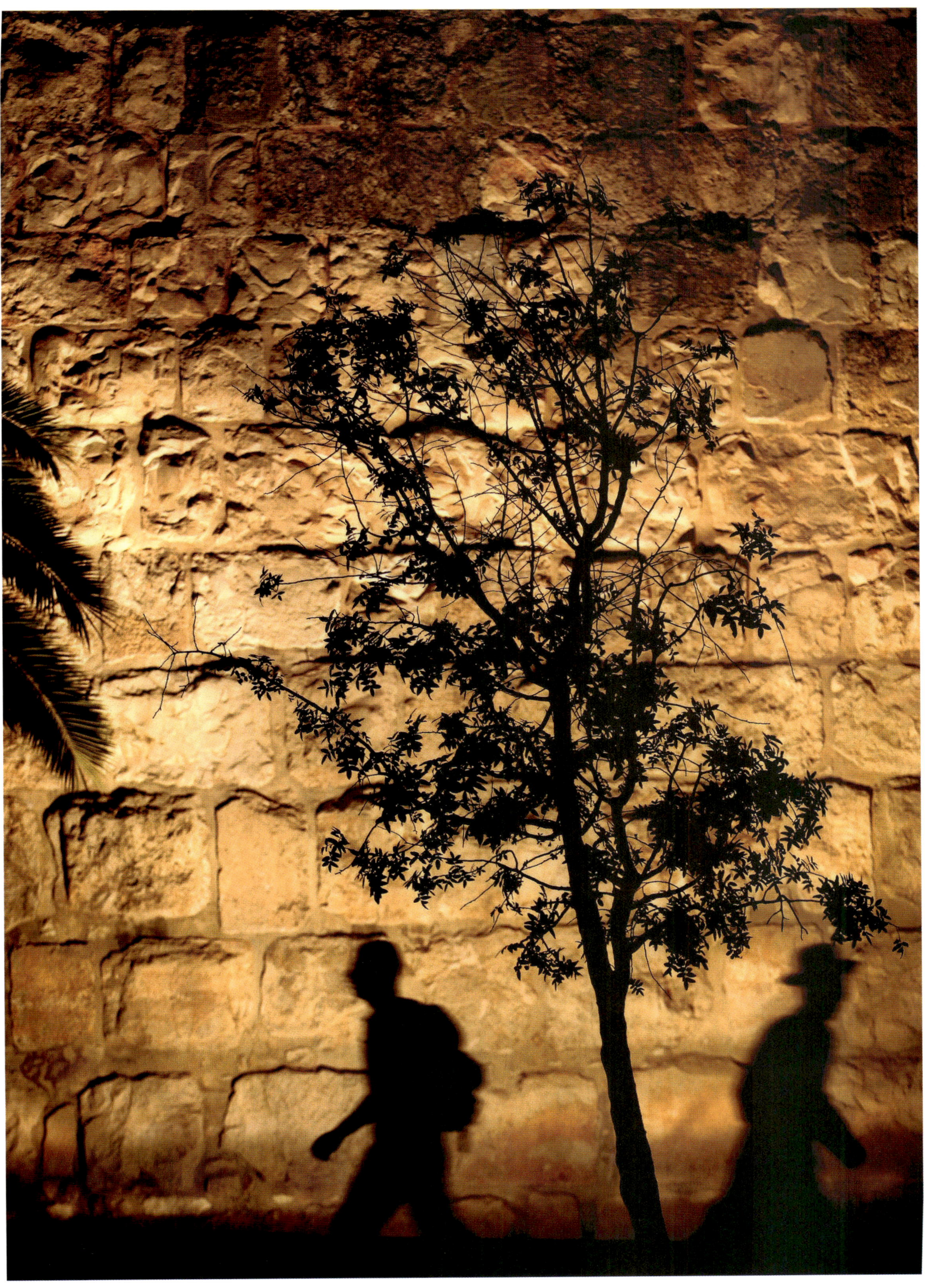

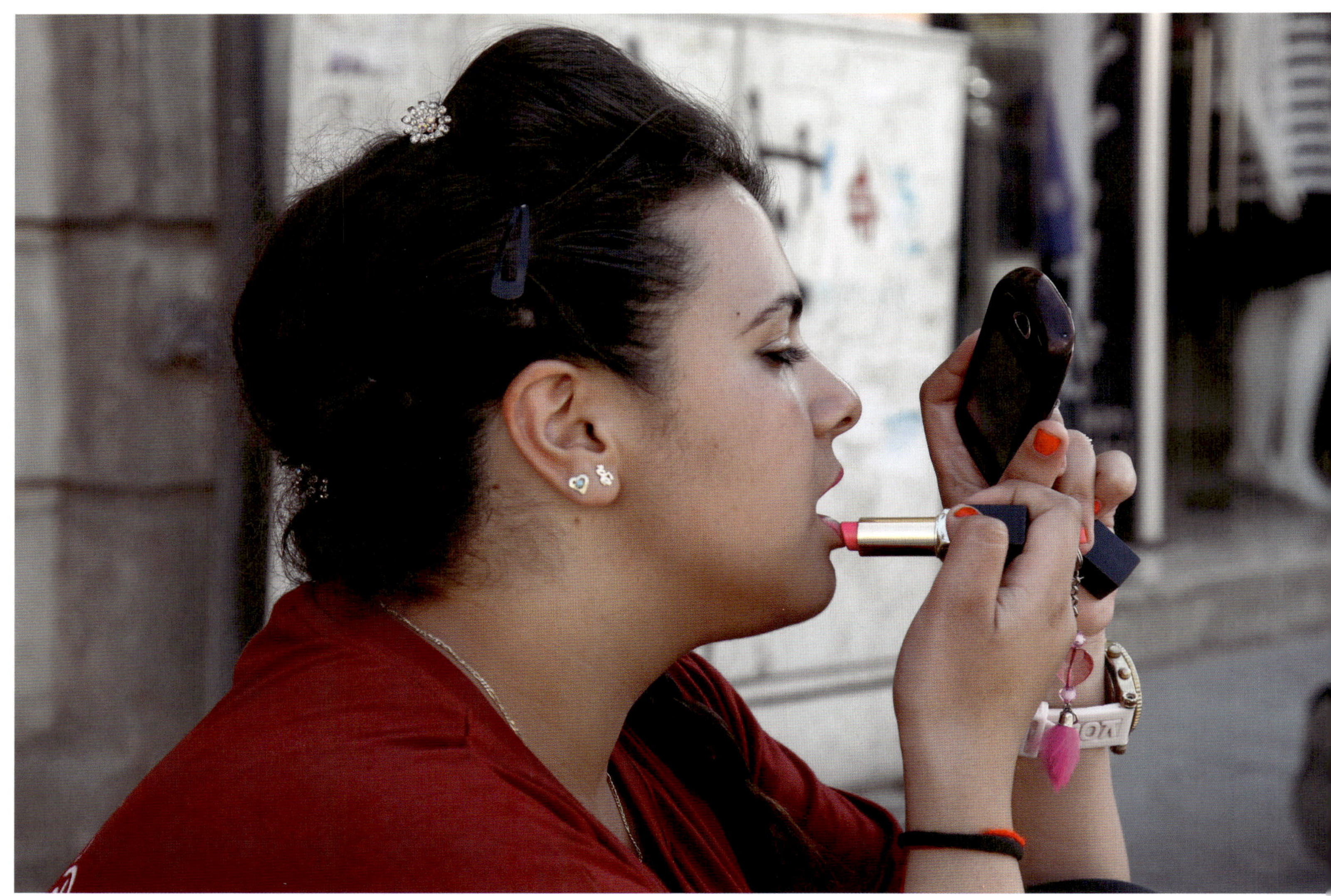

Multitasking with a cellphone.

Marc Israel Sellem

2011

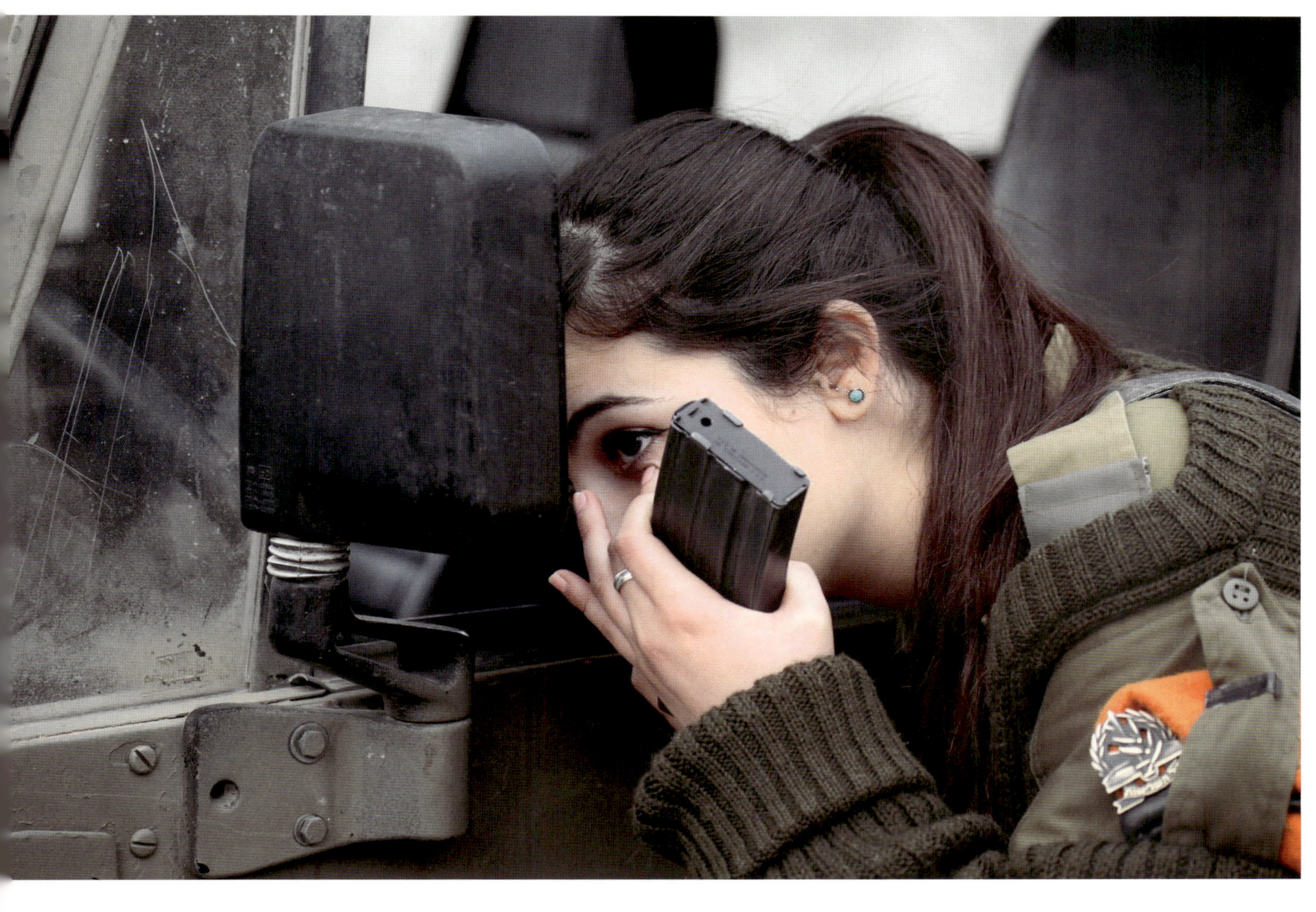

Side-view mirrors are a
military necessity.
Marc Israel Sellem
2011

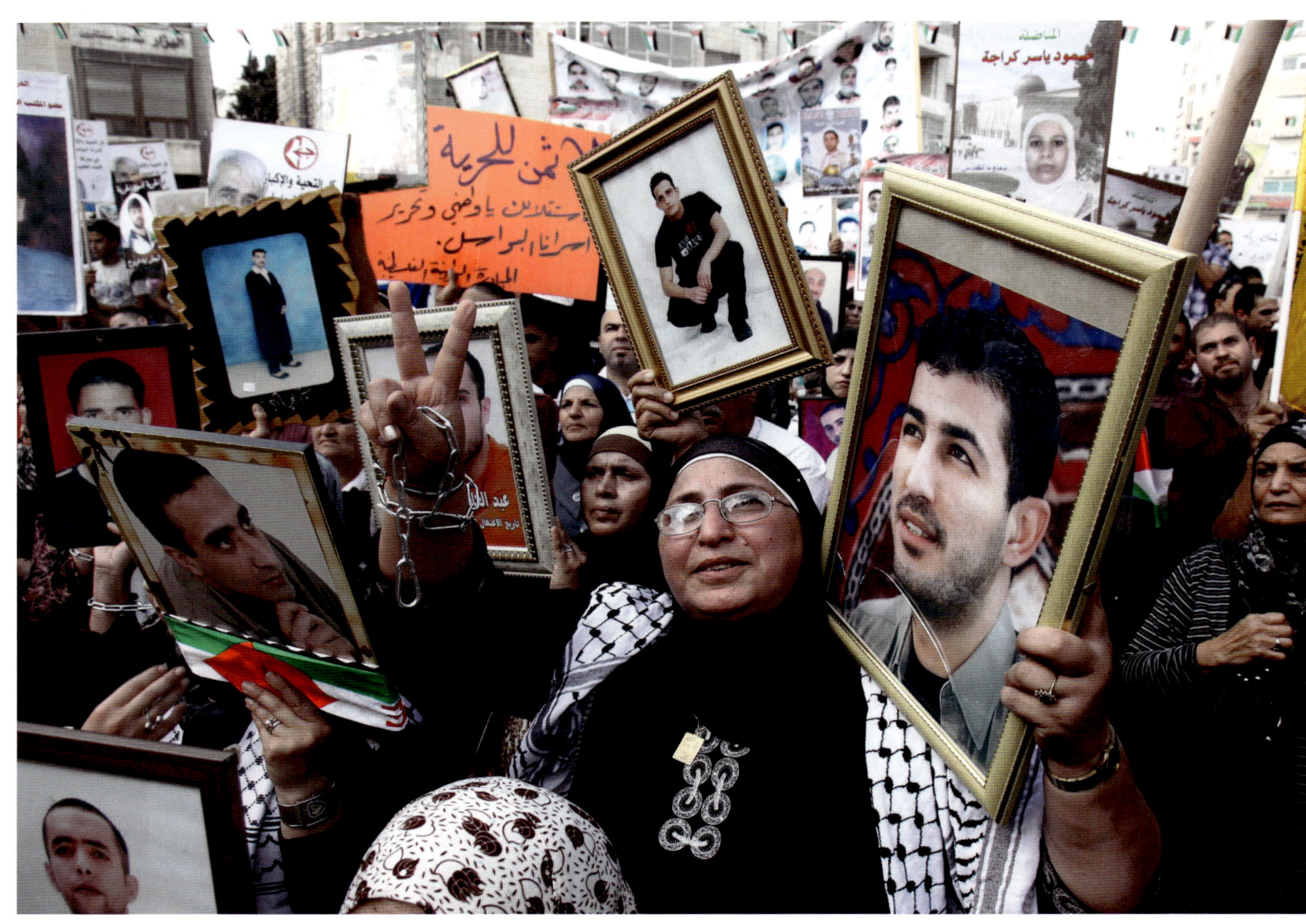

One happy picture for
the boys in Ramallah.
Marc Israel Sellem
2011

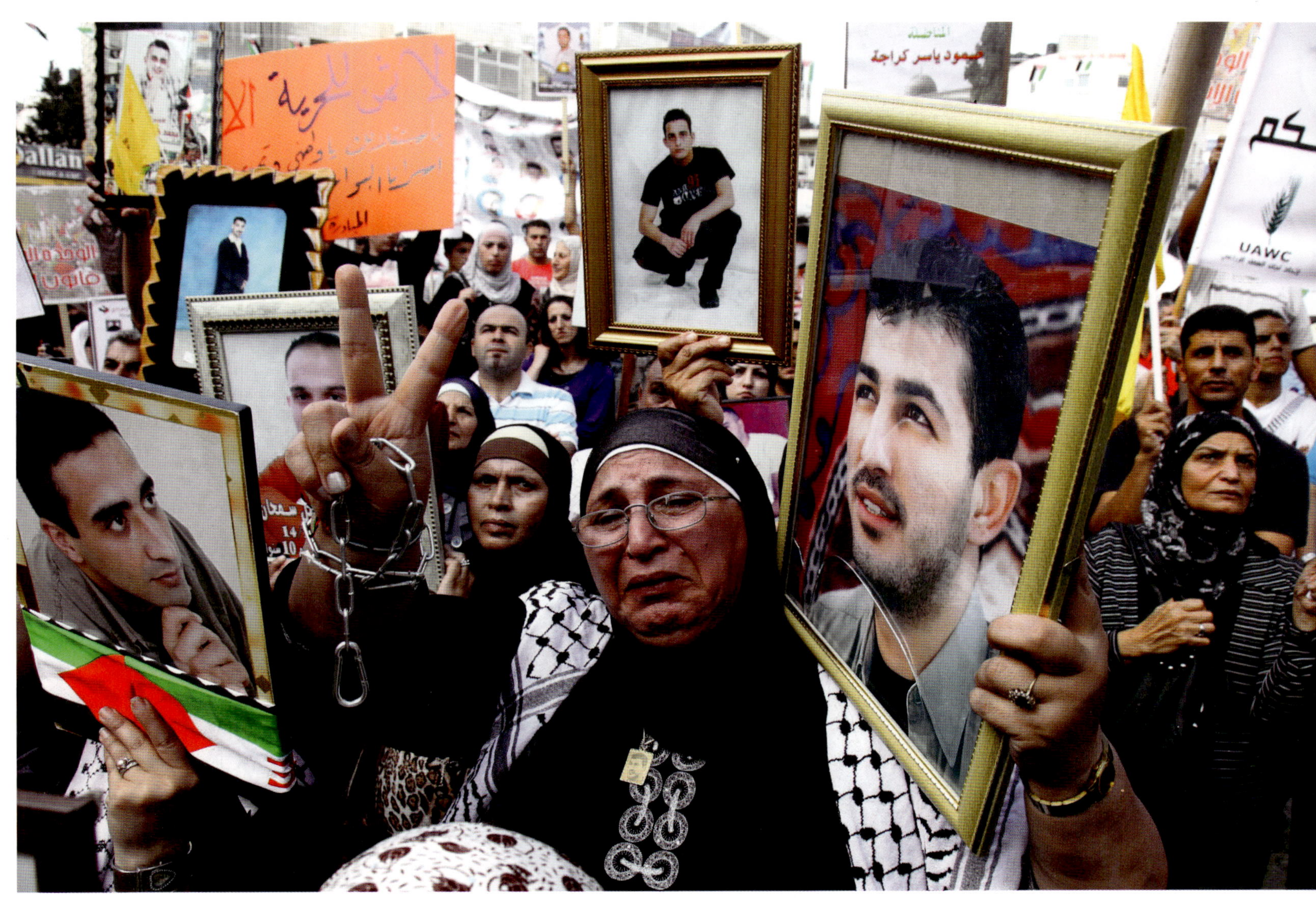

And one staged photo for
the foreign media.

Marc Israel Sellem

2011

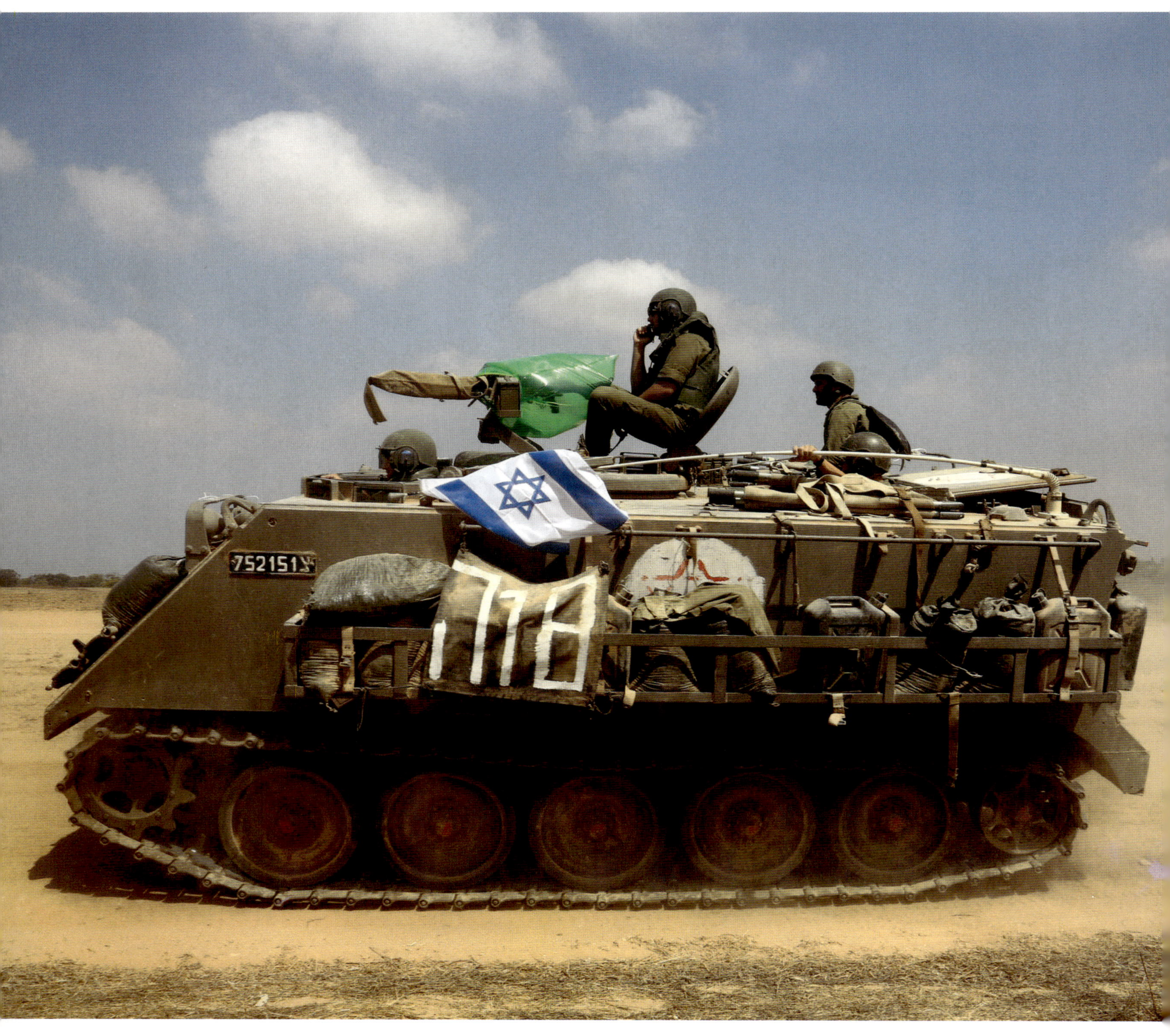

Waiting to enter the
battle in Gaza.

Marc Israel Sellem

2014

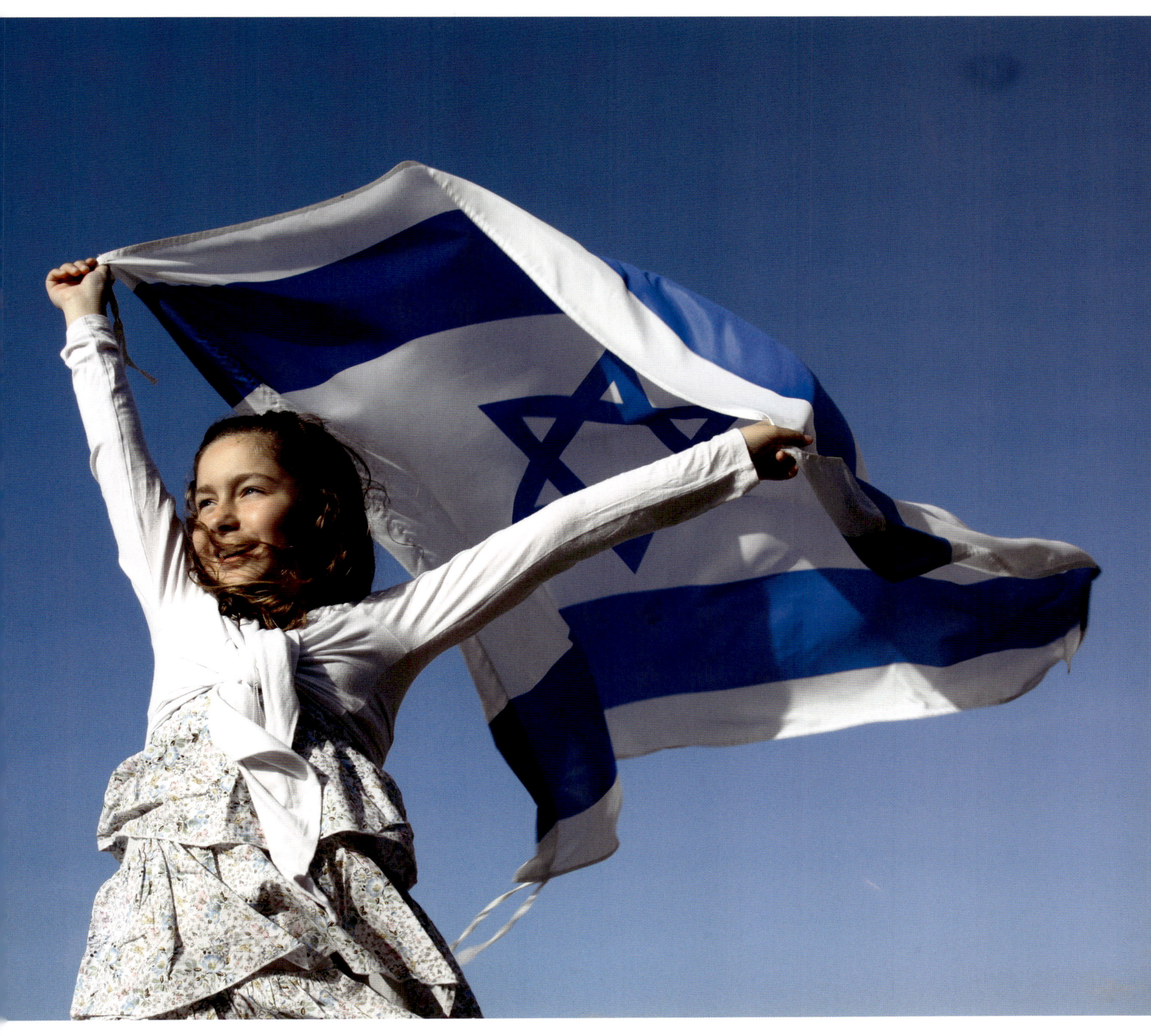

A proud Israeli.
Marc Israel Sellem
2011

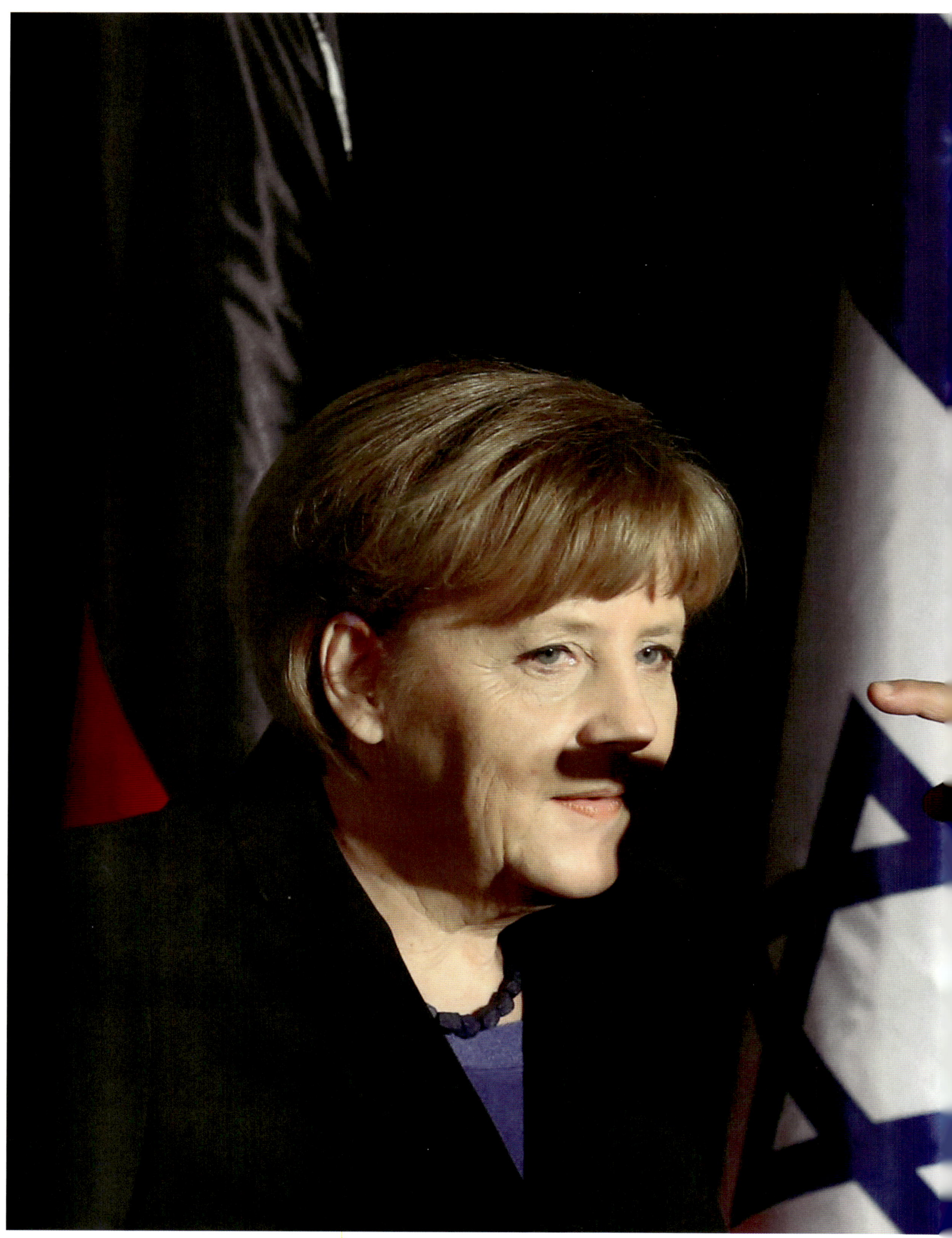

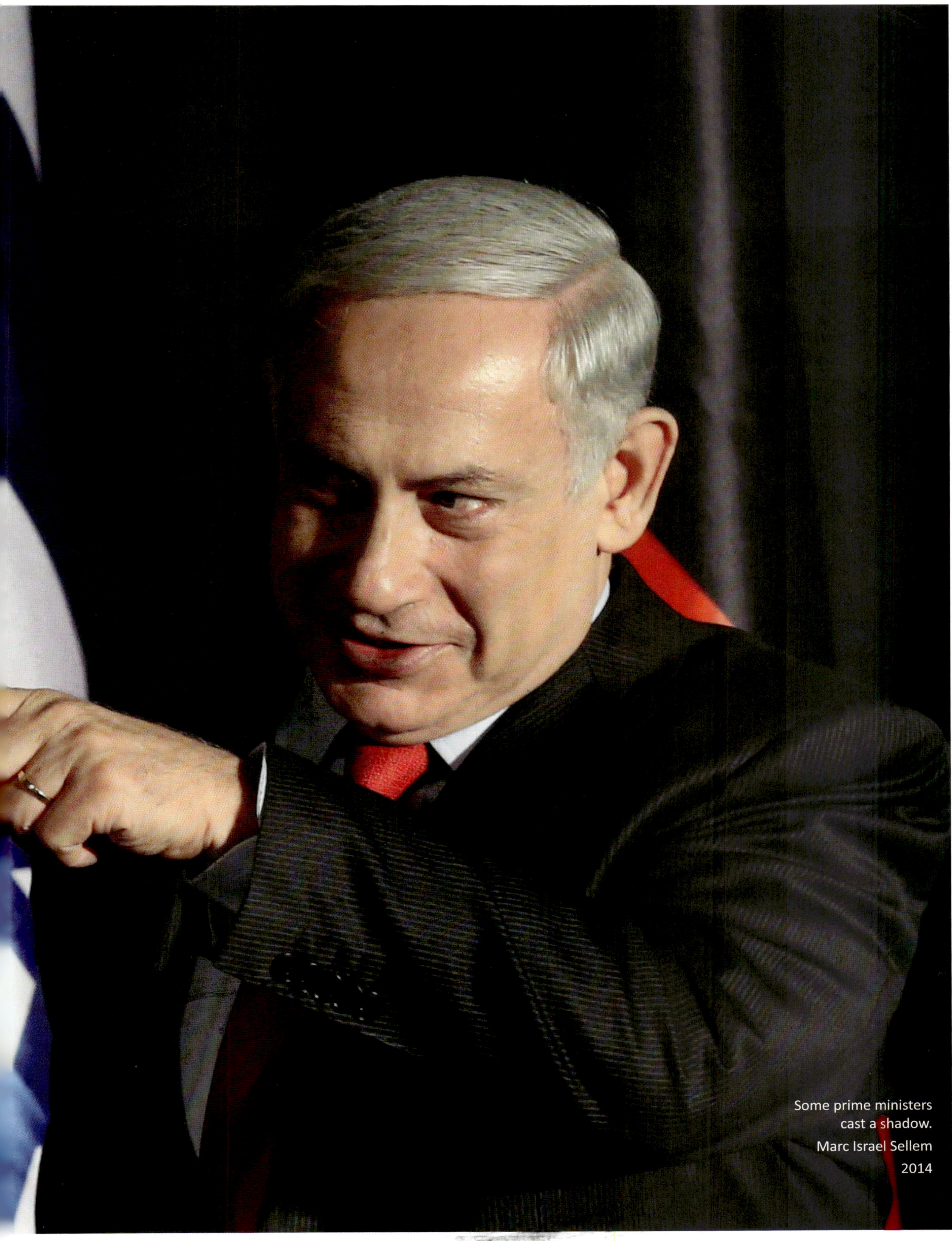

Some prime ministers cast a shadow.
Marc Israel Sellem
2014

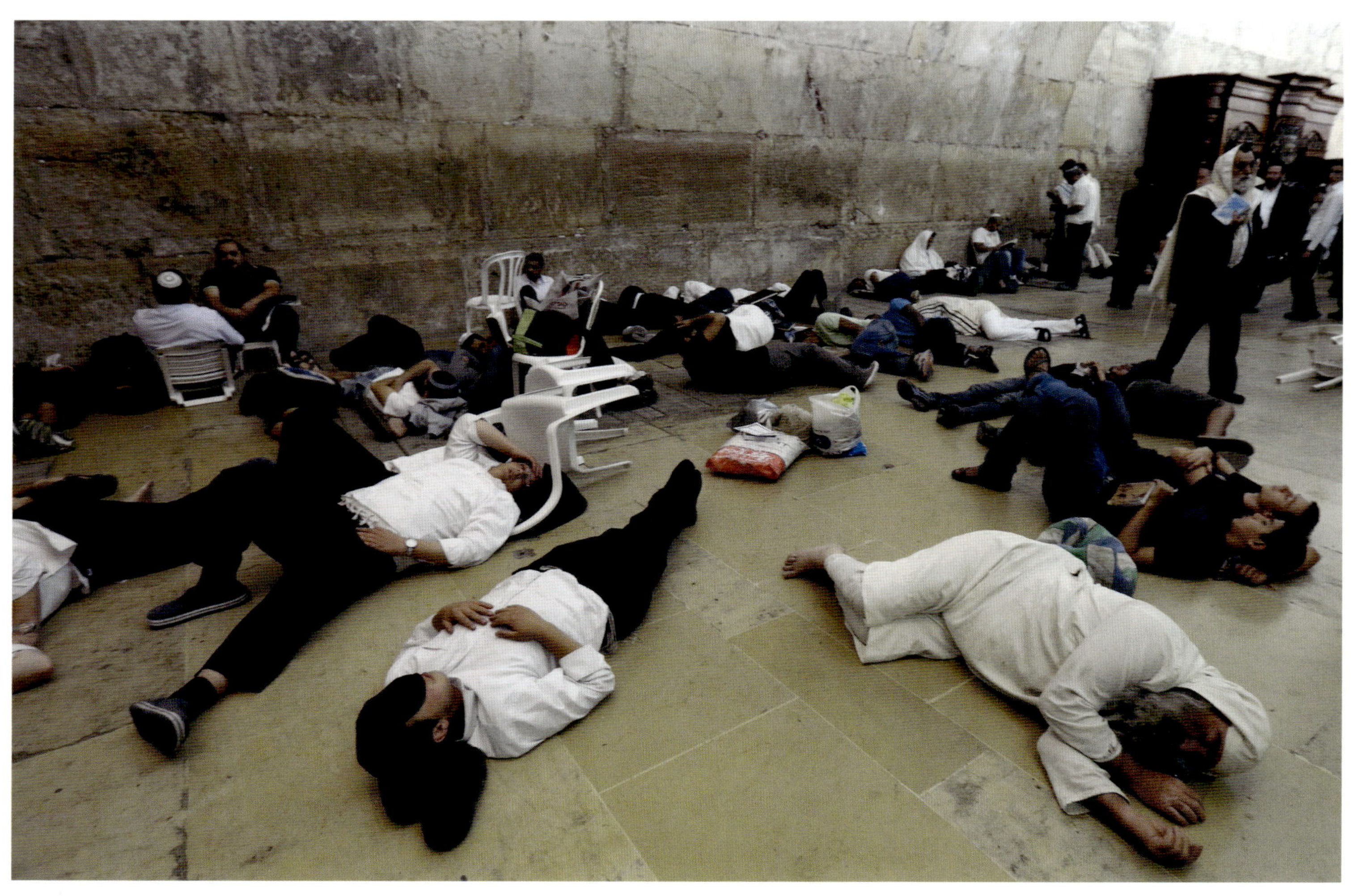

Worshipers at the
Western Wall take a
break during the long
Tisha Be'av night.

Marc Israel Sellem
2013

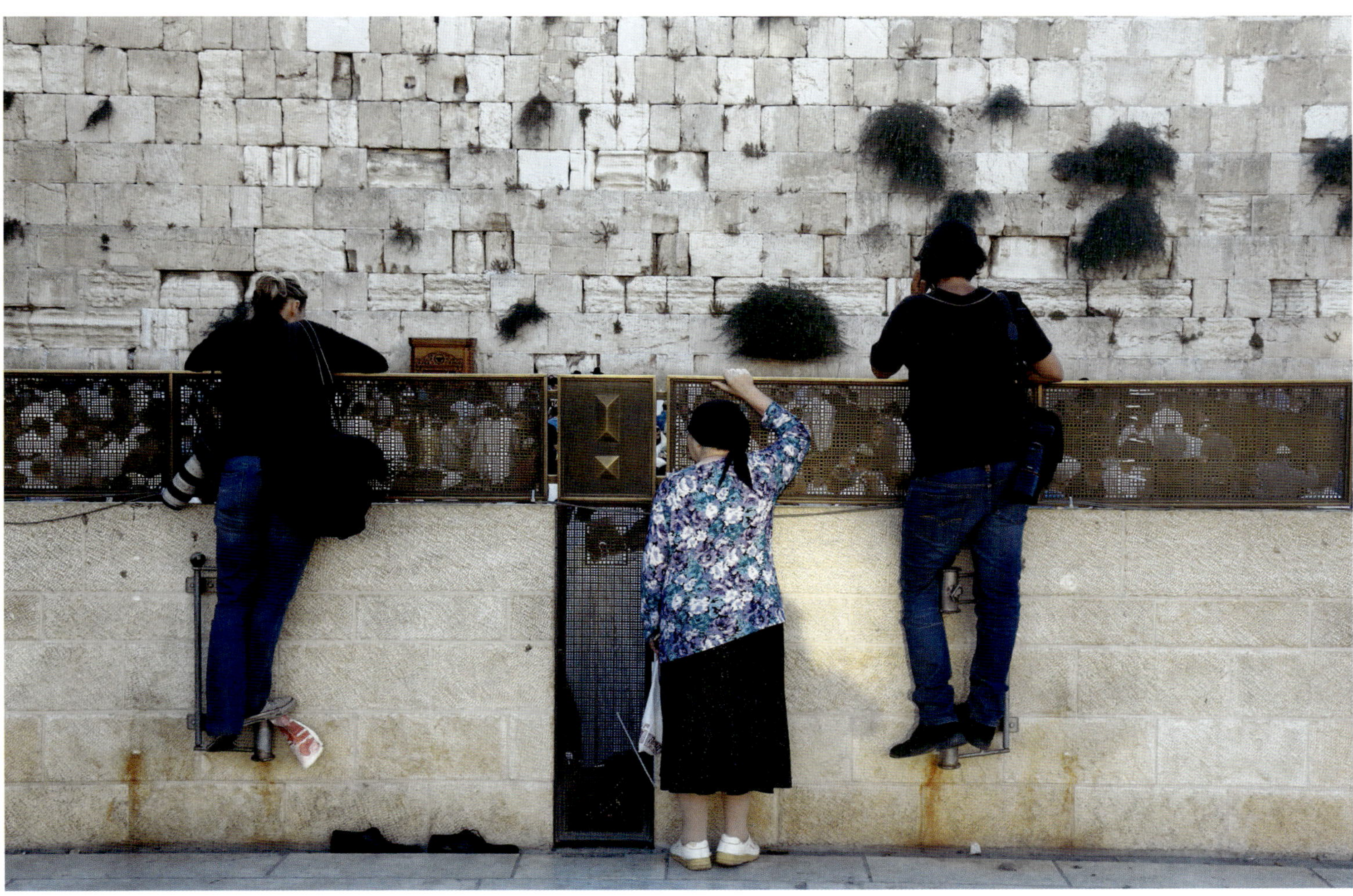

You have to be a photographer to see what goes on at the Western Wall.

Marc Israel Sellem

2013

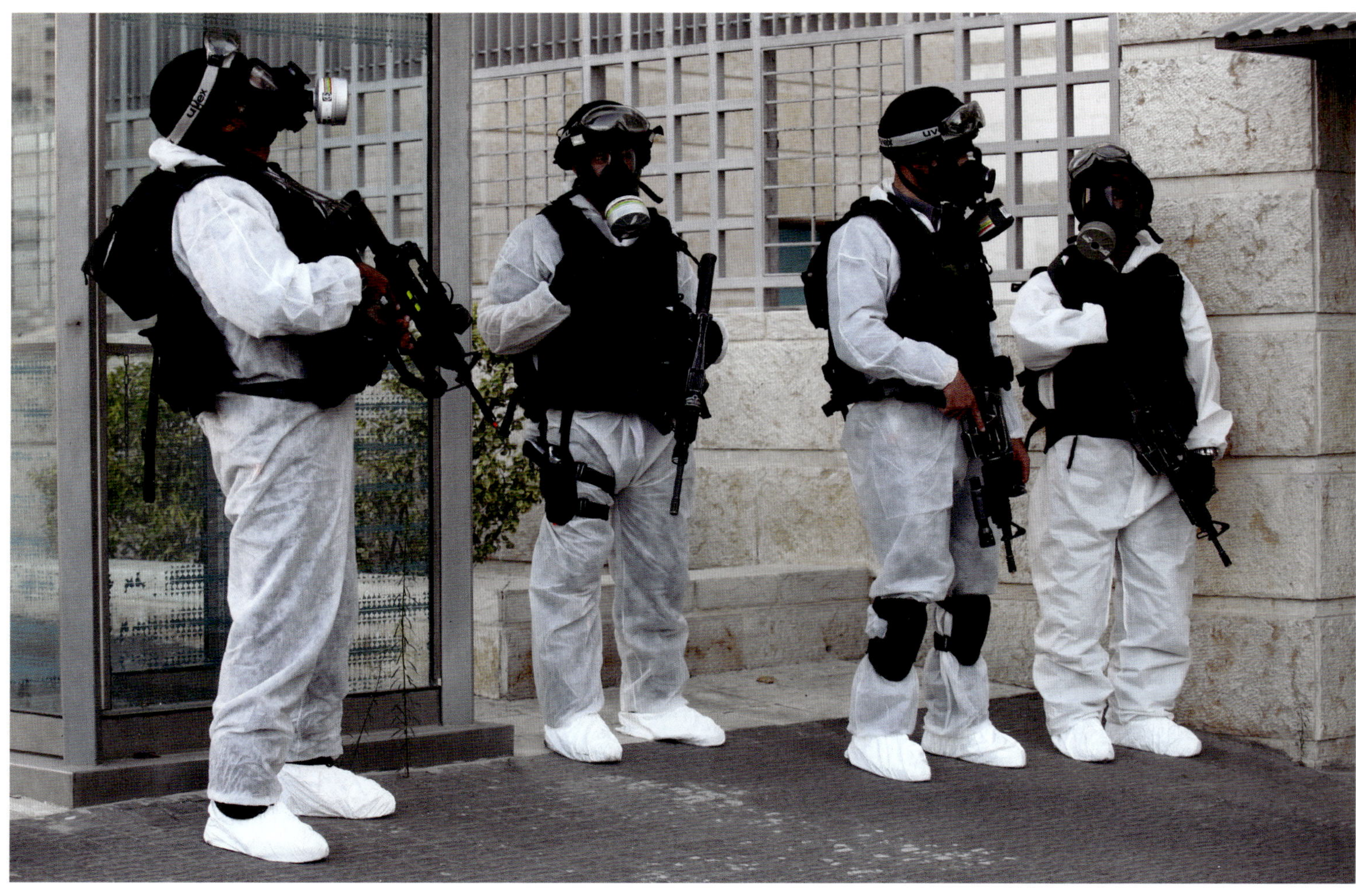

A Home Front Command
unit drills for a biological
or chemical attack.
Marc Israel Sellem
2010

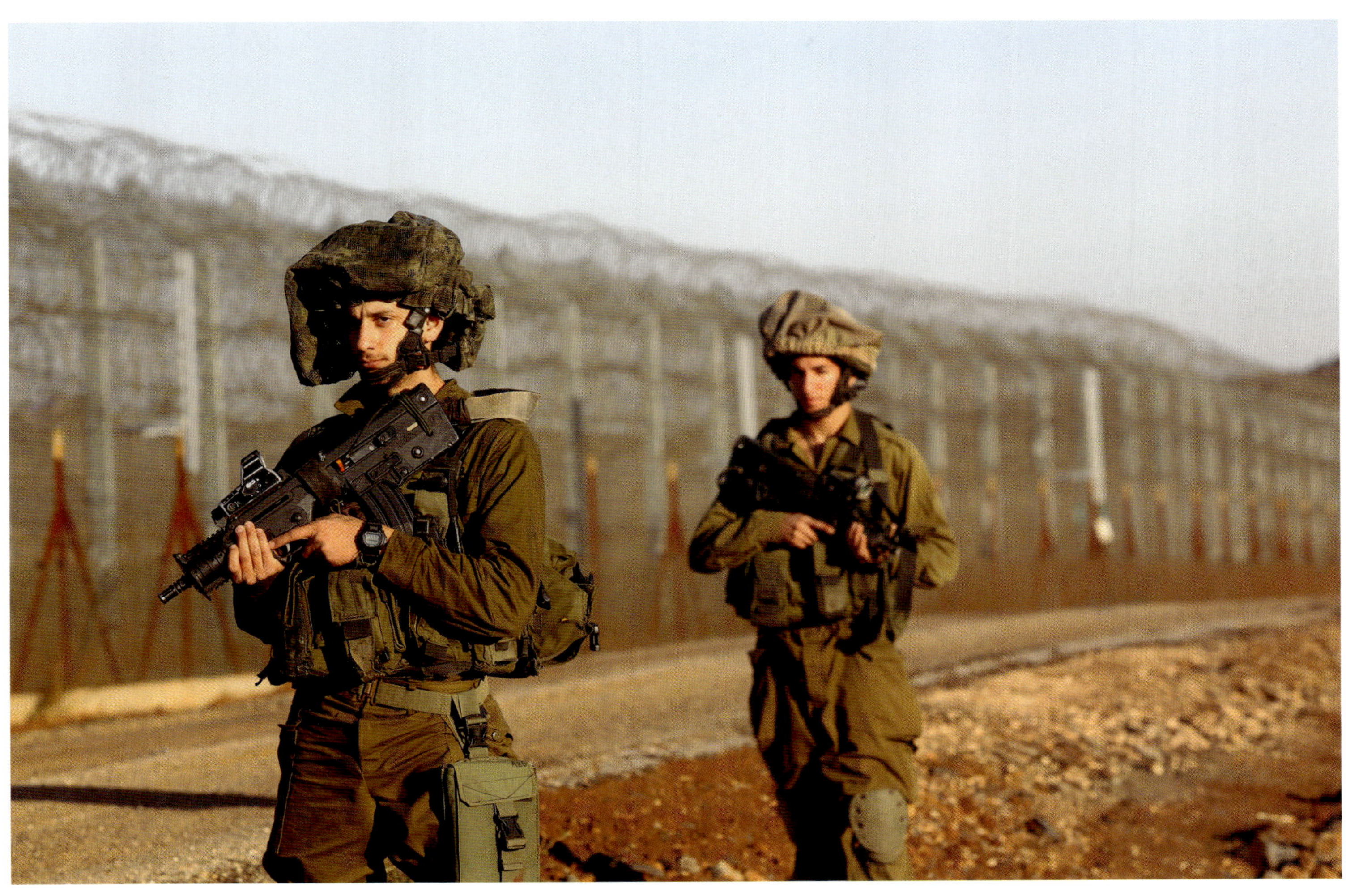

Soldiers patrol along the
security fence in the Golan
Heights opposite Kuneitra.

Marc Israel Sellem

2013

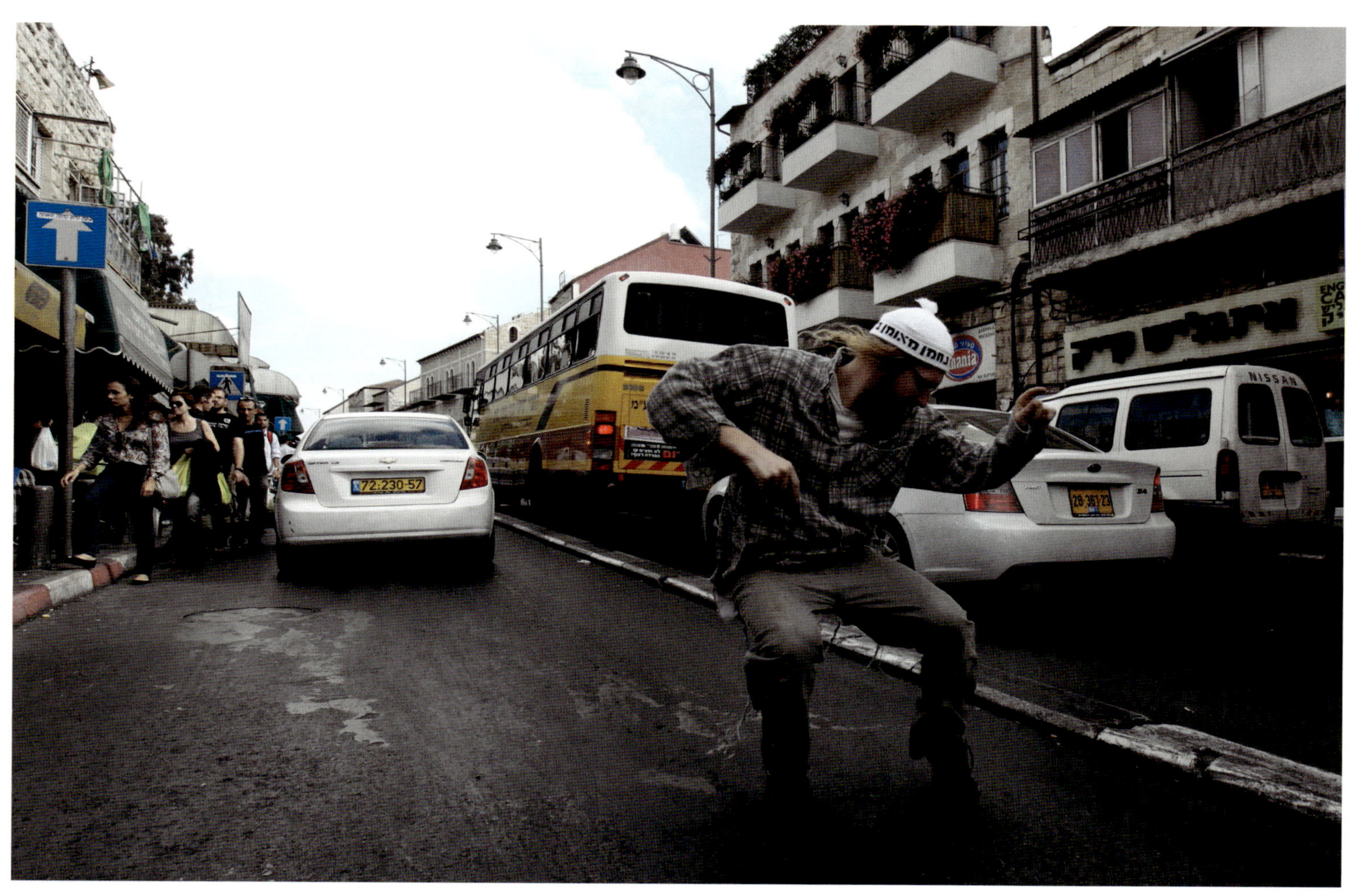

A Breslover hassid dances before the Lord in traffic.

Marc Israel Sellem

2010

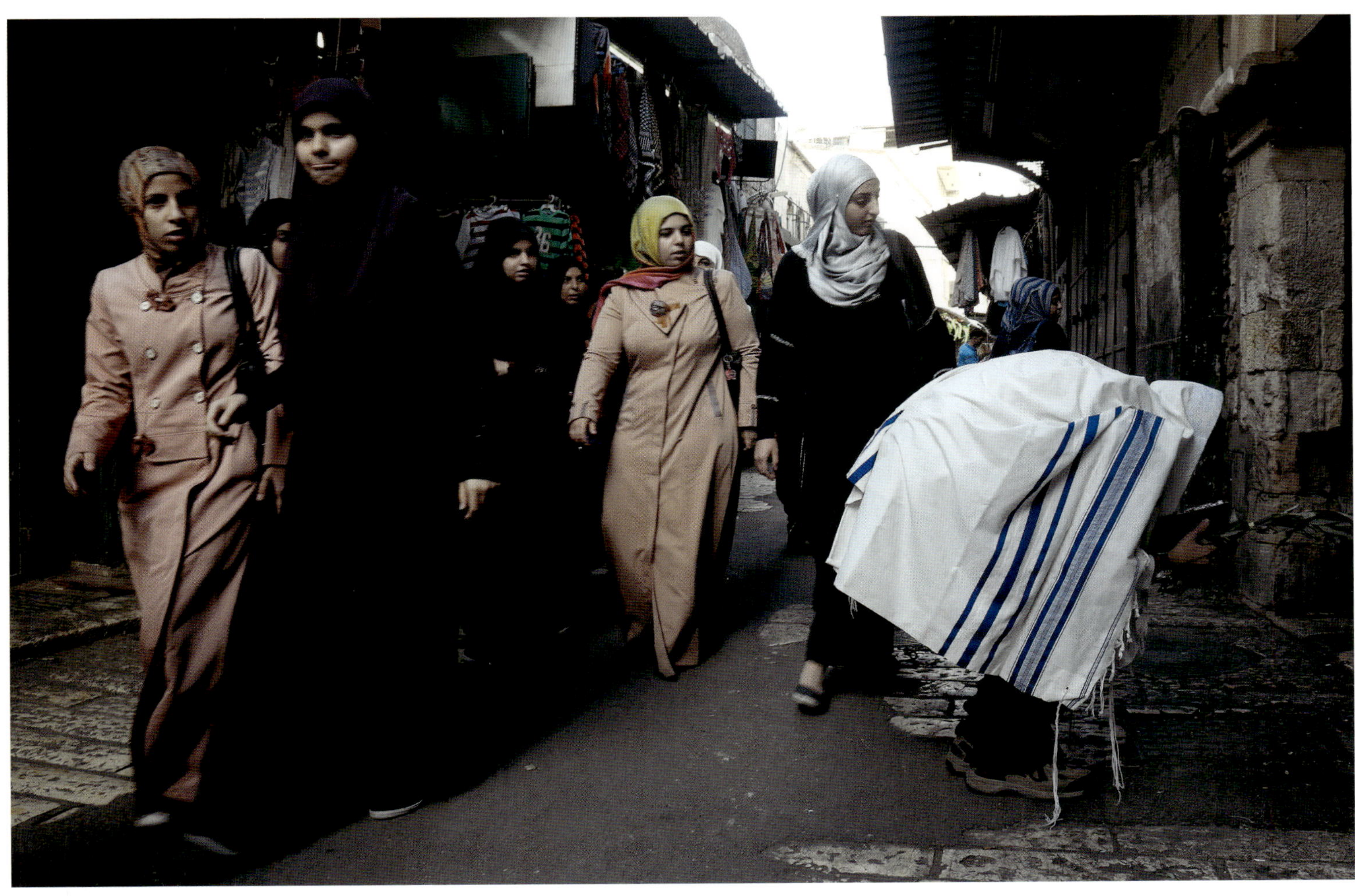

Peaceful coexistence In
Jerusalem's Old City.
Marc Israel Sellem
2013

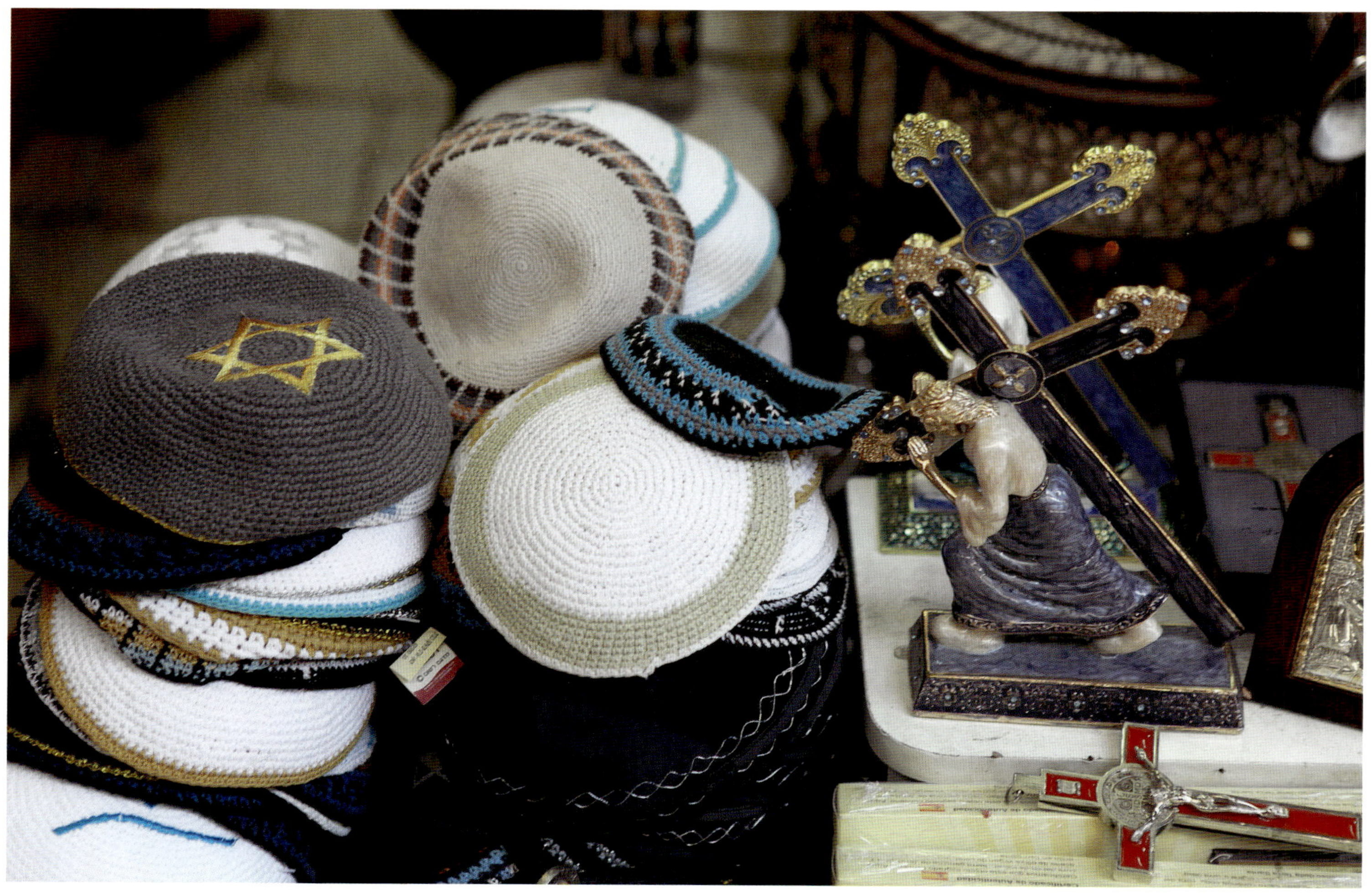

Jerusalem's Old City
caters to all religions.
Marc Israel Sellem
2013

You don't have to be
Jewish to love the Wall.
Marc Israel Sellem
2013

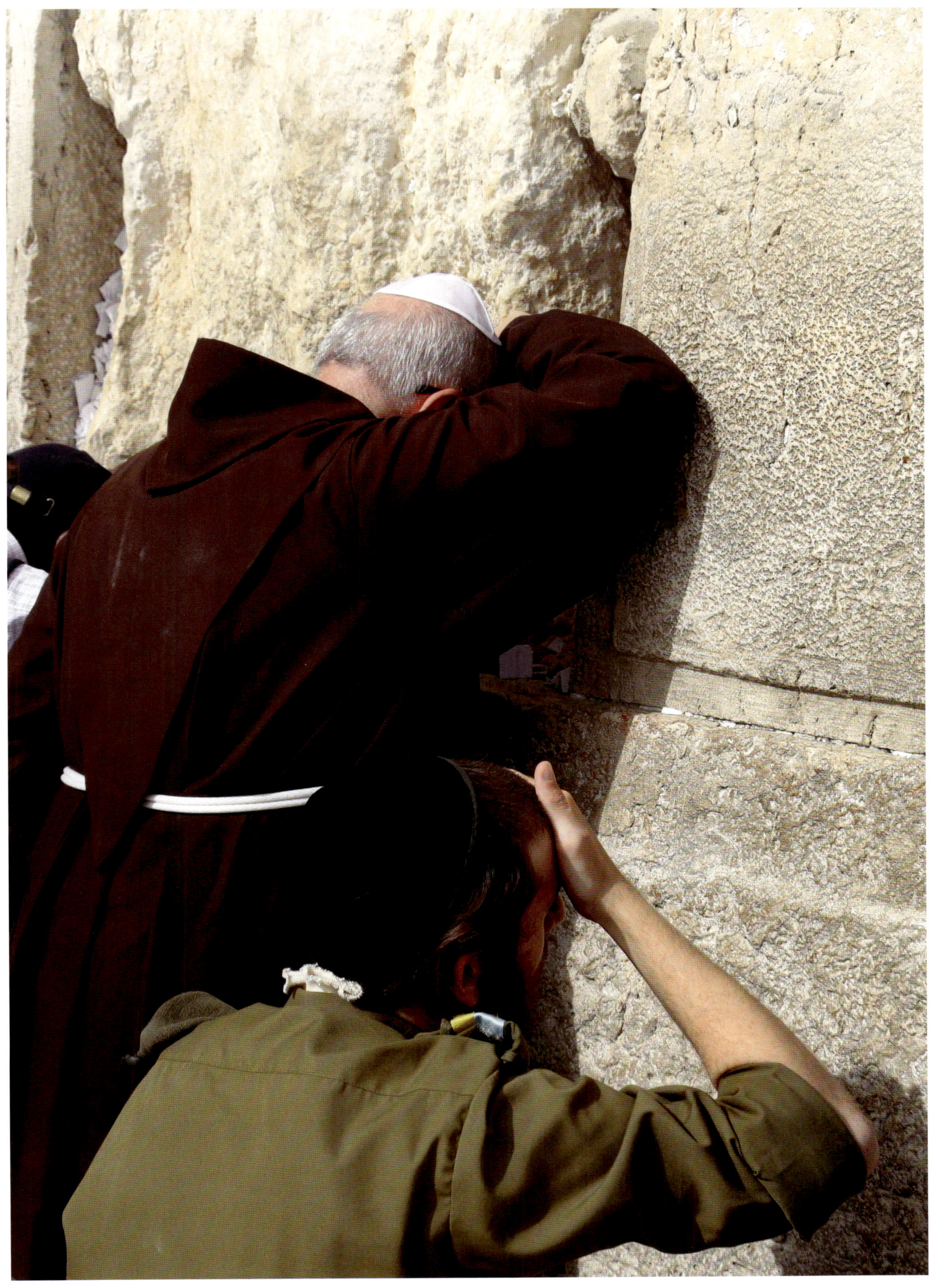

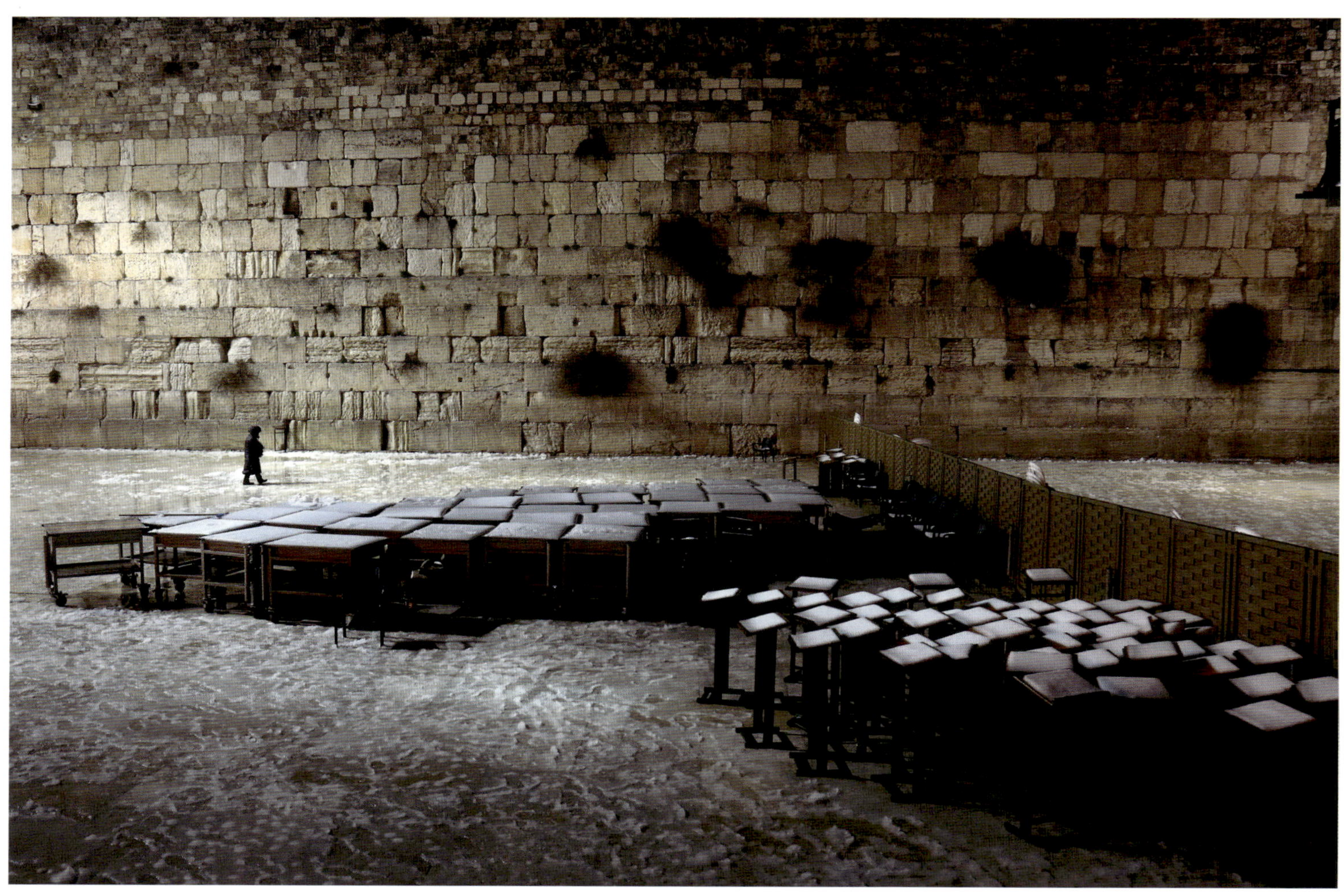

At least one early
worshiper is not daunted
by the snow.
Marc Israel Sellem
2015

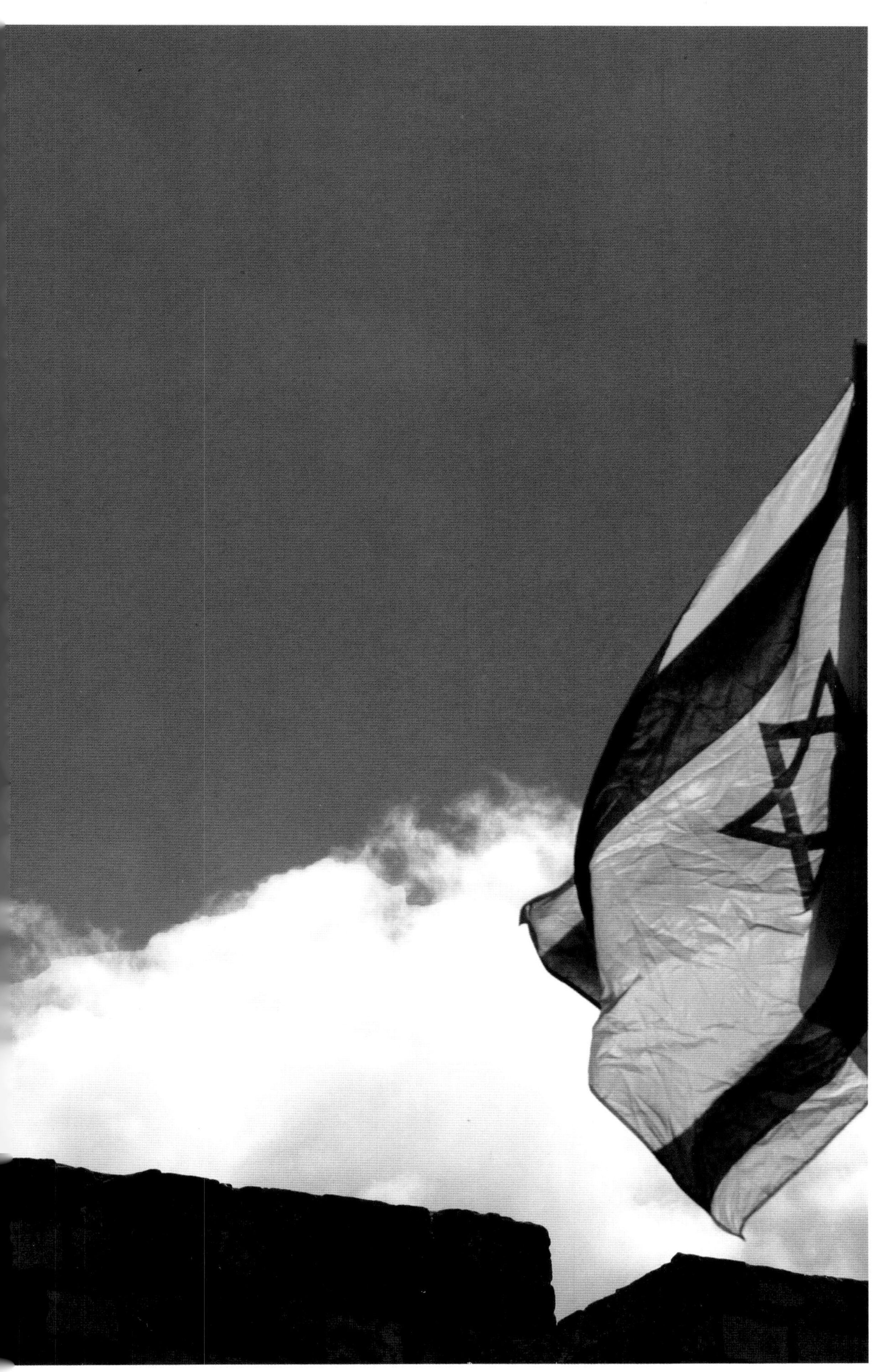

Batman is called to
Jerusalem's Old City.
Marc Israel Sellem
2013

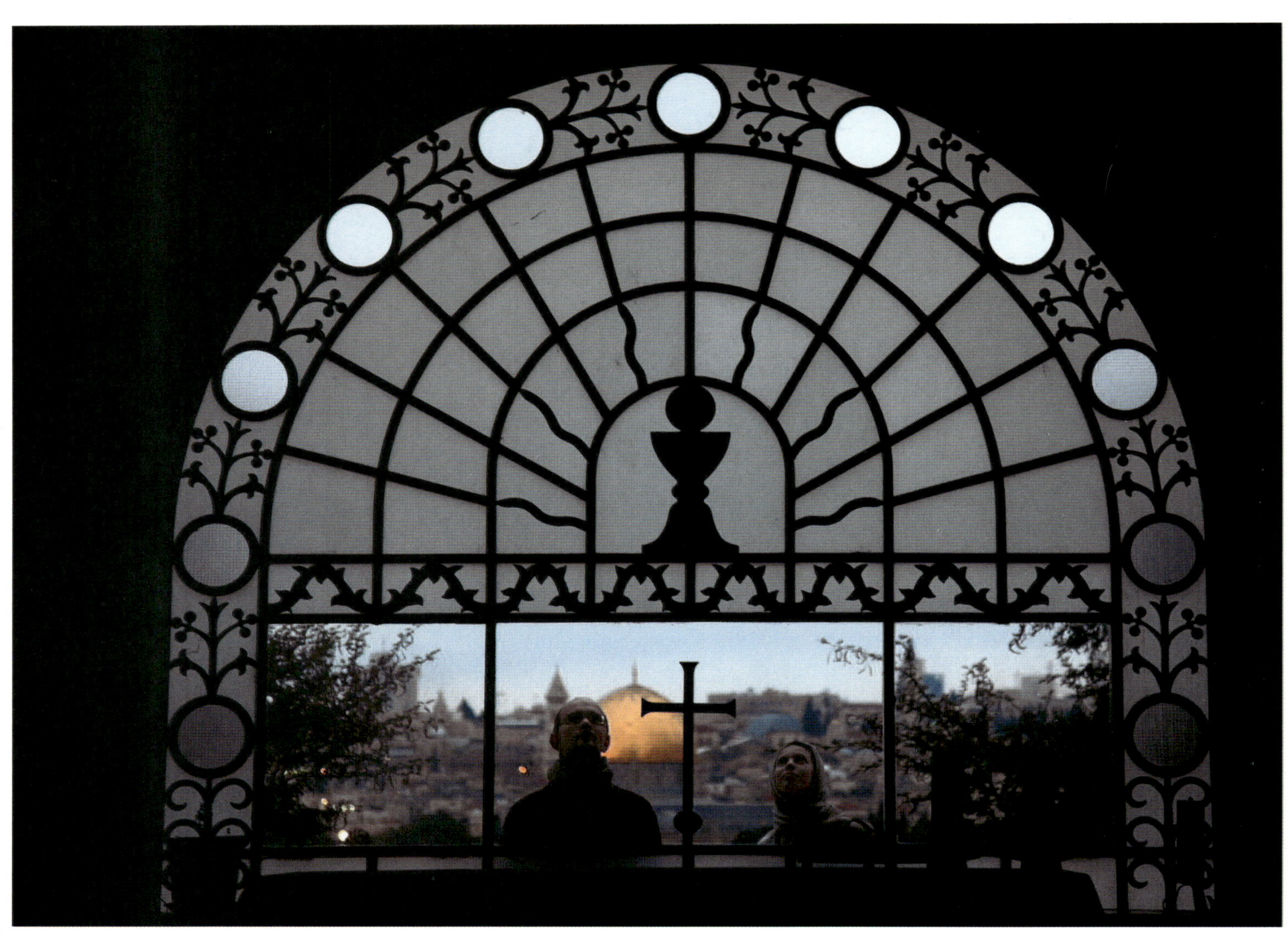

Jerusalem's Old City
caters to all religions.

Marc Israel Sellem

2013

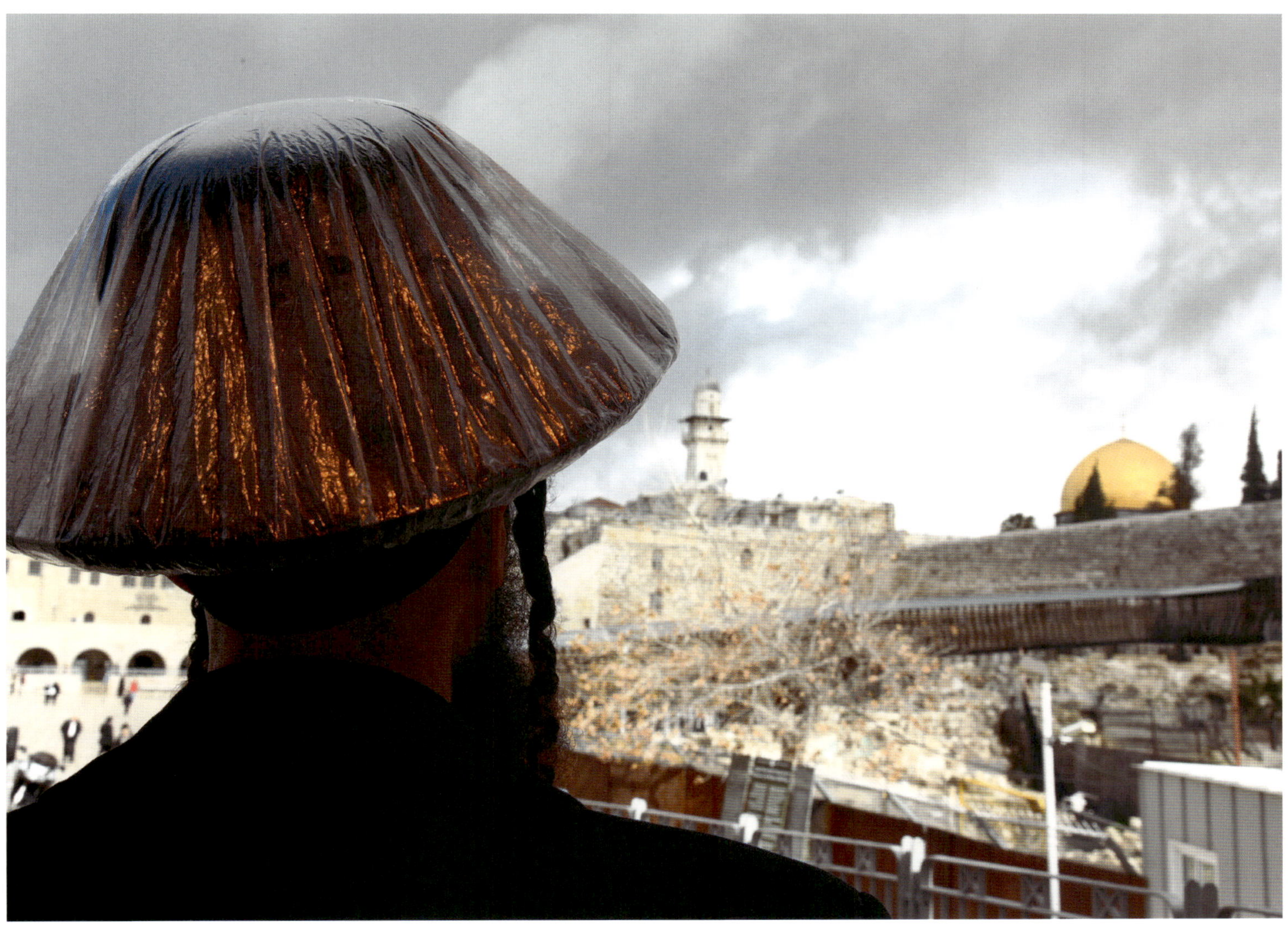

Ready for rain opposite
the Western Wall.

Marc Israel Sellem

2011

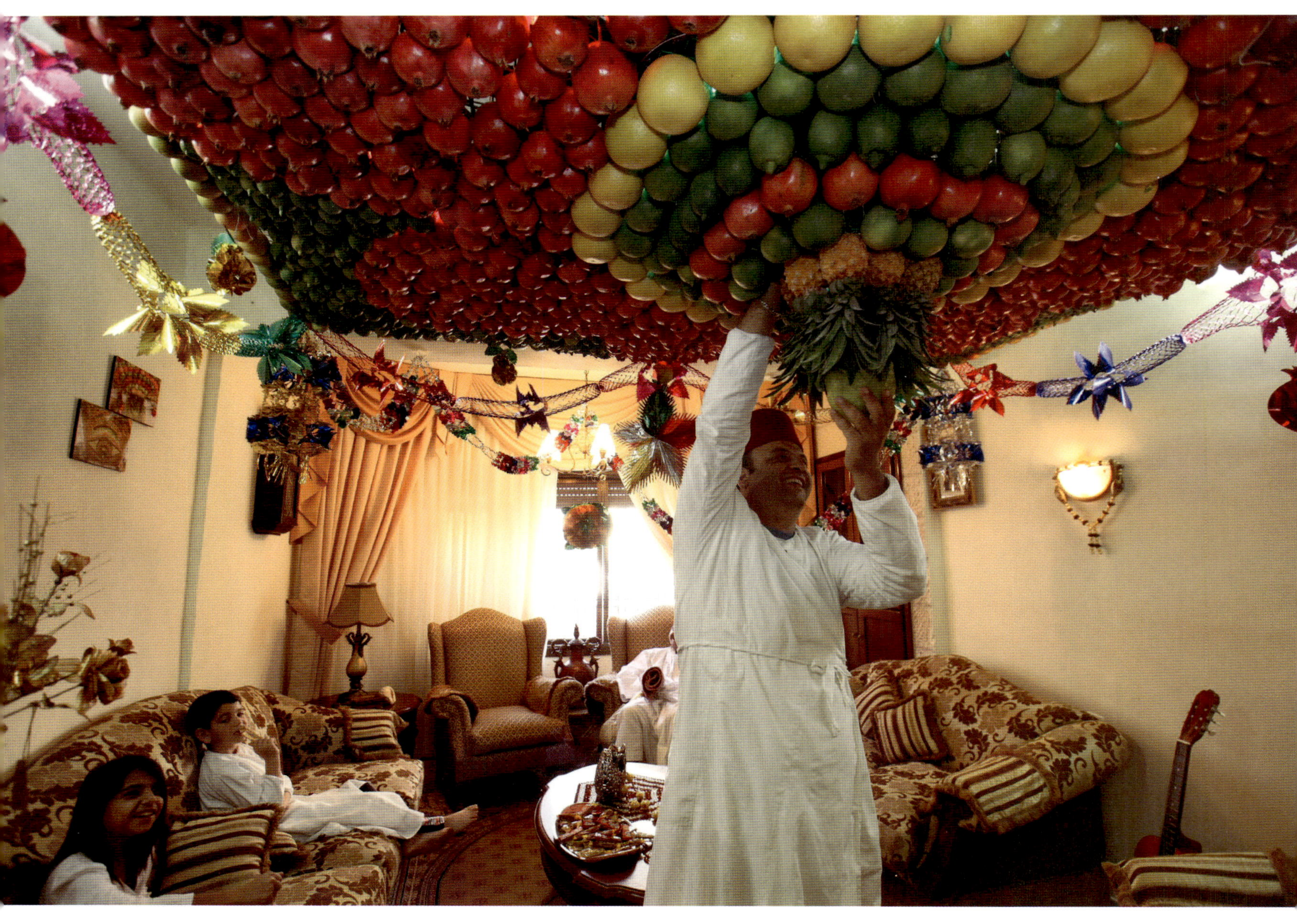

Preparations for the Succot festival will soon bear fruit.

Marc Israel Sellem

2011

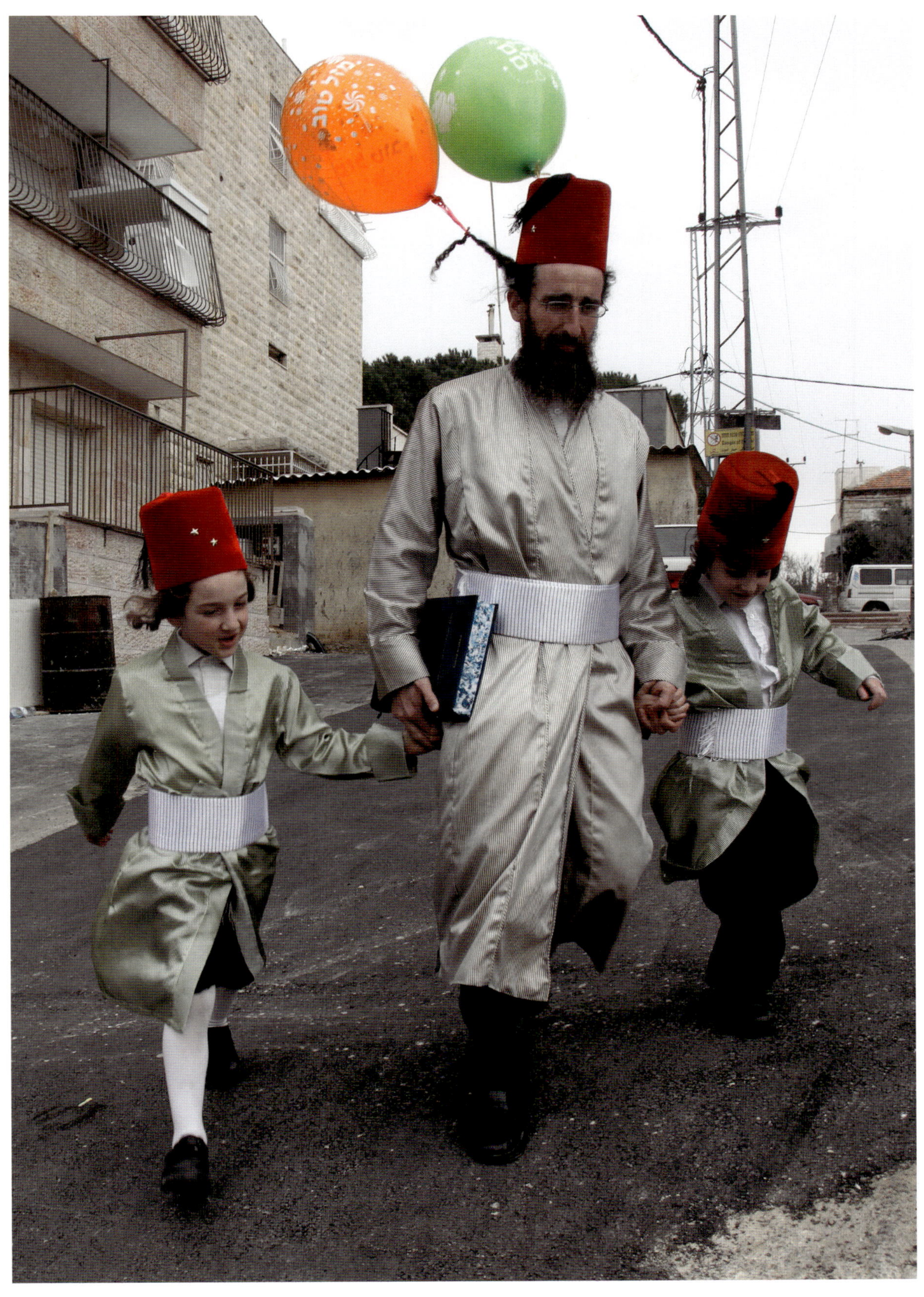

With every Purim fez
package you get two free
balloons.

Marc Israel Sellem

2011

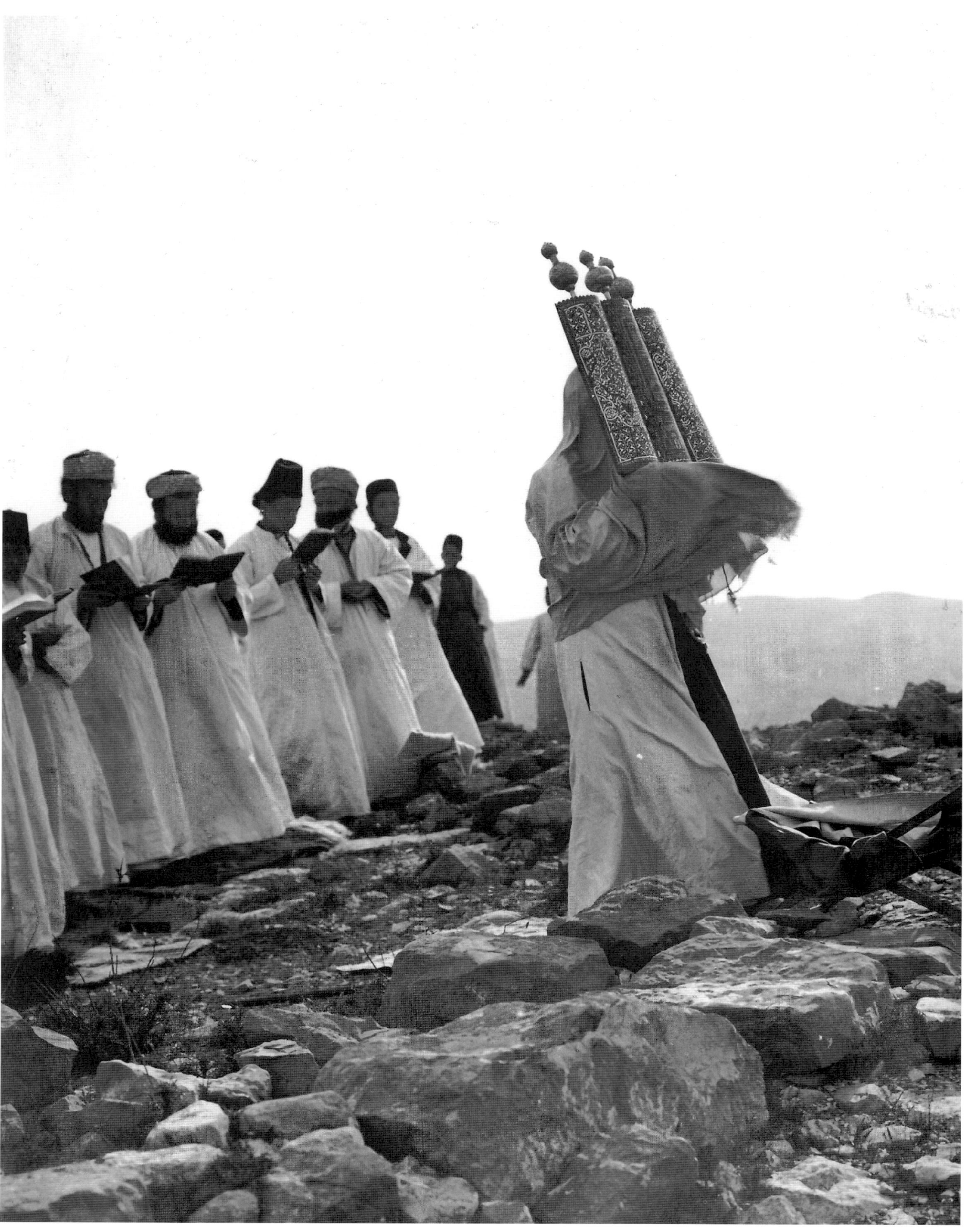

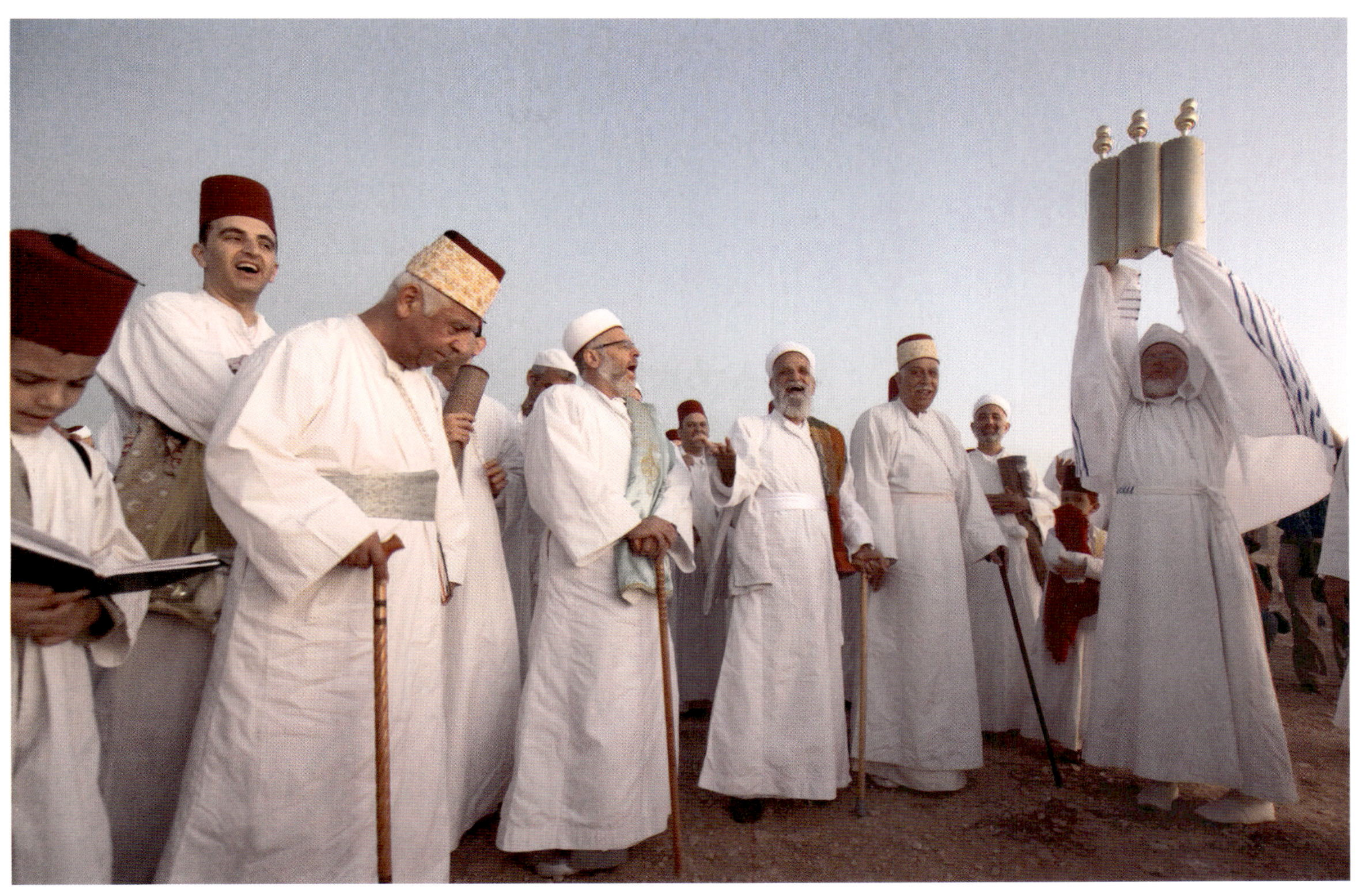

Samaritans on Mount Gerizim prepare to read the Samaritan Pentateuch on Succot.

Marc Israel Sellem

2011

Samaritans prepare to read their Torah on Mount Gerizim before Passover.

Ralph Fried

1927

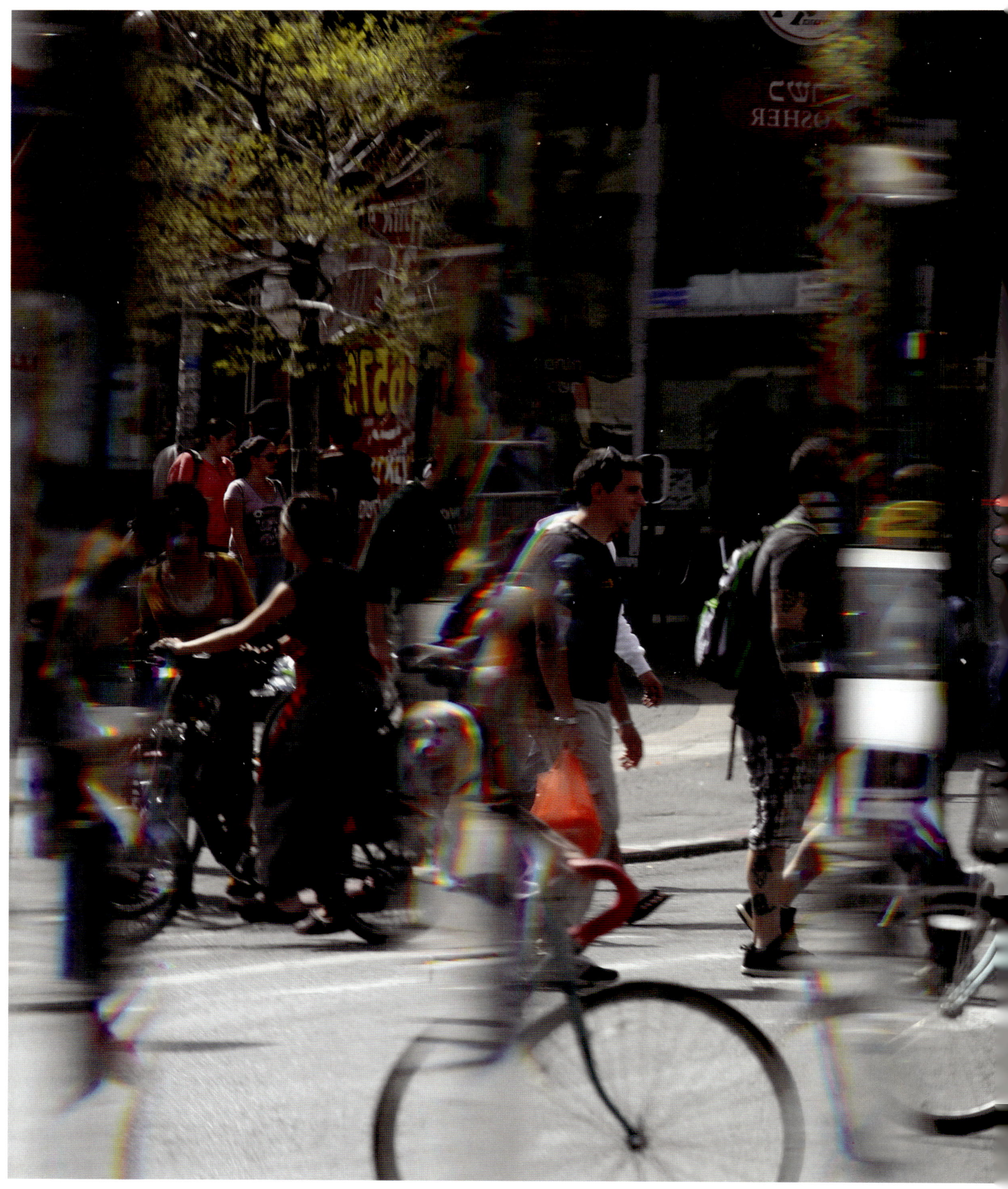

Easy riding on Tel Aviv's
Allenby Street.
Marc Israel Sellem
2014

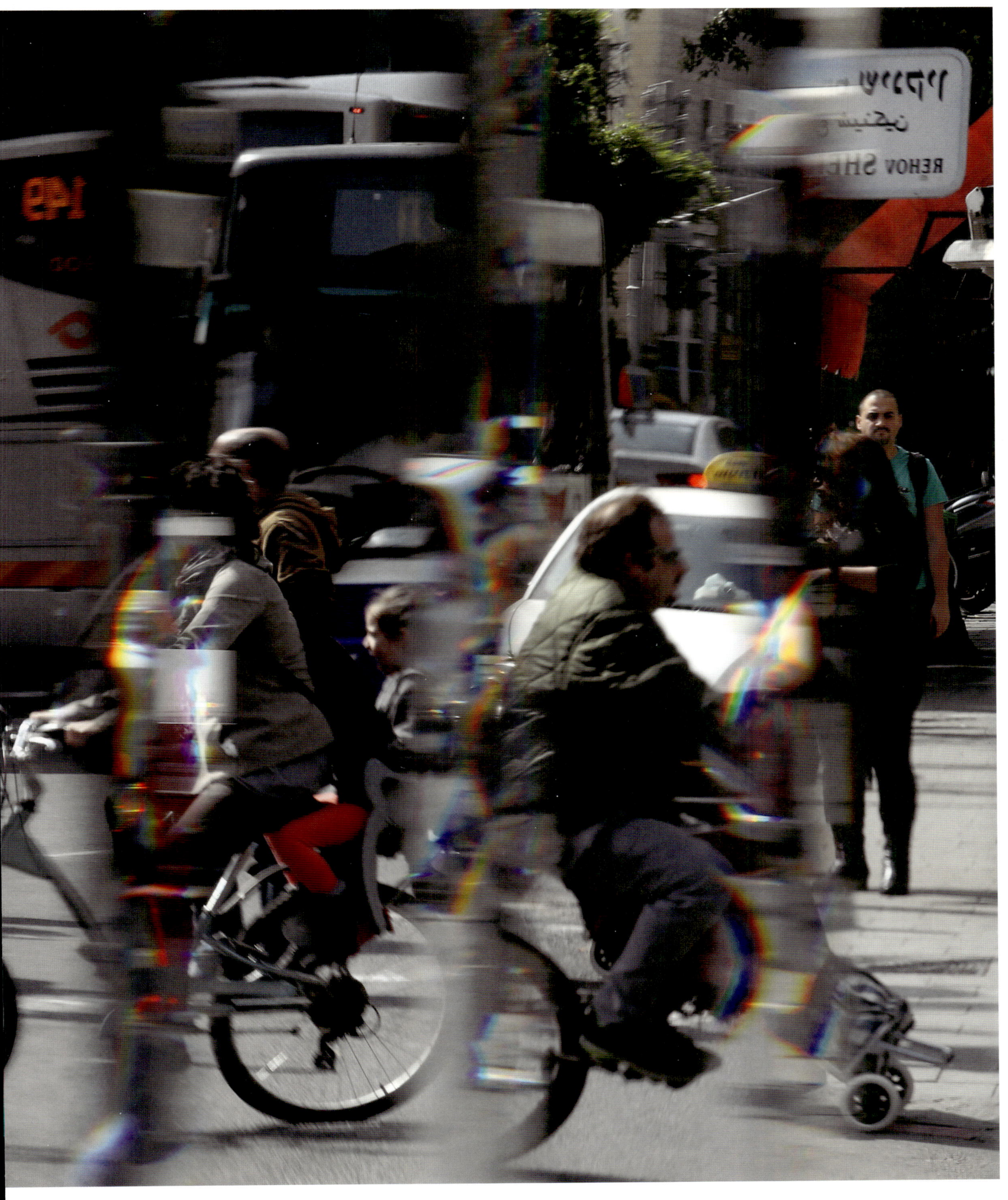

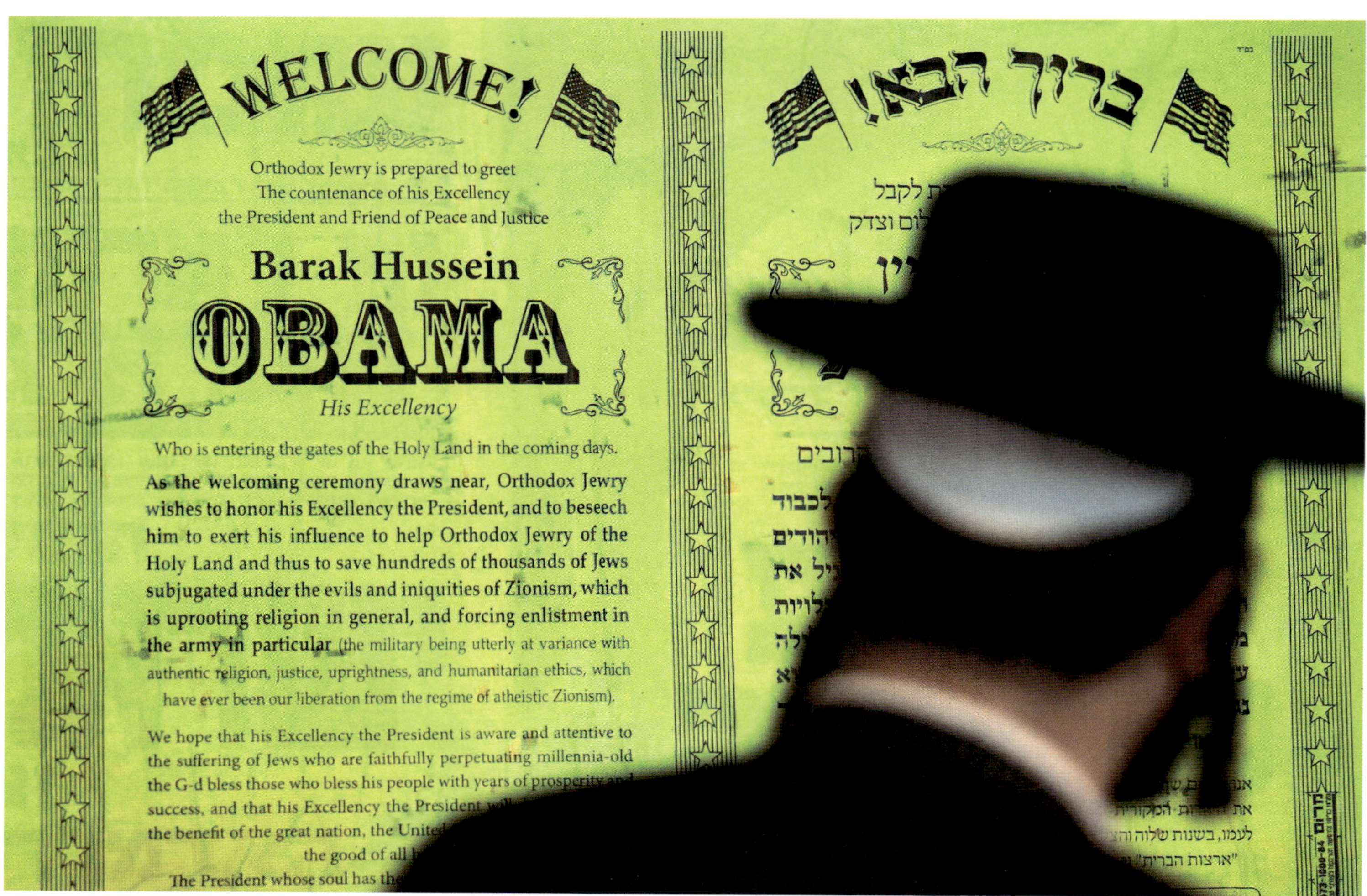

A poster in Jerusalem's Mea She'arim implores President Barack Obama to help residents fight the 'evils and iniquities of Zionism.'

Marc Israel Sellem

2013

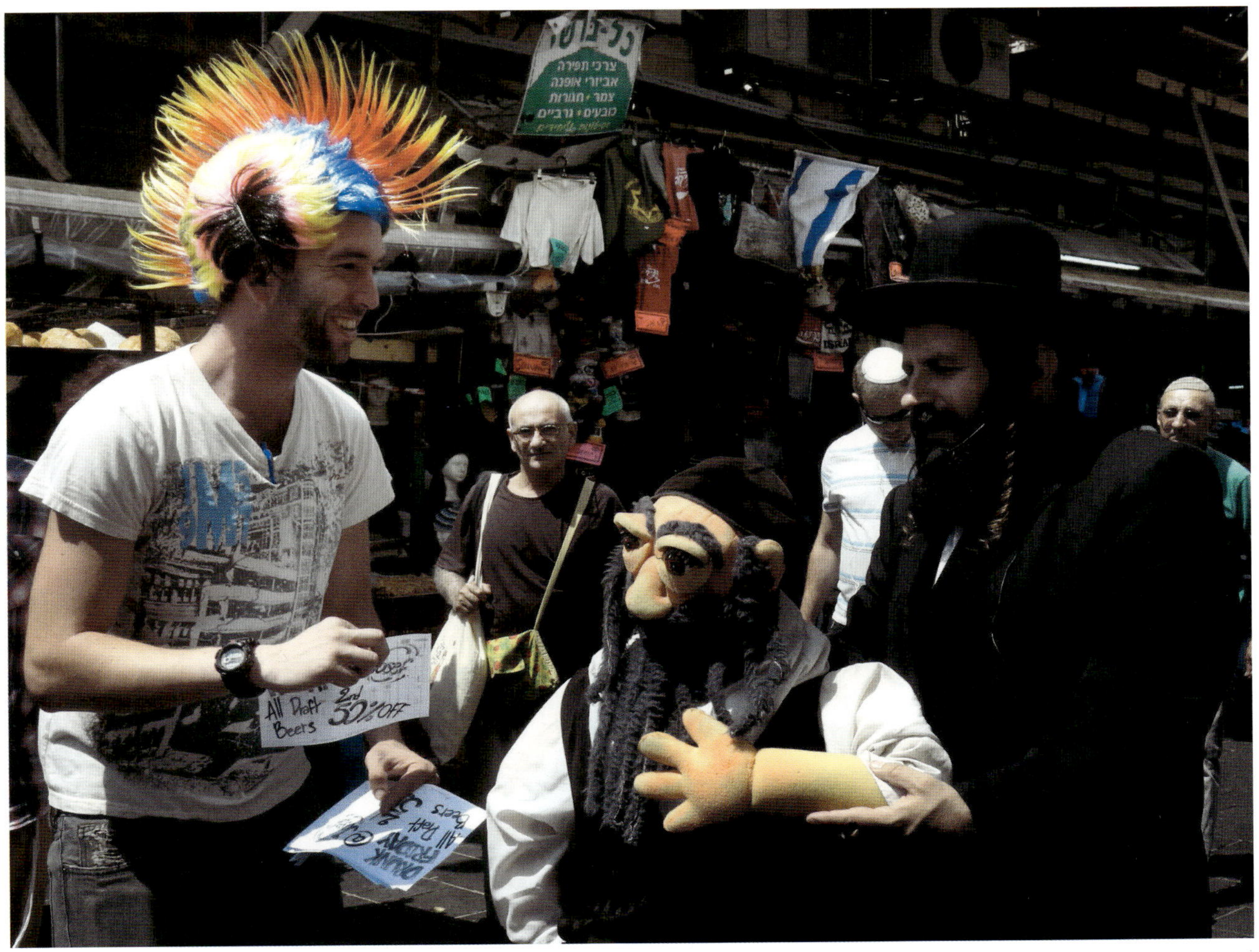

A meeting of the minds at the Mahaneh Yehuda market.

Marc Israel Sellem

2014

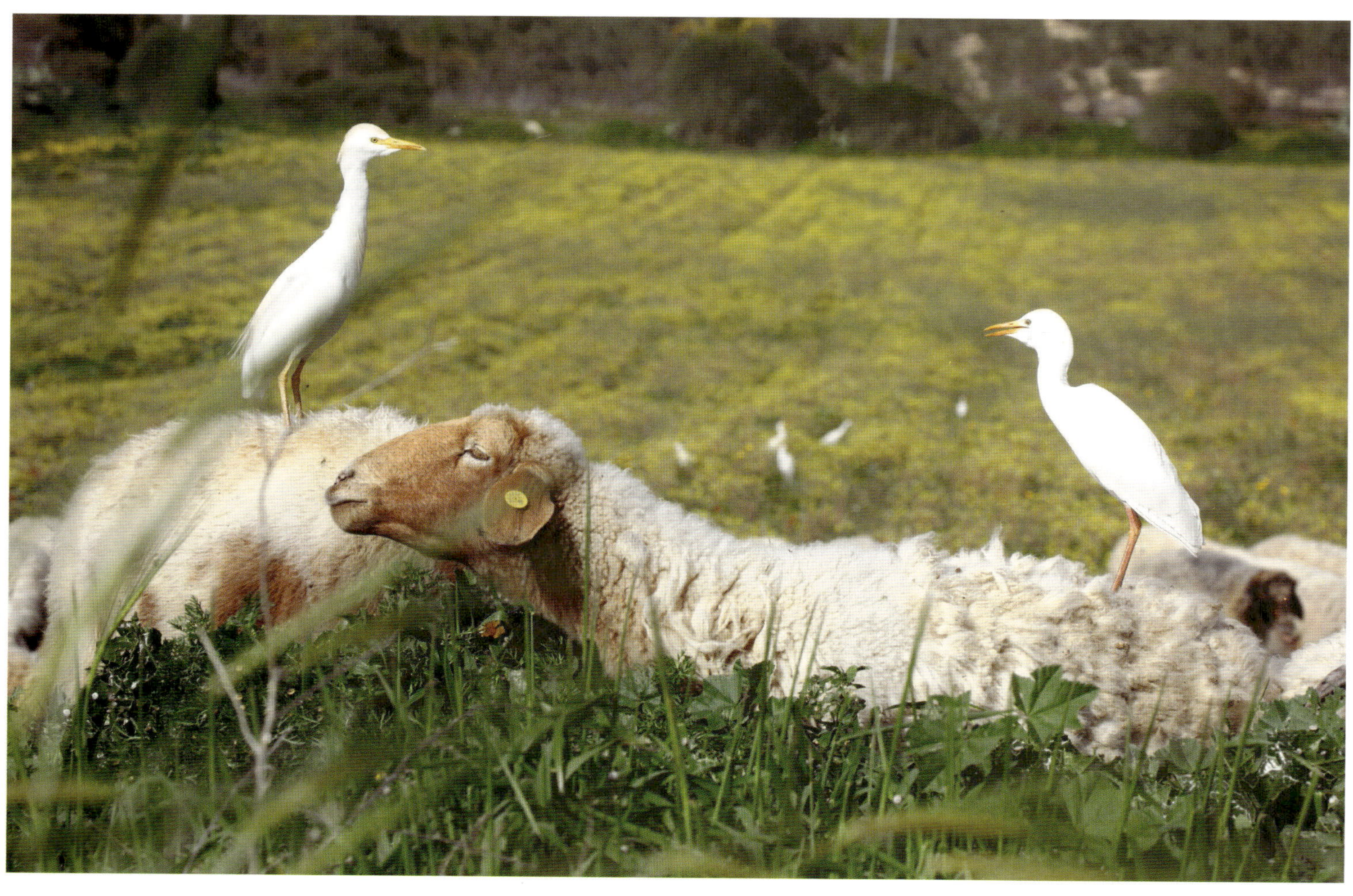

Hitchhiking is a time-
honored practice in Israel.
Marc Israel Sellem
2015

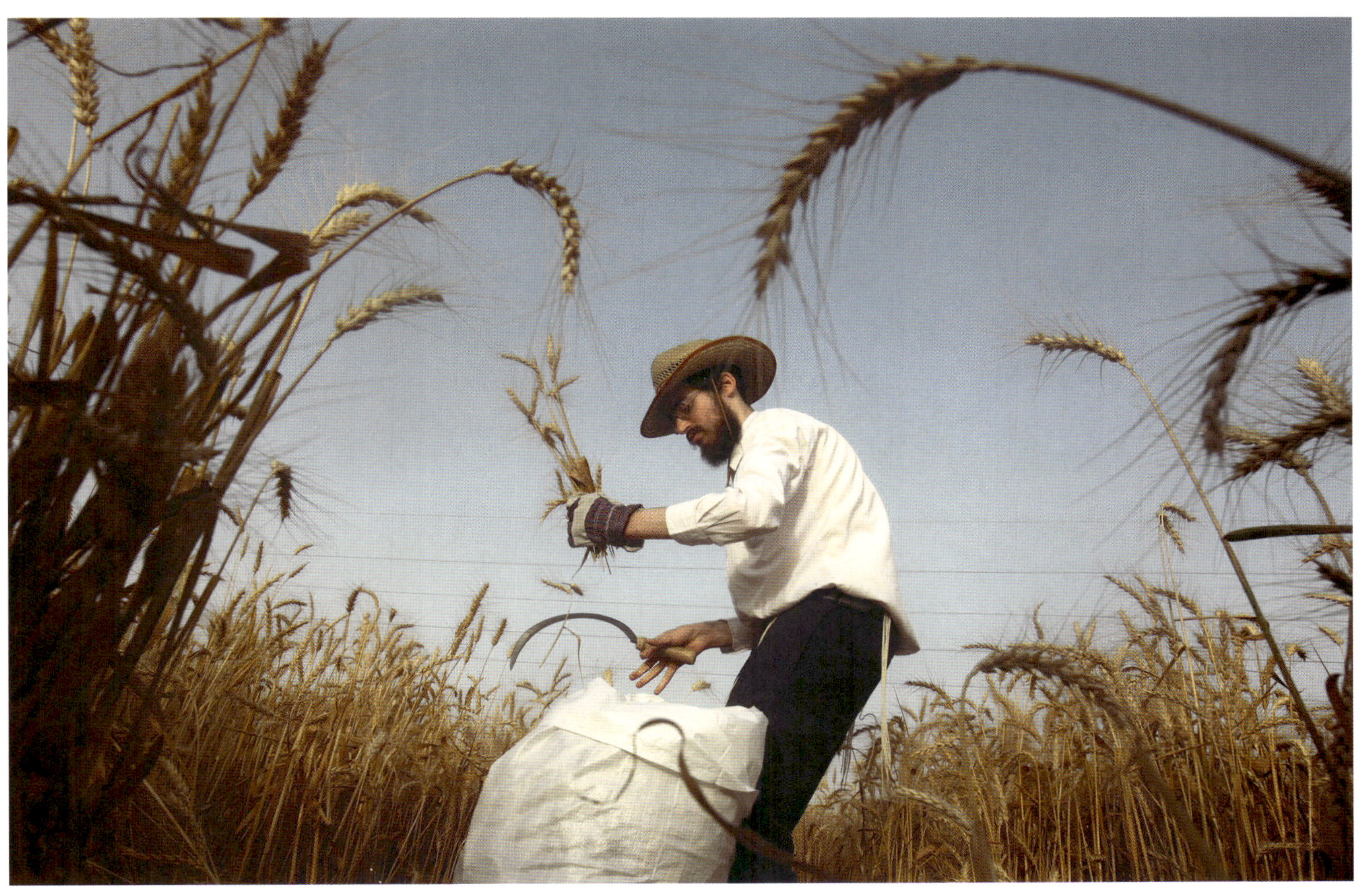

King harvest has surely come.
Marc Israel Sellem
2015

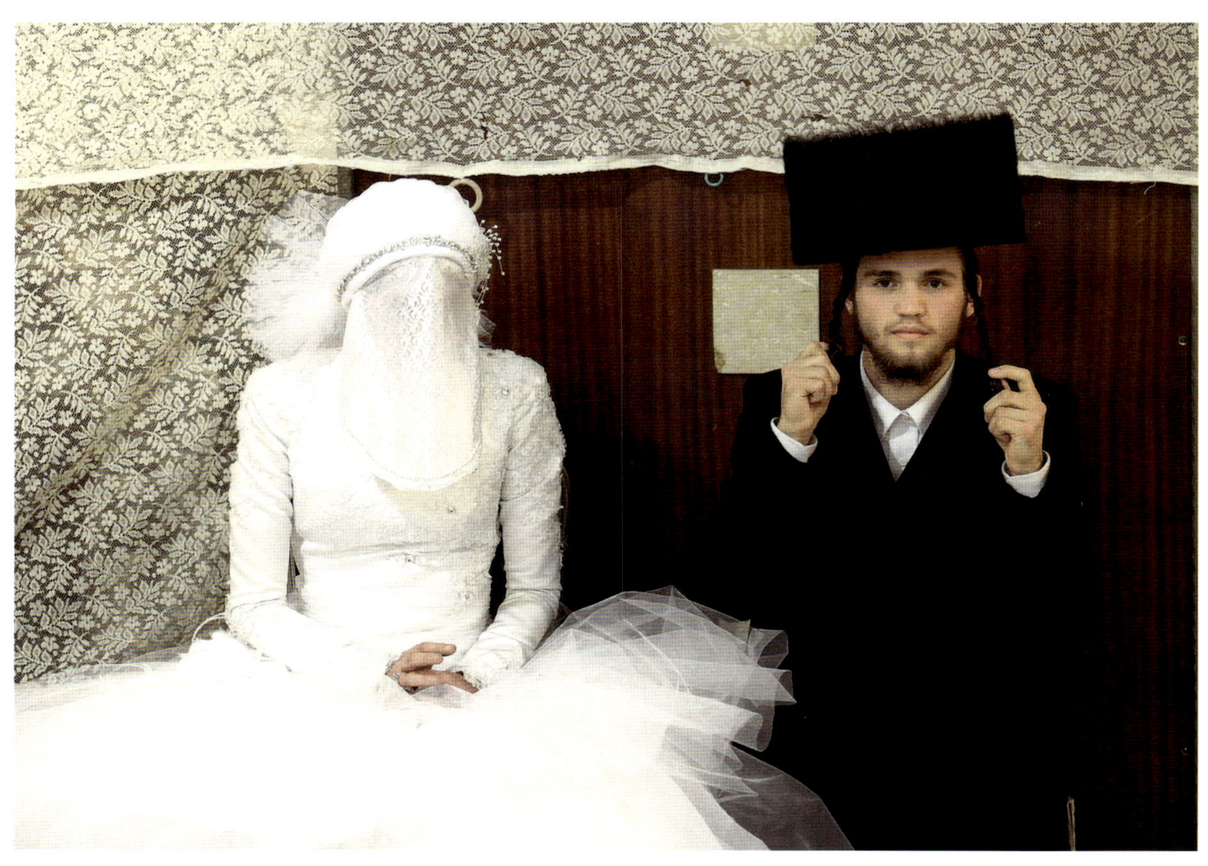

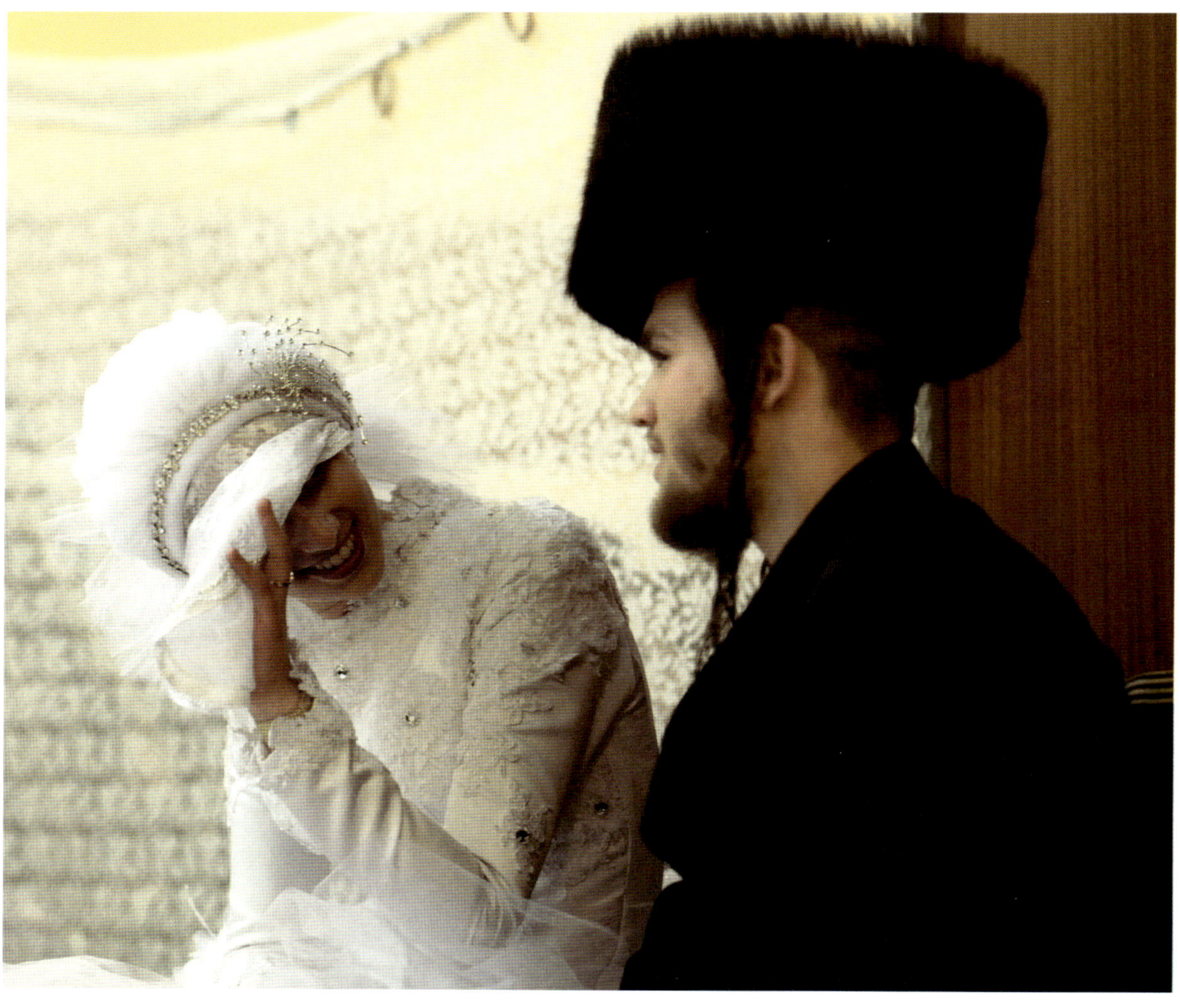

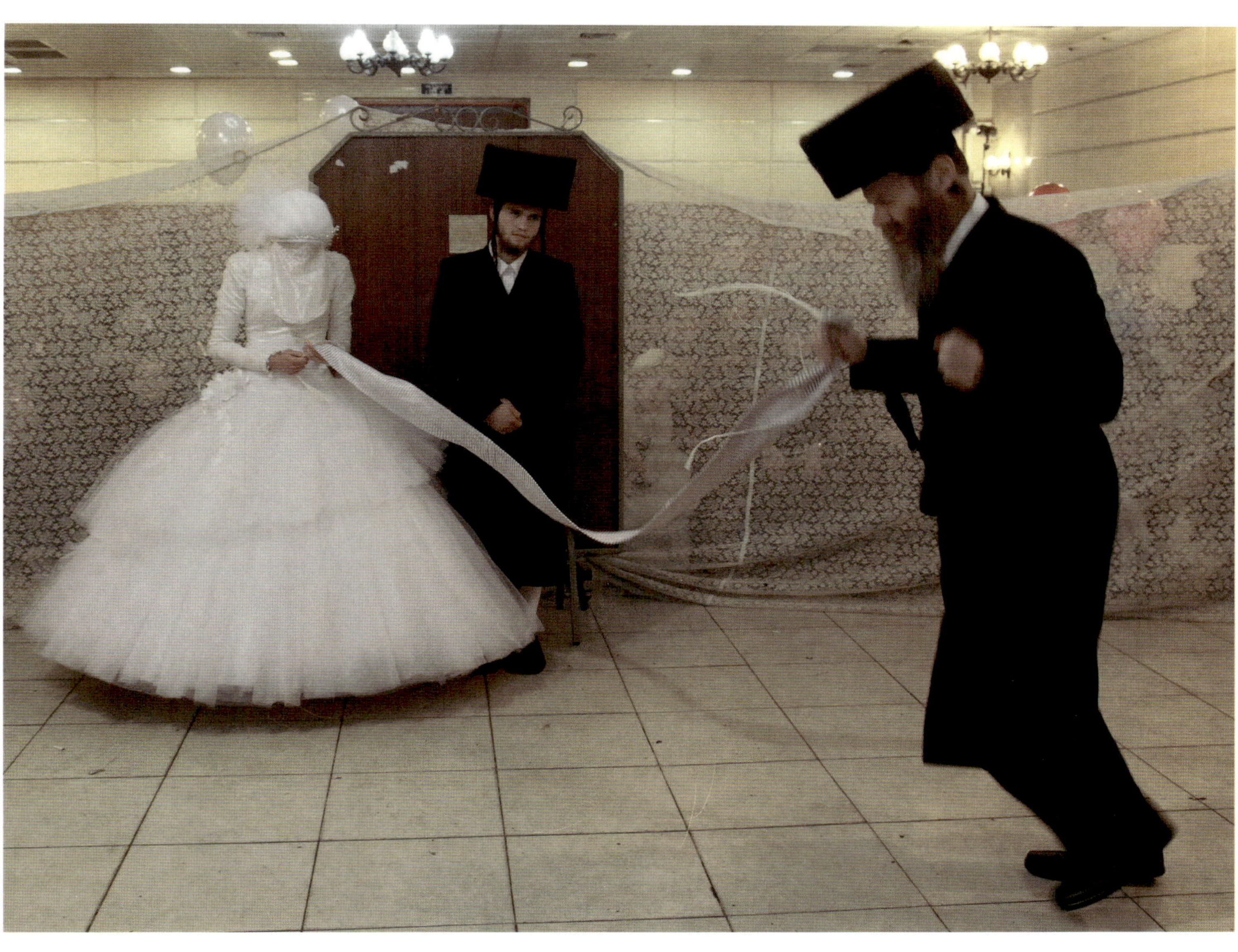

A hassidic wedding in
Bnei Brak.
Marc Israel Sellem
2012

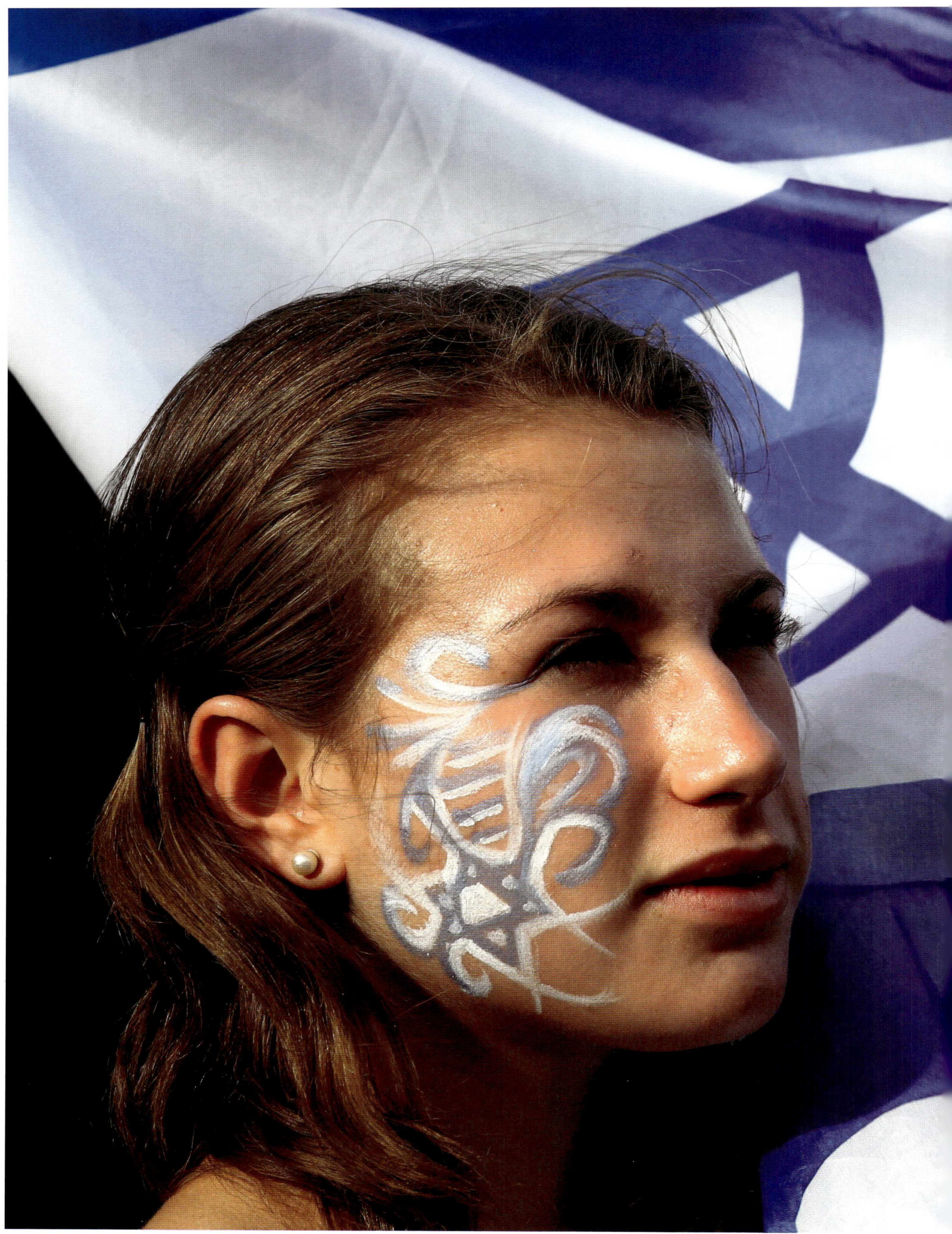

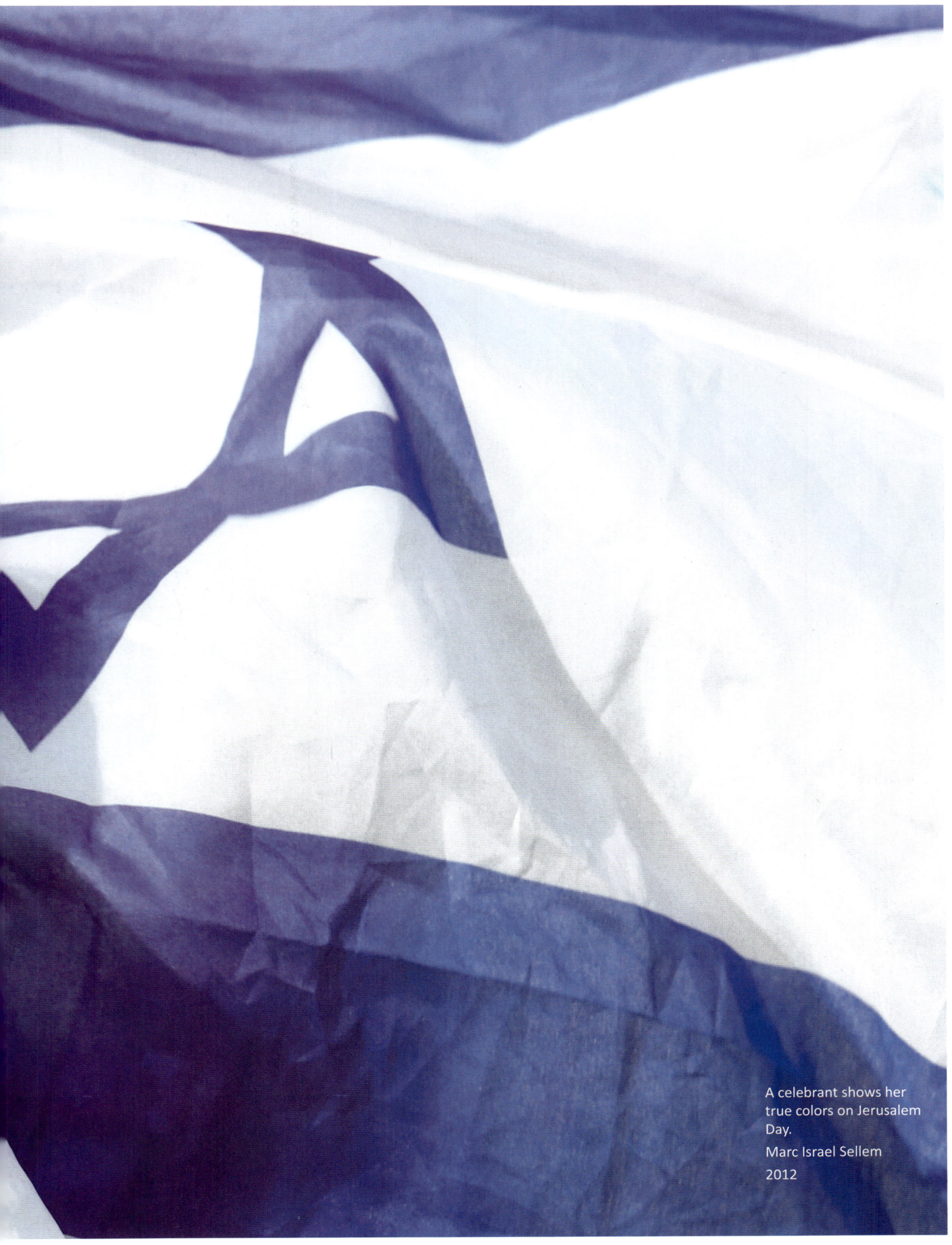

A celebrant shows her true colors on Jerusalem Day.

Marc Israel Sellem

2012

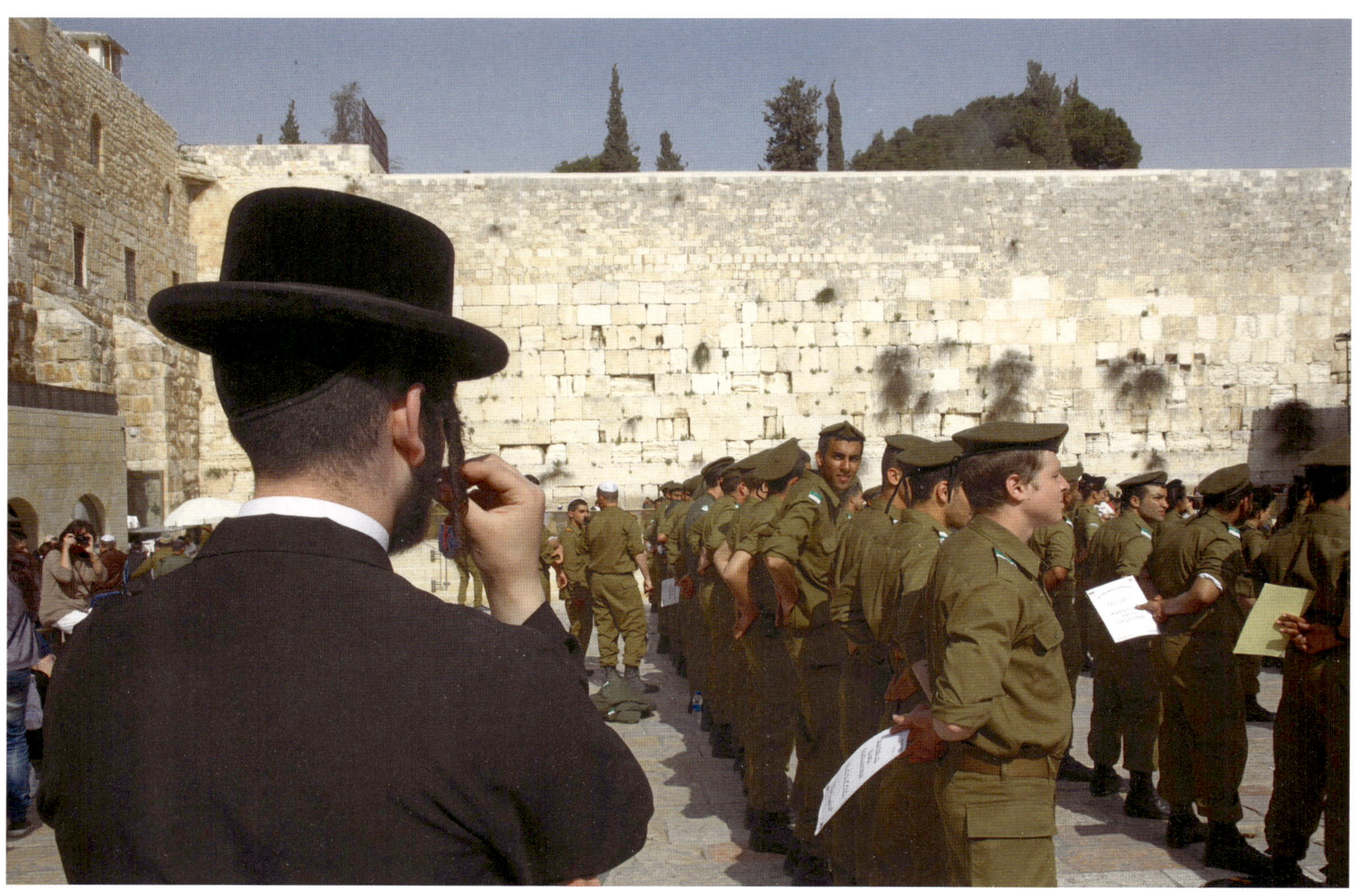

Observing an IDF
ceremony at the Western
Wall.

Marc Israel Sellem

2010

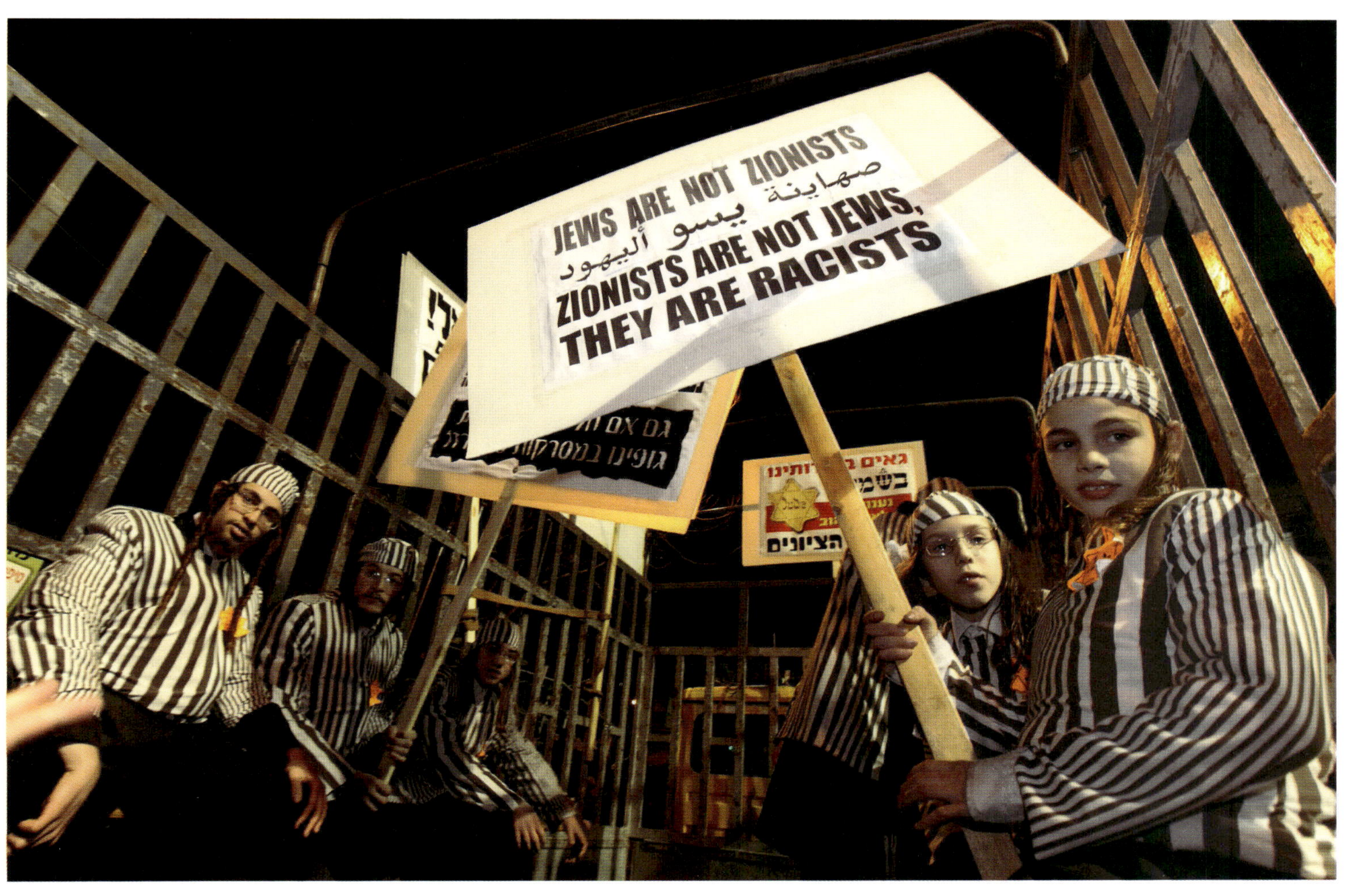

Members of the anti-Zionist Natorei Karta sect transmit their views to the next generation.

Marc Israel Sellem

2015

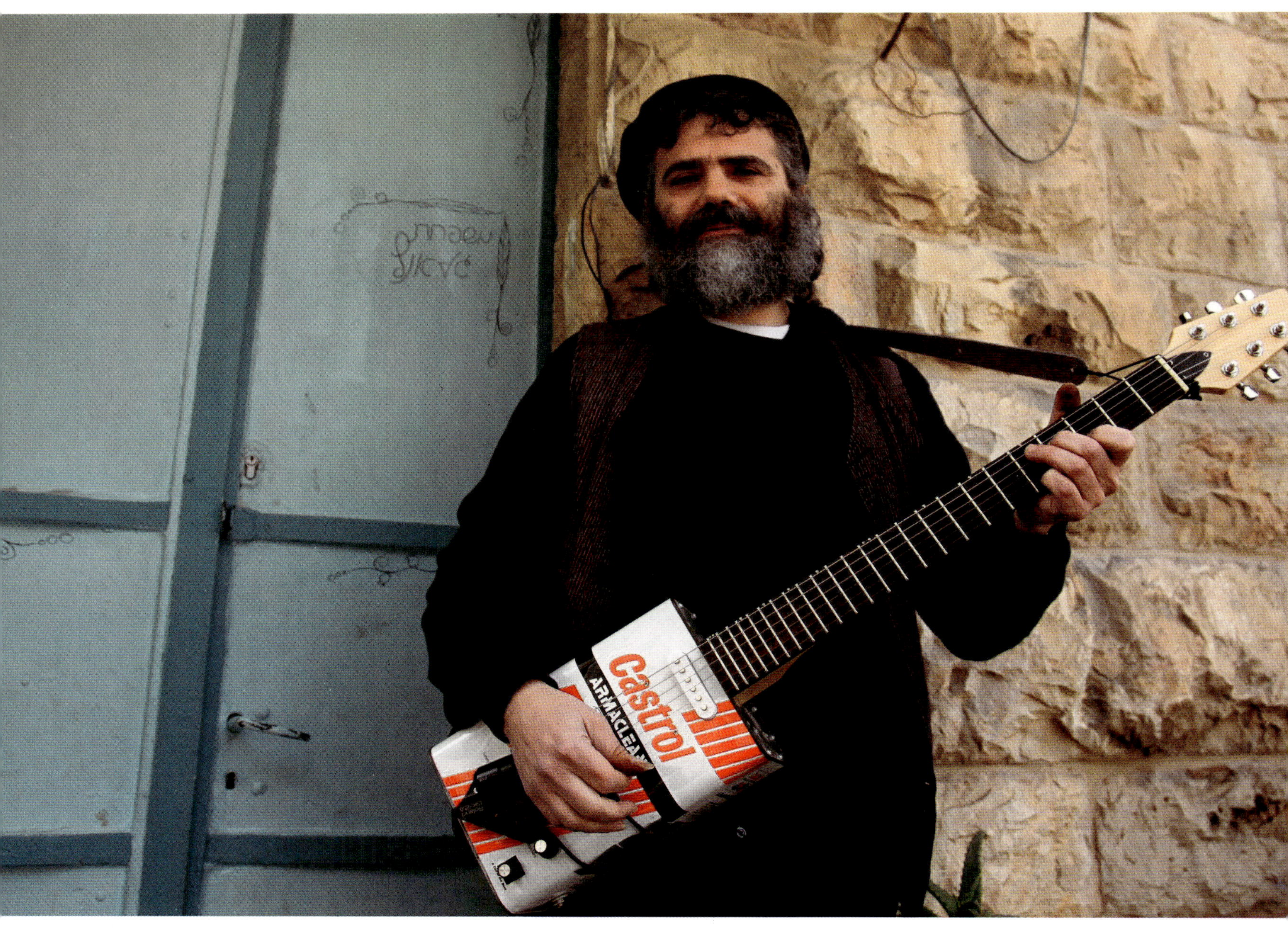

This guitar sounds best when played in a motor vehicle.

Marc Israel Sellem

2012

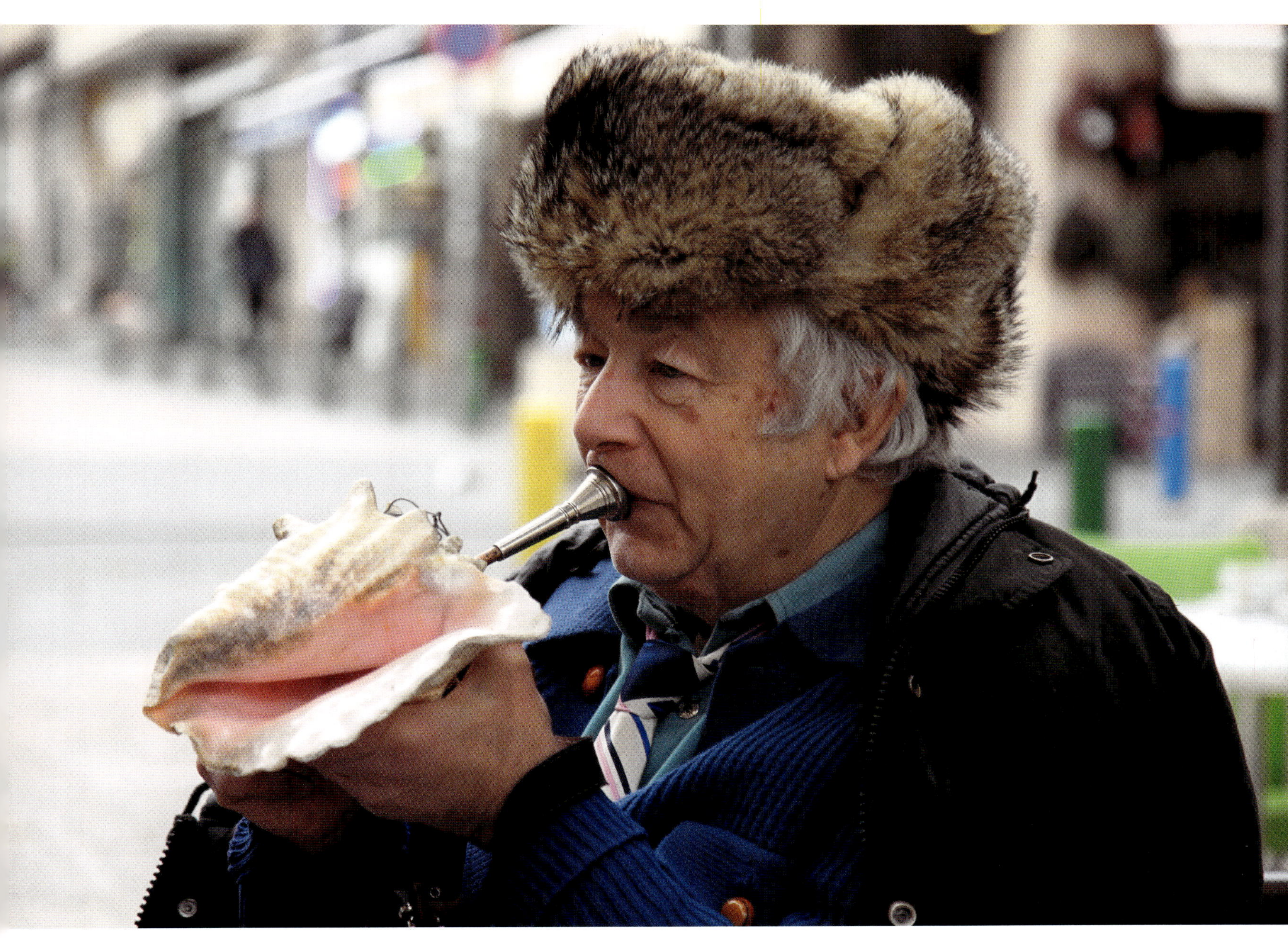

This instrument is best
played at the seashore.
Marc Israel Sellem
2012

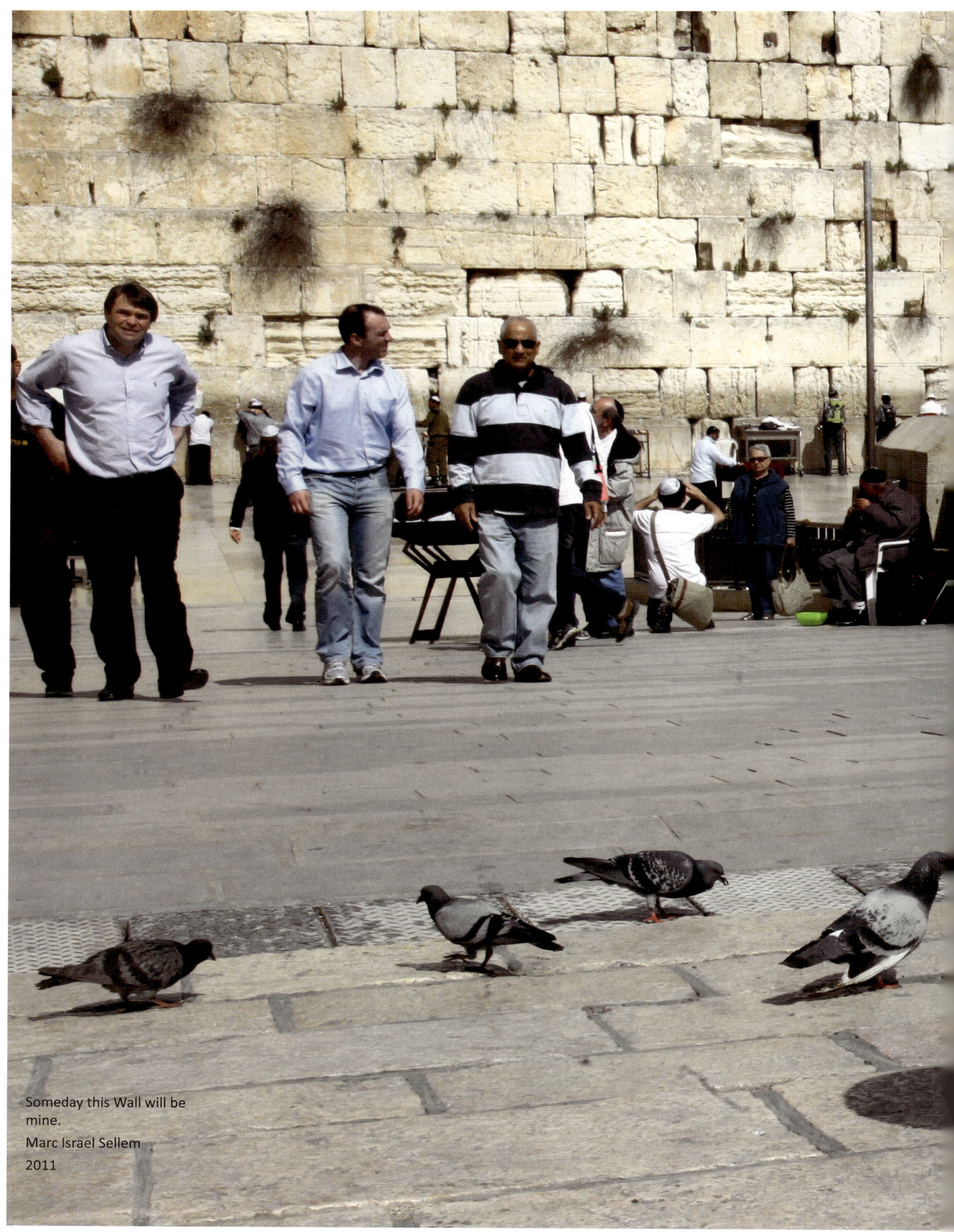

Someday this Wall will be mine.
Marc Israel Sellem
2011

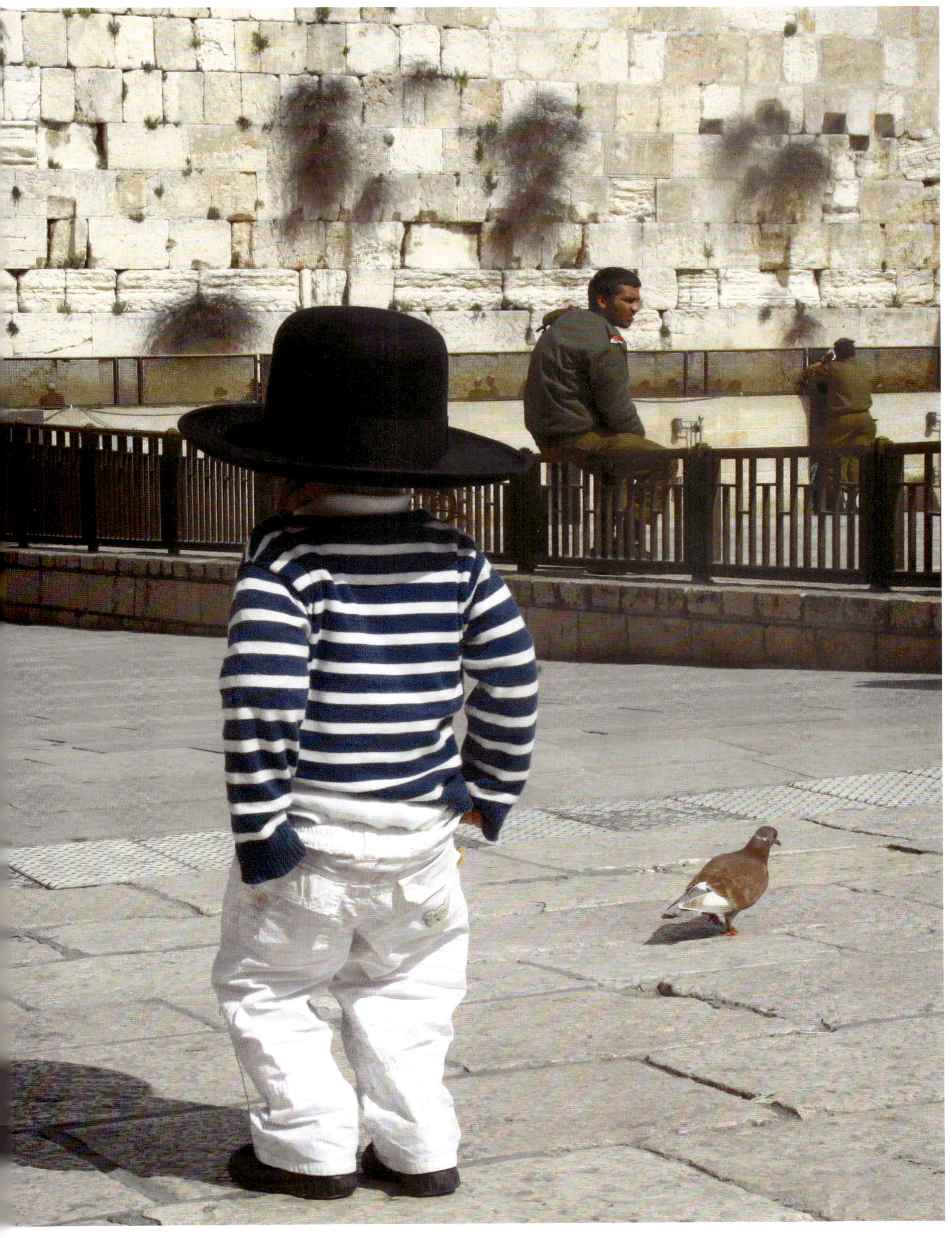

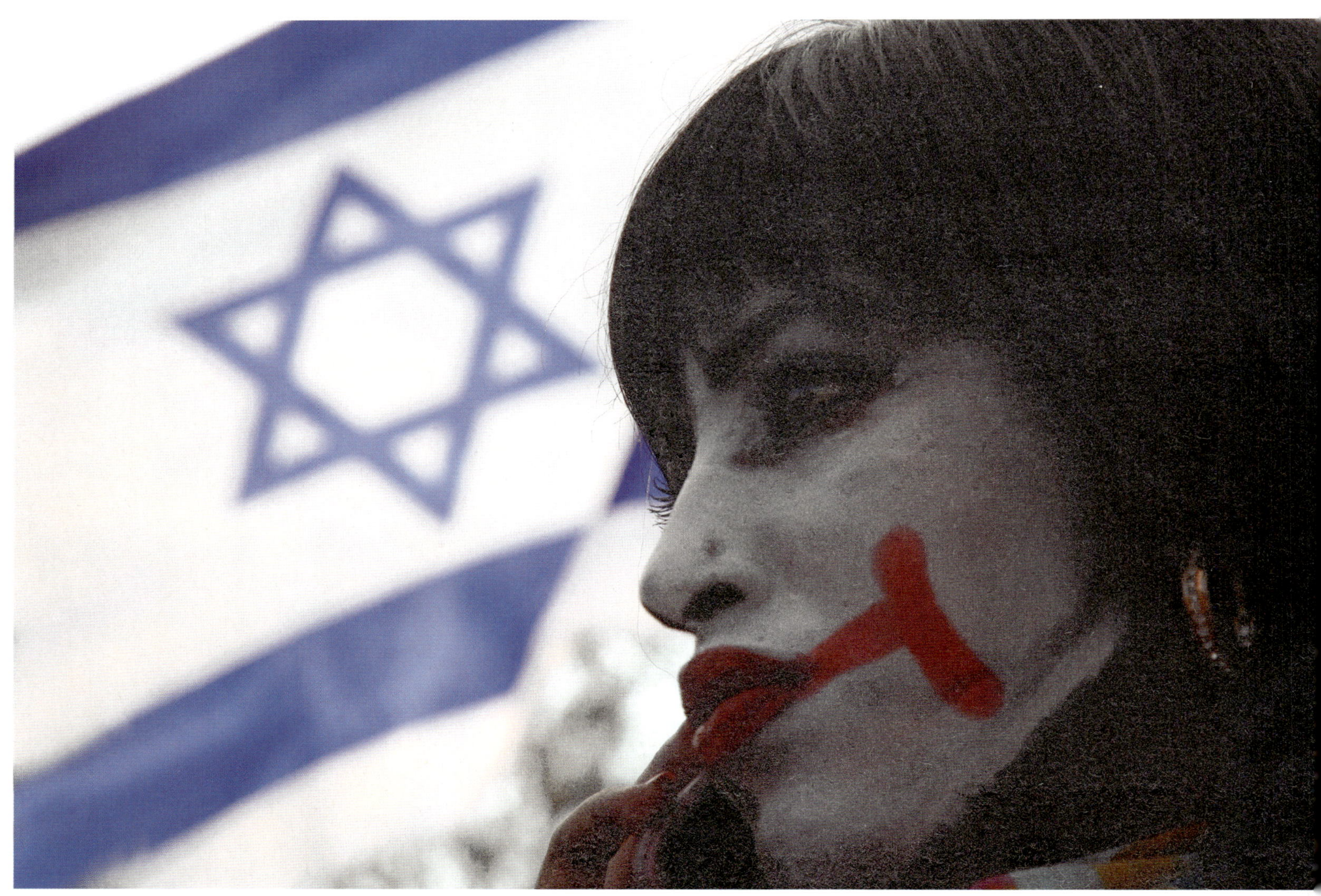

A punk-Zionist.
Marc Israel Sellem
2015

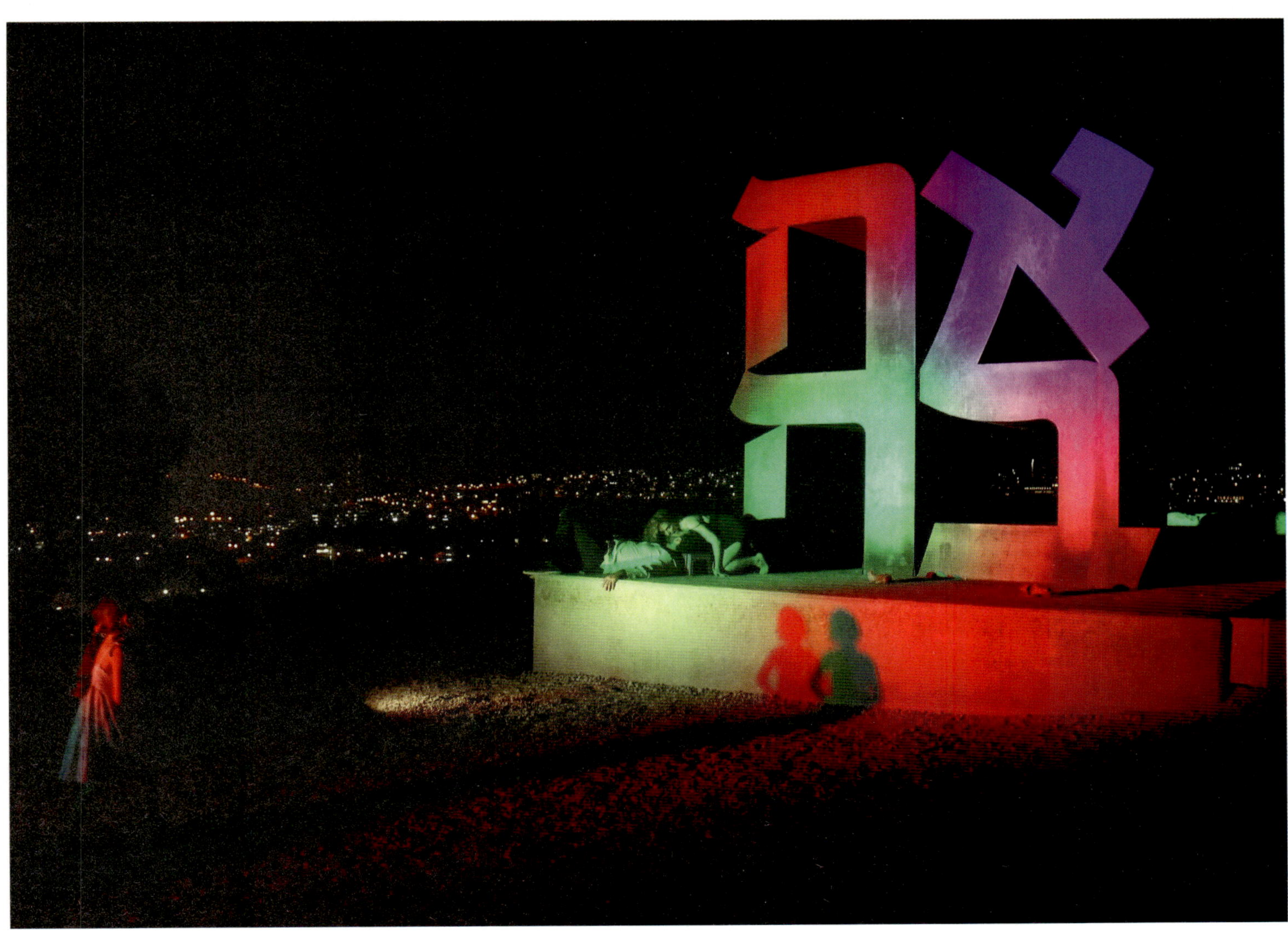

Catching an intimate embrace at the Israel Museum.

Marc Israel Sellem

2014

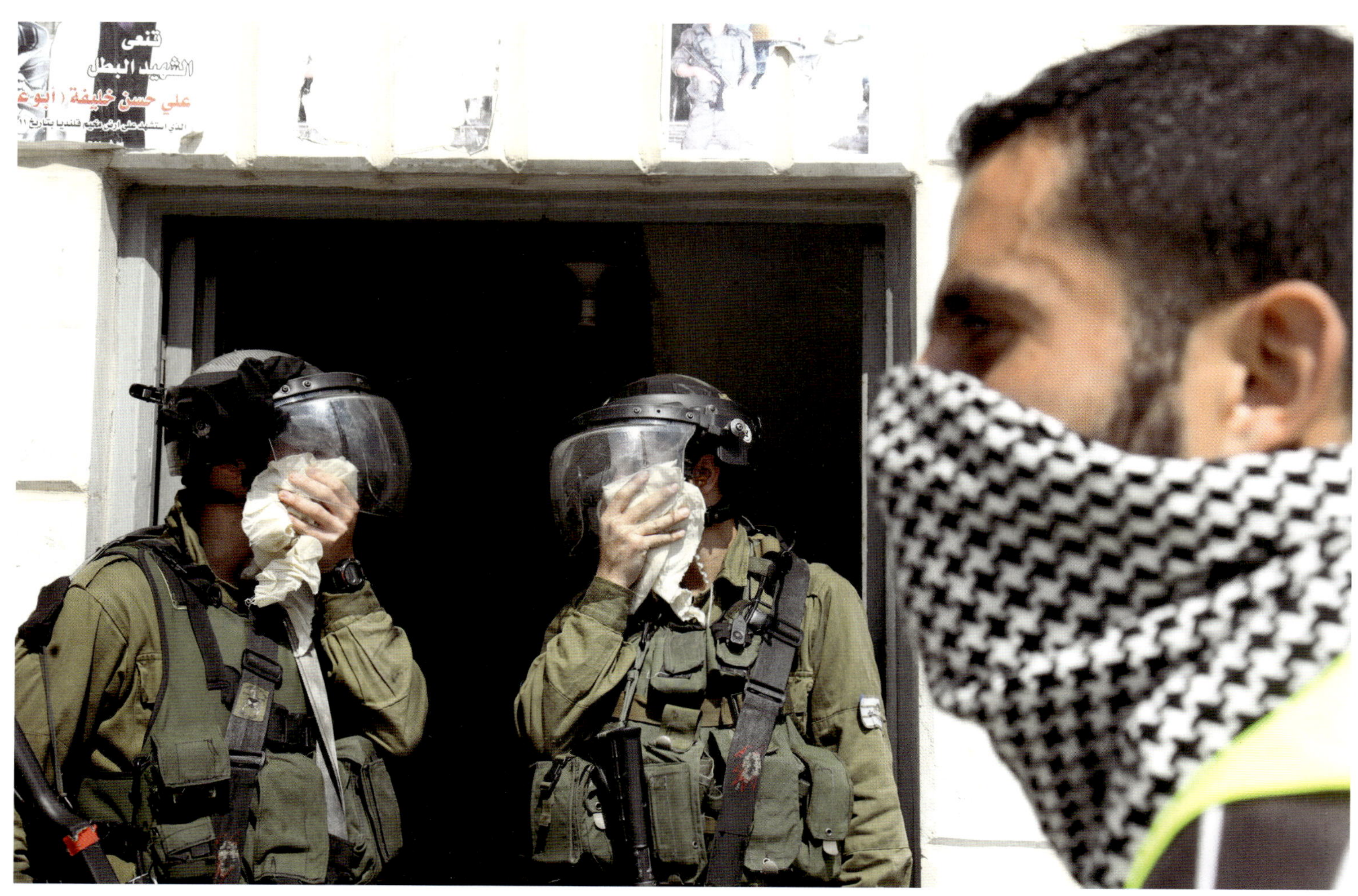

Land Day brings a
tear(gas) to the eyes.
Marc Israel Sellem
2011

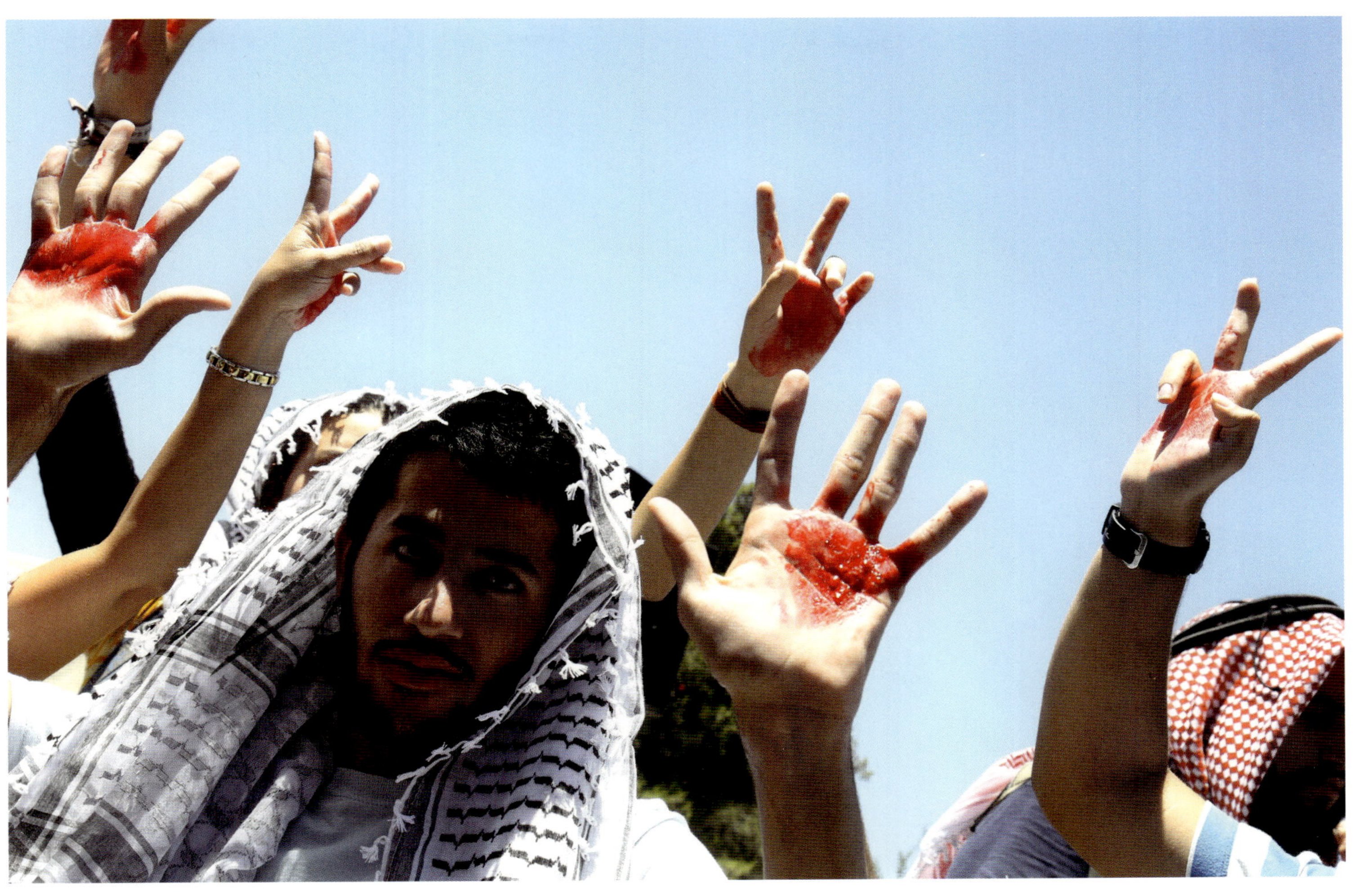

Israelis demonstrate against freeing security prisoners with blood on their hands.

Marc Israel Sellem

2013

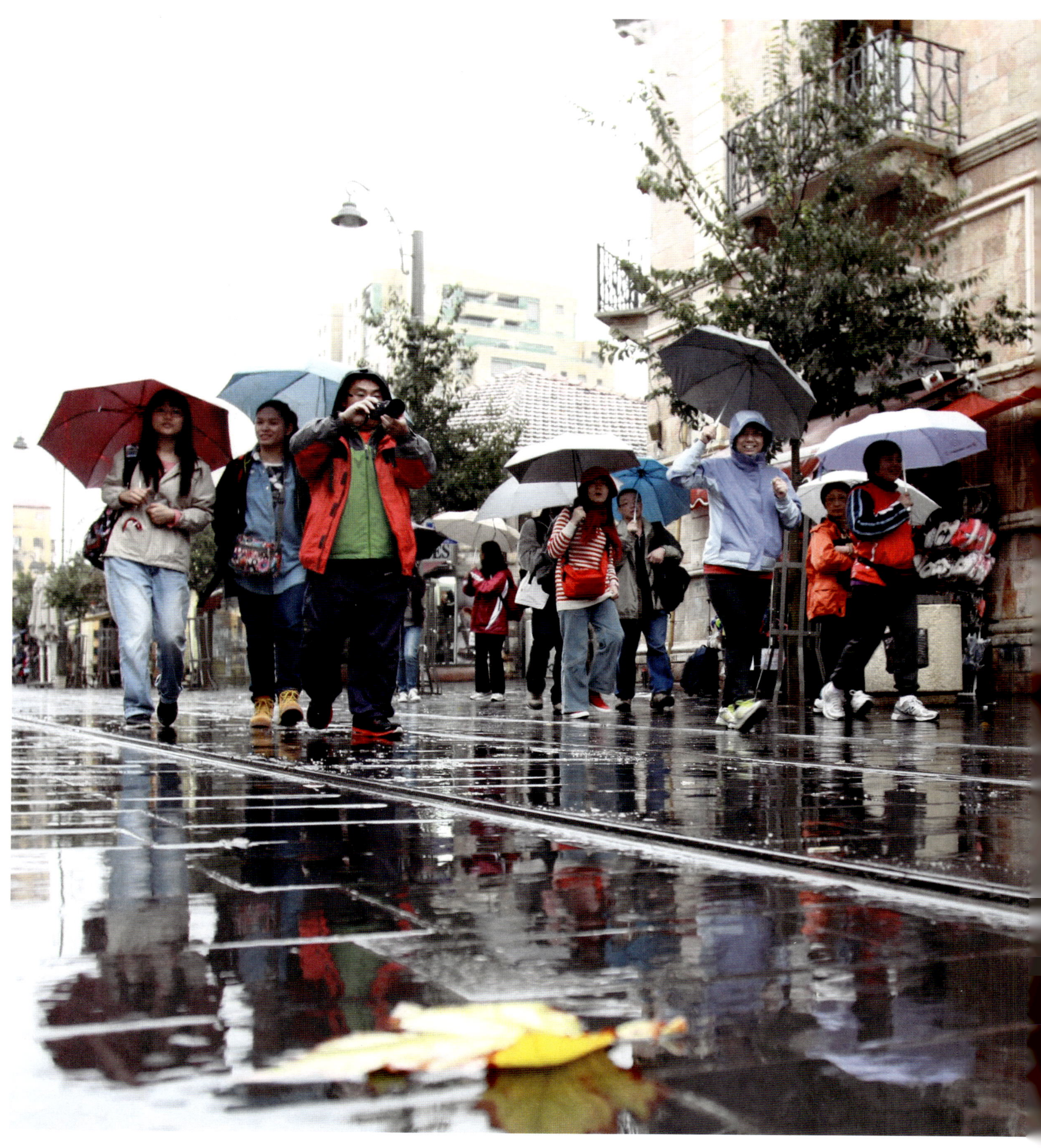

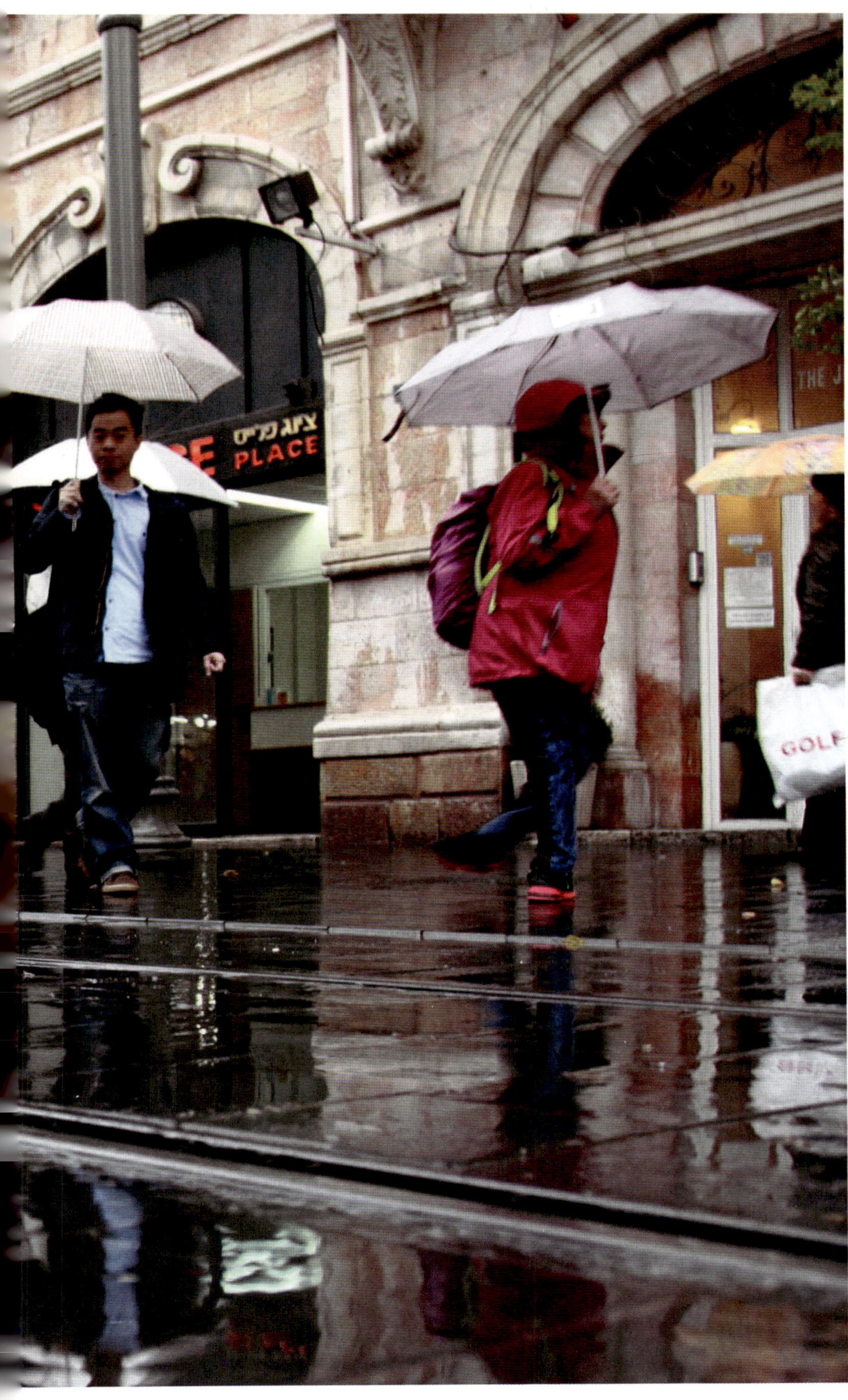

Visitors from the Far East look for a station of the Jerusalem Light Rail.
Marc Israel Sellem
2013

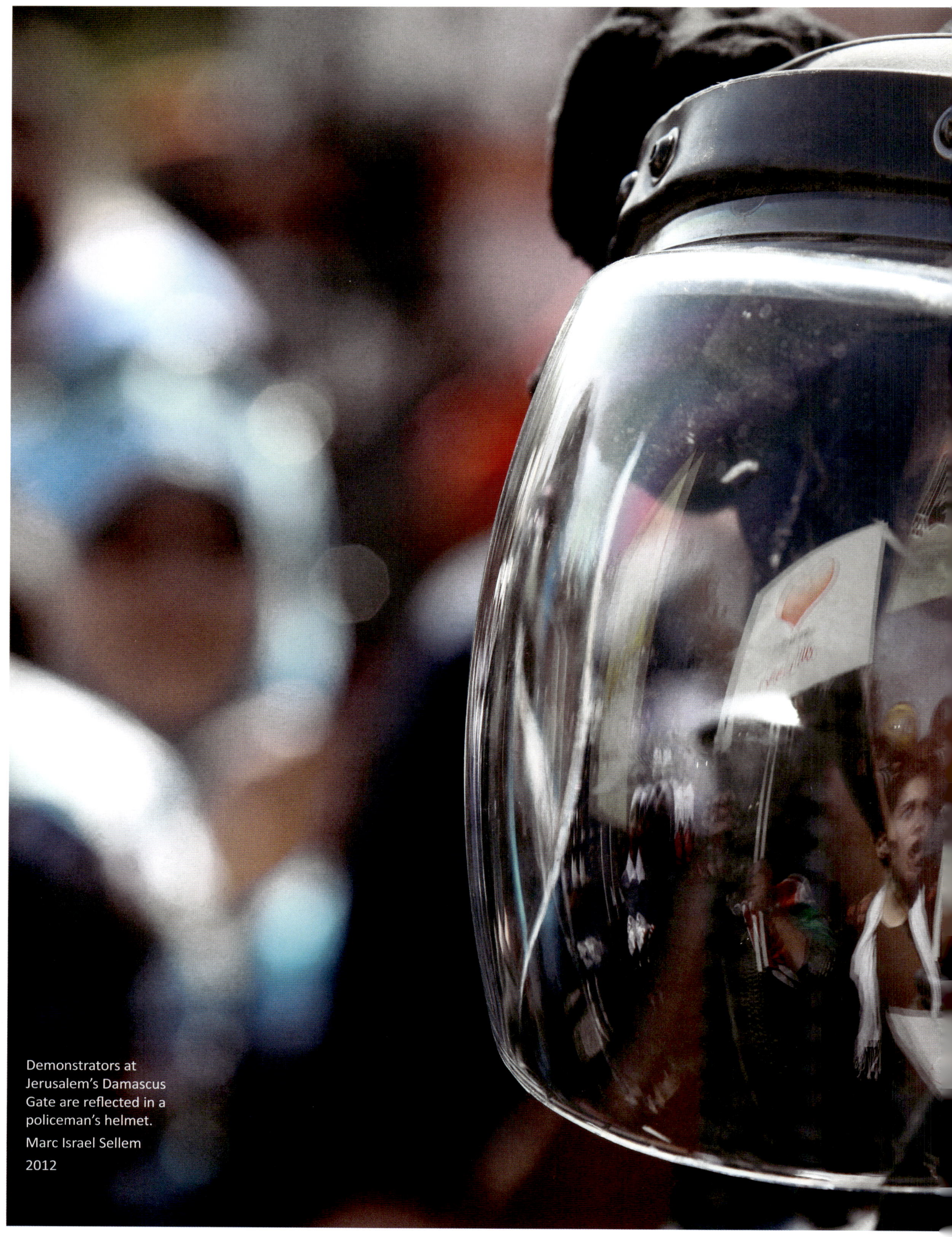

Demonstrators at Jerusalem's Damascus Gate are reflected in a policeman's helmet.

Marc Israel Sellem

2012

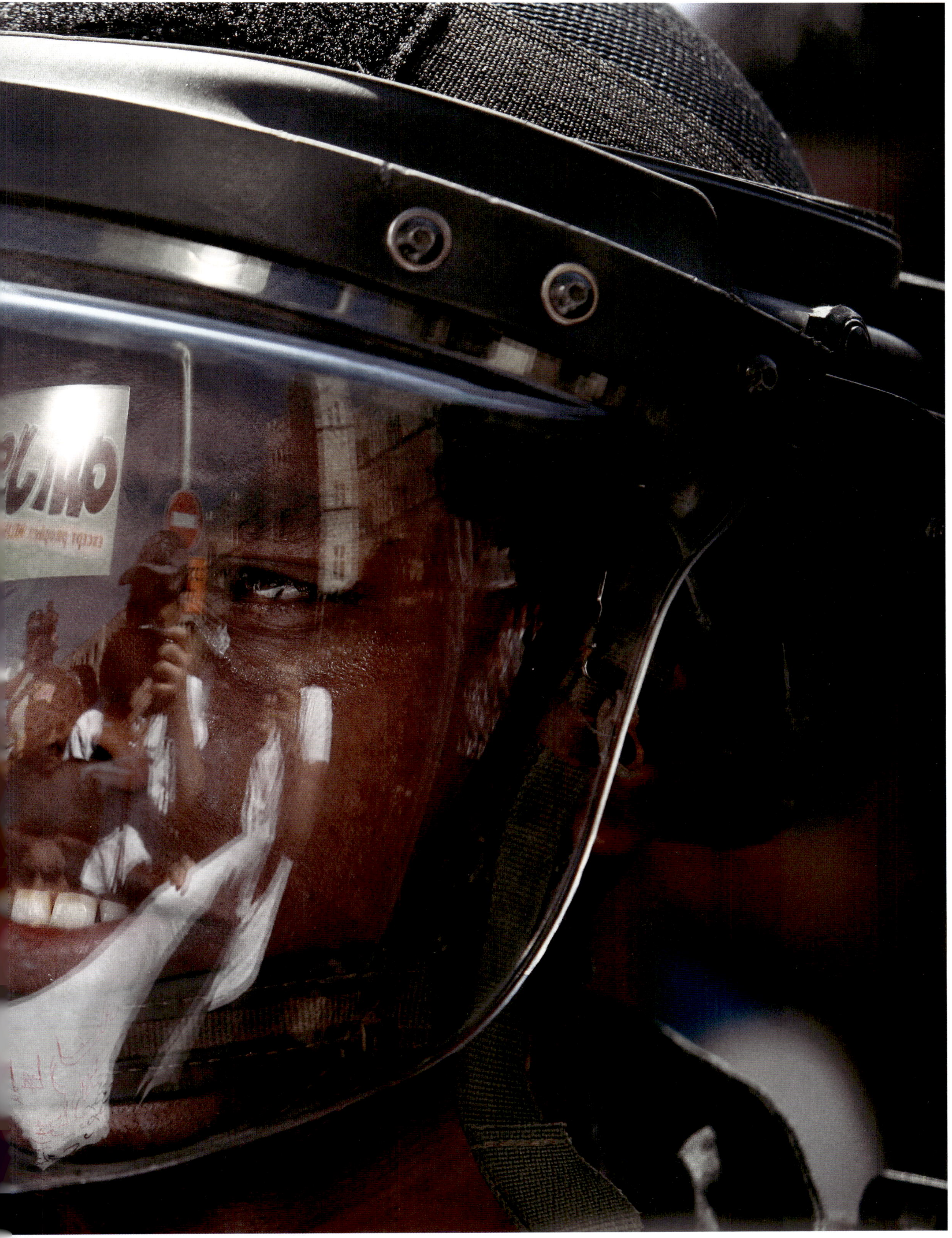

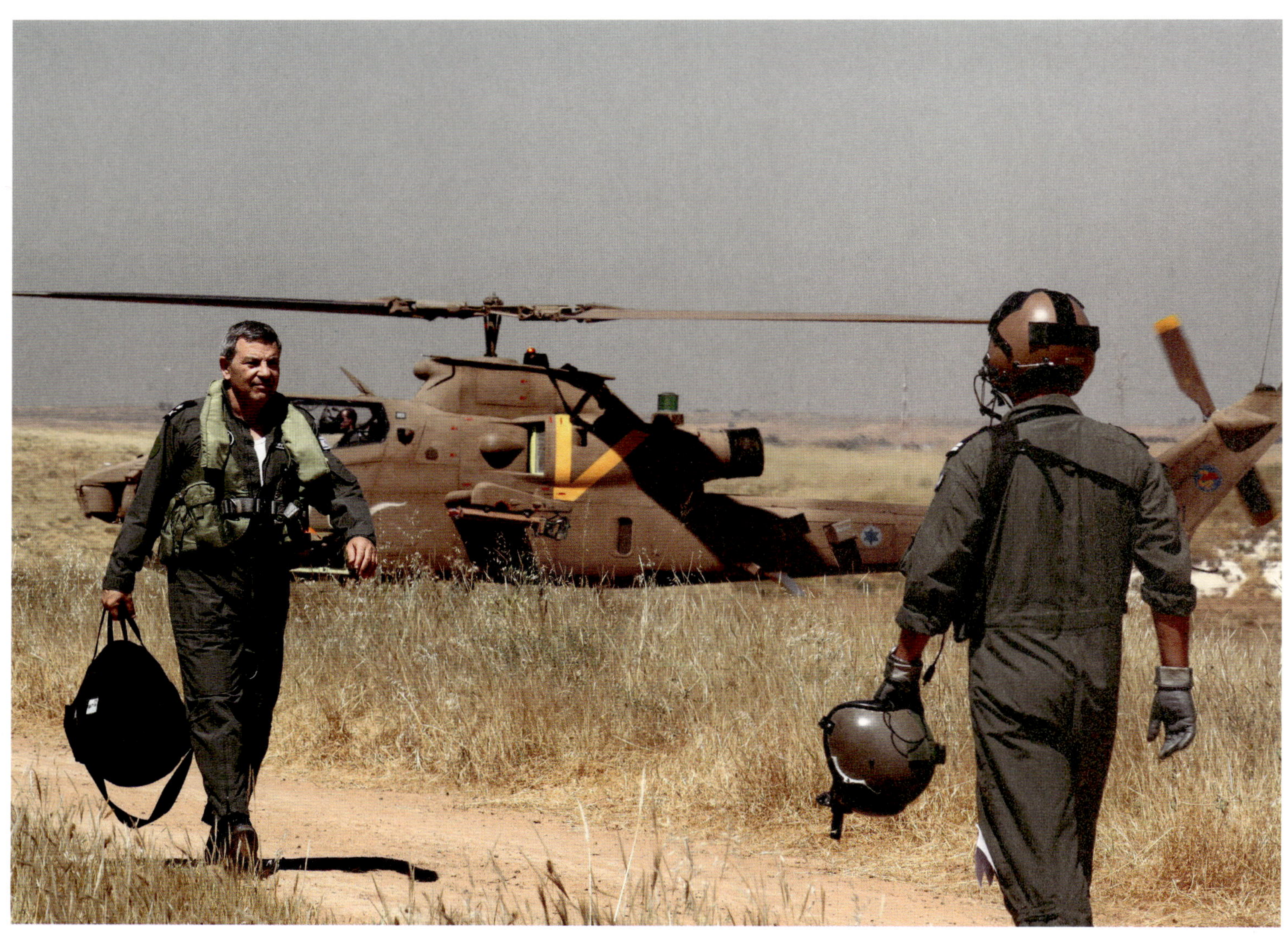

Outgoing air force chief Maj.-Gen. Ido Nehoshtan hands over a Cobra combat helicopter to another pilot after a farewell flight.

Marc Israel Sellem

2012

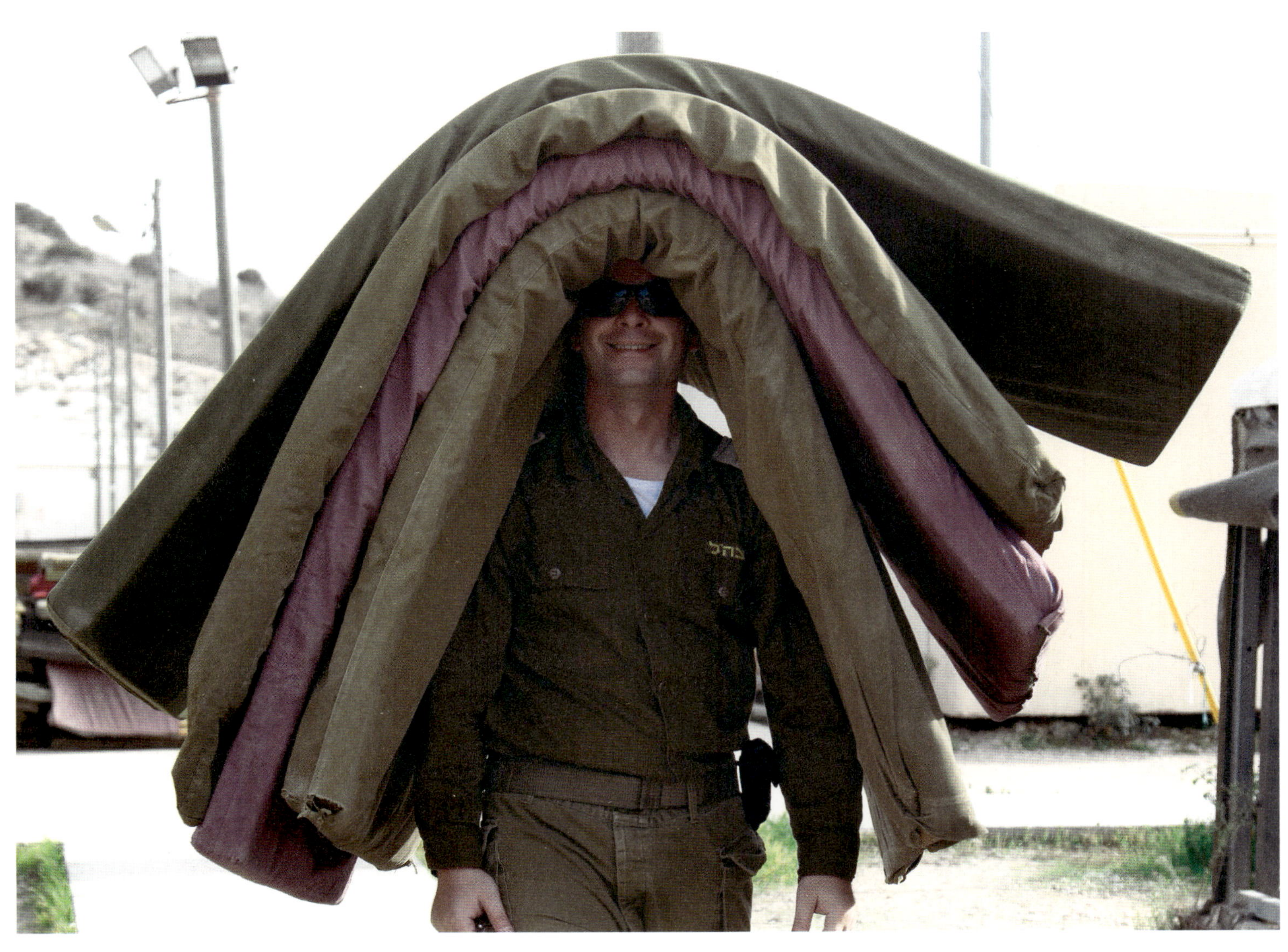

Looking forward to a
restful reserve duty.

Marc Israel Sellem

2010

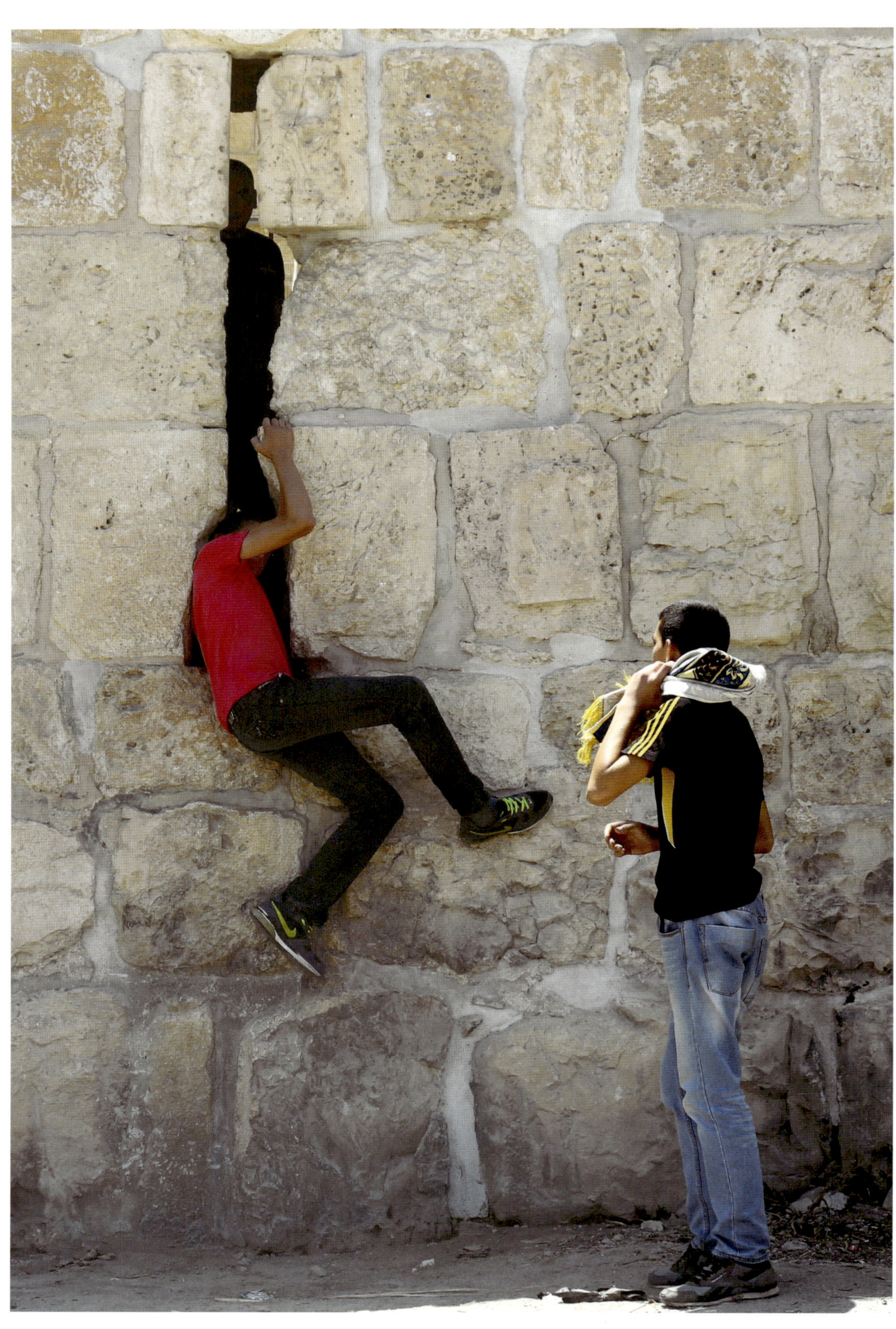

Taking a peek through
Jerusalem's Old City wall.
Marc Israel Sellem
2014

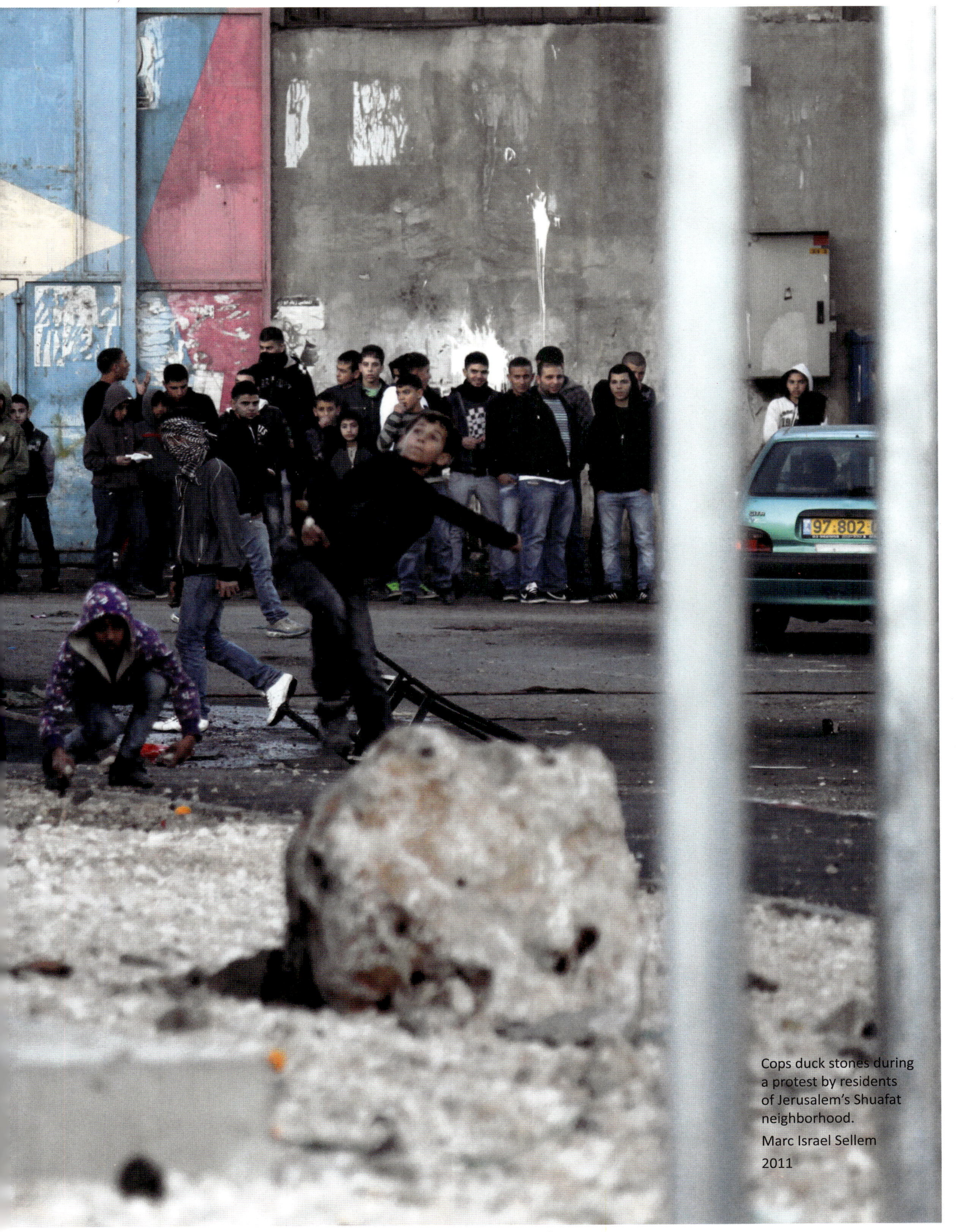

Cops duck stones during a protest by residents of Jerusalem's Shuafat neighborhood.

Marc Israel Sellem

2011

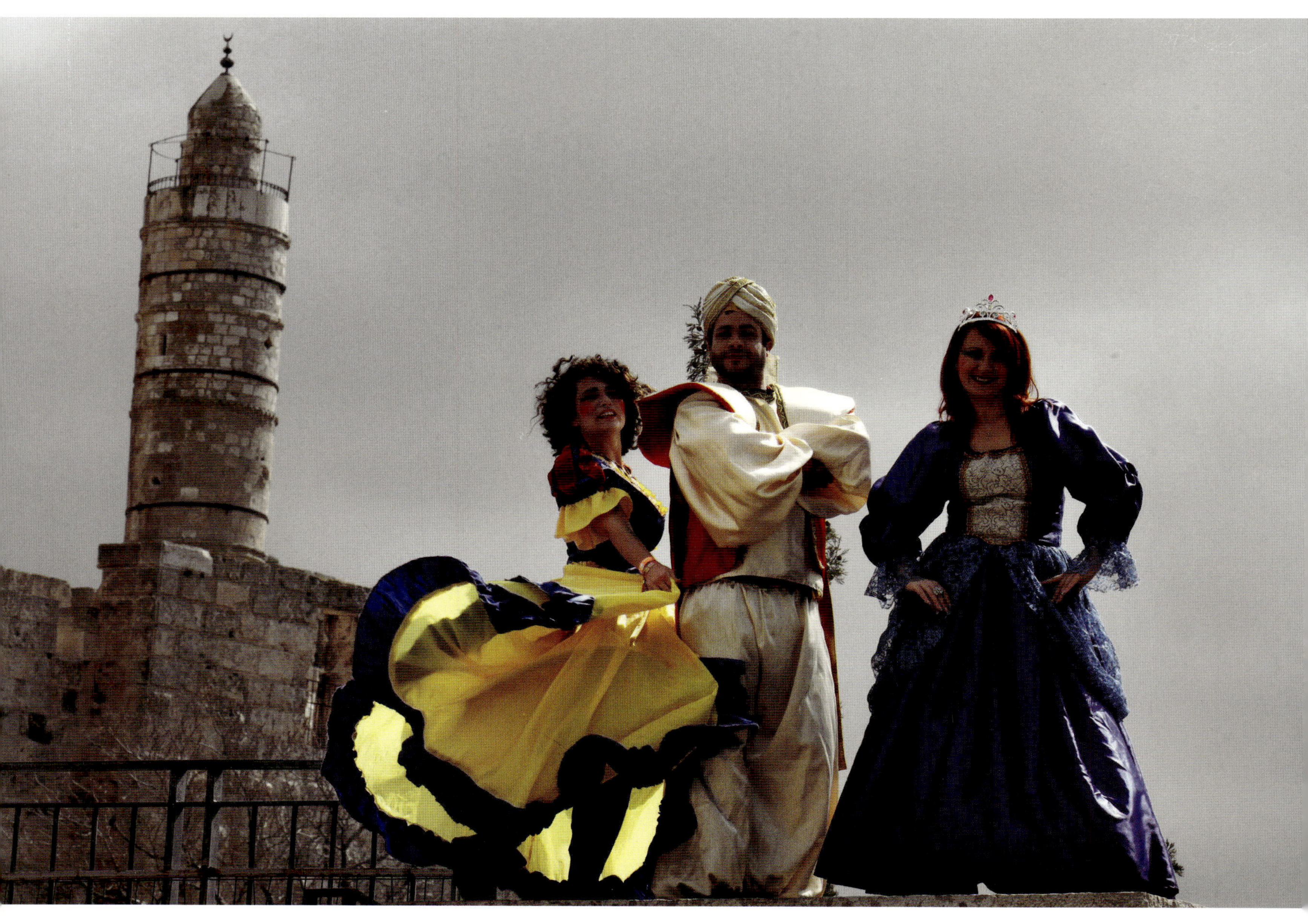

Purim revelers pose
opposite David's Citadel
at the Jaffa Gate of
Jerusalem's Old City.

Marc Israel Sellem

2013

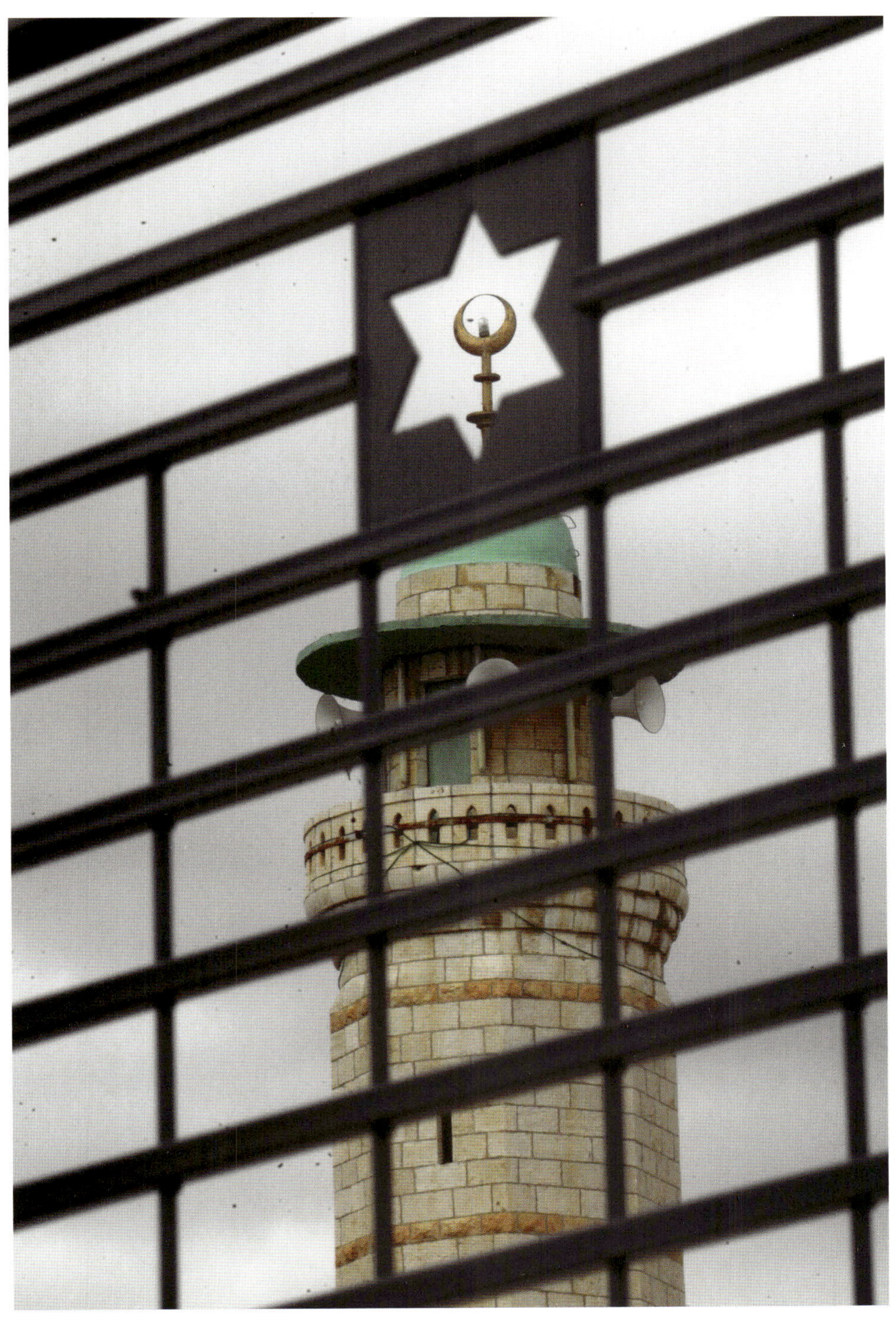

A mosque on the Mount of Olives is seen through a gate to the oldest Jewish cemetery in the world.

Marc Israel Sellem

2012

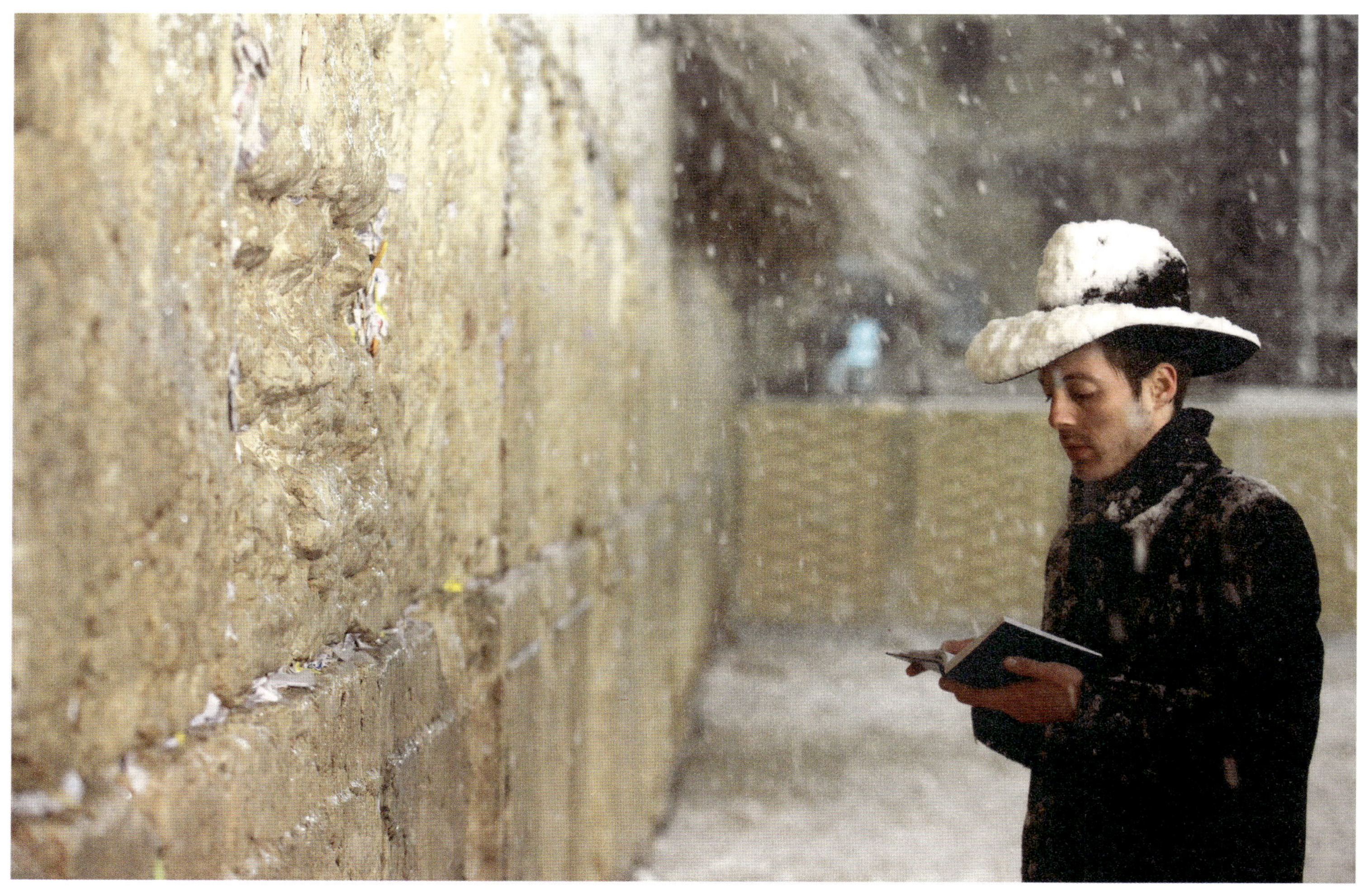

‘Neither rain, nor snow, nor sleet, nor hail’ shall keep this worshiper from the Kotel.

Marc Israel Sellem

2013

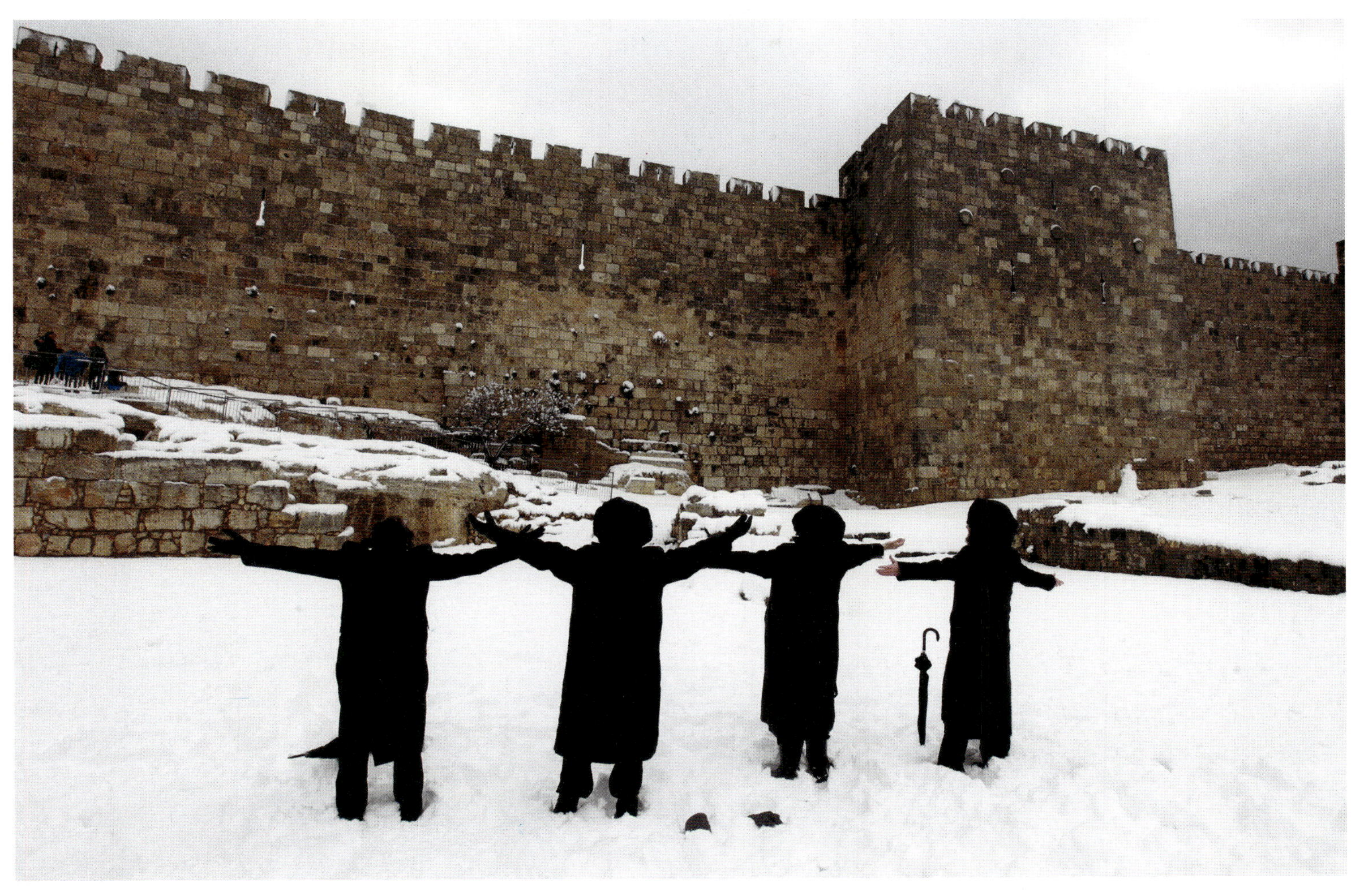

A Jerusalem snowfall
brings out the snow
angels in all of us.
Marc Israel Sellem
2013

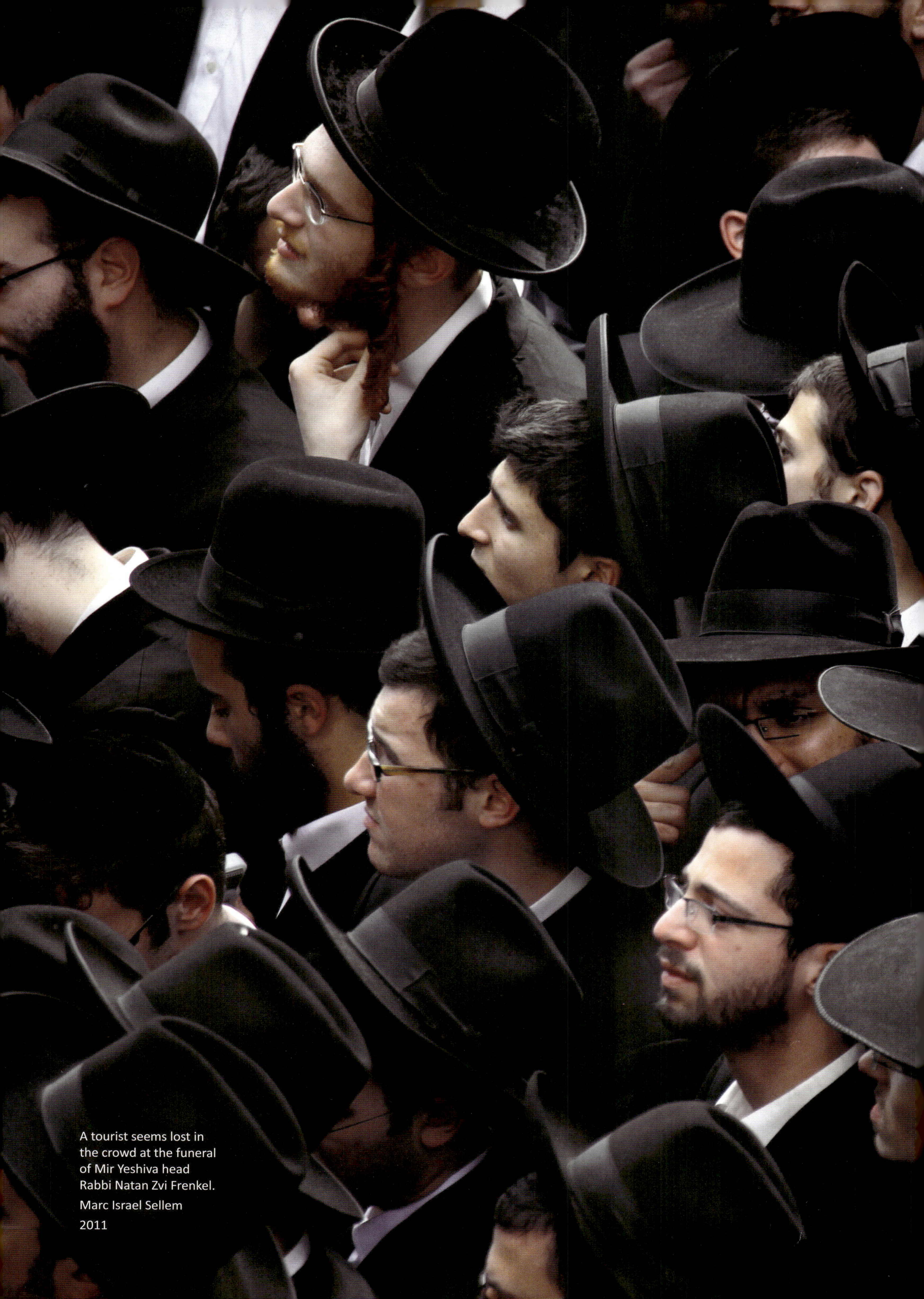

A tourist seems lost in the crowd at the funeral of Mir Yeshiva head Rabbi Natan Zvi Frenkel.
Marc Israel Sellem
2011

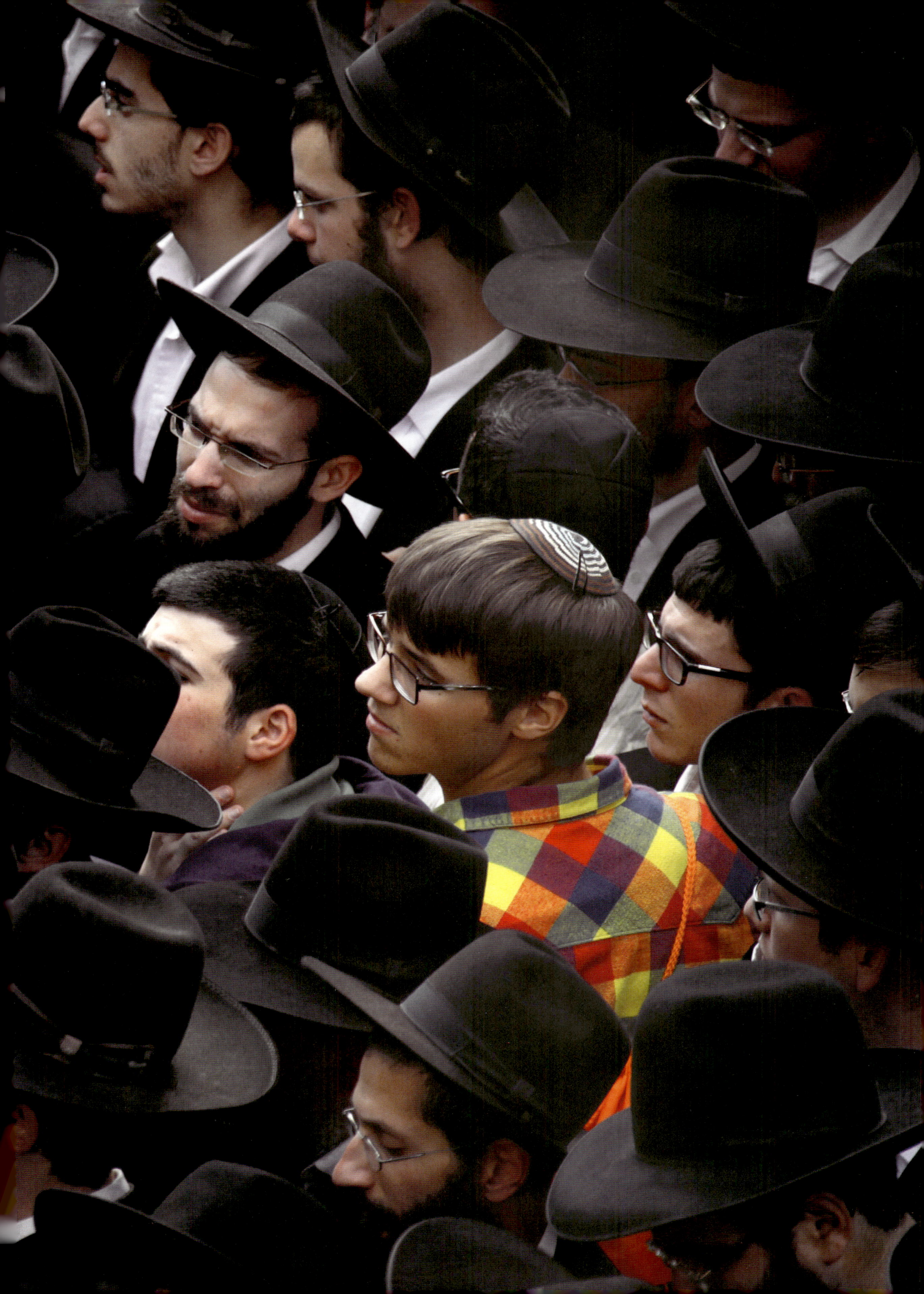

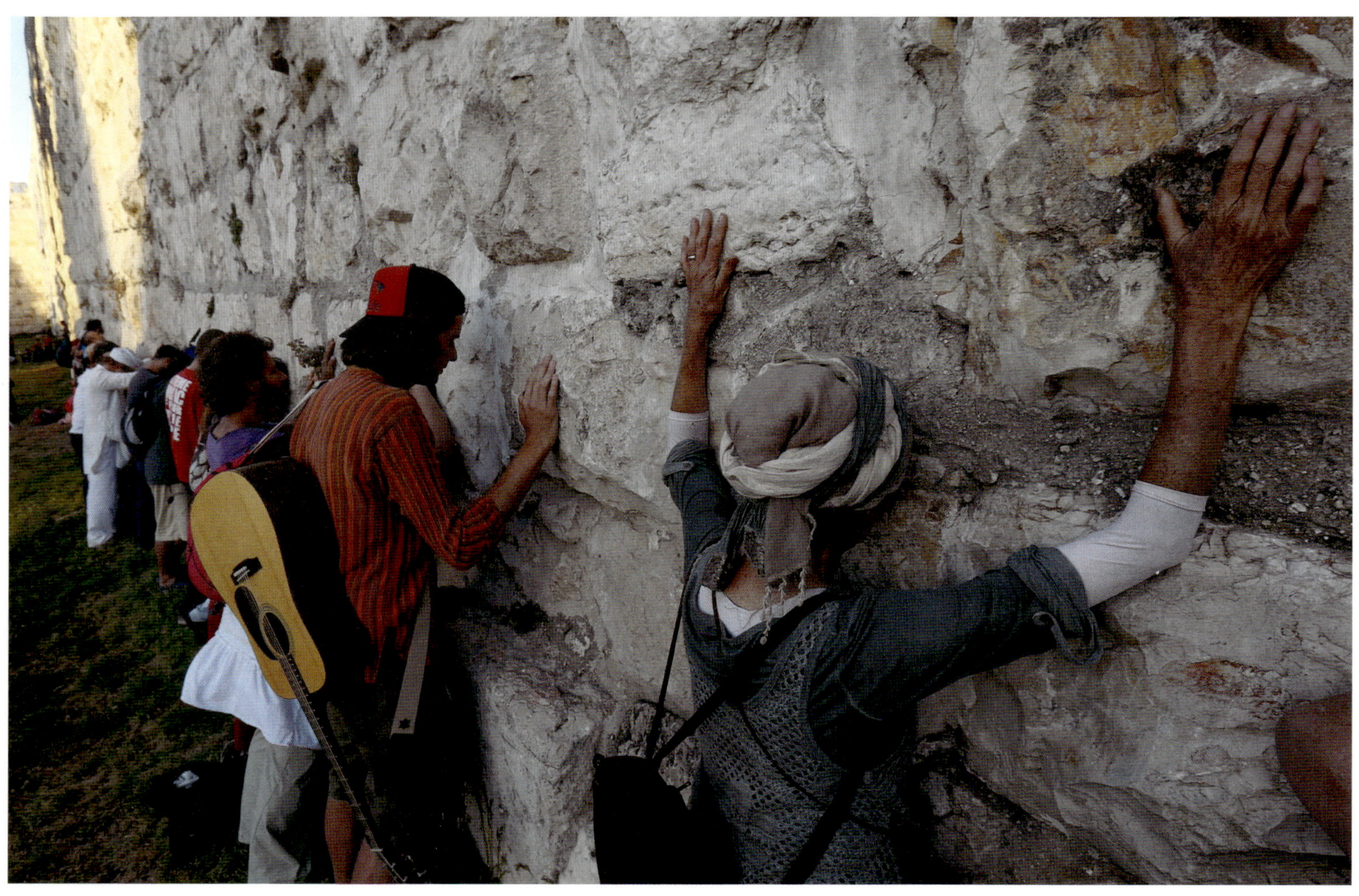

Activists commune with the walls of Jerusalem's Old City as they prepare to surround it in a 'ring of peace.'

Marc Israel Sellem

2014

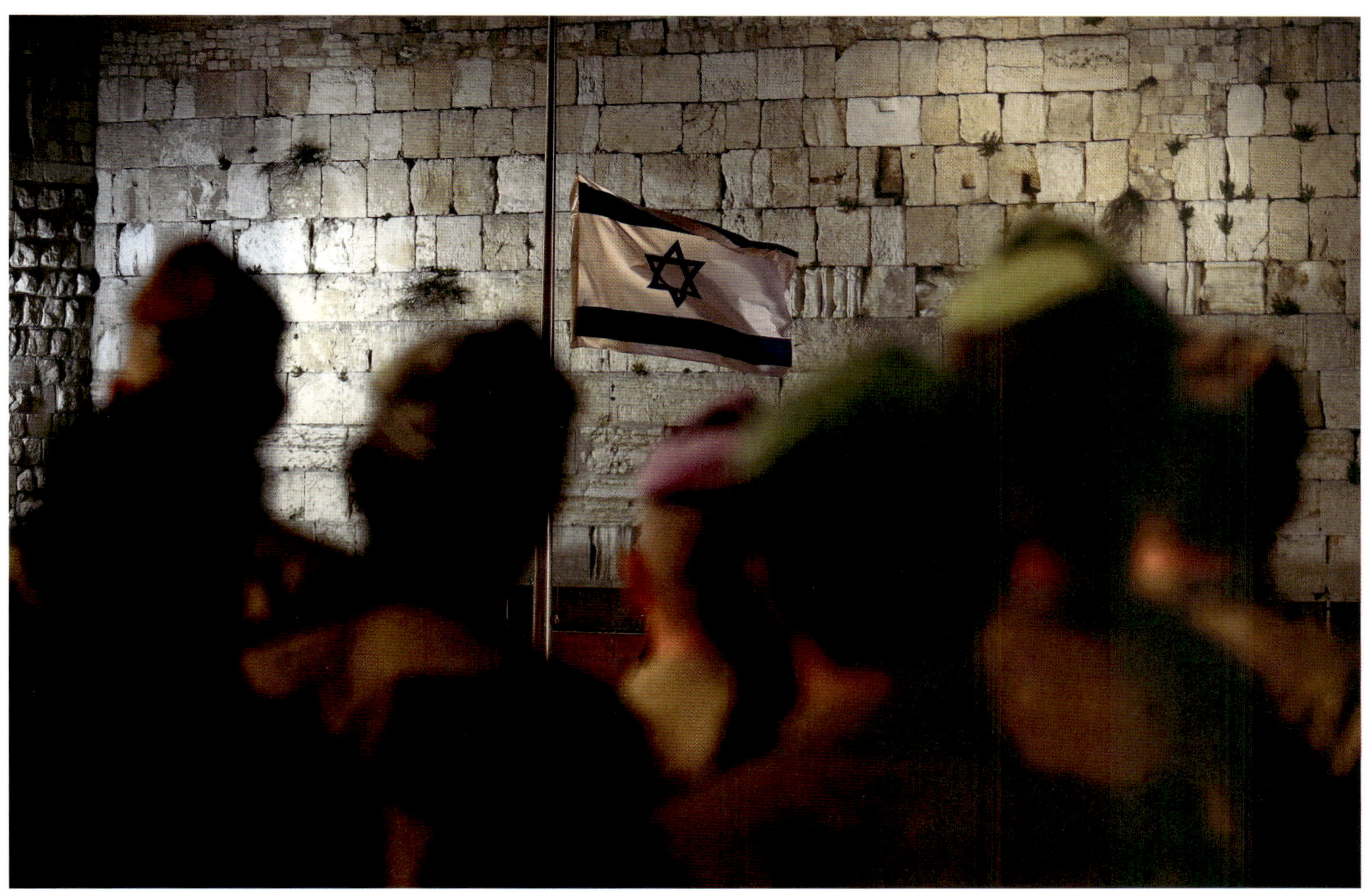

The flag is lowered to half-mast at a Remembrance Day ceremony at the Western Wall.

Marc Israel Sellem

2010

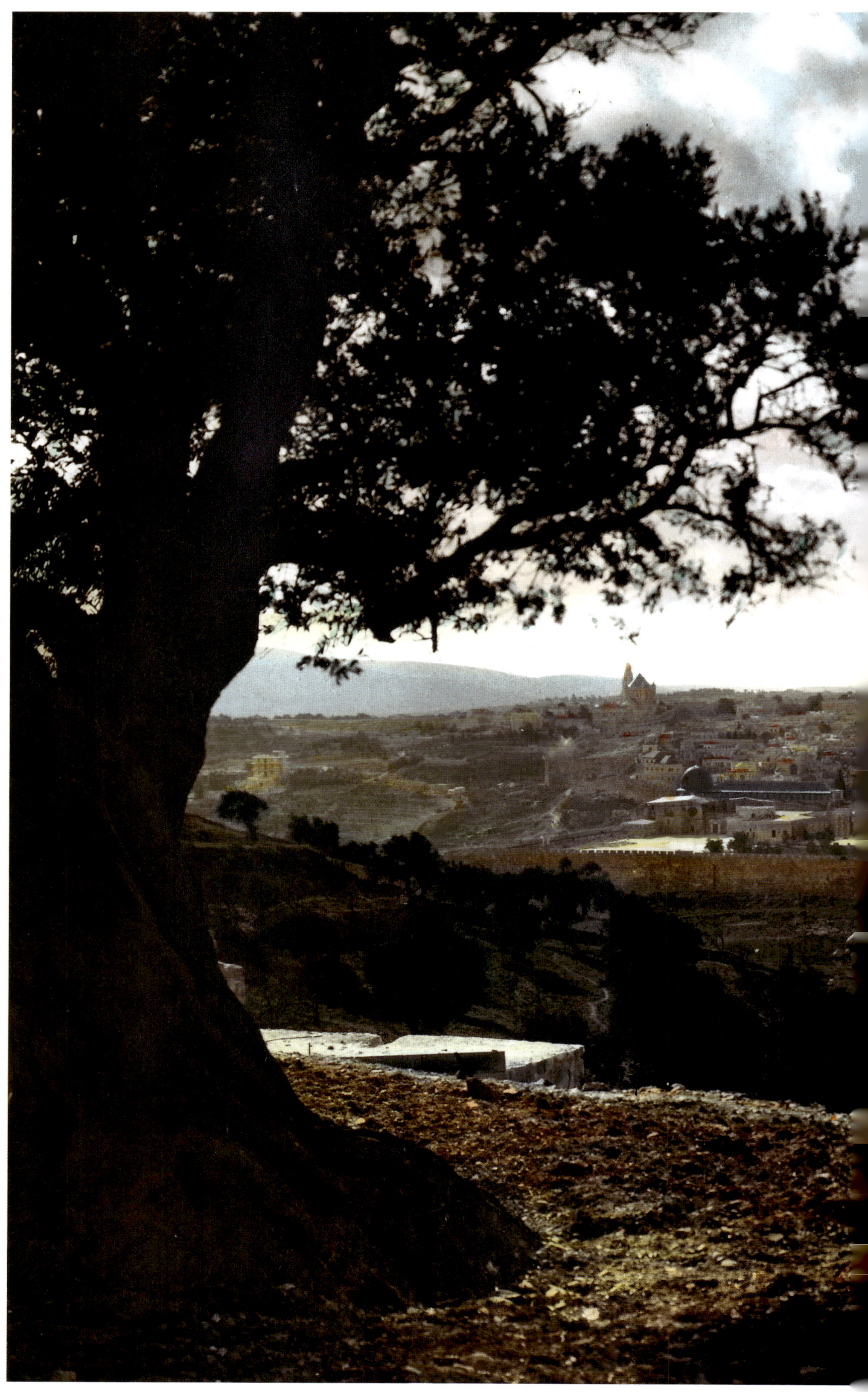

A panorama of the Temple Mount as seen from the Mount of Olives; one of the first full-color photos of the city.
Ralph Fried
1923

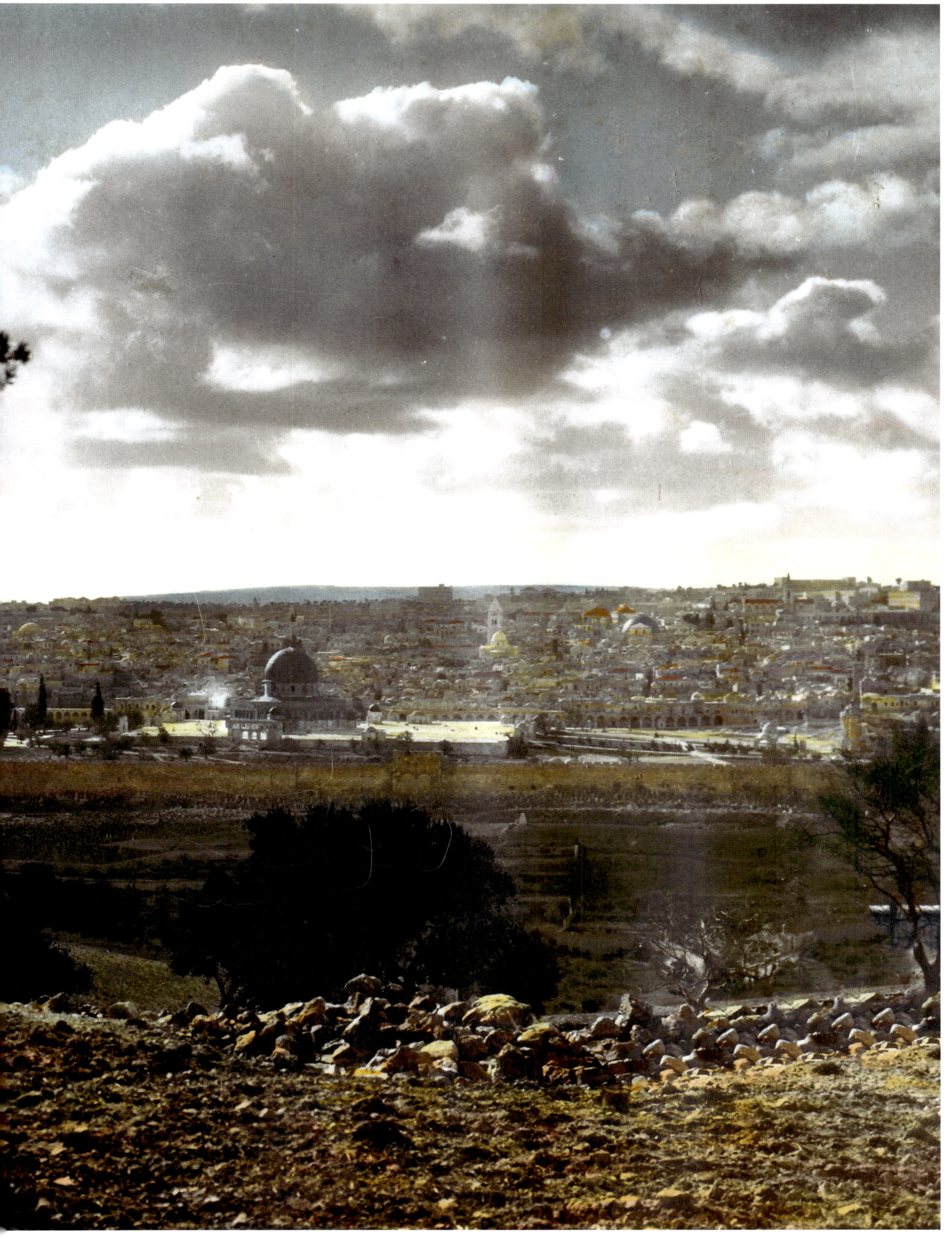

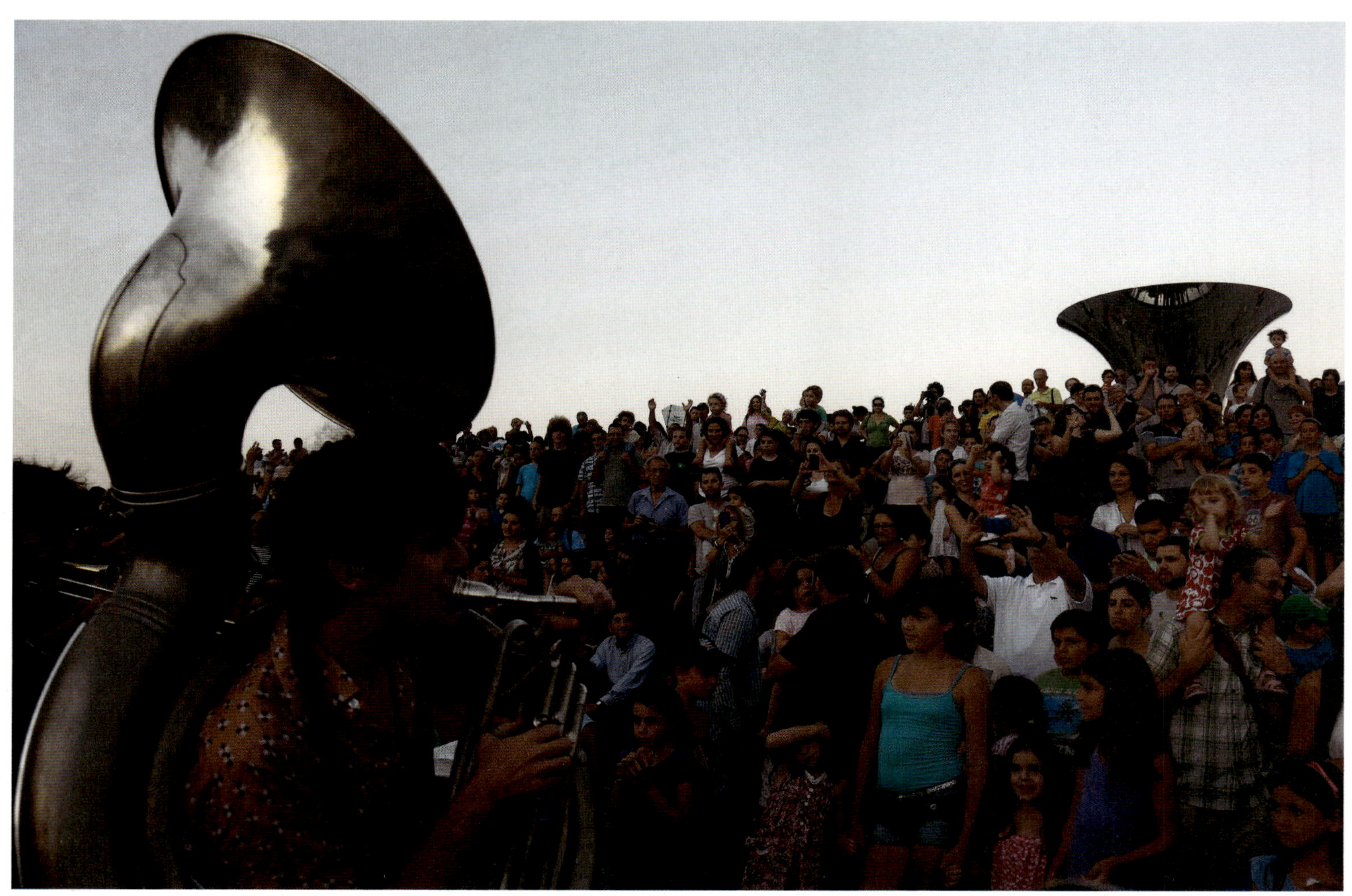

An outdoor concert at the Israel Museum in Jerusalem.
Marc Israel Sellem
2013

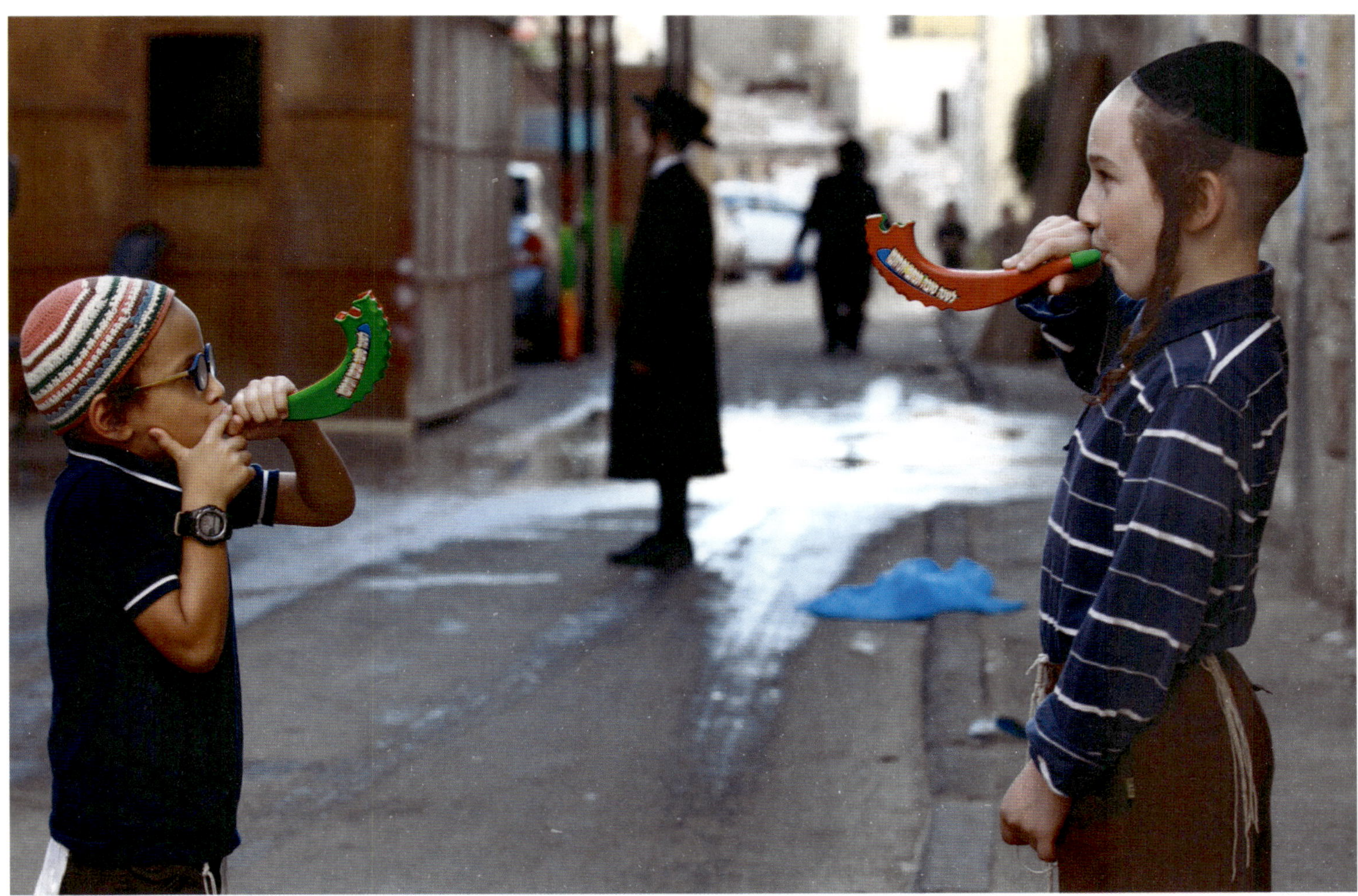

It's never too early to practice for the High Holy Days.

Marc Israel Sellem

2012

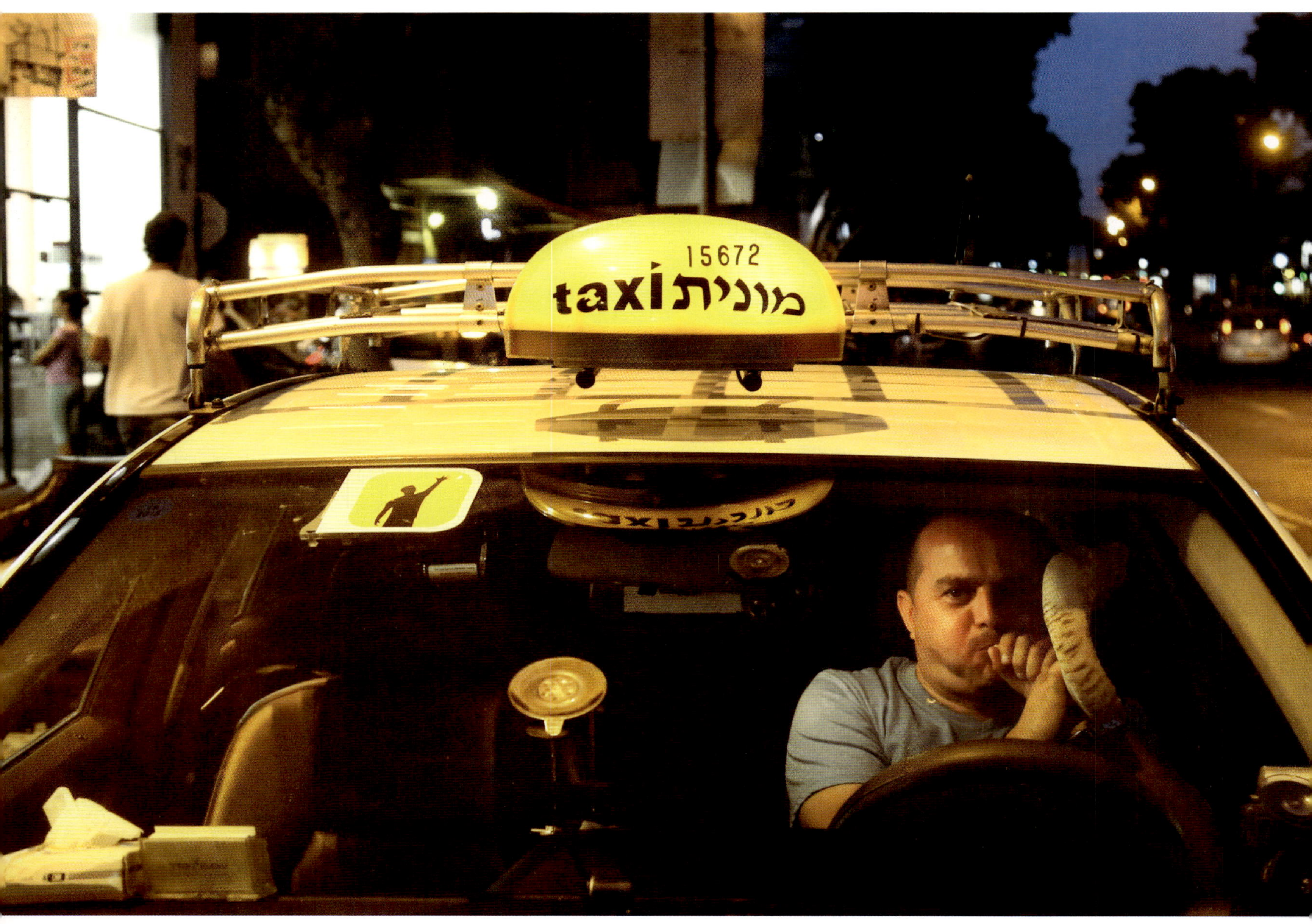

Israeli taxi drivers are
never without a horn.
Marc Israel Sellem
2014

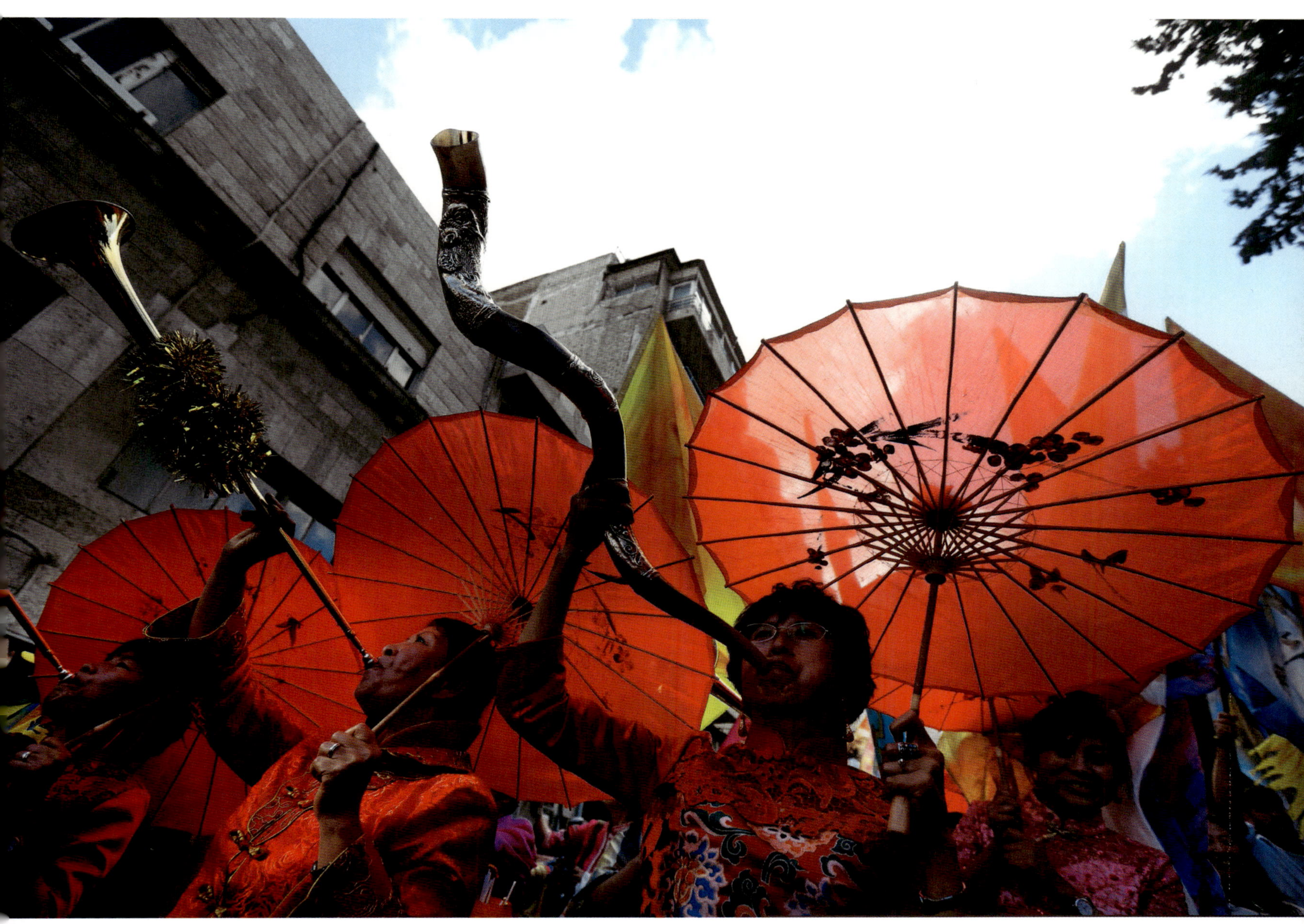

Christians from abroad
celebrate the Feast of
Tabernacles in Jerusalem.

Marc Israel Sellem

2014

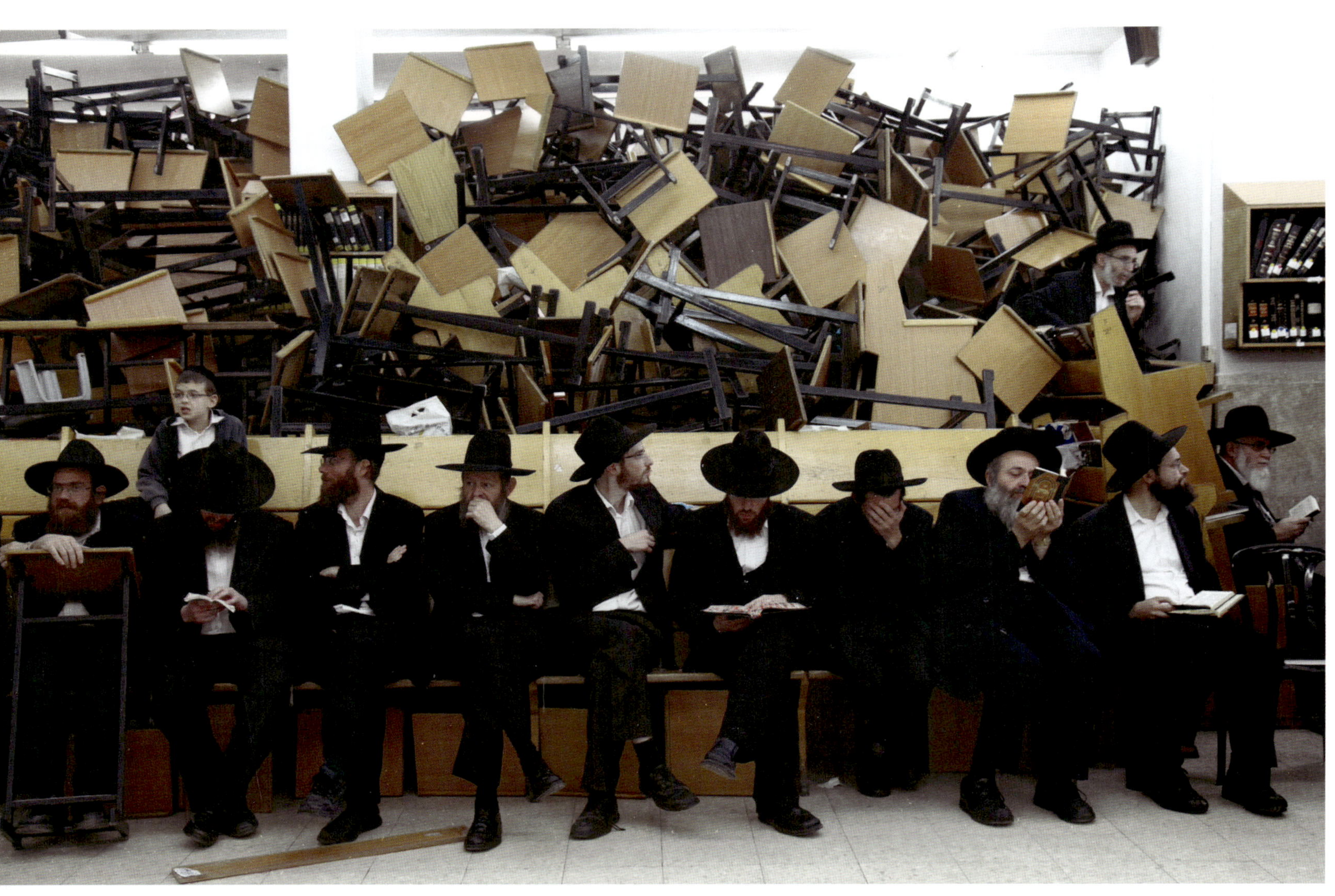

Students at Jerusalem's Mir
Yeshiva.
Marc Israel Sellem
2011

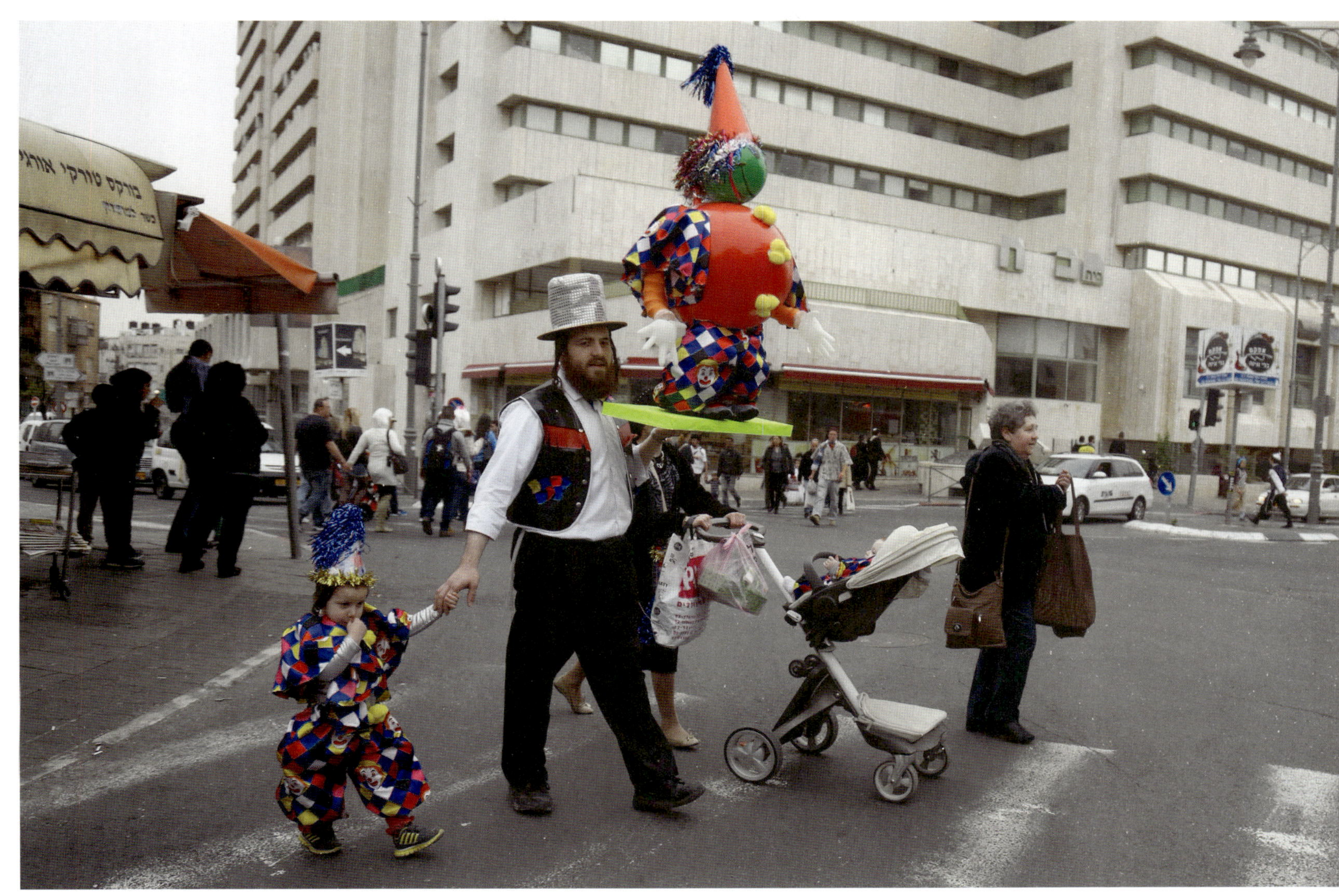

On Purim it's time to
send in the clowns.
Marc Israel Sellem
2014

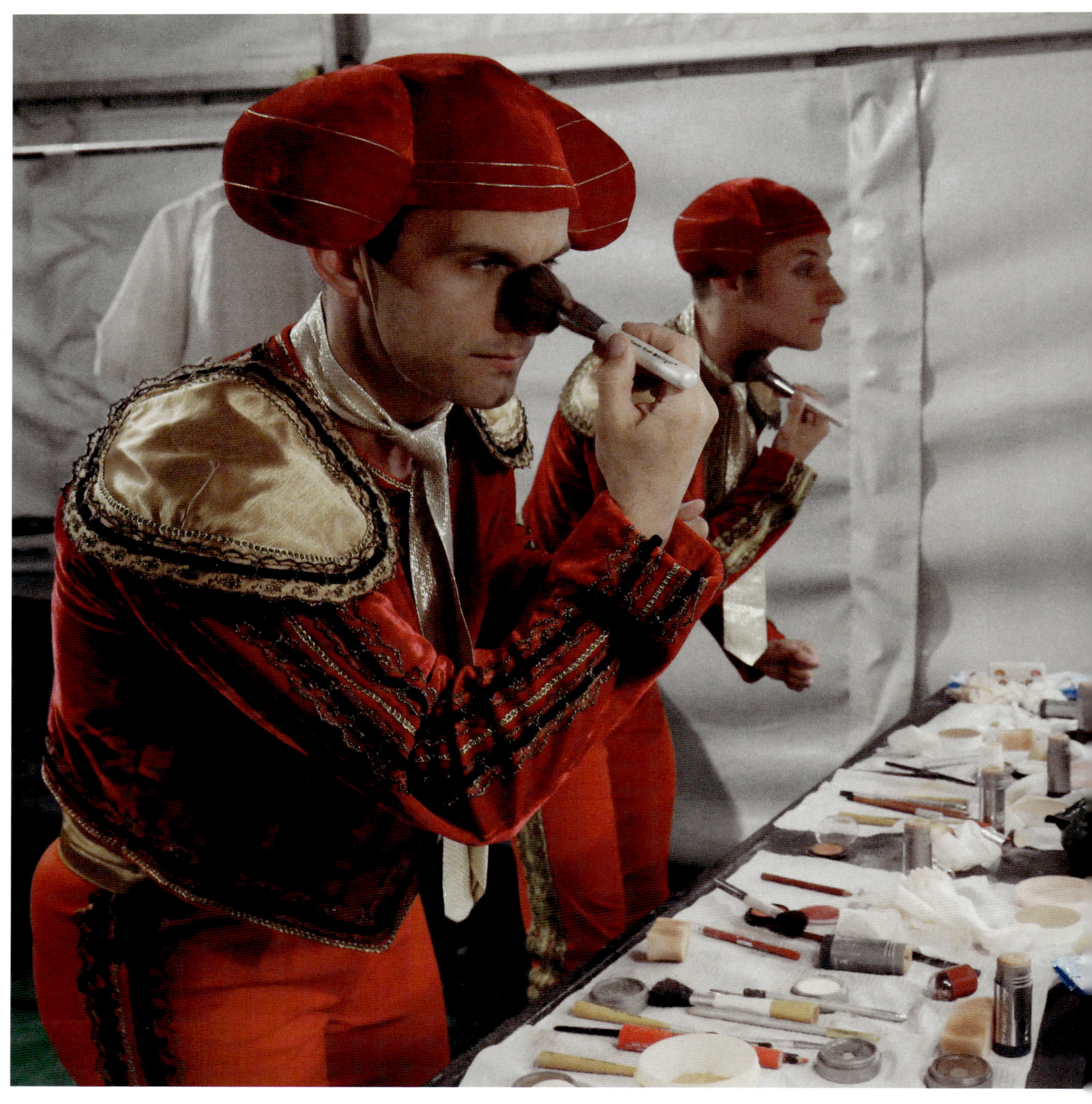

Performers in the opera 'La Traviata' dress backstage at Masada on the Dead Sea.
Marc Israel Sellem
2014

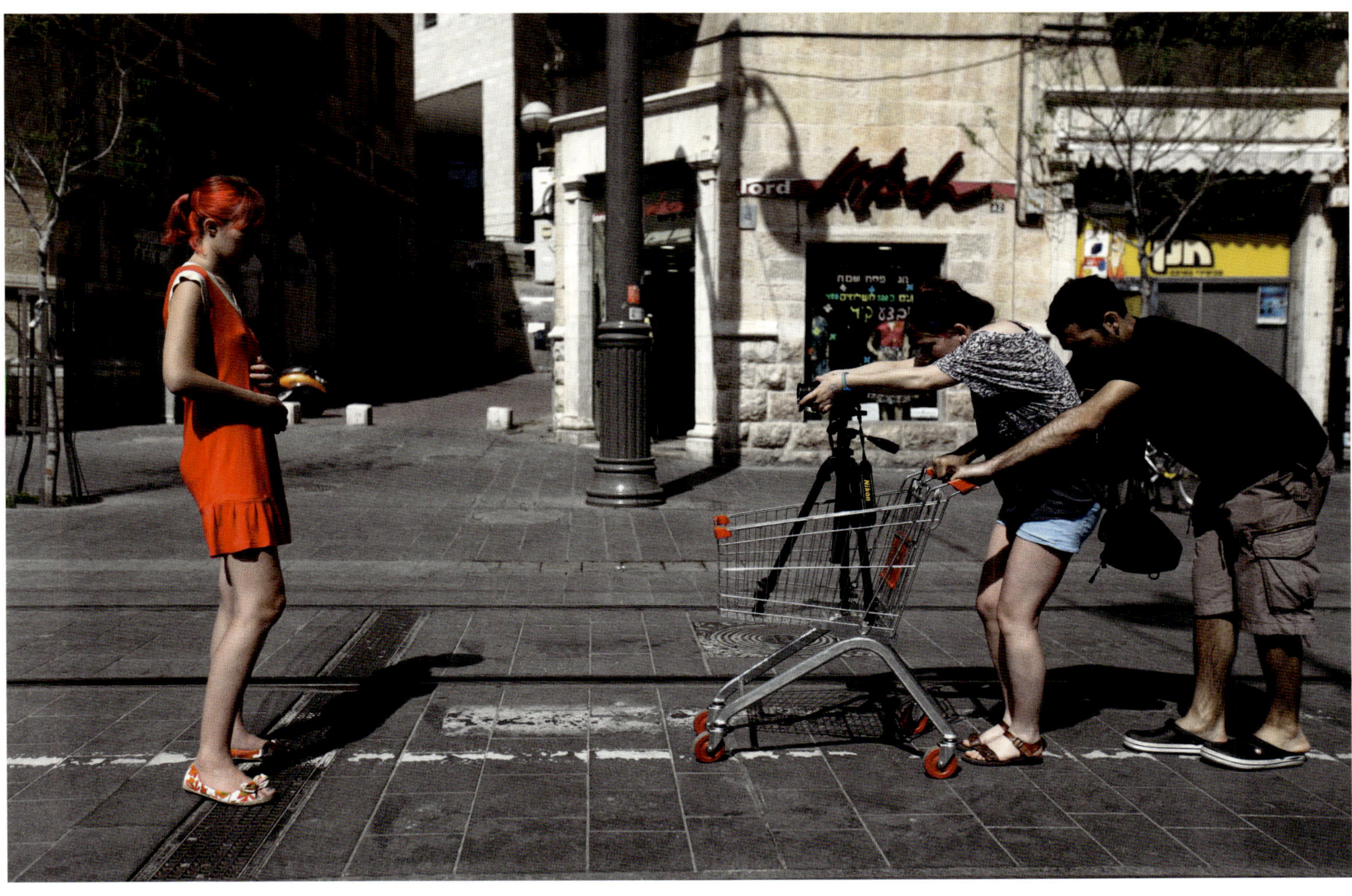

Students film a
presentation in
downtown Jerusalem.
Marc Israel Sellem
2012

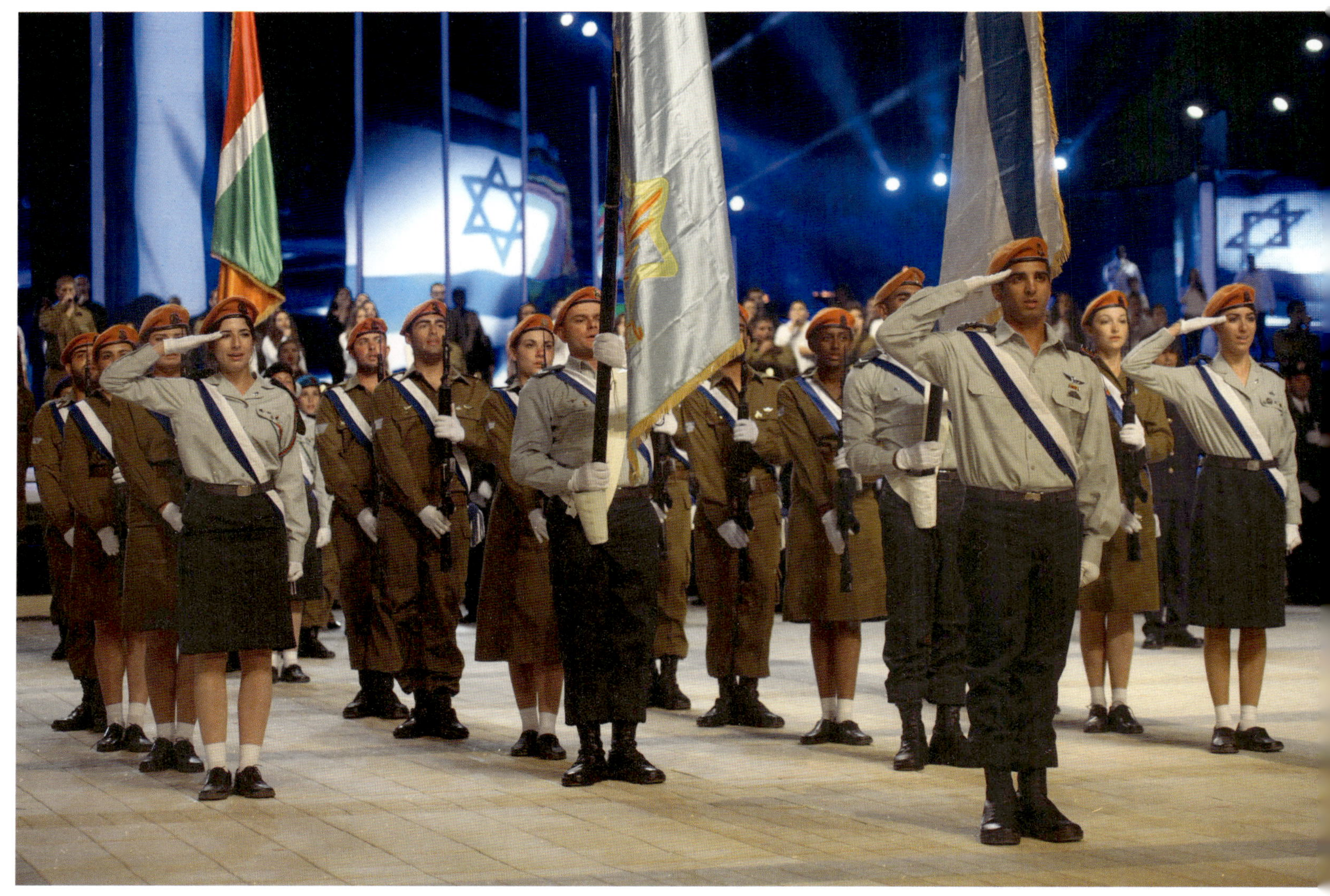

Flag bearers march
and dancers perform
at Independence
Day celebrations on
Jerusalem's Mount Herzl.

Marc Israel Sellem

2013

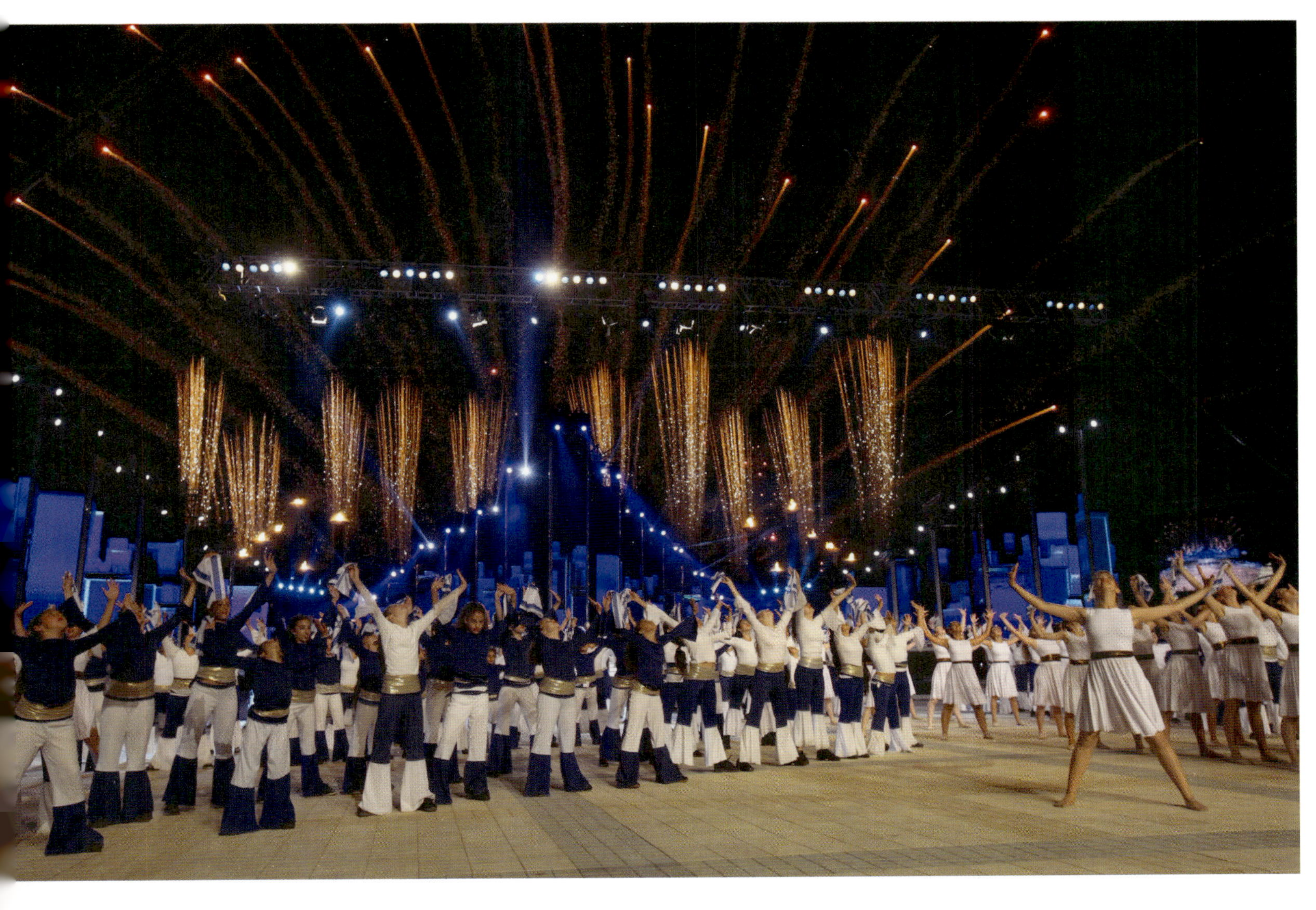

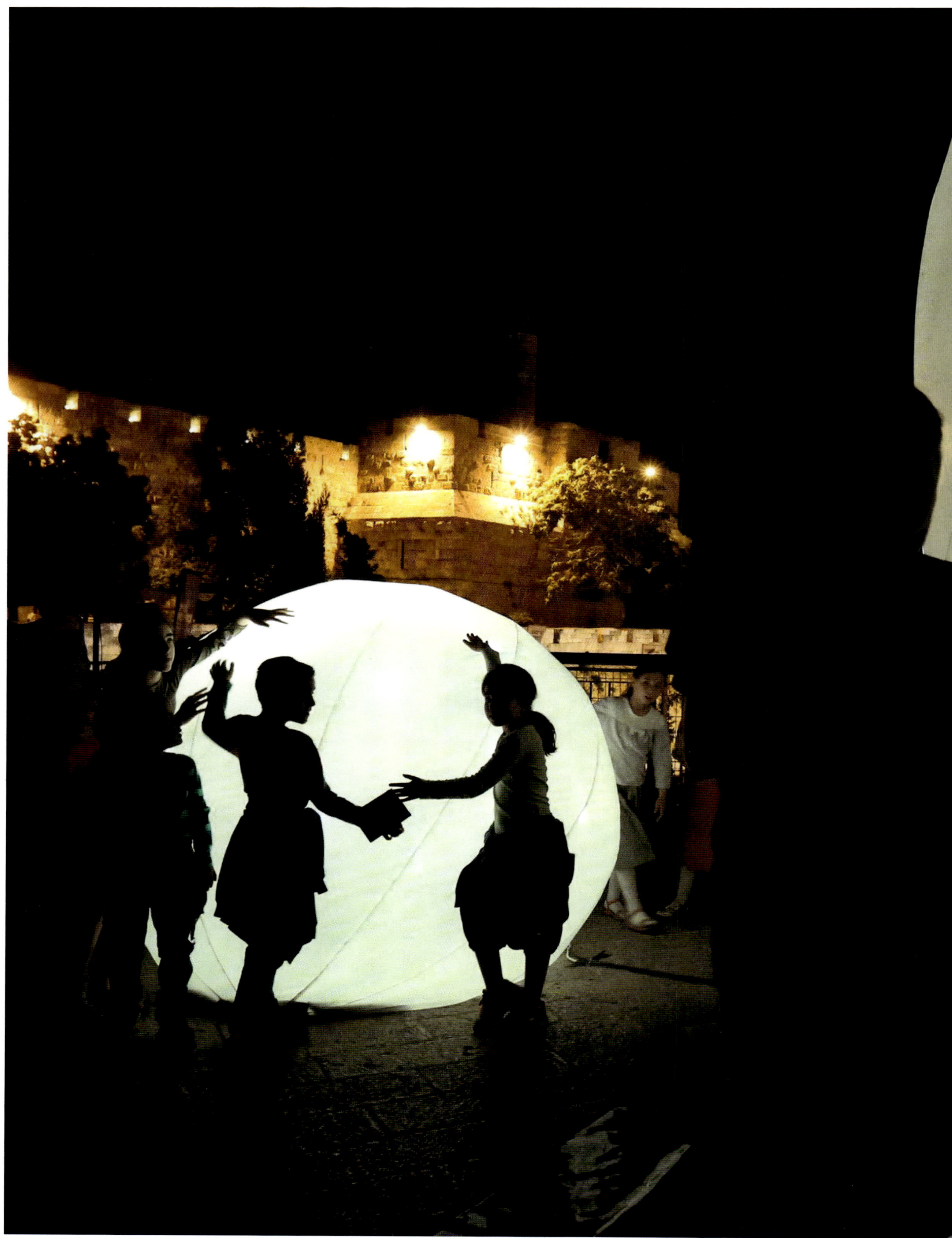

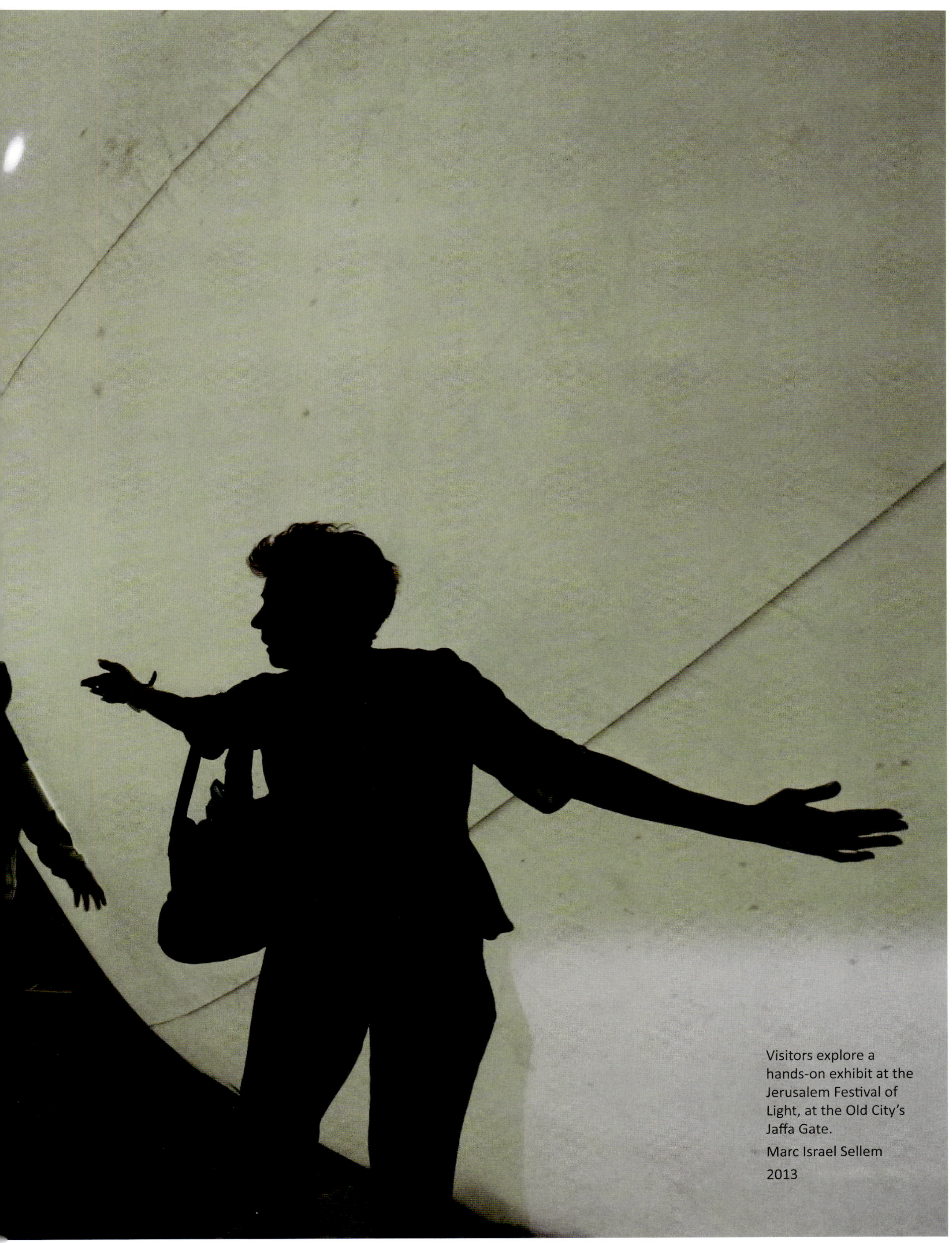

Visitors explore a hands-on exhibit at the Jerusalem Festival of Light, at the Old City's Jaffa Gate.

Marc Israel Sellem

2013

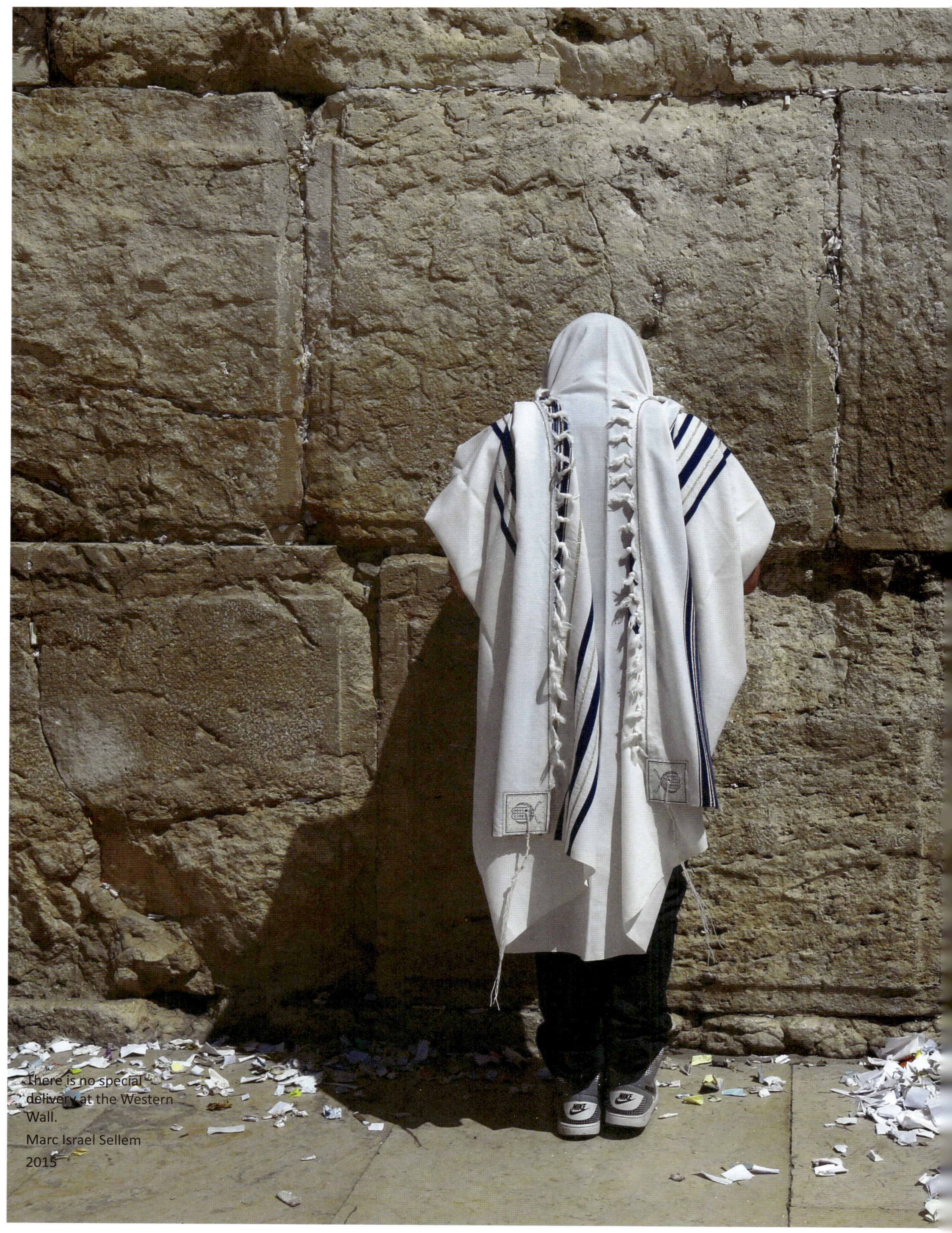

There is no special delivery at the Western Wall.

Marc Israel Sellem
2015

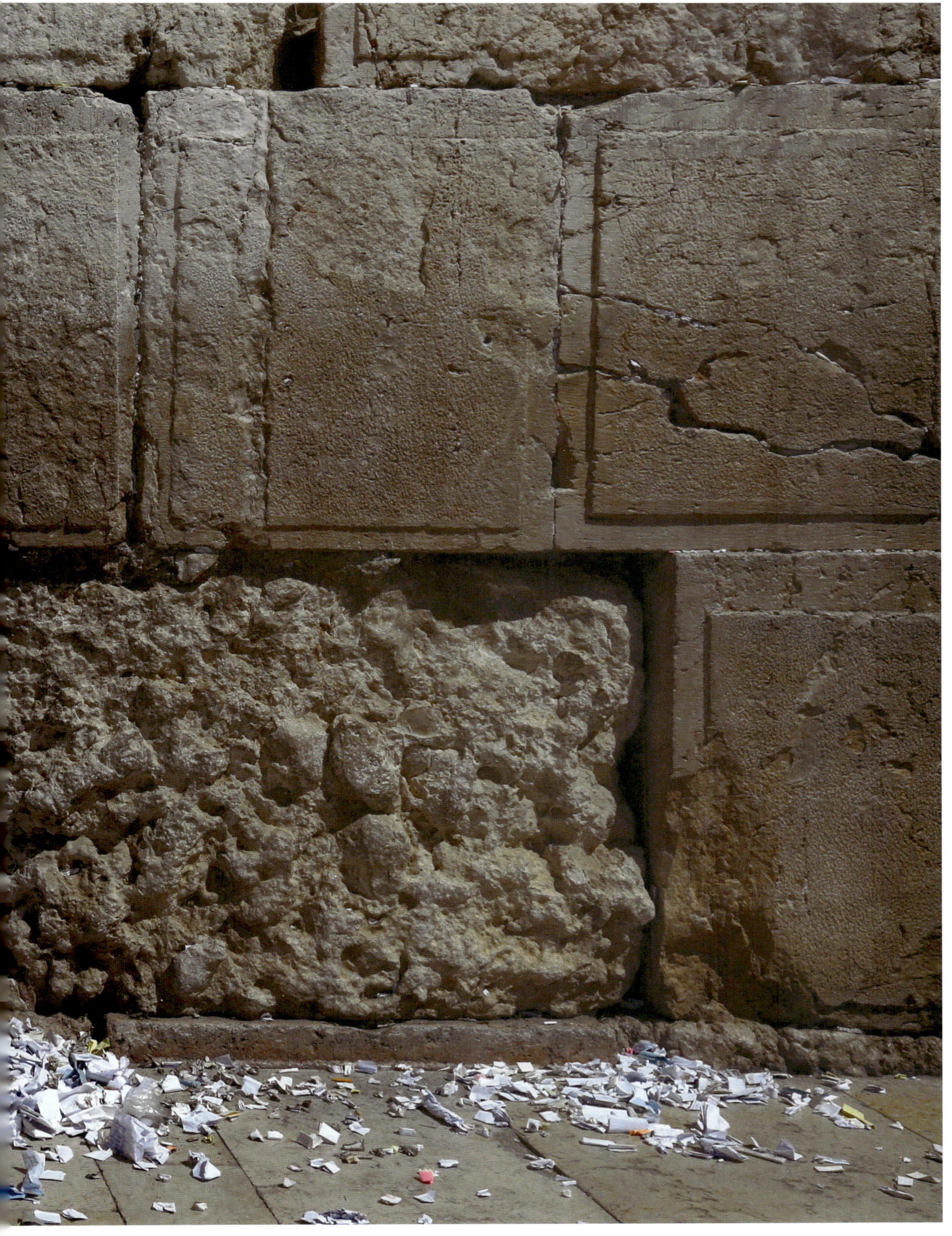

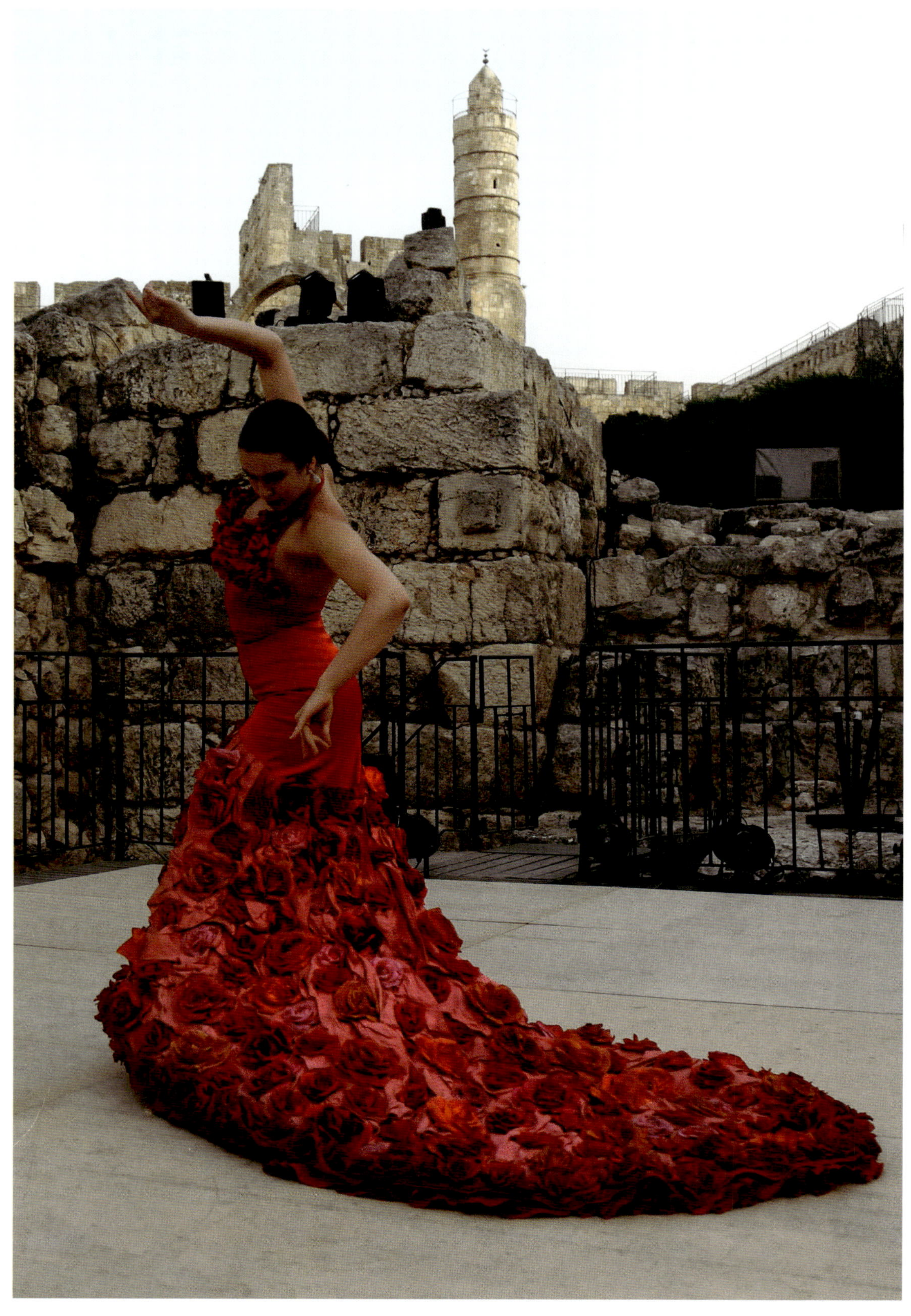

A flamenco dancer warms up before a performance at David's Citadel in Jerusalem's Old City.

Marc Israel Sellem

2013

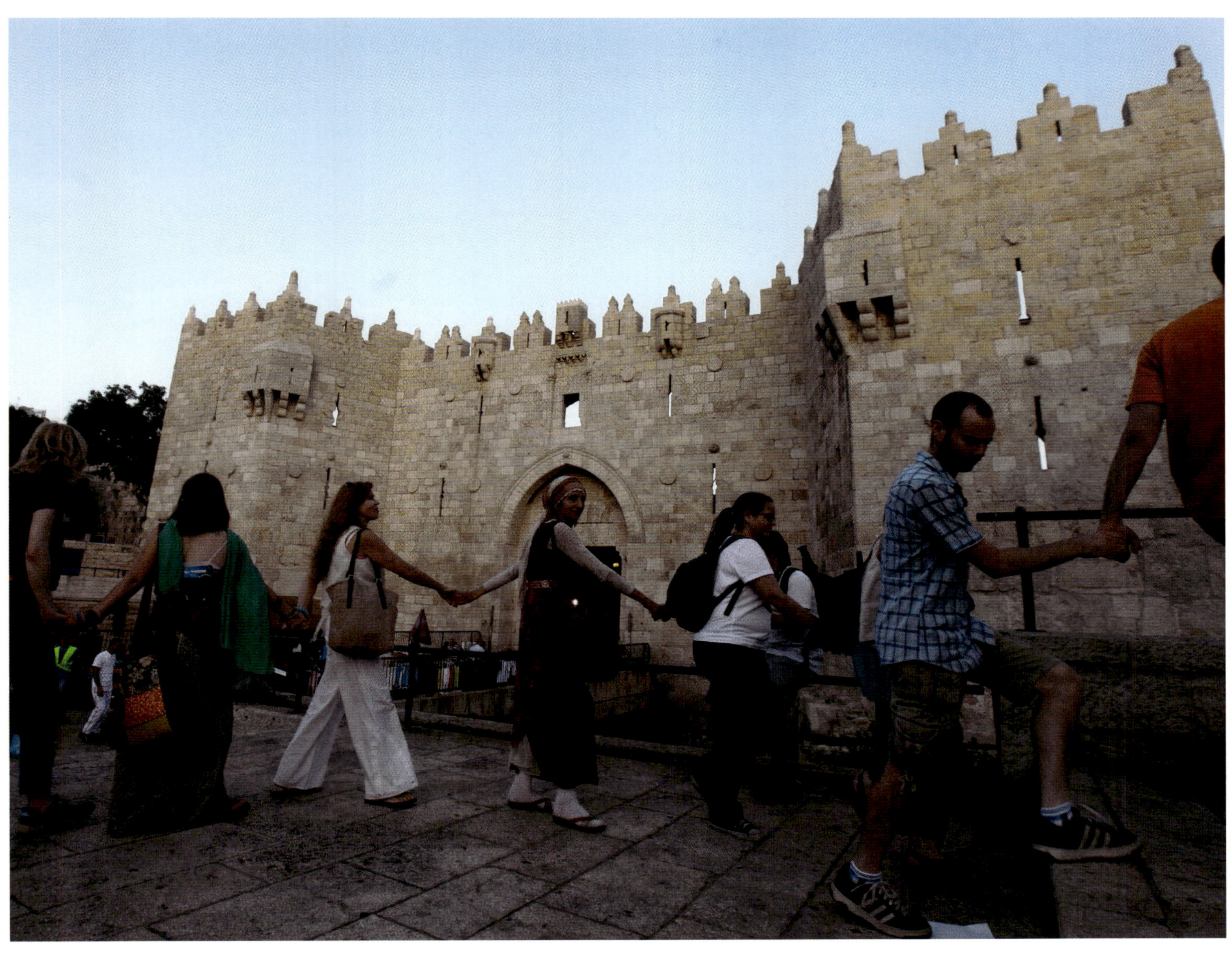

Activists join hands to form a 'ring of peace' around Jerusalem's Old City.

Marc Israel Sellem

2013

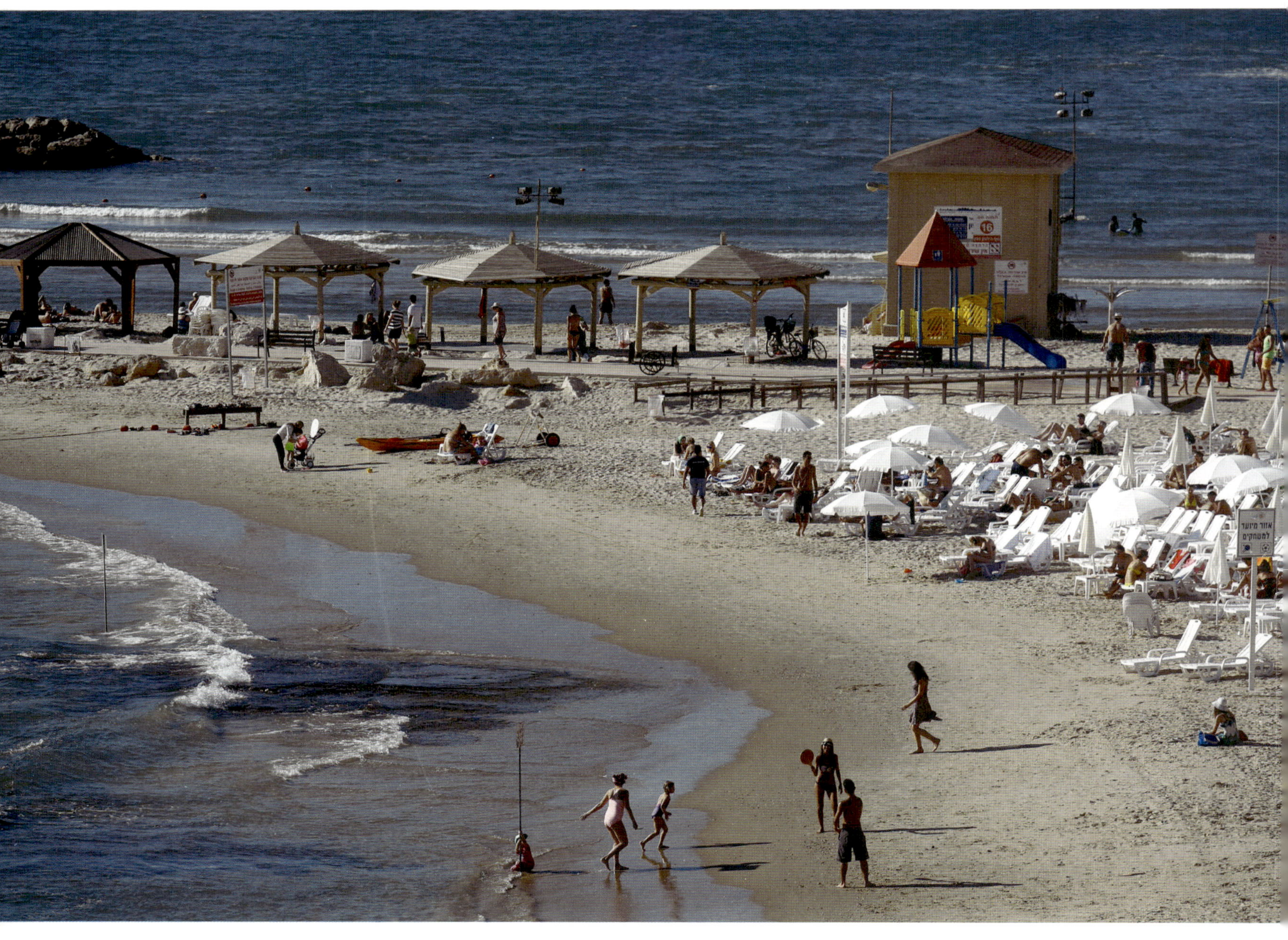

At the beach in Tel Aviv.
Marc Israel Sellem
2014

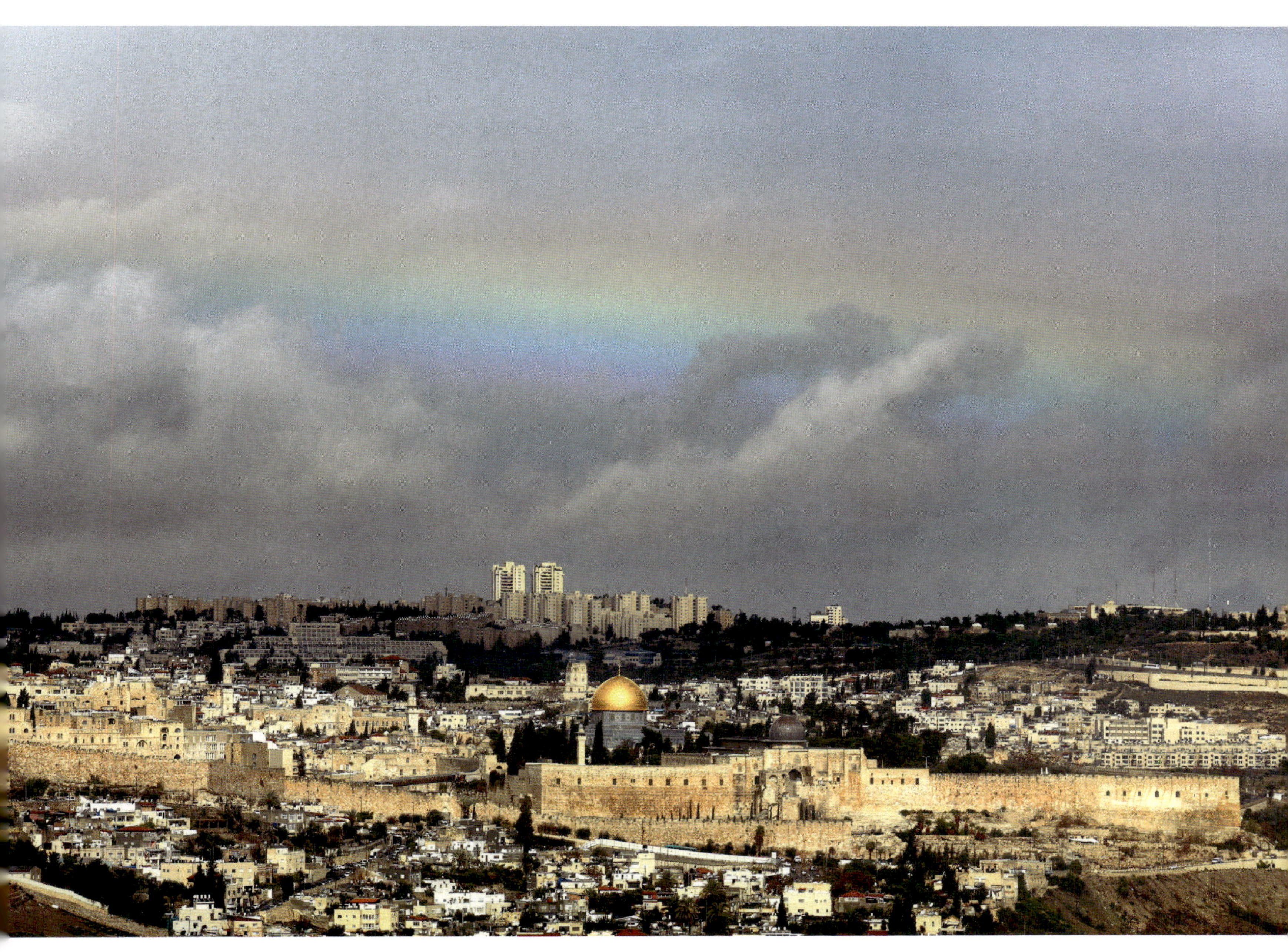

A Jerusalem panorama across the City of David, as seen from the Haas Promenade in the capital's Talpiot neighborhood.

Marc Israel Sellem

2014

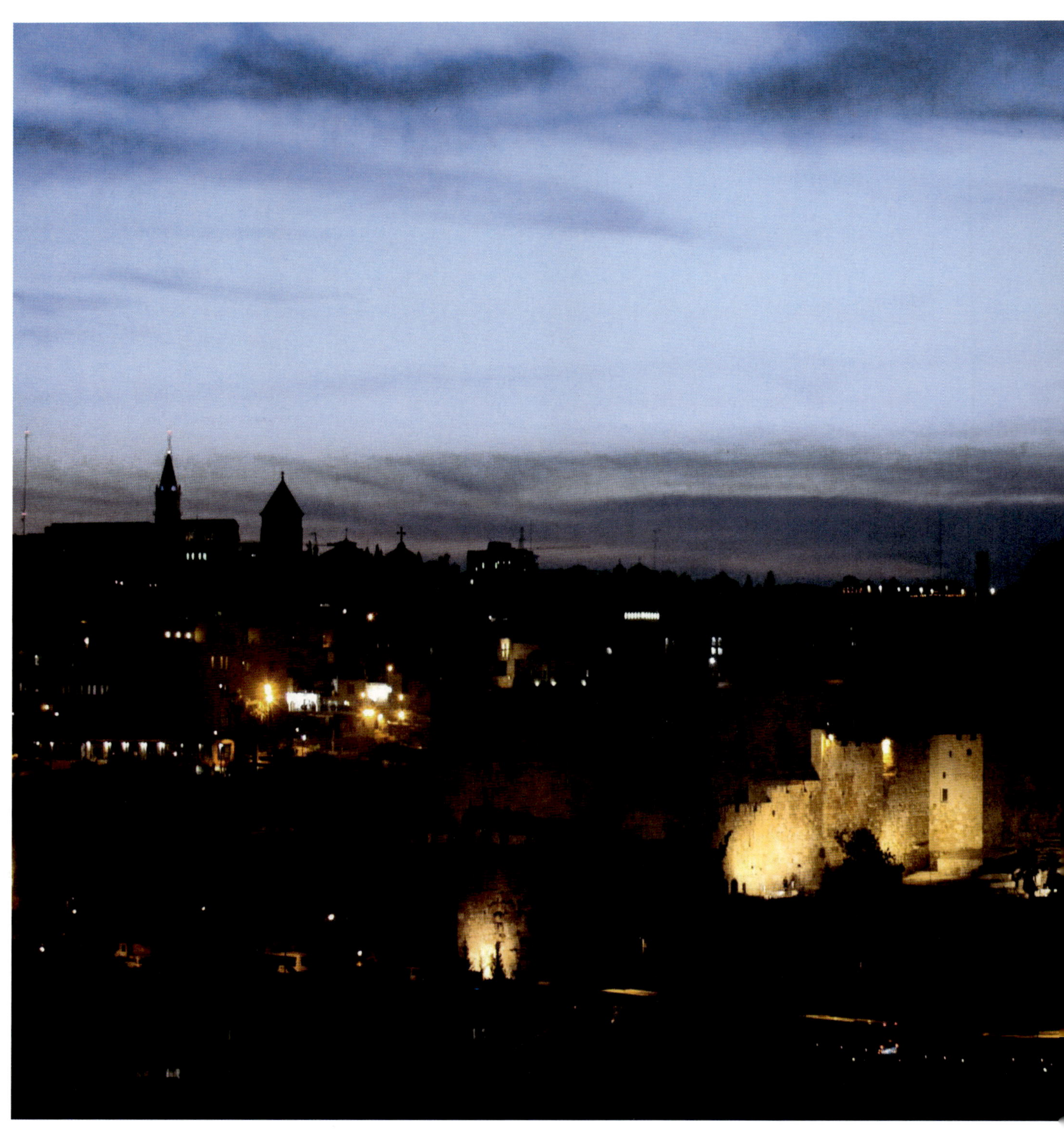

A panorama of Jerusalem's Old City as seen from the Mount Of Olives.

Marc Israel Sellem

2012

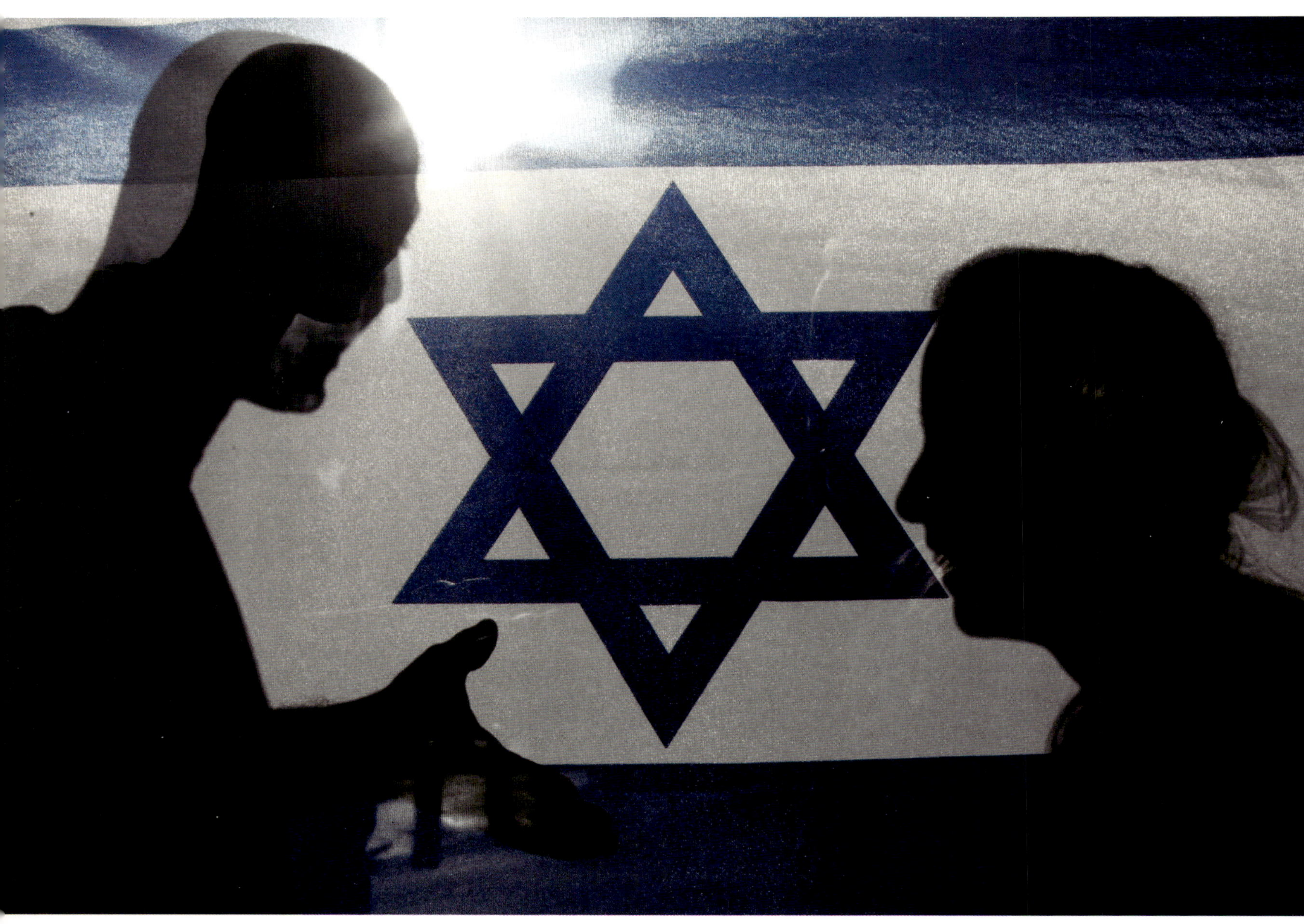

Independence Day revelers
chat on Jerusalem's Ben-Yehuda
Street pedestrian mall.

Marc Israel Sellem

2012

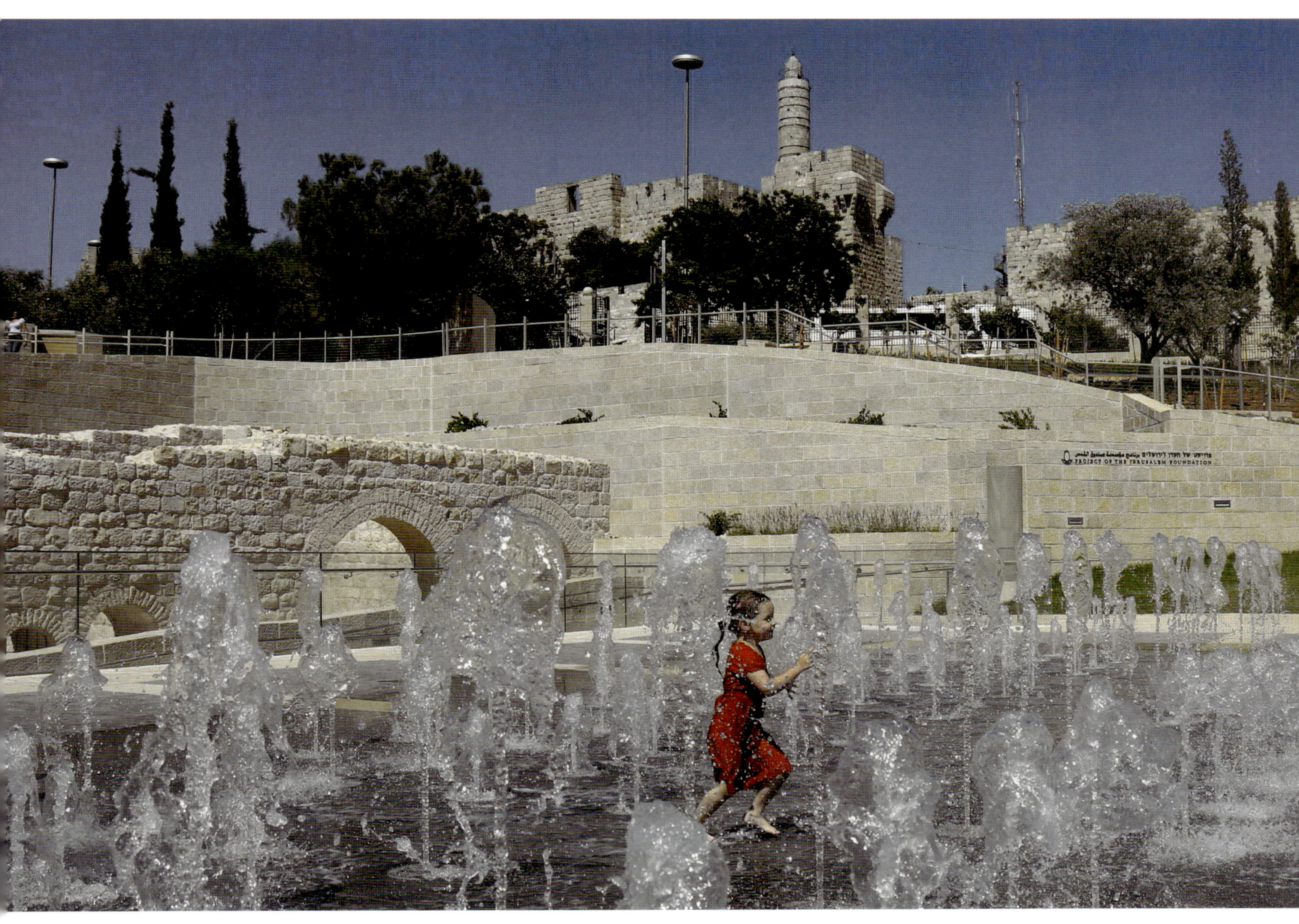

The best way to cool off in Jerusalem is at Teddy Park opposite the Old City.

Marc Israel Sellem

2013

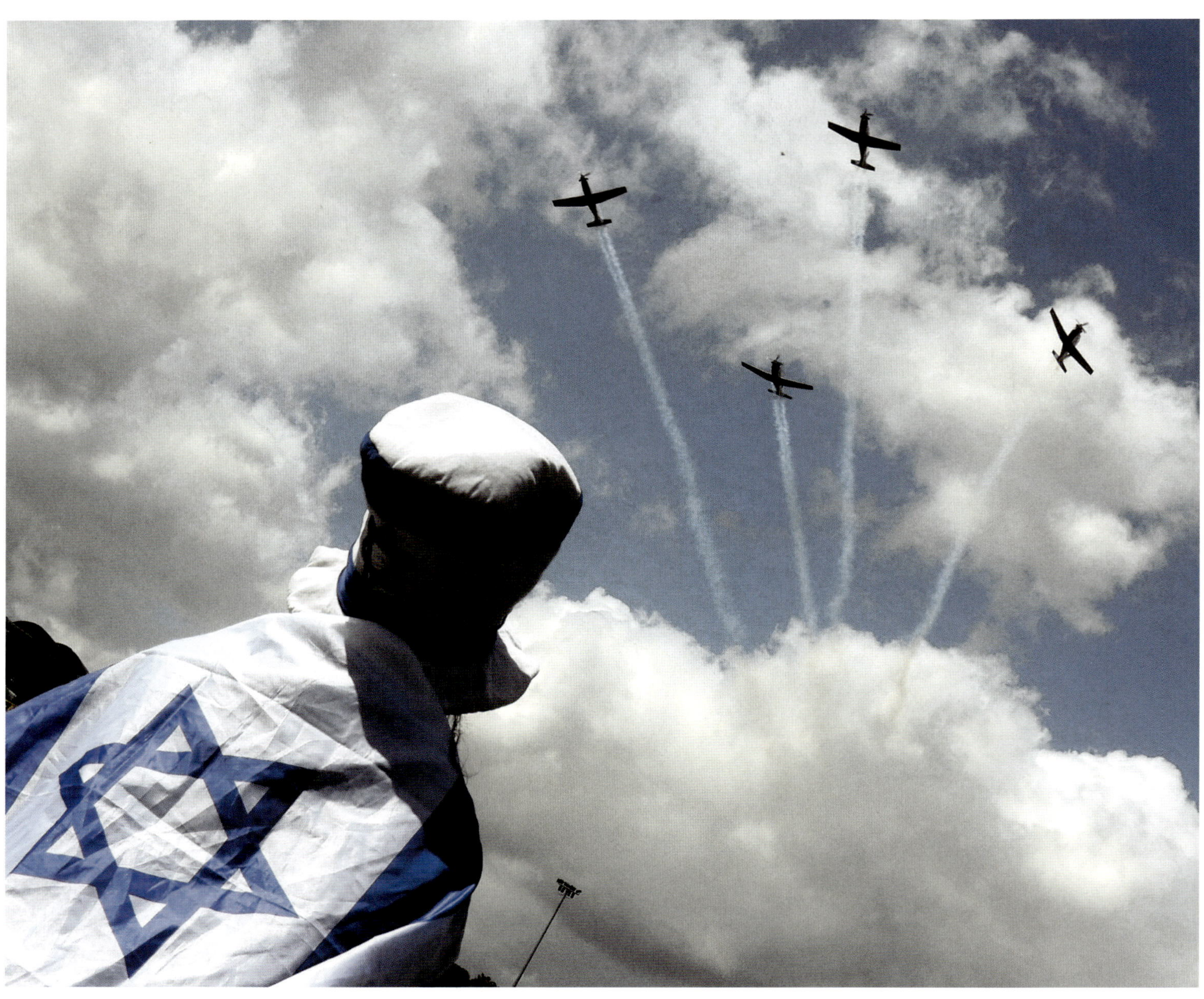

An Independence Day
reveler watches the air
force aerobatic team
perform over Jerusalem.
Marc Israel Sellem
2015

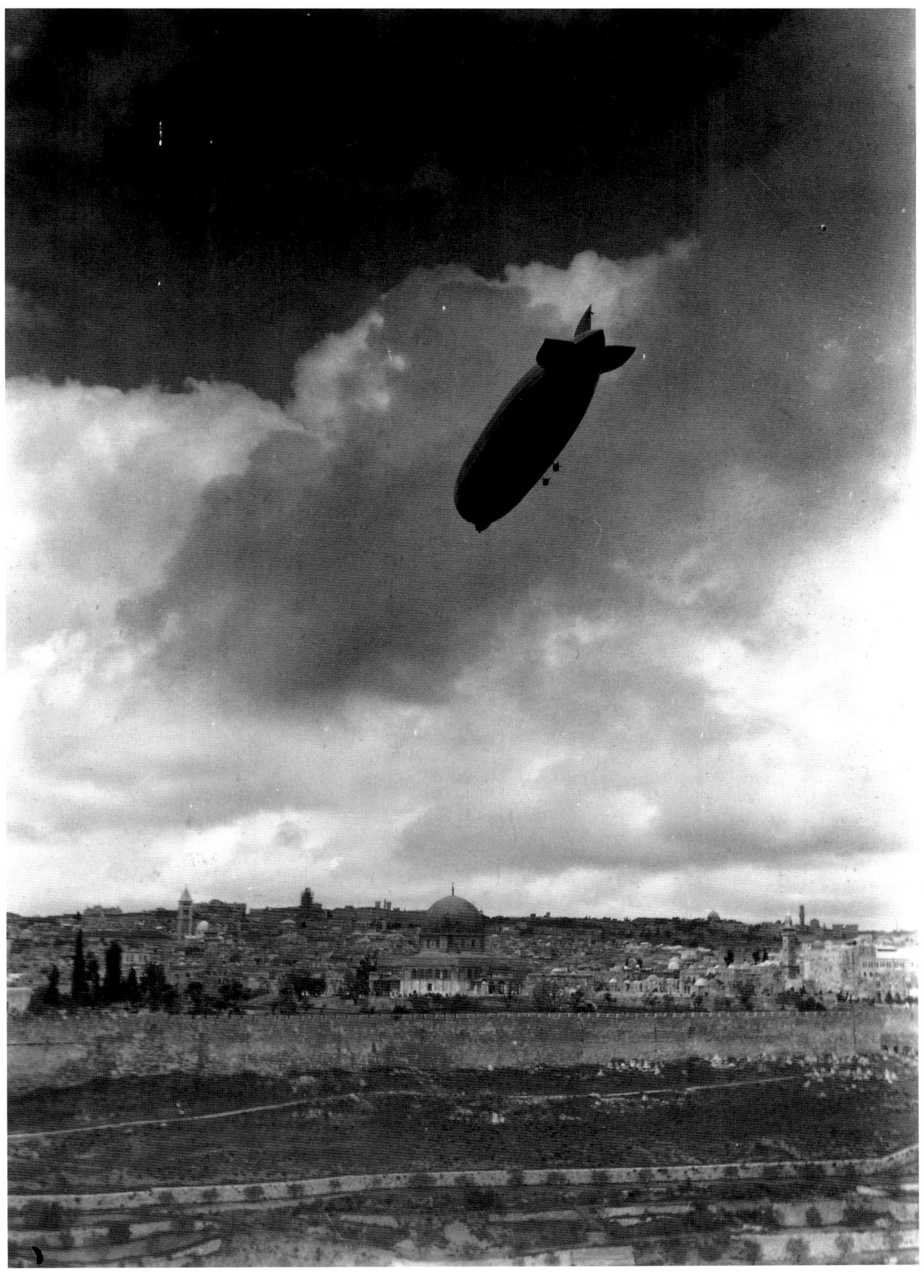

The Graf Zeppelin passes over Jerusalem on its world tour.

Ralph Fried

1929

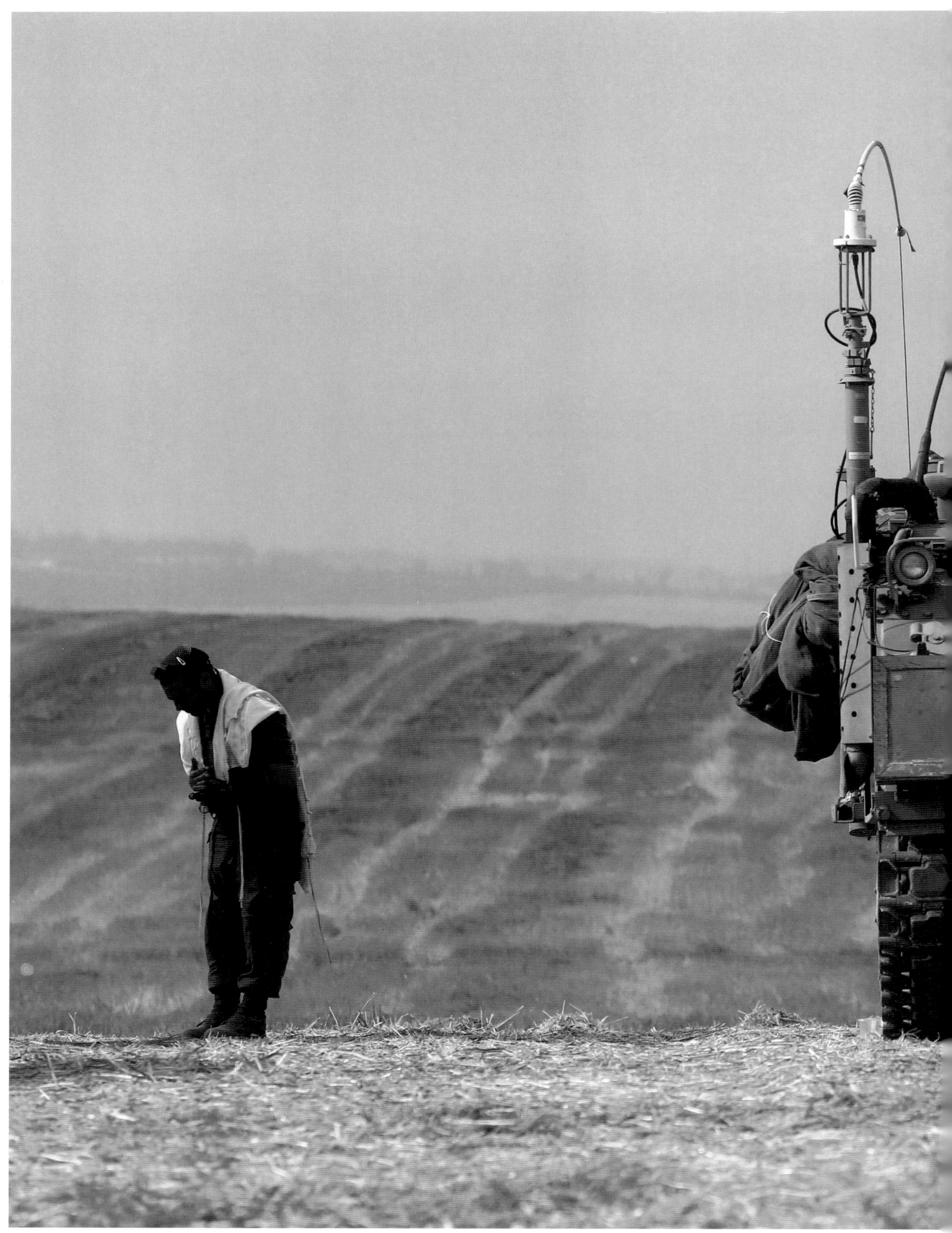

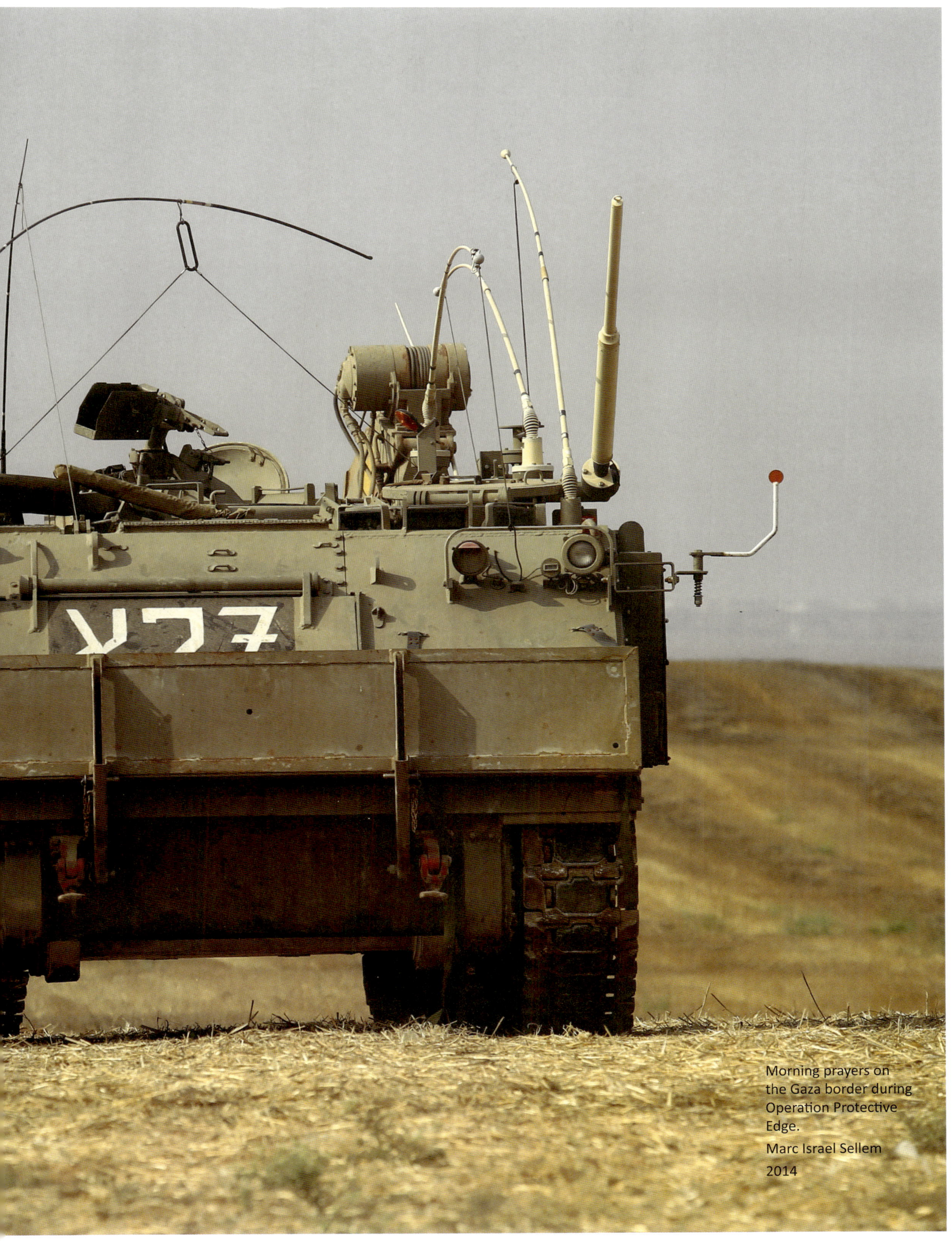

Morning prayers on the Gaza border during Operation Protective Edge.

Marc Israel Sellem

2014

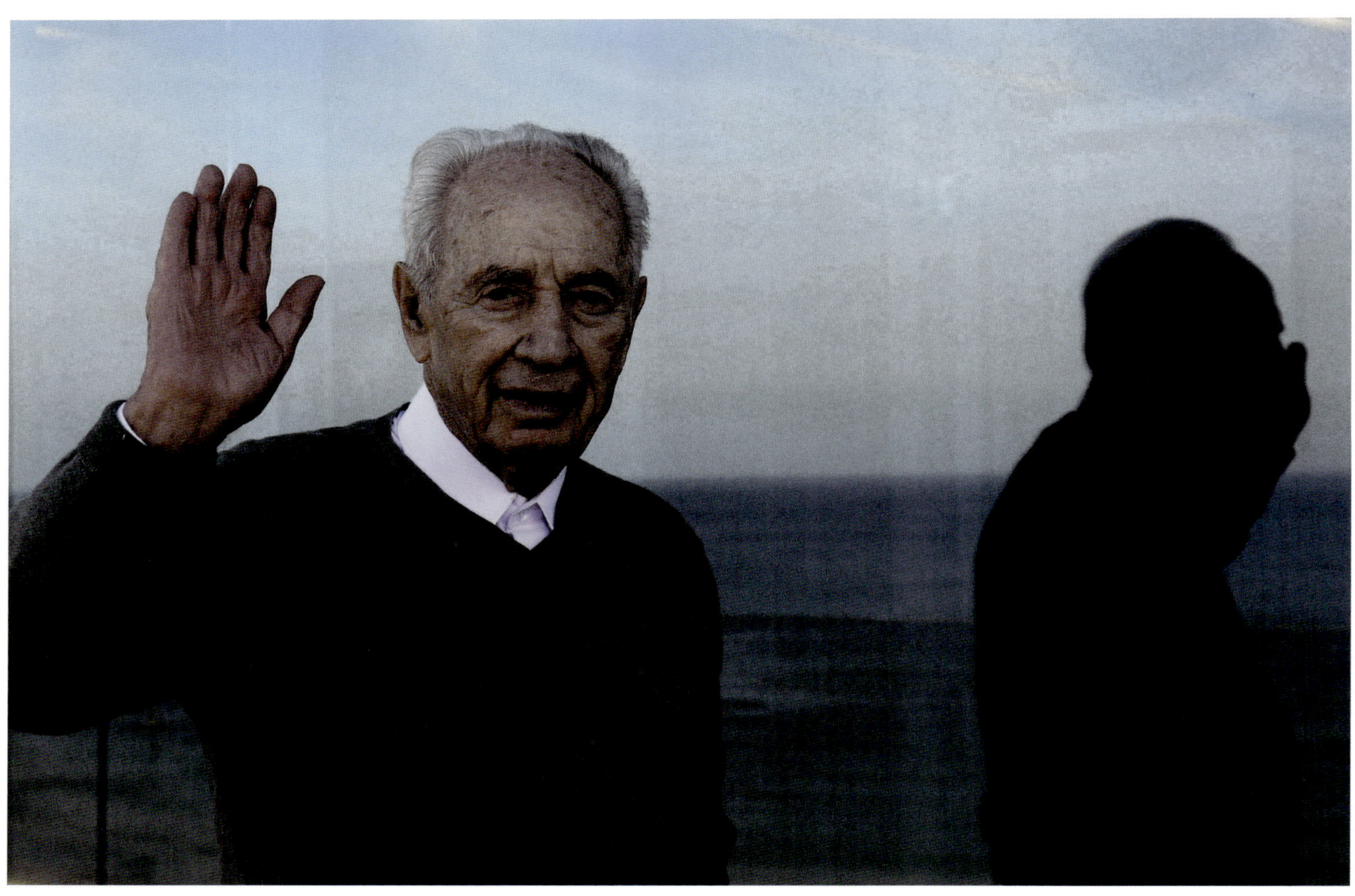

Former president Shimon Peres waves from the porch of the Peres Center for Peace in Jaffa.

Marc Israel Sellem

2014

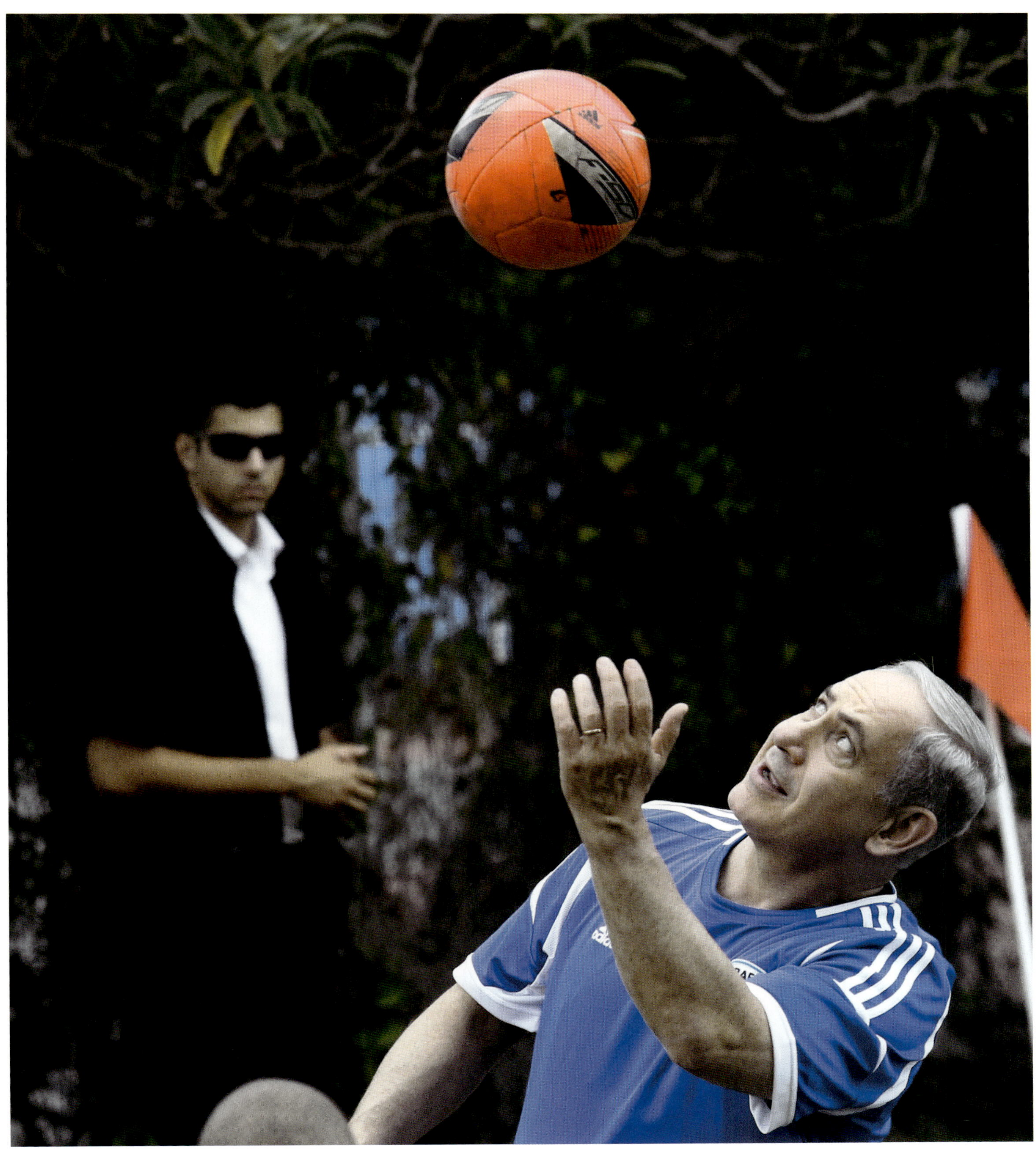

Prime Minister Benjamin Netanyahu plays ball under tight security.

Marc Israel Sellem

2013

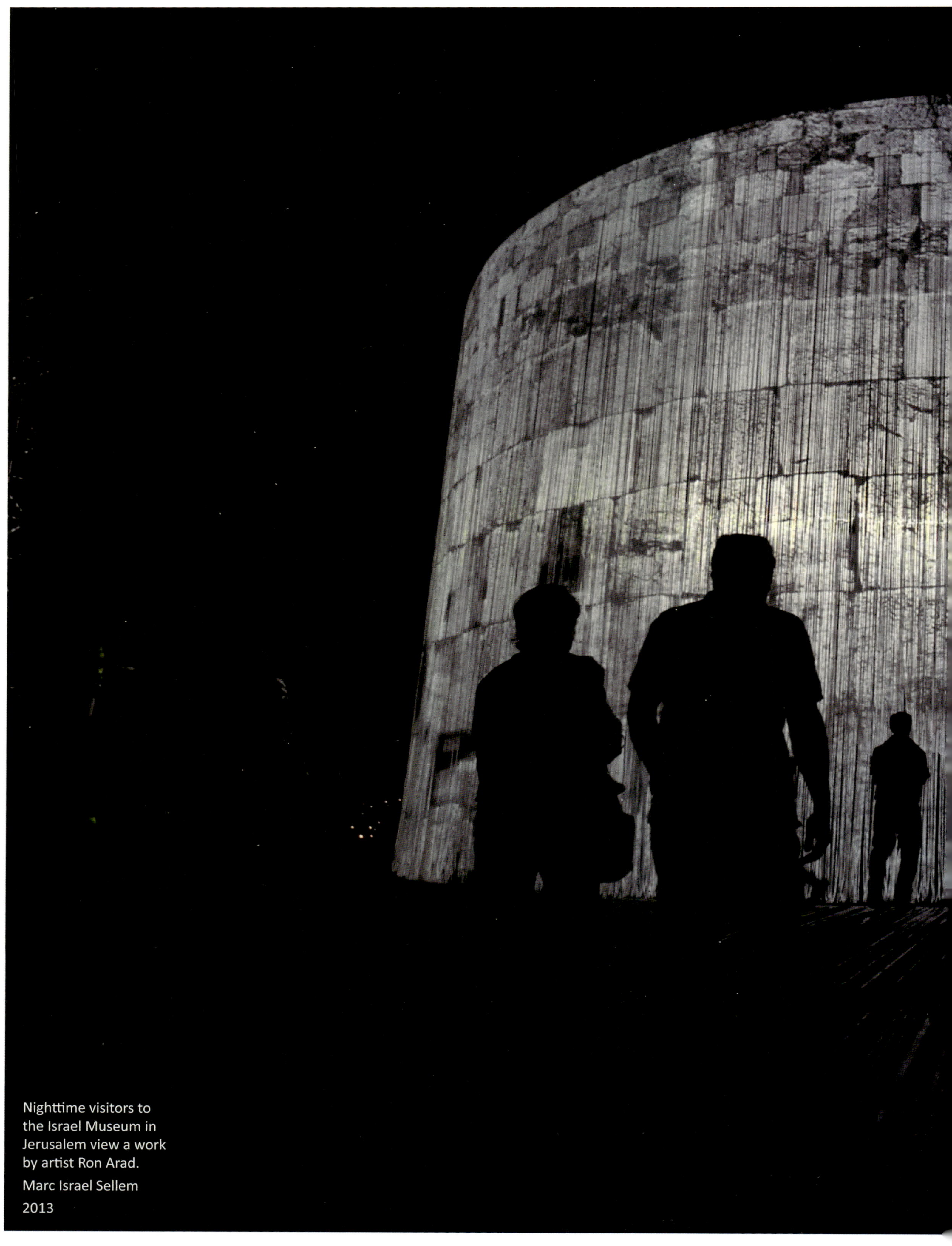
Nighttime visitors to the Israel Museum in Jerusalem view a work by artist Ron Arad.
Marc Israel Sellem
2013

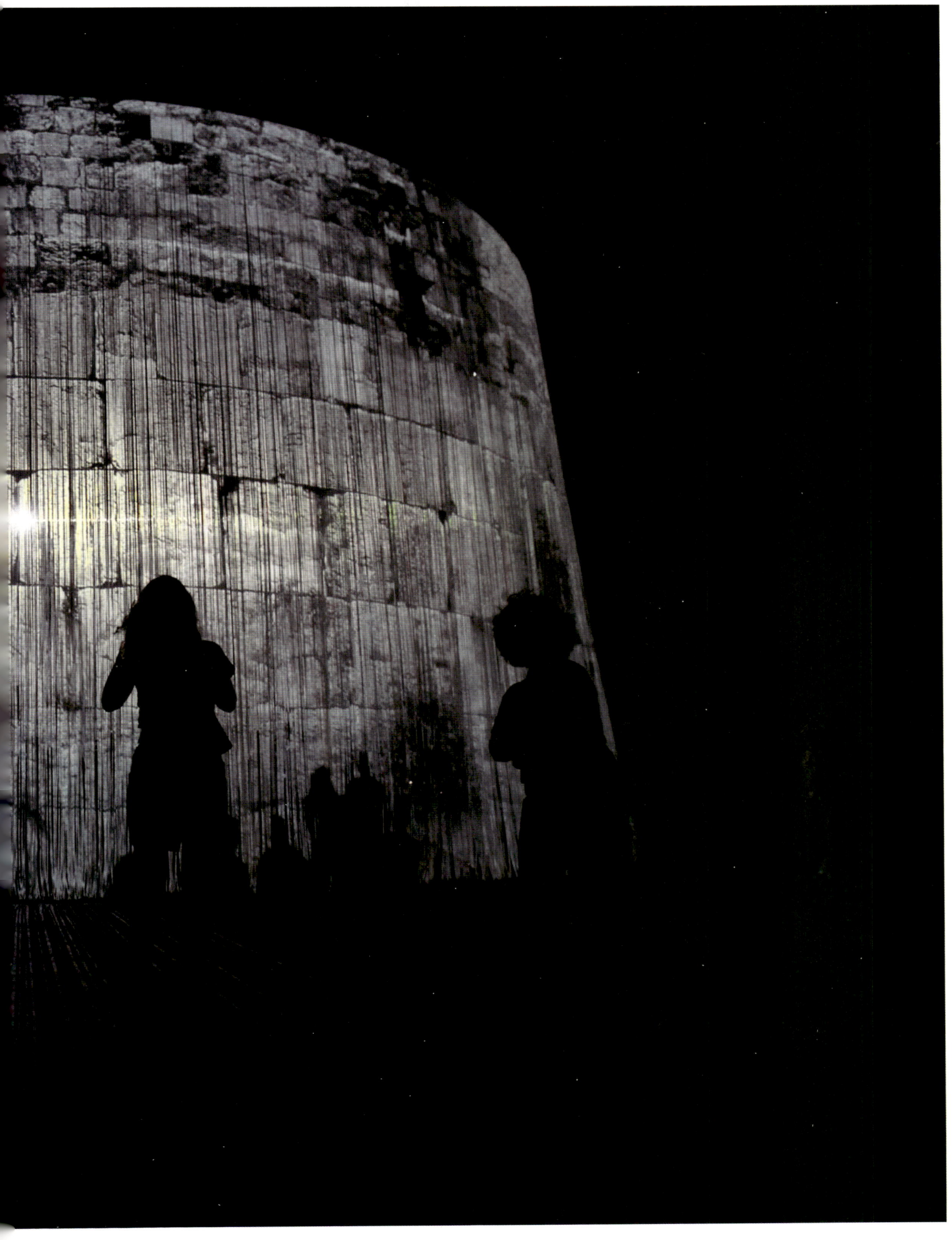

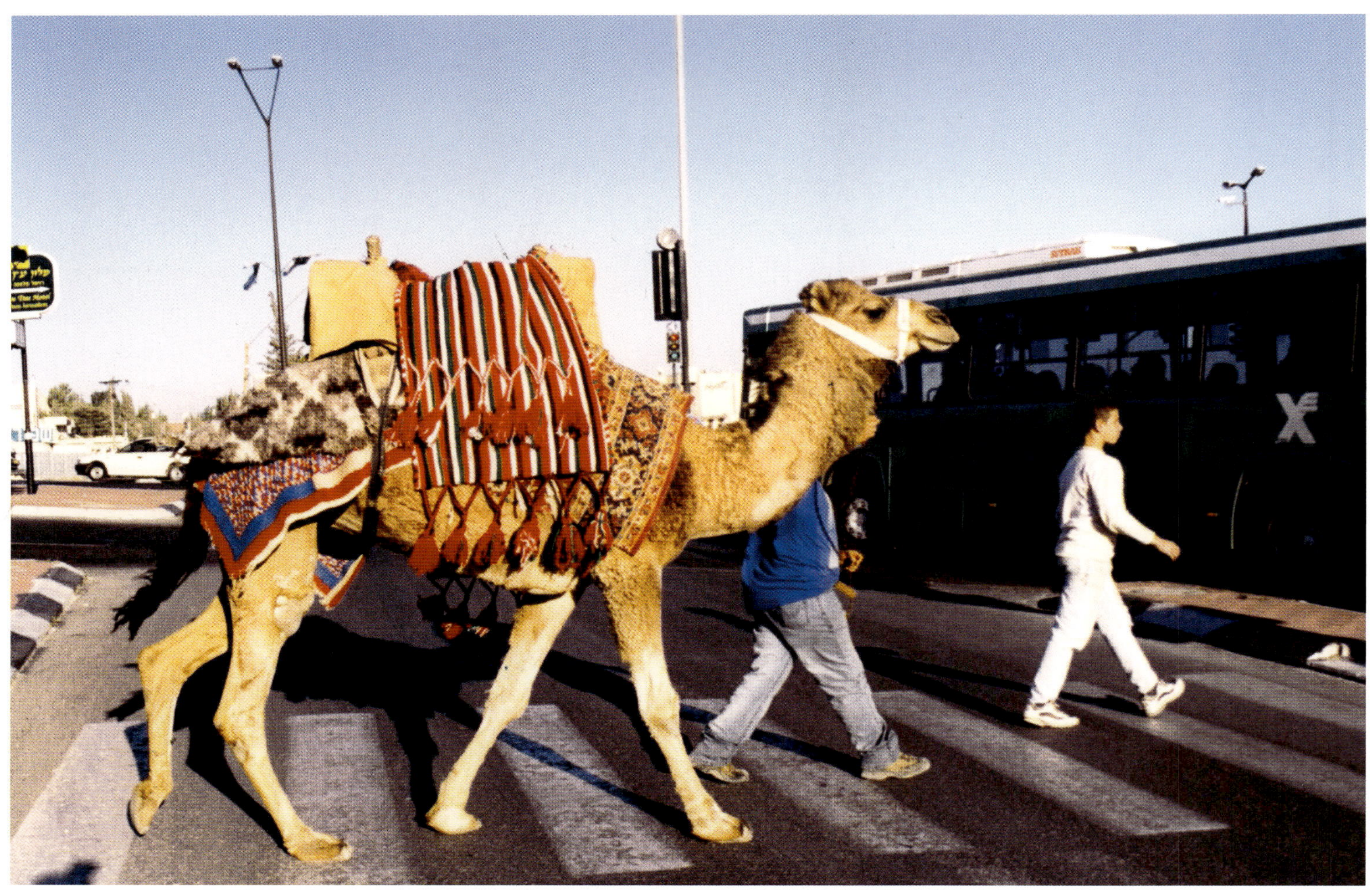

A polite camel uses a crosswalk in Jerusalem's Ramot Eshkol neighborhood.
Ariel Jerozolimski
2001

A traveler enjoys ice cream at a Jerusalem bus stop.
Ariel Jerozolimski
2001

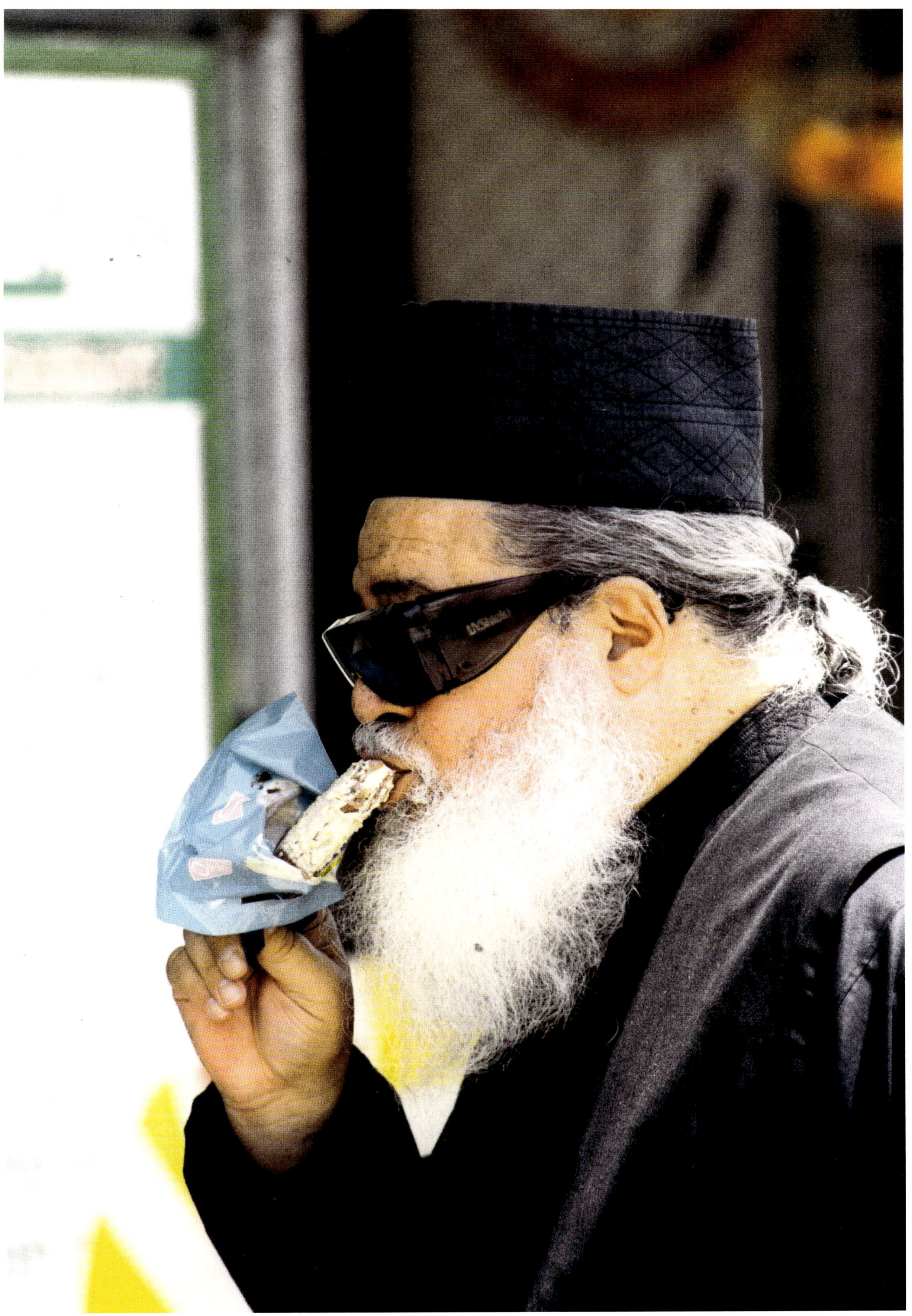

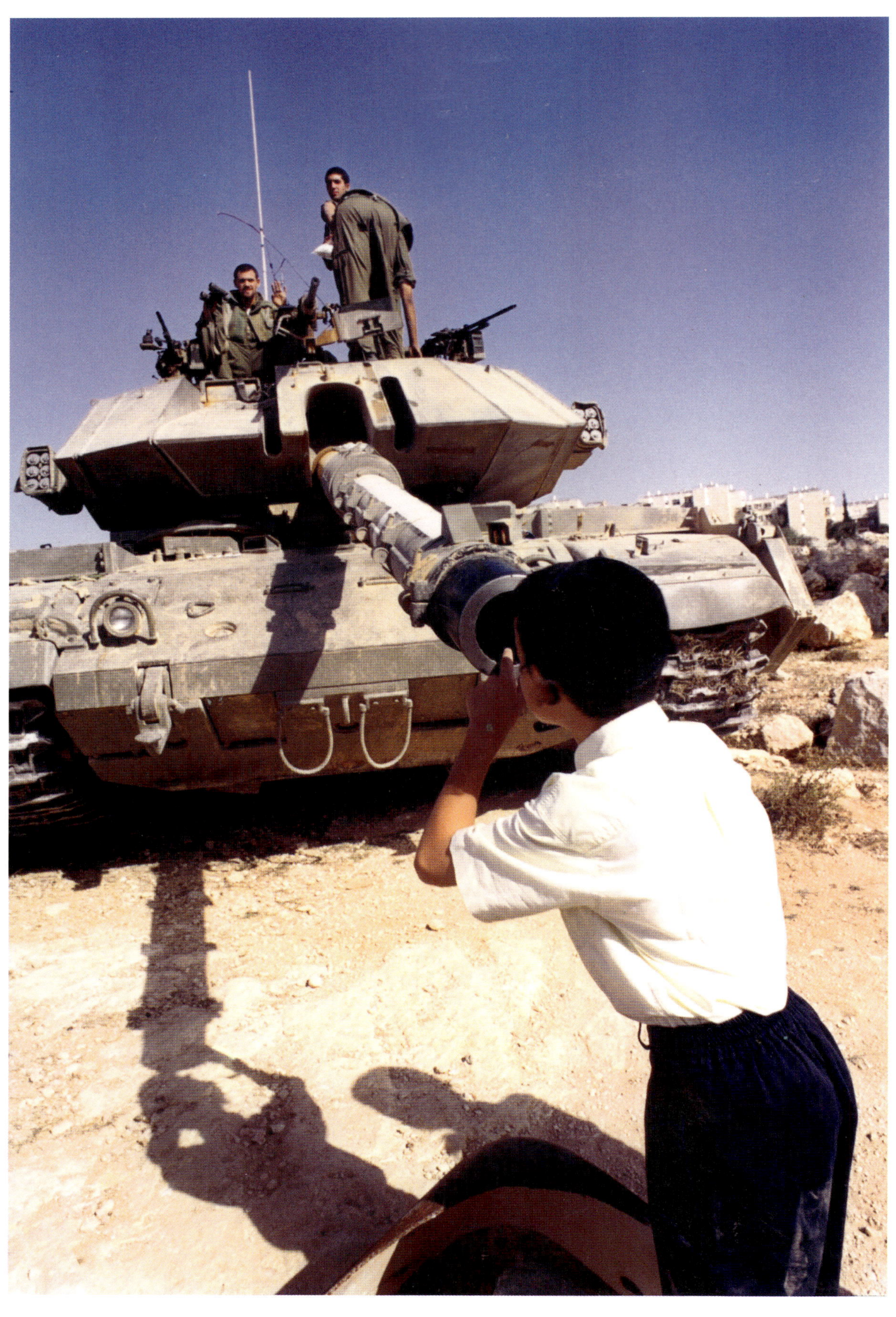

A tank is deployed
in Jerusalem's Gilo
neighborhood after firing
by Palestinians in Beit Jalla.

Ariel Jerozolimski

2000

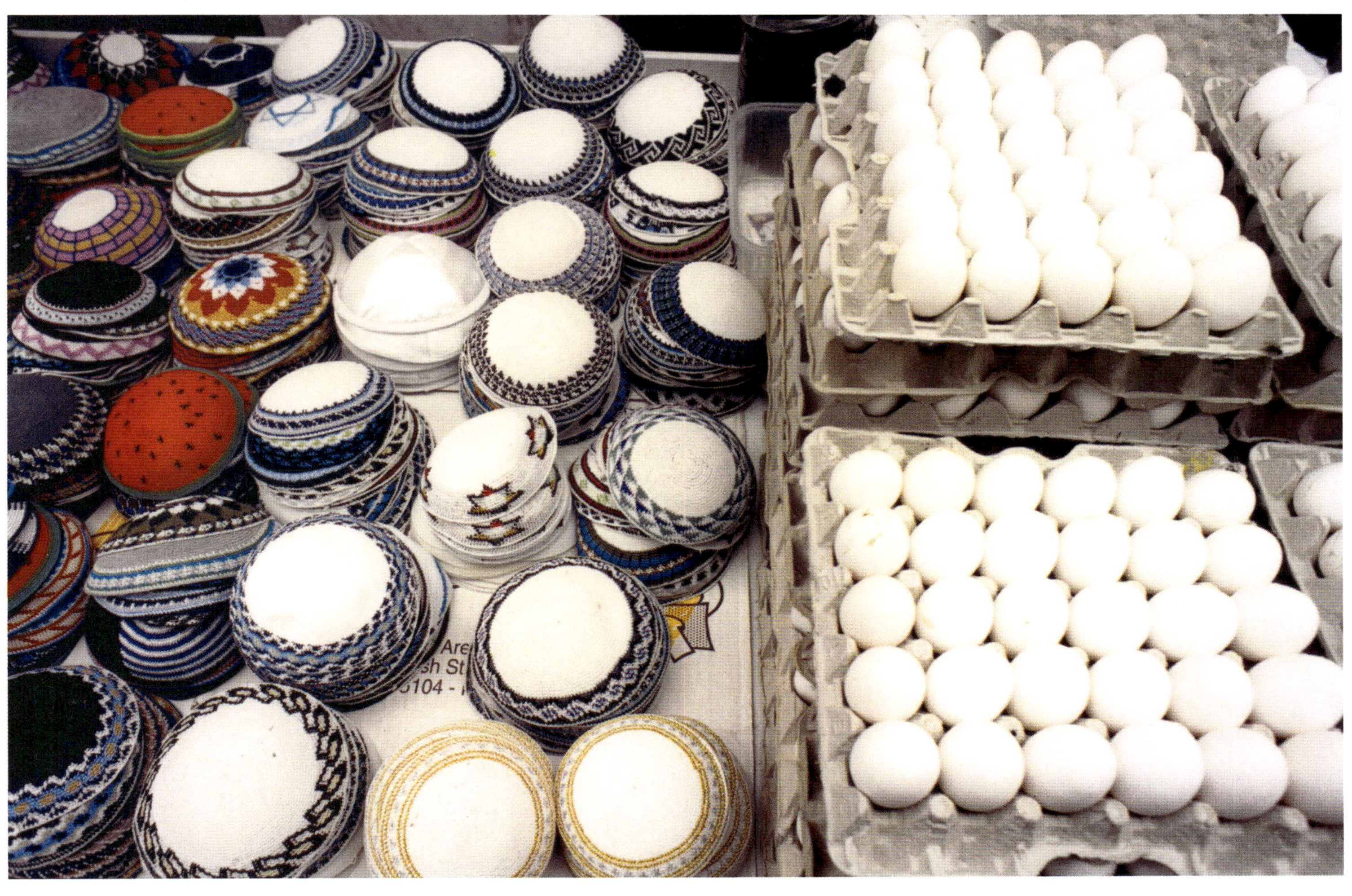

Jerusalem's Mahaneh
Yehuda Market has
something for everyone.
Ariel Jerozolimski
2001

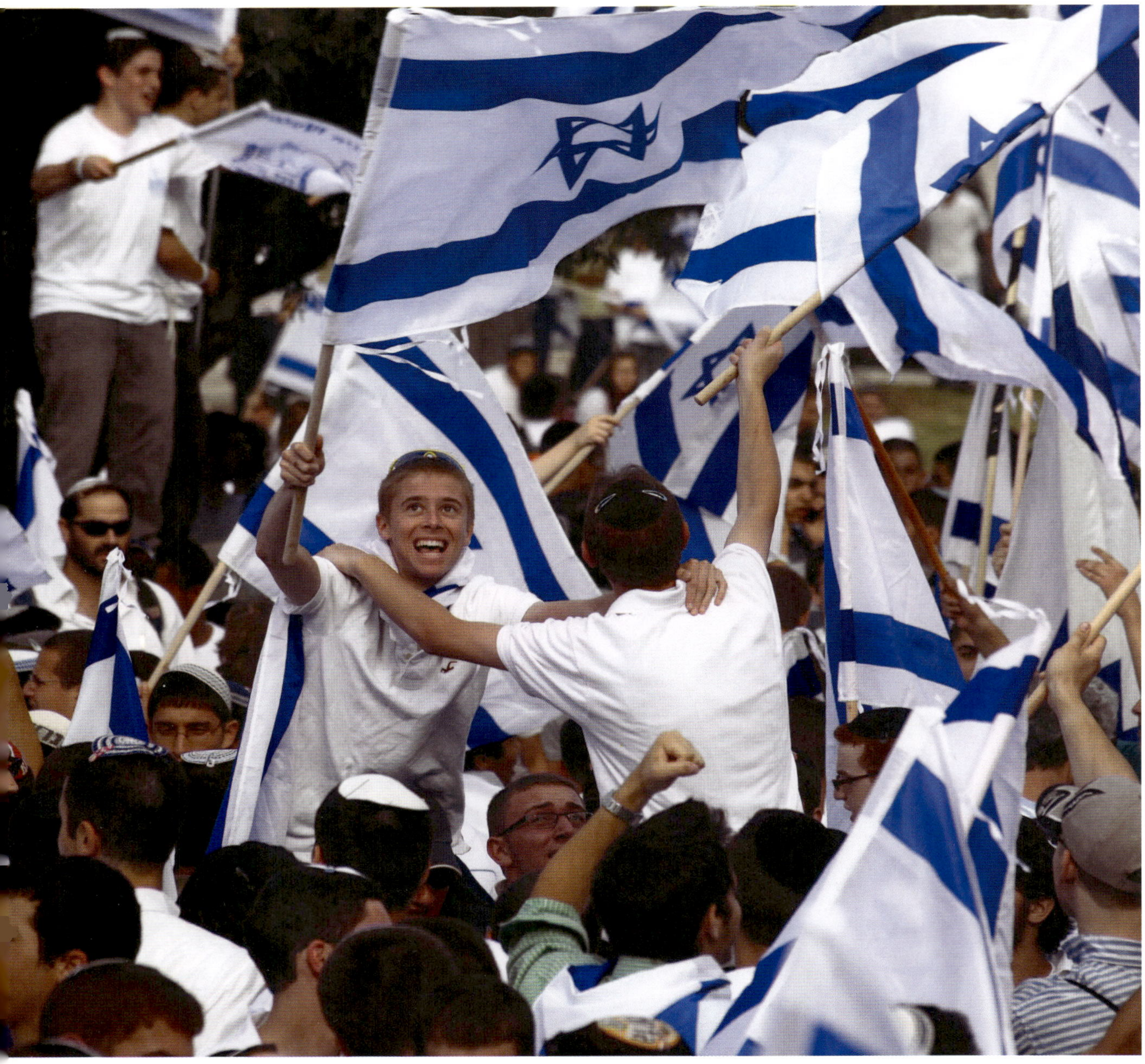

Independence Day celebrants party on Jerusalem's King George Avenue.

Marc Israel Sellem

2013

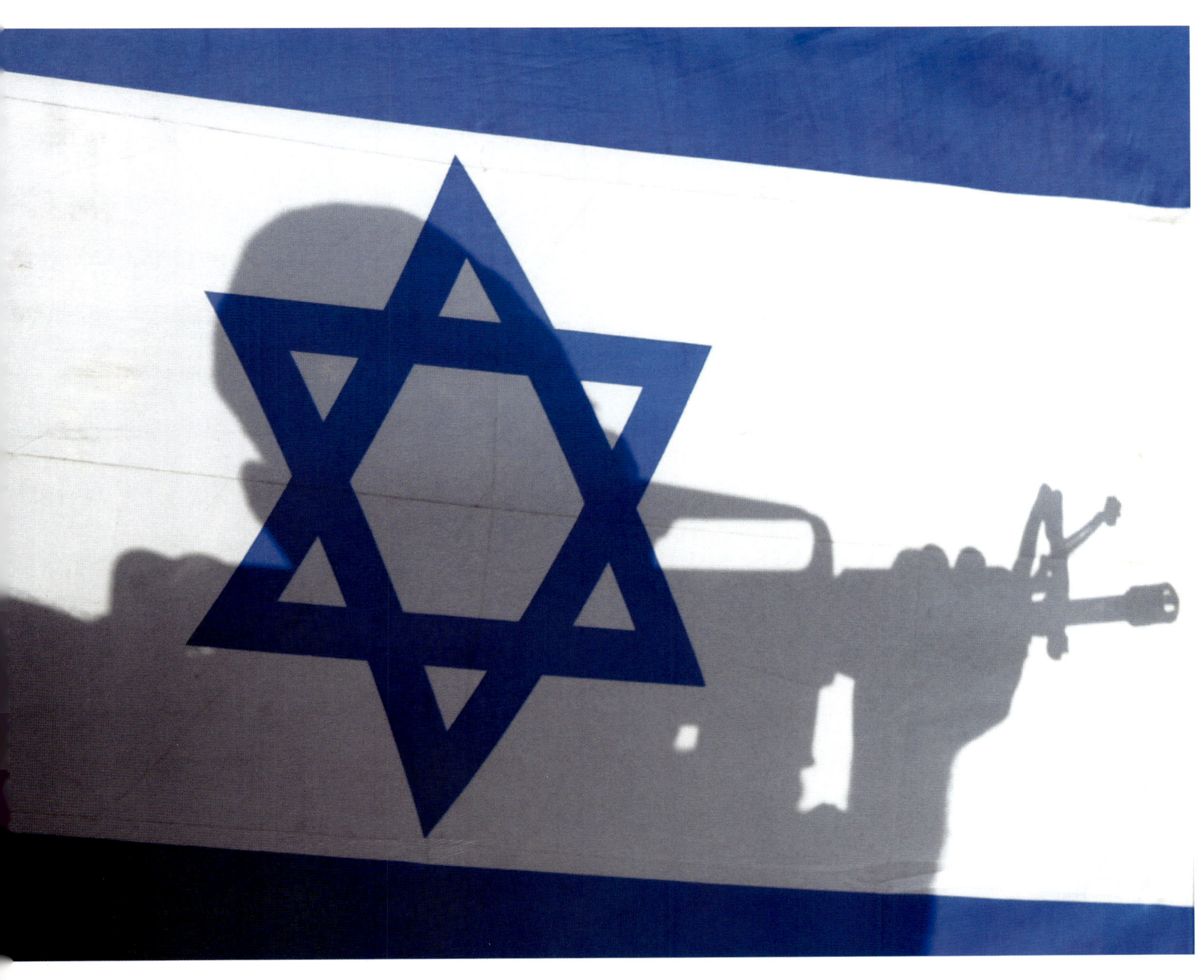

Eternal vigilance is the
price of liberty.
Marc Israel Sellem
2005

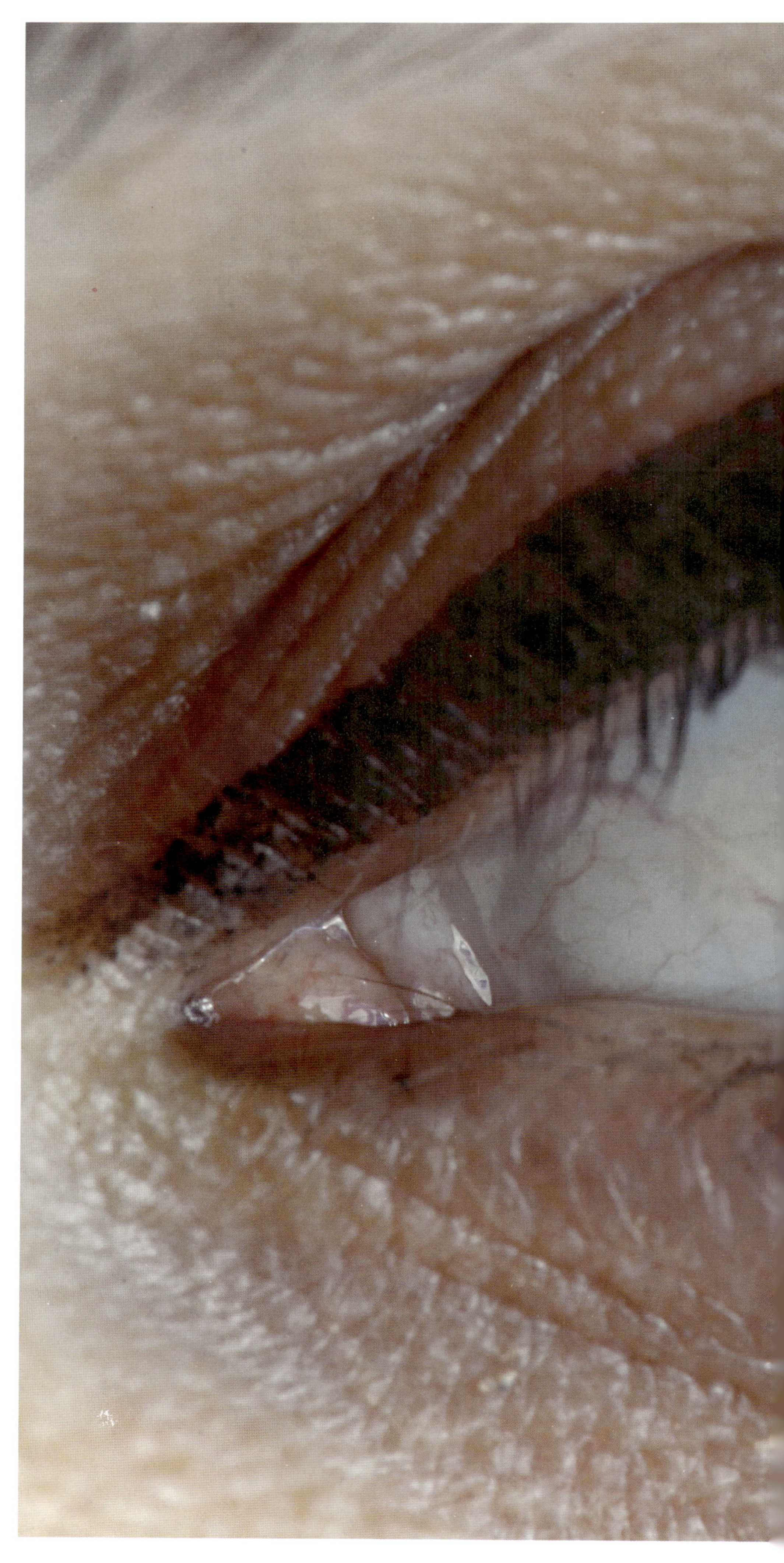

Beauty is indeed in the eye of the beholder.
Marc Israel Sellem
2014

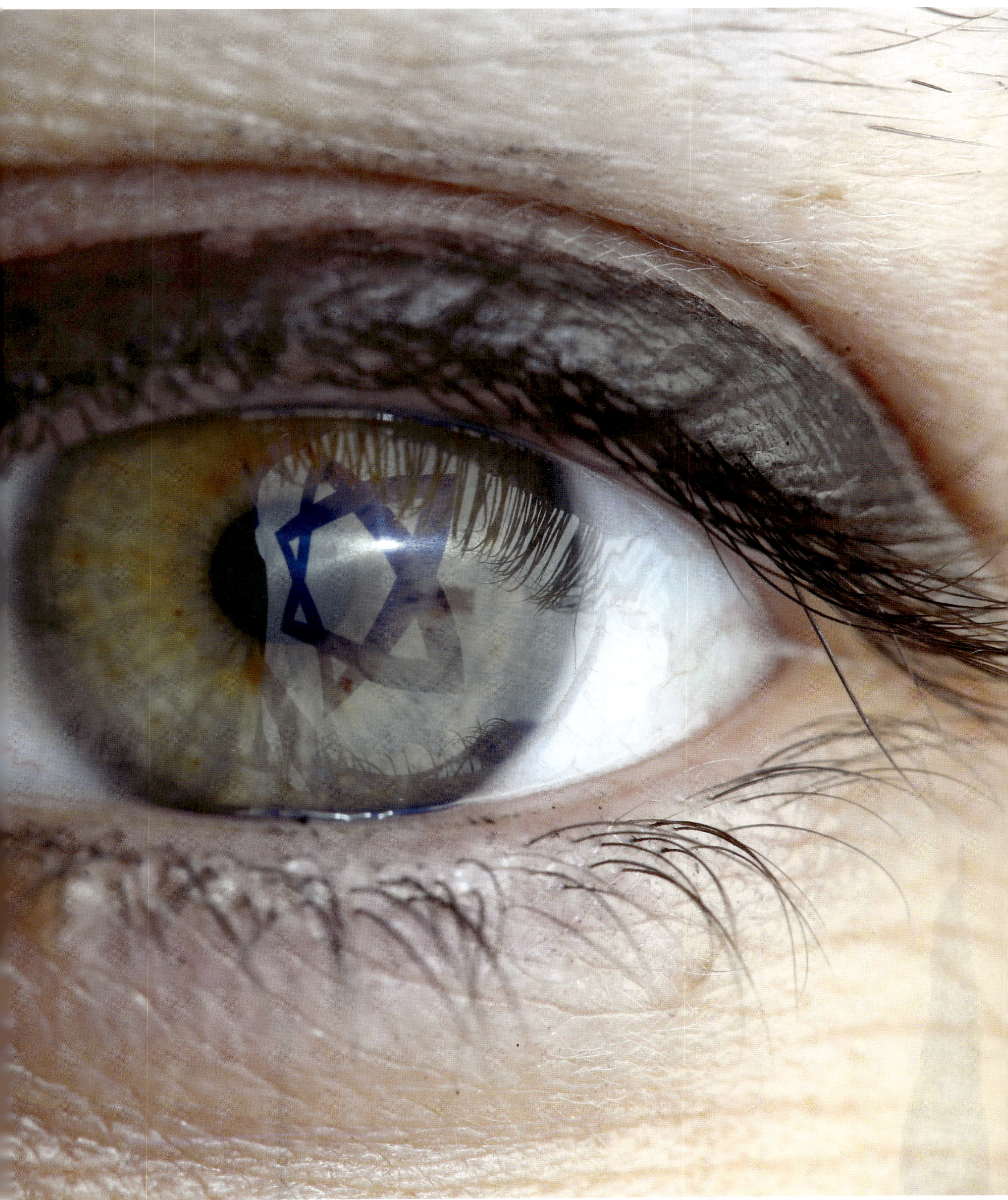

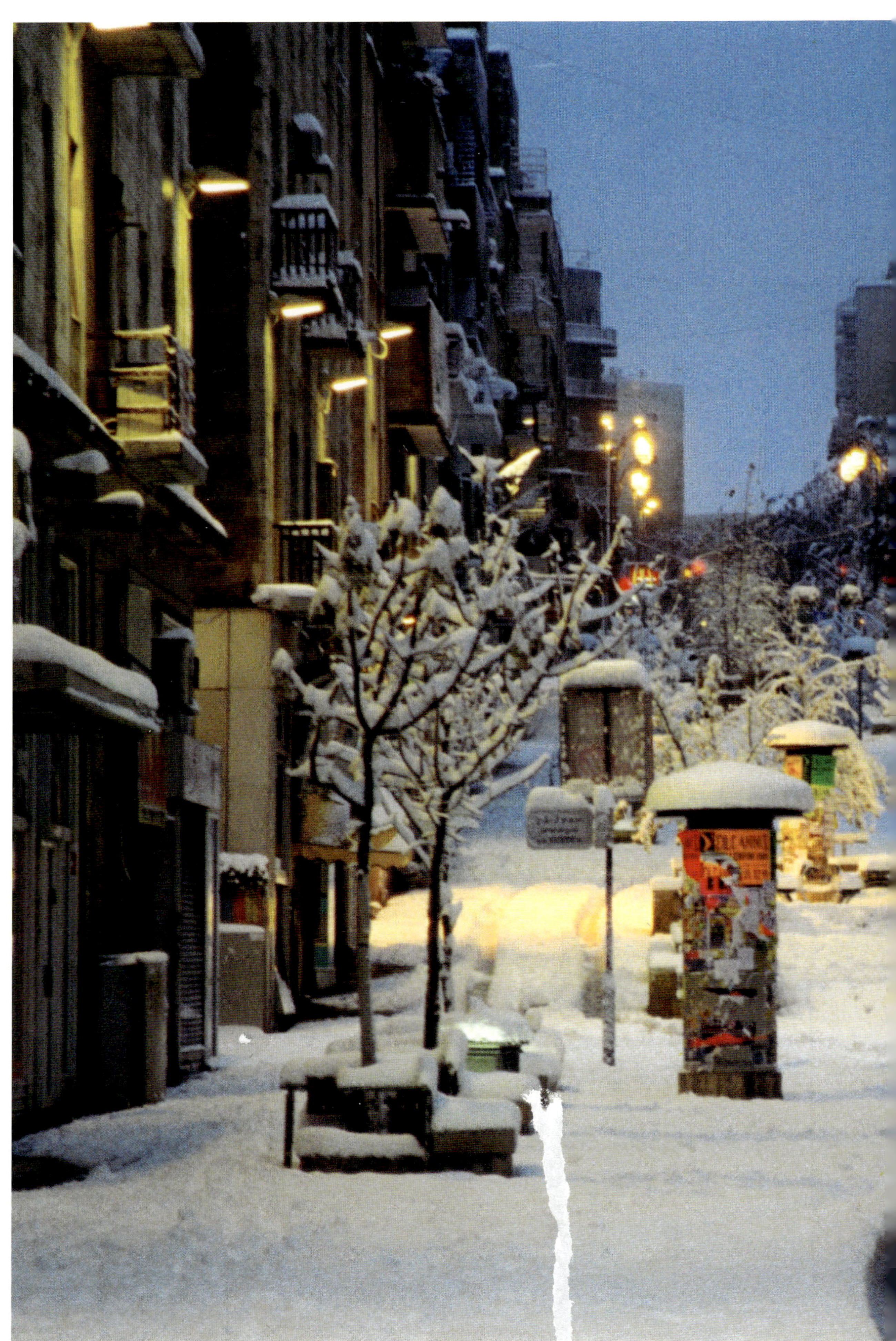

A lone pedestrian braves the elements on Jerusalem's Ben-Yehuda mall.

Marc Israel Sellem

2000

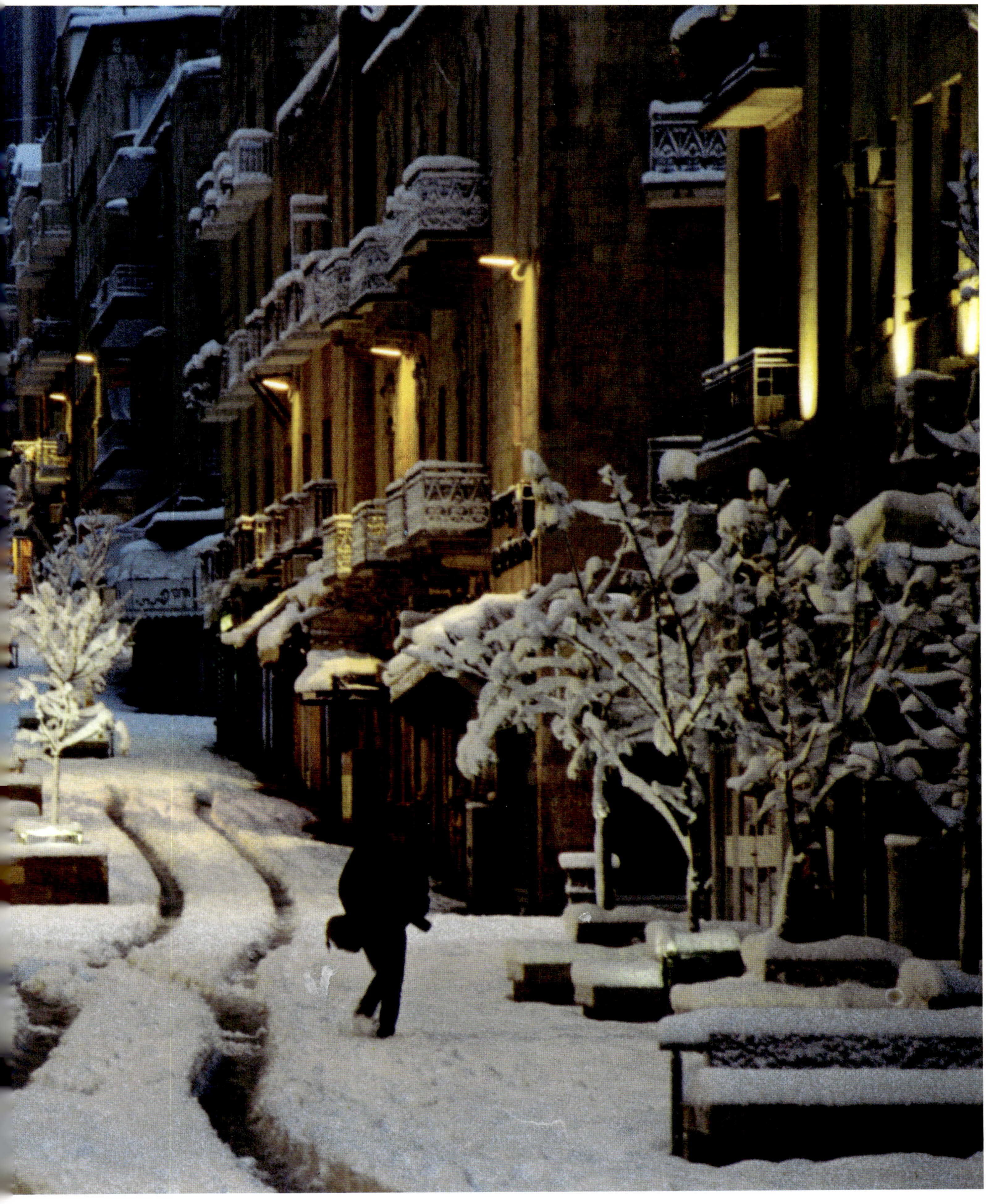

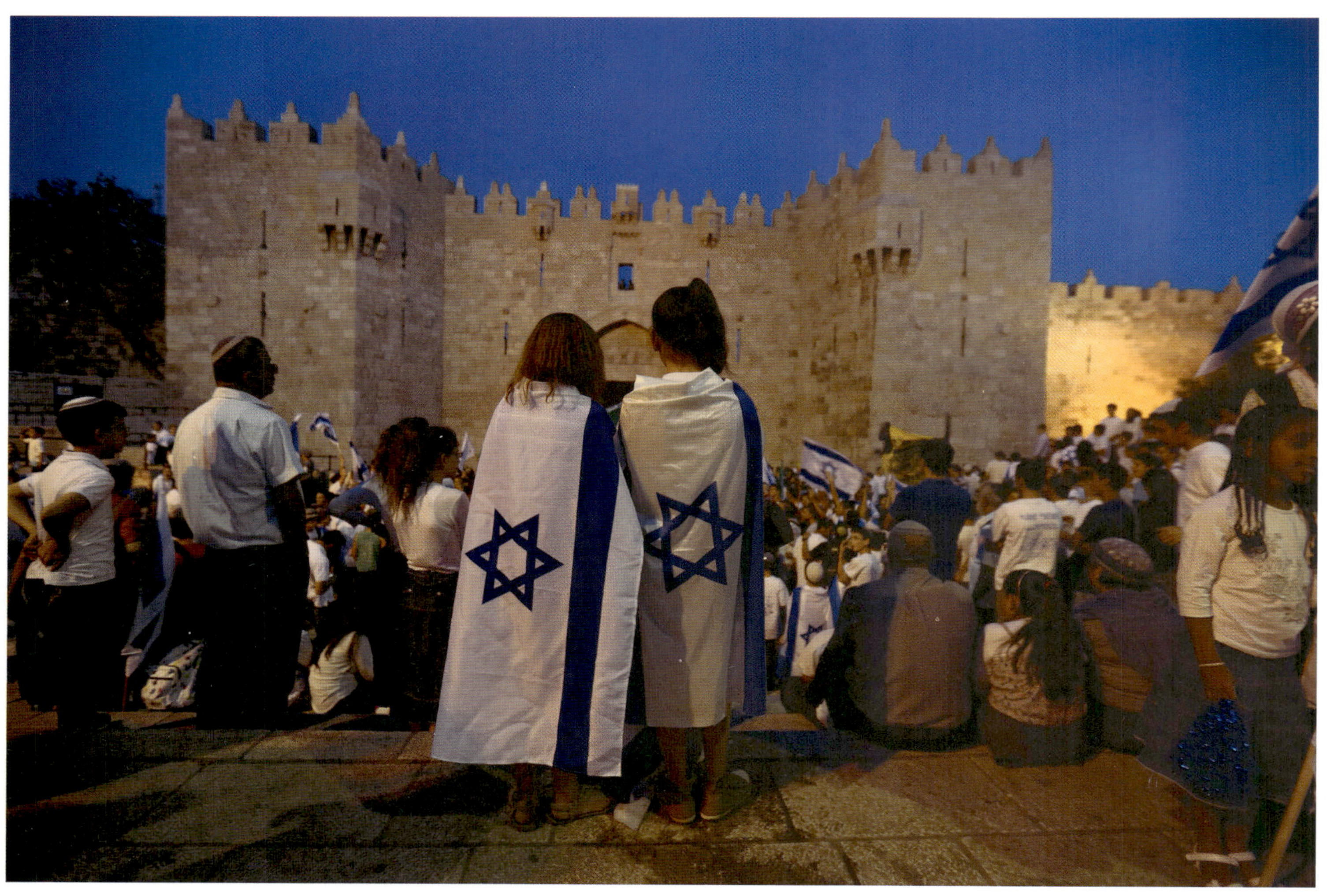

Revelers gather at Damascus Gate
on the eve of Jerusalem Day.
Marc Israel Sellem
2013